VARIANTS
10

The Journal of the European Society for Textual Scholarship

The Journal of the European Society for Textual Scholarship

Editor

Wim Van Mierlo

Associate Editor

Alexandre Fachard

AMSTERDAM - NEW YORK, NY 2013

Variants 10 was published with the support of the Institute of English Studies, School of Advanced Study, University of London.

The cover image is the second annotated proof of the Finnish poet Aaro Hellaakoski's "Dolce far Niente". Reproduced with kind permission from the Literary Archives of the Suomalaisen Kirjallisuuden Seura [Finnish Literature Society].

The paper on which this book is printed meets the requirements of "ISO 9706: 1994, Information and documentation - Paper for documents - Requirements for permanence".

ISBN: 978-90-420-3632-1
E-Book ISBN: 978-94-012-0902-1
ISSN: 1573-3084
©Editions Rodopi B.V., Amsterdam - New York, NY 2013
Printed in The Netherlands

Variants 10

Editor's Preface

This is the 10th volume of *Variants*. This is also the first non-themed issue in ten years. The choice to create a general issue was more by accident than design, although the reason was in part to streamline the production process and further clear our backlog. In future, we may well stick with this format, which will enable us to attract the best scholarship in the field on the widest variety of topics. That this is in keeping with the Society's mission, to study all aspects of textual scholarship regardless of language, period or school of thought, is reflected in the subject matter of the present volume, which includes essays on (for the first time) historical linguistics, digital scholarly editing, classical philology, Dutch, English, Finnish and Swedish Literature, book history, ballad editing, and editorial traditions in Japan.

Even though the articles were originally written for specific occasions, there are interesting and surprising overlaps. The article by Annemarie Kets, for example, on the editing of Dutch literary correspondences of a group of nineteenth-century Dutch writers and artists called "De Tachtigers" ["The Eighties Movement"] using the *eLaborate* tool nicely follows from the more general discussions by Tara L. Andrews and Franz Fischer on digital tools and editorial rationales available to the digital editor. Andrews' desideratum — that digital tools will alter the way we edit — and Fisher's — that digital editions involve much more than putting texts online — find their culmination in Peter Robinson's "Towards a Theory of Digital Editions", which is itself a rejoinder to his own "What is a Critical Digital Edition" that was published in the inaugural issue of *Variants* in 2002. Likewise, the articles by Veijo Pulkkinen and Jon Viklund, which are detailed investigations of the bibliographical codes of two modernist, Northern poets, Aaro Hellaakosken and Gunnar Ekelöf, enrich not only my own consideration of the role of the book in scholarly editing but also Kyoko Mijoyo's study of *zenshu* in Japanese literary history. *Zenshu*, meaning complete works, comprises a form of editing that situates itself between the book and authoritative text. The medium of the book further resonates in Giedrė Jankevičiūtė and Mikas Vaicekauskas' tracing of the bibliographical code through the use and re-use of illustrations in the Lithuanian idyll *Metai* [*The Seasons*] by Kristijonas Donelaitis.

The contributions by Andrews and Fischer are based on presentations at a Roundtable on the topic "Digital or Critical / Digital and Critical", organized by the Laboratory for Critical Text Editing at the Lectio center of the Katholieke Universiteit Leuven, Belgium, on 21 November 2011. The two essays explore, with reference to Greek and Latin texts, the apparent contradiction between the advances in computer technologies and their application to textual editing and the relative scarcity of truly critical and truly digital scholarly editions. Andrews addresses the issue head on by saying the scholars have not yet "articulated a clear idea of what a digital edition would look like" and that a lot of textual work on classical texts remains "fundamentally non-digital". Like Andrews, Fischer argues that a change in mentality is needed, particularly in terms of acknowledging what makes an edition "truly critical". The default option in the digital world still often seems to create archives, but "the plurality of equally legitimate texts" does not obviate the establishment of a critical text.

The largest number of articles — those by David Atkinson, Arianna Antonielli and Mark Nixon, Pietro Beltrami, Annemarie Kets, Teresa Marqués-Aguado and Kiyoko Miyojo — were originally written for the Society's 8th International Conference on "Texts Worth Editing" which was hosted by the Consiglio Nazionale delle Ricerche in Pisa, Italy on 25–27 November 2010, and which focused its inquiries on the fundamental idea of choice in the editorial process: what texts are worth editing? And why? And how do we defend these choices? What value lies in these choices? Atkinson takes this question to go right to the core of the editorial problem that he has previously described in his significant portfolio of articles on the editing folklore ballads: "Are Ballads Worth Editing?" The question deals with the inevitable tension between the fluidity of oral text and the impermeability of the printed word: why would one edit and fix a text in print that was never intended to be thus recorded? Kyoko Miyojo also addresses the problem head on when she confronts the various contradictions present in Japanese literature culture. In her highly interesting essay, she talks about the need for an editorial tradition, which does not yet exist in Japan. *Zenshū* is a form of publication that is concomitant with Japan's modernity.

As part of country's nation-building, Japan's publishing houses have produced prestigious, multivolume and authoritative editions of its major authors. None of these editions, however, is concerned with variants or revisions. But while textual editing may offer the *zenshū* a new legitimacy, as a Western concept, it is not at all clear whether these Western methodologies can be easily and justifiably adapted without disrupting the indigenous literary culture.

My own article on "Textual Editing in the Time of the History of the Book" and that of Peter Robinson, Giedrė Jankevičiūtė and Mikas Vaicekauskas and Veijo Pulkkinen were based on papers delivered at the Society's 9th International Conference in Bern 15–18 February 2012. This conference, which was organized in association with the German Arbeitsgemeinschaft für germanistische Edition, on "*Inter*National and *Inter*Disciplinary Aspects of Scholarly Editing" reflected on the theoretical and practical implications of our discipline in the broadest manner possible. In particular, it sought to address the increasingly hybrid nature of the methodologies employed by textual scholars, something that is at the heart of the articles by Pulkkinen, Robinson and myself. All three of us place critical editing and textual scholarship in broader perspectives: for me this is the history of the book, for Robinson this is computer-assisted scholarly editing, and for Pulkkinen this is genetic criticism looked at in the context of C. S. Peirce's semiotics.

The article by Arianna Antonielli and Mark Nixon on the history of *The Works of William Blake: Poetic, Symbolic and Critical*, edited by Edwin Ellis and W. B. Yeats, was also presented at the Pisa conference, but is given here its own section. A project study rather than a critical essay in the proper sense, this article inaugurates what I hope will be a fixture in future numbers of *Variants*. Work in Progress intends to give space for detailed treatments of a particular case, project or document whose description may be of practical interest to the textual scholarship. Such a section, ties in with our intent to include in the reviews section as many formal assessments of interesting digital editions and tools for scholarly editing as possible. The current book reviews, for example, have a double review of the first module on *Stirrings Still / Soubresauts* and *Comment dire / what is the word* in the Beckett Digital Project at the University of Antwerp and Dirk Van Hulle's accompanying genetic essay.

Following the resignation of Barbara Bordalejo as Editor of *Variants* in February 2012, I was appointed Editor *ad interim* to deliver the current volume. I invited Alexandre Fachard from the University of Lausanne, and an editor of the work of the English novelist Joseph Conrad, to be the Associate Editor. I would like to take the opportunity to thank Barbara for her contribution to the journal and the Society. During the past five years, she led *Variants* with considerable acumen, dedication and enthusiasm, and her efforts are greatly appreciated by the membership. At the November Board Meeting a new Editor and Associate Editor will be elected.

October 2012
Wim Van Mierlo

Notification and Corrigendum

It was brought to the Society's attention that the article by Purificacíon Ribes, "Tieck's 1793 German Version of Volpone: A Challenge for the Editors", which was published in volume 9 of *Variants* (2012), pp. 89-114, had appeared previously in near-identical form in *Sederi: The Yearbook of the Spanish and Portuguese Society*, volume 20 (2010), pp. 121-42. At the time of publication, neither the Editor of Variants, nor the guest-editors of the volume, had been made aware by Dr. Ribes that she had published her work elsewhere.

In David Atkinson, "The Secret Life of Ballad Manuscripts", *Variants*, 8 (2012), pp. 183—206, an unfortunate typographical error occurred on p. 188, where the cross deleting the stanza should have been printed over stanza 1a, not over stanza 2.

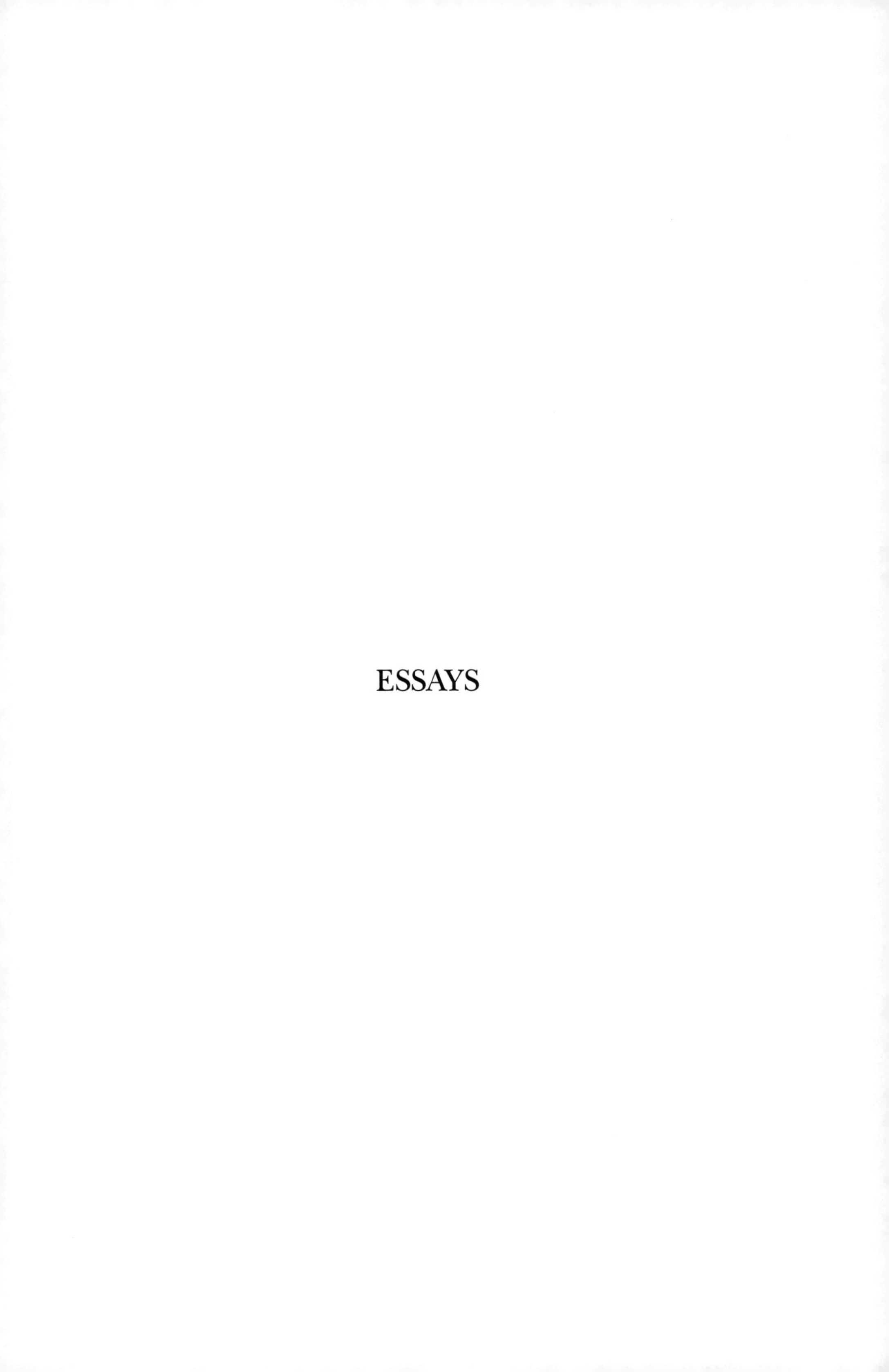

ESSAYS

Editions of Middle English Texts and Linguistic Research

Desiderata regarding Palaeography and Editorial Practices

Teresa Marqués-Aguado[1]

EDITIONS OF MIDDLE ENGLISH texts, rather than the manuscripts that hold them, are the instruments that have generally facilitated scholars' and students' understanding of medieval literature, and on many occasions even of the whole period. This is the claim that opens Tim Machan's work (1994, 9) on the relationship between textual criticism and Middle English texts.

Nonetheless, Middle English texts were first left aside from editorial tradition at the time of the humanists on the grounds that they appeared to lack the literary qualities and moral values (Machan 1994, 40) which by contrast were found in classical works.[2] This is one of the reasons why Middle English textual studies have traditionally lagged behind those in other vernacular languages. A different perspective with two contending views came to the fore in the modern era: either to make the texts available to a wider audience, who were unacquainted with the grammatical, orthographic and syntactic peculiarities of the texts of the period; or else to preserve the texts (Machan 1994, 41).[3]

---

[1]   This research has been carried out with the support of the research projects "Desarrollo del corpus electrónico de manuscritos medievales ingleses de índole científica basado en la colección Hunteriana de la Universidad de Glasgow", grant number FFI2008–02336/FILO (Spanish Ministry of Science and Innovation) and "Corpus de referencia de inglés científico-técnico en el período medieval inglés", grant number P07–HUM–02609 (regional government of the Junta de Andalucía). These grants are hereby gratefully acknowledged.

[2]   Old English literature, for example, has received more scholarly attention according to Machan (1994, 48).

[3]   Machan provides an example for both tendencies: on the one hand, the early editions of Chaucer's *The Canterbury Tales*, which often included a glossary or were modernized; on the other, Caxton's second edition of this work, who claimed that it preserved the original text (1994, 41–42).

Most editorial matters discussed in the relevant literature concern literary works. A completely different picture, however, emerges if the main interest lies not in literature, but language, the study of linguistic expression. Are the same editions equally suitable? Are the edited texts equally representative? If the perspective changes, the features and prospective users of these editions will necessarily vary. For instance, the edition and subsequent research on texts that belong to fields of knowledge other than literature (such as science or law) have progressively gained ground over the last decades, as evinced by the projects referred to in the third section below.[4] Texts like these provide a different insight into the language of the period, away from literary nuances (and convoluted language), and may be extremely useful for linguistic studies focusing on real language use.

In the light of this, the aim of this paper is to discuss editions of Middle English texts that serve the needs of linguists. I will first survey the palaeographical aspects to be taken into account, as well as editorial matters like the use of a particular apparatus or the needs of the audience. Although my emphasis will rest on scientific texts, especially on Glasgow, University Library, MS Hunter 513 (ff. 37v–96v), other types of text will be mentioned as well in passing.

Basic aspects of editions of Middle English texts

Machan's comments on the copies of Chaucer's major work (1994, 10–13) evince some of the differences that result from accessing a medieval manuscript and a modern edition: while each manuscript holding a relatively complete copy of *The Canterbury Tales* is different in terms of size, quality and content, published modern editions represent a particular editor's text. Conversely, modern editions typically present the works by one single author, whereas in the medieval period manuscripts usually compiled works by several authors in accordance with the commissioner's needs and wishes. Finally, modern editions seem to present texts in a stable and finished form which is not the one found in the Middle Ages. Hence, the stability of modern editions is in sharp contrast with medieval manuscripts, many of which underwent copying, correction, excision and/or

---

[4]   See, for example, Dossena and Lass's claim that "the importance of accessing documents beyond literature is indeed of crucial relevance in dialectological studies" (2004, 11).

compilation. By presenting a medieval text transmitted in manuscript form like a modern printed book, we are witnessing "the transformation of one document and text combination into another" (Machan 1994, 12).

This leads us to consider the material dimension of Middle English documents. If this dimension is left aside when editing, the text is detached from the object and from the context (time and place) in which it was produced and used (see Verweij 2006). Not only do editions tend to overlook codicological and palaeographical aspects, like the use of a particular script or the presence of certain decorations, but also the manuscript's social origins. Who commissioned the manuscript? Why was that person interested in having a copy of a particular work, or of a particular set of works in a bound volume? What was it going to be used for — for display, for consultation, for reading?[5] All of these circumstances played a role in the final configuration of the text from the points of view of content and *mise-en-page*. At any rate, if readers get access to a work through a particular edition, then it is only reasonable that material conditions are somehow taken into consideration.

In the case of critical editions, and as explained by Hanna (1992, 111), the distance between the edited text and the manuscript (object) is apparent if compared to a transcription or a diplomatic edition; the edition provides access to the variant readings in the witnesses, but little information about the objects themselves (both physically and socially) is preserved.[6] The material circumstances differ in several respects, e.g. the modern presentation does not fully suit that of Middle English works, the immediate audience of a medieval text has been replaced with a wider and more heterogeneous public, and the non-professional medieval authorship has disappeared (see Hanna 1992, 112–15). Yet the validity of a critical edition is by no means questioned, despite these remarks, if it is going to be used for textual or critical purposes (see Tanselle 1989,

---

[5]   An analysis is provided in Vázquez and Marqués-Aguado (2012, 130–33). See also Sutherland (2009, 108) on the social aspects (production, distribution network, etc.) that are concealed in many editions.

[6]   The same idea is found in Machan (1994, 65), who stresses the uniformity of modern critical editions as opposed to the variability of medieval manuscripts. As Robinson points out, it is difficult to encode "non-textual" elements in textual transcriptions (2009, 47), although attempts have been made (see Robinson's comments on *The Canterbury Tales* below).

92; in Machan 1992, 65). Access is provided to the work, rather than to the document that holds it, which seems to vanish with so much data on variables and interplay of variance. One of Machan's suggestions that addresses these losses is to publish a series of editions "each, perhaps, reflecting a different version of a work" (1994, 79).

The terms I have used this far — "work", "version", "text" or "document" — need to be defined before proceeding any further. This article will be mostly concerned with what Machan classifies as "documents" (1994, 6–7), insofar as these are copies of texts, regardless of the accuracy of their (presumably) original wording, for it is on these documents that subsequent editorial work relies. The edition may, in turn, be presented under a variety of formats. The classical division into diplomatic and critical editions is not completely faithful to reality, since as Hudson explains, "most modern editions are rightly a compromise between them" (1977, 39).[7] Generally speaking, while critical editions include more variant readings and stress textual relations between witnesses, diplomatic editions focus on the single document offering a reproduction that is as close to the original text as possible. As Elena Pierazzo puts it: "a diplomatic edition comprises a transcription that reproduces as many characteristics of the transcribed document (the diploma) as allowed by the characters used in modern print" (2011, 463–64).[8] This statement does not allow us to conclude that the original document is being imitated at all levels, even in diplomatic editions.[9]

---

[7]   A placatory view is offered by Petti, for whom half-way editions represent "a useful compromise [...] which provides nearly all that a diplomatic transcription would, but in a more continuous process. It gives scope for editorial interpretation while clearly indicating where this has been carried out" (1977, 34). Nonetheless, other options are available: facsimiles (see Machan 1994, 78 and Pierazzo 2011, 472, among others) or what Pierazzo labels as "superdiplomatic or type-facsimile" editions, which try to represent aspects like the location of each piece of writing on the writing surface, but set within the limits imposed by the printing medium (2011, 464).

[8]   Pierazzo's distinction between *transcription* as "a derivative document that holds relationship with the transcribed document" and *diplomatic edition* as the formal, public presentation of this document (2011, 464) will be kept in mind and employed in this article, since it will address linguistic use of public documents (hence editions, rather than transcriptions). For a detailed consideration of definitions of transcription, see Pierazzo (2011, 467).

[9]   In Charles Moorman's words, a diplomatic edition entails "the faithfully transcribed reproduction as in a facsimile of a single [manuscript] including

Indeed, all editorial work entails modifying somehow the original document (hence distorting its material conditions, as explained above), and this task varies depending on the prospective edition. Hence, editors must take decisions as to the choices available when transcribing, which on the palaeographical side range from how to reflect the different shapes of a particular letter-form, the distance between letter-forms, or the amount of ink used to execute them on the writing surface; to deciding that a particular group of minims must be rendered in a particular way. In turn, readers must be conveniently informed about these judgements so that they may follow and understand the editorial process. These choices will be justified in the context of the prospective edition, that is, its use and its users (Robinson 2009, 46). This unavoidable process of choosing and selecting has been widely reported in the relevant literature (Sperberg-McQueen 2009, 31; Pierazzo 2011, 466–67; to mention but a few), and implies that modifications or alterations will inevitably become part and parcel of editing. As Machan affirms, all editions of medieval texts bear the editor's fingerprint to a greater or lesser extent (1992, 1; see also Pierazzo 2011, 466). Peter Robinson and Elizabeth Solopova (1993, 21; see also Robinson 2009, 45) have analyzed these alterations in the light of editing as a process of translating, whereby the system of the original document is translated into a different, modern system, a thought which takes us back to Machan's idea of transformation (at the beginning of this section).

Linguists may still feel comfortable (though a graphologist or palaeographer clearly would not) about a diplomatic edition that ignores the distance between letter-forms or the amount of ink employed in each penstroke, but they must be made fully aware of any editorial interpretations, like those pertaining to minims for instance. Yet a critical edition featuring modernized spellings or reconstructed texts, or loaded with editorial notes on variance, can by no means serve as the basis for linguistic research (see also Vázquez and Marqués-Aguado 2012, 128–29).

---

every spelling variant, every mark of punctuation, every scribal error" (1975, 48). This statement, therefore, is not completely accurate in view of our discussion.

Palaeographical aspects

Although editions have been recurrently used in language studies, it would be convenient to assess their validity in achieving this aim considering palaeographical details, and propose any changes, if necessary, so that they may fully address linguists' research needs. As Robinson explains, "decisions about what one should encode and should not encode are to be determined according to the purpose of our editing" (2009, 46), which is, in our case, linguistic research. He further claims that by revising aspects like manuscript punctuation or script, among other features, "a rationale for a new edition of the [*Canterbury*] *Tales*" has been developed" (2009, 49), a statement that stresses the importance of palaeographical issues even for critical and textual work.[10] That these aspects are important in relation to the editing of this work is explained by both Machan and Robinson. The former argues that manuscripts clearly diverge in terms of their quality, and that this may relate to the finished or unfinished state of the work itself, or to the progressive rise of Chaucer's status (compare the Hengwrt manuscript, the earliest extant copy of the work and of poor quality, to the Ellesmere manuscript, a high-quality copy) (1994, 85–87). The latter acknowledges that, even though the differences in the ornamentation of the copies are not strictly relevant for a critical edition focusing on textual transmission, they provide an insight into conditions of production and use, which are also important for modern readers (2009, 47).

In what follows I will analyze the impact palaeographical issues associated with scripts (e.g., minims), abbreviations (including tildes and specialized brevigraphs) and the treatment of post-copying activity (marginalia, corrections of errors and additions) have on linguistic research.[11] These will concern the initial transcriptions, as well as what appears on (diplomatic) editions.

Scripts may pose problems even to the most skilled editor. Besides getting to know the script and the handwriting of a particular

---

[10]   On this premise, in the digital edition of the autograph materials by Jane Austen, layout, handwriting, spelling, diacritics, capitalization and punctuation are respected as in the original "with the aim of favouring the study of the genetic process of such manuscripts along with the linguistic and orthographic habits of the author" (see Pierazzo 2011, 496–70).

[11]   Some of these have been also highlighted by McCarren and Moffat (1998).

document, other elements have to be examined. First, a distinction between graphemic and graphetic transcriptions should be made: while the former "translate" (in Robinson's words) medieval letters into modern printed ones, the latter attempt to reproduce the exact shape of the letter-form (see McIntosh 1989). This means that the various letter-forms for <a>, <r> or <s> used in Hunter 513 (positionally-conditioned and related to two different scripts, i.e. Anglicana and Secretary) would be preserved in a graphetic transcription but not in a graphemic transcription, like the one in Marqués-Aguado (2008). Typographical constraints, along with those imposed by printing houses (Pierazzo 2011, 467) normally promote graphemic transcriptions, which normally suffice for purely linguistic studies, but not for graphological studies or for studying scribal habits, since the specific shape of letter-forms is needed for accurate analysis.[12] This does not pave the ground, however, for substitutions or modernizations of Middle English characteristic letters like yogh or thorn.[13]

Complications may arise, especially with medieval scripts like Anglicana, from the presence of minims, and at this point expert knowledge of the Middle English linguistic system may be useful to elucidate "the only reading which makes sense" (Robinson 2009, 43). As Robinson exemplifies, "[a]n 'i' is an 'i' not because it is a stroke with a dot over it. An 'i' is an 'i' because we all agree that it is an 'i'" (2009, 44). Recalling the idea of editing as choosing, Robinson provides a clear case in which the editor is forced to take a stance on these sequences of minims. Scribes themselves seem to have occasionally experienced the need to make sense of the strokes employed, hence devising mechanisms and visual aids to prevent confusion and misreading. The scribes of Hunter 513, for instance, added at times acute accents over <i>, or used <w> in the place of <u> (Figures 1 and 2, respectively). When confronted with practices like these, the editor should respect (that is, decode, interpret and inform the reader about) the use and significance of these strokes

---

[12]   See, among others, the extensive research carried out by Linne Mooney or Simon Horobin.

[13]   For example, dialectal studies have been carried out assessing the contextual uses of <þ> and <y>, for instance (Benskin 1982). Similarly, in Nevalainen and Raumolin-Brunberg's words, "spelling in modernization may sometimes have [...] unpredictable effects on morphology", to the extent that it may render variation studies impossible (1996, 45).

over <i>, especially when carrying out a transcription, since these sometimes solve ambiguous readings.

Figure1: "emínctories" (f. 53r)   Figure 2: "brawnches" (f. 59v)

Yet linguistic knowledge may not suffice to decode certain minims. Words like present-day English "betony" or "colophony" are occasionally represented in this manuscript with a series of strokes that may be read as either <betonie> or <betoine> (Figure 3) due to the absence of accents. Comprehensive dictionaries like the *Middle English Dictionary* may normally help the editor find the way out, but not in this case, since both spellings are registered. The likelier and less compromising solution is to transcribe the word modelled on the most frequent spelling used by that scribe in that manuscript, hence reducing the chances of editorial mistake (though not avoiding them). At any rate, this entails again editorial interpretation.

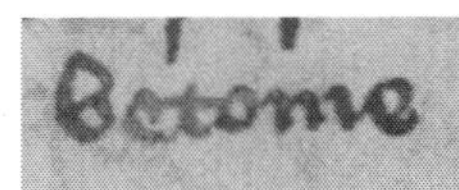

Figure 3: "betonie" or "betoine" (?) (f. 88v)

Abbreviations are also difficult to transcribe, since new ambiguities may arise: the same brevigraph may represent different readings (as with the plural number marker brevigraph that may be expanded as *-es, -is* or *-ys*; Figure 4) or altogether different abbreviations (as with *-er* and *-re*; Figure 5).[14] Once again, the reasons why one or the other expansion is preferred must be given to the users of the edition, such as using the most frequent ending in expanded forms (in the case of plural number markers), the linguist's knowledge (which may bar a spelling form as unattested or impossible), etc. Editorial interpretation is therefore introduced when expanding abbreviations, in which case the expanded letters should be conveniently

---

[14]   The choice between <-es> and <-is> is a difficult one, as reported by Voigts (1989, 94).

italicized. Typography permitting, symbols could be reproduced to avoid expansions, although this is not a common feature in editions, as explained further down.

Figure 4: doyng*es*/doyng*is* (f. 63r)   Figure 5: "pr*æ*sence" (*"p*er*sence") (f. 66r)

Particularly tricky in scientific texts are the abbreviations of weights and apothecaries measures, although systematically summarized by Voigts (1989, 101). Expert knowledge on science, botany or medicine may allow correcting the text from a conceptual point of view and proposing more convenient alternatives, but these are not required to transcribe what is on the manuscript surface.

The last case in point to be sketched within abbreviations is the ever-present problem in late Middle English texts of word-final penstrokes which may have been intended by the scribe as true marks of abbreviation or else as otiose strokes (Parkes 1969, xxvi). Although Parkes himself decided not to transcribe them as letters but as apostrophes to represent the flourish (1969, xxx), most editions take a stance on this aspect, owing again to the difficulties of encoding them properly in modern typography. These apostrophes may lead to a clear misinterpretation of the text, if they are added by the editor where they were not intended by the scribe, or if they are deleted where they are significant for the text. A comprehensive study on this aspect is again the reasonable course of action to decide whether to include or discard these abbreviations.

Modernized punctuation in any edition may suggest an interpretation of the text that might not have been intended by the scribe of the text, let alone the author (Moorman 1975, 85). The fact that present-day and Middle English prose are so different is the reason why scholars like Hudson (1977, 50–51) object to modernizing punctuation, even though it contributes to bringing the text closer to the modern reader. Let us take an example from the edition of MS Hunter 513 (Marqués-Aguado 2008, 113) which illustrates two common cases. First, the editorial distinction between commas (to separate noun phrases in a list) and semicolons (to separate sets of noun phrases) can only be made after some knowledge is gained on the conceptual nature of medieval science: the semicolons in the quotation serve to distinguish groups of plants from seeds, types of animal grease and gums:

> These ben*e* symple medecines: camomylle (the whiche medecine by hersylfe owe to be clepyd worthy, for she drawith neu*e*more ther*e* she resoluith), mellilote, peritorie, wylde malewe o*þer* white malue, ffumeterr*e*, dille,| wyrtes, netles, helena campana, borage, longede-beoff, ellerne, walworte, valeriane; cole sed, dille sede, nettle sede, malue seed, p*er*cille seed, smalach sed, and ffenell sede; *and* brenne, barly flour*e*, ffflour*e* of chykes, and of benes, cro*m*mes of grete brede; the fat|nes of a gander, and of a dukke, and a henne and a swyne; and allmaner of maries, mastik, frankencense, myrr*e*, armoniak, serapine, galbanu*m*, opoponak and all sotyll go*m*mes (lapdanu*m*, isopus humida, terbentine, wexe and the fece of wexe,| butter and o*þer* suche).

Second, this passage also reflects the problems posed by relative clauses (lines 1 and 2), particularly in specialized texts, where it may be difficult to discern whether they are restrictive or not. While modernization clarifies the text for the reader, it also modifies the original document, which had no punctuation.

Therefore, linguists who use editions that offer no specific explanation or rationale about their treatment of punctuation may find it difficult to process the data, which may eventually lead them to study syntactical structures not present or intended in the original document. Besides, studies on punctuation practices would be impossible, and these may be especially fruitful to study authorship or shared practices between manuscripts.[15] Likewise, studies on patterns of line division (this being a result of the use of punctuation) may also be helpful, but these cannot be carried out with editions that modernize punctuation.

Finally, most medieval texts underwent revision to some extent, either by the scribe, by a contemporary of the scribe, or by somebody at a later point in time; these revisions often consisted of the correcting of errors or the addition of new material (glosses in the main text or marginal notes). A modern editor must devise some

---

[15]   Robinson notes that Solopova managed to determine the authorial punctuation of the Hengwrt and Ellesmere manuscripts, but that this was possible only with reference to the original punctuation in the manuscript itself (2009, 49).

mechanism to represent each type of intervention accurately so that the linguist (or any user) may clearly discard unnecessary information. This is especially true of marginal notes: whereas scribal corrections may reflect the scribe's afterthought, a marginal note that was added some time after the text was written (because of its spelling, grammar system, etc.) is completely alien to the original system and, much as it may be of value, it cannot be considered part of it. It may therefore be convenient to collect marginal notes under one system (distinguishing also each hand or annotator), and provide different systems for errors and scribal corrections (specifying the method — expunction, alteration, cancellation, etc.) and for scribal insertions.

Likely solutions to these individual problems have been put forward, but it is clear that transcriptions (or diplomatic editions) are preferred to any other type of edition for linguistic research. Additionally, a complementary detailed palaeographic study is definitely of help when editing texts. If any changes are made, by following systematic mechanisms, we may give way to a systematic "translation" (in Robinson's terms) from the system in the manuscript to the system in modern print. Synoptic editions are also useful when several witnesses are of interest and a critical edition is to be avoided, but these increase costs and general audiences are left to decide for themselves about too many aspects, such as the hierarchy of witnesses, when the edition provides no complementary guidance on them (Hudson 1977, 39).[16]

The use of edited texts for linguistic research

As Hanna points out, "one can thus visualize, not An Edition, but a range of use- or interest-driven possible editions" (1992, 122). Indeed, one of the major decisions to be taken is the scope of the edition, which inevitably implies considering the edition's prospective use and users.[17] An edition without a clear rationale and a defined

---

[16]   An example of this practice is the conscientiously conceived synoptic edition of Benvenutus Grassus's Middle English tradition, which is supplemented with various palaeographic and linguistic studies (Miranda-García and González Fernández-Corugedo 2012).

[17]   Though applied to digital editions, these have been included as part of Pierazzo's five-item list of parameters to consider: (a) purpose of the edition; (b) needs of others; (c) nature of the document; (d) publishing technology; and (e) cost and time of the venture (2011, 468).

audience, as Alois Pichler explains, is of little use: "[W]hat we are going to represent, and how, is determined by our research interests [...] and not by a text which exists independently and which we are going to depict" (quoted in Robinson 2009, 45). These aspects will be analyzed in this section by combining the intended user of the edition, the edited object and the procedure to edit it, bearing in mind the linguist's needs.

Who are we editing for? Locating the linguist

The intended user of the editions surveyed in this article needs to be specified from among the wide range of possible end-users.

John Lavagnino identifies what he calls "the problem of the two audiences", i.e., "readers who are editors, and readers who are not editors but who study English-language literature" (2009, 65); the latter are also called "the popular audience" or "the common reader". To produce an edition that satisfies the needs of both groups is a tricky task, as he explains. Pierazzo has recently taken the idea of the two audiences up again with reference to digital editions, with some differences: the intended audience comprises both scholars and students, and the "Others" are a group that encompasses scholars of other disciplines and generic readers (2011, 470–71). It is clear that both classifications grant a privileged position to scholars and/or editors.

For my purposes, the identity of these two audiences needs some modification. To begin with, since linguistics rather than literature is the main concern, the scope and nature of the edition will be manifestly different, especially if the editor is a linguist herself.[18] Therefore, in addition to the editor — who, according to her own wishes and expectations, models the type of edition — there are other scholars, who can in turn be split into two groups. On the one hand, there are those who are likely to be interested in issues of textual criticism — how and why the edited text was constructed, how its rationale and apparatus work, and so on. On the other hand, there are the linguists (sociolinguists, historical linguists, pragmatists,

---

[18]   As illustrated below in the section on "What to edit?", Lavagnino's remark that "scholars in any field are inclined to address, first of all, other scholars of the same type" (2009, 65) holds true; the projects I discuss are devised by linguists for linguists.

etc.) whose interest lies in language use. Besides the scholars, the second group comprises all other readers, which includes students and experts from other knowledge fields.[19] How can an editor possibly manage to cater for the diverse needs of these "other" readers? Pierazzo's advice should be kept in mind: "[I]f it is a matter of simplifying the lives of readers by decrypting the idiosyncratic habits of textual scholarship, the answer should probably be: 'quite a long way'. [...] if it is a matter of considering the needs of possible future scholars in other disciplines and providing special markup for them, the temptation is to say: 'not far'" (2011, 471). Indeed, addressing what an editor might consider to be an expert need in any field of knowledge will be a taxing activity, if she ever manages to elucidate what is expected at all.

What to edit? Types of texts and editions of specialized texts

In contrast to editions of literary works, which may have a narrow or a wide readership depending on genre, tradition and the canonical status of the author, editions of scientific and legal works, among other specialized fields, may find it more difficult to garner a broad audience.[20]

The compilation of specialized historical corpora, either synchronic or diachronic, has witnessed a boost in the last decades, with some projects already finished and others still under way.[21] Some of the most notable recent projects worth mentioning are the *Corpus of Early English Medical Writing* (split into three sub-periods, i.e. Middle [Taavitsainen et al. 2005; MEMT], early Modern [Taavitsainen and Pahta 2010; EMEMT] and late Modern English), compiled at the University of Helsinki (Finland); or the *Reference Corpus of Late Middle English Scientific Prose* and the *Málaga Corpus*

---

[19] O'Donnell demonstrates that editions of Old English texts for students tend to show "the normalization of certain unusual linguistic and orthographic features" (2009, 116), since students are not for the most part acquainted with the language of the period, its conventions, the socio-historical context, etc.

[20] Lavagnino suggests that scholars are normally faced with the "everything or nothing" dichotomy when building an edition when it comes to deciding what kind of data to include (2009, 70).

[21] Since the compilation of the *Helsinki Corpus of English Texts* (Rissanen et al., 1991), a wealth of historical corpora has been created. A survey of a representative sample of historical corpora can be found in Vázquez et al. (2011).

of Late Middle English Scientific Prose, two sister projects led by the University of Málaga (Spain). The aim of these projects is to compile field-specific corpora (on science), with very precise time-spans, but with varying aims (diachronic, syntactic and morphological, dialectal, etc. studies). Nonetheless, they also allow for wider diachronic linguistic issues.

Irrespective of the specific linguistic use of these corpora, the compilers share the view that not all available editions prove equally valid as raw material for their purposes, a situation that led them on some occasions to transcribe and edit the texts of interest themselves. For instance, the compilers of MEMT used published editions, omitting "the textual notes and the critical apparatus, including variant readings in other manuscripts" (although some information about changes of scribal hands and of the source texts they used was retained and encoded) (Tyrkkö n.d., <http://www.helsinki.fi/varieng/CoRD/corpora/CEEM/MEMTeditorial.html>). The EMEMT subcorpus, however, was "keyed-in by hand from facsimiles or originals" (Tyrkkö n.d., <http://www.helsinki.fi/varieng/CoRD/corpora/CEEM/EMEMTtexts.html>) in view of the shortcomings of the available editions. Likewise, the *Reference Corpus of Late Middle English Scientific Prose* made its own transcriptions to produce texts that are "accurate, readable, and hopefully based on clearly defined and well-explained criteria" (O'Donnell 2009, 117) and, therefore, suitable for linguistic research.

The situation with historical sociolinguistic studies is slightly different, since linguistic information needs to be paired with sociological information on the informants (identity, age, gender, and so on) and the context in which the message was produced (time, place, social background, relation between informants and the like).[22] Letters are best suited for this type of research, and they constitute the focus of the *Corpus of Early English Correspondence* (Nevalainen et al. 1998).[23] Its compilers found roughly the same drawbacks as

---

[22]   In fact, the sociological dimension may pose a two-fold problem: first, not all texts suit sociolinguistic studies; second, these texts, if taken from existing editions, need to include information on these parameters.

[23]   Kohnen argues that "[l]etters have proved to be among the few historical genres which are open to sociolinguistic investigations" (2007). However, guild charters, certificates and other legal texts may also lend themselves well to sociolinguistic research, as shown by Toon (1992).

other historical linguists had observed when using existing editions (besides the specific need for sociolinguistic data) and selected for inclusion only those editions that retained the original spelling of the manuscript materials, although in many cases a comparison of the sources was carried out (Tyrkkö n.d., <http://www.helsinki.fi/varieng/CoRD/corpora/CEEC/compilation.html>; see also Nevalainen and Raumolin-Brunberg 1996, 45–46).

Therefore, although these editions are subservient to the ultimate purpose of corpus compilation, linguists share the view that texts need to be preserved in a state as close as possible to the original. This illustrates that if an edition is envisaged to serve as part of a corpus, Lass's remark that "the ideal model for a corpus or any presentation of a historical text is an archaeological site or a crime-scene: no contamination, explicit stratigraphy, and an immaculately preserved chain of custody" (2004, 46) holds true.[24] Linguistic studies cannot (or should not) rely on editions which diverge in their scope and editorial conventions, since reconstructed spellings or readings borrowed from other witnesses normally create a text that never existed as such and, hence, alter the results of the analysis.

How to edit? Editorial intervention and the apparatus

As I said earlier, and as among others Hudson (1977, 49) and Voigts (1982, 40) confirm, for decades there has been a clear gap (and, consequently, a niche for research) in the production of editions of scientific texts (generally known as *Fachprosa*), although work in this area has recently increased.[25] As a result, new documents (in Machan's terminology) or copies of already identified texts have been located, and altogether new textual traditions have emerged; besides, some documents have been found to be inadequately catalogued (Voigts 1995, 185–86). In this scenario, critical editions are difficult to produce if all the extant witnesses must (ideally) be

---

[24] Nevertheless, he concedes that "[m]y objection throughout is to the reconstruction of *texts*, and their subsequent use as witnesses – not to reconstruction as a source of knowledge of earlier language states at 'system' level" (Lass 2004, 24).

[25] See for instance Voigts and Kurtz's expanded and revised version of their electronic database (available online), released only a few years after the first edition (2000).

first transcribed and assessed, and their variant readings collated in the edition, or if the best text must be picked from those available (Reynolds and Wilson 1978, 195).

This view is shared by scholars like Voigts, who advises using the best text but without producing a full critical edition with variant readings. Her argument to create "a good base text edition, perhaps cautiously emended" (1982, 56) is also based on the premise that much scientific writing (particularly scholarly writings, as opposed to popular remedy books) was "Englished" (1982, 40), normally from Latin or from a Romance language like French (as in the case of Hunter 513). Whenever a text was imported from a different language, as with "Englished" texts of Romance provenance, different texts (i.e., translations into Middle English) were likely to emerge in the target language as potential exemplars, even almost simultaneously (Voigts 1982, 43–44 and 51–52). From these translations could then stem separate textual traditions.[26] This situation may obviously complicate the task of finding a single exemplar for the English tradition. These translations may as a consequence be examined in their own right, rather than be used to evaluate the similarities between witnesses, since no common exemplar may exist.

This picture is further compounded by the very purpose of scientific texts, which were "almost certainly measured by a criterion of truthfulness, of accuracy", so that their aim was not to reproduce the original author's spelling or grammatical constructions, but rather to offer "readings [...] which were authoritative and therefore likely to give good results when applied to healing patients" (Crossgrove 1982, 57). This may help understand the processes whereby additions were made to the base text by later users, not necessarily to emend textual errors, but maybe to offer new medical information or to make some more precise readings from the specialized standpoint. Scribes could occasionally conflate two exemplars to offer more accurate and comprehensive readings to facilitate medical practice, as Crossgrove also points out (1982, 45–46). In this line, compilations gathered from various materials and sources were

---

[26]   A case in point is that of the four Middle English versions traditionally identified for Guy de Chauliac's surgery, such as the one by Wallner (1995). Taavitsainen even refers to one document containing this scientific treatise as "the only extant manuscript of version two [...] and a different translation from the other versions" (2004, 216).

typical of medieval times, giving way to completely new textual traditions (as with the antidotary in Hunter 513; see Marqués-Aguado 2008, 58–64), which suggests that traditions were to a certain extent open to modifications (see also Reynolds and Wilson 1978, 193). This casuistry clearly poses more difficulties to identify an author, not to mention to establish what a text is.[27]

Linguists (especially historical linguists) are interested in how the individual documents may reflect synchronic or diachronic changes in the language (Lucas 1998, 171): every copy may contribute to the general understanding of the development of the English language (see also Voigts 1982, 53–54). So, tracing back the archetype or devising a stemma is not the main aim (see also Crossgrove 1982, 56–57), but rather the ability to study lexical items, grammatical structures, or even the evolution of scientific thought in this case.[28]

Hence the question, what should an edition for linguistic purposes look like? As explained above, a graphemic transcription may suffice for purely linguistic analysis, but this des not imply that editorial intervention must be completely ruled out. The following remarks, in part developed from Petti's guidelines (1977, 34–35) and from Voigts's enlightening essay "Editing the Middle English Text: Needs and Issues" (1982), build on the suggestions made above in the section on "Palaeographical aspects" and may serve as guidance to make editions more suitable as inputs for linguistic research.

First, the apparatus must reflect any changes in scribal hands, since each scribe may have a preference for certain syntactic patterns, lexical items and, of course, spelling variants. These preferences must be carefully examined, for instance, when expanding abbreviations, since the editor must proceed according to each scribe's spelling habits. Similarly, any scribal fingerprint (such as, possibly, the use of <i> with a diacritic or of <w> instead of <u> in ambiguous words, which we find in Hunter 513) must be respected. The preservation of these features and the addition of notes where relevant may pave the ground for the identification of some scribes at work in the Middle English period (a field in which further research is still

---

[27]   This concern is also addressed by Voigts (1982, 54–56).

[28]   In this line, Keiser has focused his attention on a text that he defines as not very reliable on account of its scribal errors and the like, but which is important inasmuch as it may help understand the circulation of medieval medical writing (2005, 38).

needed), and it may also provide hints about whether scribes worked in isolation or not (see Voigts 1986, 327).

Second, it is not advisable to standardize orthography or to modernize punctuation, because spelling variation is required for dialectal analysis, and punctuation (including word-division) can reveal patterns of use whose development may be measured over time. If any modernization occurs, a separate list of the emendations should be included in the edition to allow for the reconstruction of the manuscript's authentic readings. Likewise, if lineation is modified at all, then some mark (like a vertical stroke) should be employed to indicate the original line divisions, even if this takes place in the middle of a word.

Third, scribal errors, together with their analysis and the implications that these may have for the text, have traditionally been at the heart of textual criticism. In the types of text and edition under discussion, a substantial amount of errors (particularly alterations) may be caused by the scribe being unacquainted with the technical language employed in this type of text, hence leading to misreadings, as suggested by Keiser (2005, 33). These errors must be clearly categorized (deletions, additions, etc.), and may be emended by taking the scribe's own linguistic system as a model in an attempt not to distort the original system preserved in each document, although support from other witnesses may also be gathered, in which case it is advisable to collate the variant readings available but without emending them in the main text. If any of the latter need to be introduced in the main text, they should be marked and clearly distinguished (even graphically with different marking) from the emendations based on the scribe's habits. For instance, brackets may enclose emendations based on other witnesses, and braces may be reserved for those modelled on the scribe's system. In either case, the apparatus must specify the provenance for the correction, along with the original reading, in case this is of help to reconstruct a textual tradition, or to investigate the process of copying between witnesses, hence trying to combine the likely interest of those scholars focusing on textual studies.

Finally, marginalia should never be omitted from the edition, since they are essential to assess the circulation of a manuscript or the evolution of scientific thought, among others. Of course, no modernization or standardization should be allowed here either.

Were different hands involved in rendering marginalia, notes should be introduced accordingly; the same applies to the emendation of errors, which must also be classified (i.e., expunction, deletion, and so on).

Additionally, some knowledge of medieval science is more than welcome when delving into explanatory notes, which have "the all-important purpose of making the edited text more easily accessible and comprehensible" (Keiser 1998, 122). Unclear readings or obscure passages should form part of these notes, too, offering as many interpretations as grammar constructions, textual conventions and lexical items permit. Obviously, notes of linguistic nature are essential to provide a more comprehensive view of the state of the language as found in the original text.

Conclusions

This article calls for the production of editions that may engage a broader audience that includes linguists, who are not normally taken as the potential end-users when editions are planned and published. The same applies to the types of texts that are edited: scientific texts, among others, reflect actual language use more closely than literary texts so that they may be of more interest to linguists. The level of editorial intervention in many of the available editions of medieval works is, unfortunately, not easily conducive to linguistic research: they amalgamate readings from various copies, modernize spelling or punctuation, or erase traces of changes in scribal hands and of scribal idiosyncrasies. Thus, input suitable for linguistic research that may foster studies on real language use is scarce.

With this situation, and difficult as it may seem, editions should explicitly address the material conditions that shaped the particular text as found in each manuscript in an attempt to cast light on the features of the medieval products that have come down to us. Modern editing inevitably implies presenting medieval material in modern form, but editors should aim to distort the original system as little as possible or, at least, to offer as much information as possible to allow for the reconstruction of the original system. Perhaps one of the key aspects is that palaeographical traits should become a major concern in the transcription and subsequent edition. By stating clearly the rationale followed to decode abbreviations or to resolve minims, as well as the difficulties encountered with word-final otiose strokes and the criteria used to discard or retain them as abbreviations, or the peculiarities and number of hands taking part in the correction process (if this was carried out at all), the linguist making use of the edition will be able to know how to employ the data for linguistic research. In short, the process followed for the selection of the features portrayed in the edition must be made explicit. Likewise, editorial intervention should be marked in such a way that it may be easily decoded and the original system of the document restored. A complementary study or a set of explanatory notes that treat linguistic intricacies would also be very welcome. All these remarks will allow for various types of studies (on punctuation, word-division, spelling practices, evolution of syntactic constructions and so on) that may cast light on particular developments in the English language for which we lack evidence, which should be the main goal when editing for linguistic research.

In doing this, the edition is not the final product, but becomes an agent facilitating the linguist access to the original text, hence increasing the potentialities of editing and stressing that the dividing line between textual and linguistic studies may be blurred.

Bibliography

Benskin, Michael. 1982. "The Letters <þ> and <y> in Later Middle English, and Some Related Matters". *Journal of the Society of Archivists*, 7(1), pp. 13–30.

Calle-Martín, Javier, et al., comps. 2008–2012. *Reference Corpus of Late Middle English Scientific Prose.* Málaga: University of Málaga. <http://referencecorpus.uma.es>. [Accessed 20 October 2012].

Crossgrove, William C. 1982. "Textual Criticism in a Fourteenth Century Scientific Manuscript". In William Eamon (ed.), *Studies on Medieval Fachliteratur: Proceedings of the Special Session on Medieval Fachliteratur of the Sixteenth International Congress on Medieval Studies.* Brussel: Omirel, pp. 45–58.

Dossena, Marina and Roger Lass. 2004. "Introduction". In Marina Dossena and Roger Lass (eds.), *Methods and Data in English Historical Dialectology.* Bern: Peter Lang, pp. 7–18.

Hanna, Ralph. 1992. "Producing Manuscripts and Editions". In Alastair J. Minnis and Charlotte Brewer (eds.), *Crux and Controversy in Middle English Textual Criticism*. Cambridge: D.S. Brewer, pp. 109–30.

Hudson, Anne. 1977. "Middle English". In A. G. Rigg (ed.), *Editing Medieval Texts: English, French and Latin Written in England. Papers given at the Twelfth Annual Conference on Editorial Problems*. New York, London: Garland, pp. 34–57.

Keiser, George. 1998. "Editing Scientific and Practical Writing". In Vincent P. McCarren and Douglas Moffat (eds.), *A Guide to Editing Middle English*. Ann Arbor: University of Michigan Press, pp. 109–22.

——. 2005. "Robert Thornton's *Liber de Diversis Medicinis*: Text, Vocabulary, and Scribal Confusion". In Nikolaus Ritt and Herbert Schendl (eds.), *Rethinking Middle English: Linguistic and Literary Approaches*. Frankfurt am Main: Peter Lang, pp. 30–41.

Kohnen, Thomas. 2007. "From Helsinki through the Centuries: The Design and Development of English Diachronic Corpora". In Päivi Pahta et al. (eds.), *Studies in Variation, Contacts and Change in English* 2. <http://www.helsinki.fi/varieng/journal/volumes/02/kohnen/>. [Accessed 31 July 2012].

Lass, Roger. 2004. "Ut Custodiant Literas: Editions, Corpora and Witnesshood". In Marina Dossena and Roger Lass (eds.), *Methods and Data in English Historical Dialectology*. Bern: Peter Lang, pp. 21–48.

Lavagnino, John. 2009. "Access". In Julia Flanders et al. (eds.), *Computing the Edition*. Special issue of *Literary and Linguistic Computing*, 24, pp. 63–76.

Lucas, Peter J. 1998. "The Treatment of Language". In Vincent P. McCarren and Douglas Moffat (eds.), *A Guide to Editing Middle English*. Ann Arbor: University of Michigan Press, pp. 169–83.

Machan, Tim W. 1992. "Middle English Text Production and Modern Textual Criticism". In Alastair J. Minnis and Charlotte Brewer (eds.), *Crux and Controversy in Middle English Textual Criticism*. Cambridge: D.S. Brewer, pp. 1–18.

——. 1994. *Textual Criticism and Middle English Texts*. Charlottesville, London: University Press of Virginia.

Marqués–Aguado, Teresa. 2008. *Edition and Philological Study of G.U.L. MS Hunter 513 (ff. 37v–96v)*. Unpublished PhD Thesis. Málaga: University of Málaga.

McCarren, Vincent P. and Douglas Moffat. 1998. "A Practical Guide to Working with Middle English Manuscripts". In Vincent P. McCarren and Douglas Moffat (eds.), *A Guide to Editing Middle English*. Ann Arbor: University of Michigan Press, pp. 305–18.

McIntosh, Angus. 1989. "Scribal Profiles from Middle English Texts". In Margaret Laing (ed.), *Middle English Dialectology: Essays on Some Principles and Problems*. Aberdeen: Aberdeen University Press, pp. 32–45.

Middle English Dictionary. 2001. Eds. Frances McSparran et al. Ann Arbor: University of Michigan. <http://quod.lib.umich.edu/m/med/>. [Accessed 30 October 2012]/

Miranda-García, Antonio et al., comps. 2007–2011. *Málaga Corpus of Late Middle English Scientific Prose*. Málaga: University of Málaga. <http://hunter.uma.es>. [Accessed 20 October 2012].

—— and Santiago González Fernández-Corugedo, eds. 2012. *Benvenutus Grassus' On the Well-proven Art of the Eye*. Practica Oculorum & De probatissima arte oculorum: *Synoptic Edition and Philological Studies*. Middle English Texts Series 1. Frankfurt: Peter Lang.

Moorman, Charles. 1975. *Editing the Middle English Manuscript.* Jackson: University Press of Mississippi.

Nevalainen, Terttu and Helena Raumolin-Brunberg. 1996. *Sociolinguistics and Language History: Studies Based on the Corpus of Early English Correspondence*. Amsterdam, Atlanta (GA): Rodopi.

—— et al., comps. 1998. *Corpus of Early English Correspondence*. Helsinki: Department of English, University of Helsinki.

O'Donnell, Daniel P. 2009. "Back to the Future: What Digital Editors Can Learn from Print Editorial Practice". In Julia Flanders et al. (eds.), *Computing the Edition*. Special issue of *Literary and Linguistic Computing*, 24, pp. 113–25.

Parkes, Malcolm B. 1969. *English Cursive Book Hands, 1250–1500*. Oxford: Clarendon Press.

Petti, Anthony G. 1977. *English Literary Hands from Chaucer to Dryden*. London: Edward Arnold.

Pierazzo, Elena. 2011. "A Rationale of Digital Documentary Editions". *Literary and Linguistic Computing*, 26(4), pp. 463–77.

Reynolds, L. D. and N. G. Wilson 1978. *Scribes and Scholars: A Guide to the Transmission of Greek and Latin Literature*. Oxford: Clarendon Press.

Rissanen, Matti, et al., comps. 1991. *The Helsinki Corpus of English Texts*. Helsinki: Department of English, University of Helsinki.

Robinson, Peter. 2009. "What Text really Is Not, and Why Editors Have to Learn to Swim". In Julia Flanders et al. (eds.), *Computing the Edition*. Special issue of *Literary and Linguistic Computing*, 24, pp. 41–52.

—— and Elizabeth Solopova. 1993. "Guidelines for Transcription of the Manuscripts of the Wife of Bath's Prologue". In N. F. Blake and P. M. W. Robinson (eds.), *The Canterbury Tales Project Occasional Papers* 1. Oxford: Office for Humanities Communication, pp. 19–52.

Sperberg-McQueen, C. M. 2009. "How to Teach your Edition how to Swim". In Julia Flanders et al. (eds.), *Computing the Edition*. Special issue of *Literary and Linguistic Computing*, 24, pp. 27–39.

Sutherland, Kathryn. 2009. "Material Text, Immaterial Text, and the Electronic Environment". In Julia Flanders et al. (eds.), *Computing the Edition*. Special issue of *Literary and Linguistic Computing*, 24, pp. 99–112.

Taavitsainen, Irma. 2004. "Scriptorial 'house-styles' and discourse communities". In Irma Taavitsainen and Päivi Pahta (eds.), *Medical and Scientific Writing in Late Medieval England*. Cambridge: Cambridge University Press, pp. 209–40.

—— and Päivi Pahta, eds. 2010. *Early Modern English Medical Texts [CD–Rom]*. Amsterdam, Philadelphia: Benjamins.

—— and Päivi Pahta and Martti Mäkinen, comps. 2005. *Middle English Medical Texts [CD–Rom]*. Amsterdam, Philadelphia: Benjamins.

Toon, Thomas E. 1992. "The Social and Political Contexts of Language Change in Anglo-Saxon England". In Tim W. Machan and Charles T. Scott (eds.), *English in Its Social Contexts: Essays in Historical Sociolinguistics*. Oxford: Oxford University Press, pp. 28–46.

Tyrkkö, Jukka, coord. n.d. *Corpus Resource Database (CoRD)*. Helsinki: University of Helsinki. <http://www.helsinki.fi/varieng/CoRD/>. [Accessed 31 July 2012].

Vázquez, Nila, Laura Esteban-Segura and Teresa Marqués-Aguado. 2011. "A Descriptive Approach to Computerised English Historical Corpora in the 21st Century". *International Journal of English Studies*, 11(2), pp. 119–39.

—— and Teresa Marqués-Aguado. 2012. "Editing the Medieval Manuscript in its Social Context". In Juan Manuel Hernández-Campoy and Juan Camilo Conde-Silvestre (eds.), *The Handbook of Historical Sociolinguistics*. Cambridge: Wiley-Blackwell, pp. 123–39.

Verweij, Michiel. 2006. "La matérialité des manuscrits: Consequénces pour l'histoire et pour les éditions critiques". In Tanya Van Hemelryck and Céline Van Hoorebeeck (eds.), *L'écrit et le Manuscrit à la Fin du Moyen Âge*. Turnhout: Brepols, pp. 367–77.

Voigts, Linda E. 1982. "Editing the Middle English Text: Needs and Issues". In Trevor H. Levere (ed.), *Editing Texts in the History of Science and Medicine*. New York, London: Garland, pp. 39–68.

——. 1986. "Medical Prose". In A.S.G. Edwards (ed.), *Middle English Prose: A Critical Guide to Major Authors and Genres*. New Brunswick: Rutgers University Press, pp. 315–35.

——. 1989. "The Character of the Carecter: Ambiguous Sigils in Scientific and Medical Texts". In Alastair J. Minnis (ed.), *Latin and Vernacular: Studies in Late-Medieval Texts and Manuscripts*. Cambridge: D.S. Brewer, pp. 91–109.

——. 1995. "Multitudes of Middle English Medical Manuscripts, or the Englishing of Science and Medicine". In Margaret R. Schleissner (ed.), *Manuscript Sources of Medieval Medicine: A Book of Essays*. New York, London: Garland, pp. 183–95.

—— and Patricia D. Kurtz. 2000. *Scientific and Medical Writings in Old and Middle English: An Electronic Reference [CD–Rom]*. Ann Arbor: University of Michigan Press.

——. n.d. *Voigts-Kurtz Search Program*. Kansas City: Center for Academic Research Computing: University of Missouri. <http://cctr1.umkc.edu/search>. [Accessed 16 October 2012].

Wallner, Björn. 1995. *An Interpolated Middle English Version of The Anatomy of Guy de Chauliac. Part I: Text*. Lund: Lund University Press.

Textual Criticism and Historical Dictionaries

Pietro G. Beltrami

IN THIS PAPER I wish to address some issues of textual criticism in Medieval Romance philology, taking as a starting point my experience as chief editor of the *Tesoro della Lingua Italiana delle Origini* (*TLIO*) [*Treasure of the Early Italian Language*]. *TLIO* is the historical dictionary of Early Italian that the Opera del Vocabolario Italiano (OVI, a research unit of the Consiglio Nazionale delle Ricerche [National Research Council]) is currently editing and publishing online.[1] It is my contention that historical lexicographers for their work must rely on critical editions based on sound editorial judgment or on editions of manuscripts made specifically for historical linguistics. But while not just any source will do, lexicographers sometimes cannot but use the sources that are available to them. Focusing on a handful of problems in early Italian sources, I wish to show the paramount importance of editorial judgment, and how informed editorial judgment is required, at times, to overrule the evidence embodied in documents.

Problems in dealing with sources

Most of the Italian corpus of texts written before the end of the fourteenth century is currently available in editions of varying quality, established in accordance with varying methodologies and to satisfy various agendas — some very old, others more recent. For the compiler of historical dictionaries who must rely on lexicographical evidence, such qualitative fluctuations pose considerable problems, where the core task consists of collecting each attestation of a word and its meaning. Where accuracy is a prerequisite condition, many, especially older editions prove unfortunately unreliable. A lexicographer of early Italian would find no difficulty in drawing up a wish list of texts that are worth editing to replace many of the older editions with new, more accurate ones.

---

[1]   See also Beltrami 1999 for further details on the *Tesoro* and Beltrami 2010b in which I set out in detail my views on textual criticism.

A good illustration of this quandary is the anonymous Sienese translation of Egidio Colonna's *De regimine principum* [*On the Rule of Princes*], dated 1288. The only available edition by Francesco Corazzini, dating from 1858, is utterly unreliable; however, since it is one of the oldest and most important Sienese literary texts, lexicographers have no choice but to use and cite from Corazzini's edition. The same is true of the late thirteenth-century Tuscan translation of Brunetto Latini's *Tresor*, of which the only available complete edition dates from 1878–1883 (Gaiter 1878–1883). Both the Sienese *De regimine principum* and the Tuscan *Tesoro* include the earliest, sometimes the only, attestations of many words, and a dictionary of early Italian disregarding these sources would be incomplete (see Beltrami 2010, 241–43).

There are two ways to deal with this tension between editing and philology on the one hand and lexicography on the other. The obvious solution is to prepare new editions. This is the route that *TLIO* has followed since the beginning with the addition of a number of editors to the research team. Recently, for instance, an edition of an old Sienese version of an anonymous bestiary included in the *Tresor*'s first book was published in the OVI annual (Squillacioti 2007), followed two years later by a thirteenth-century Pisan translation of Albertano da Brescia's treatises (Faleri 2009). Unfortunately, this philological solution only partially solves the problem, for unless the team would suspend work on the dictionary and concentrate on preparing new editions, only small advances will remain possible. The same goes for the revision of existing editions, as was done too in certain cases for non-literary texts surviving in only one manuscript. This still remains a big task, however. Thanks to this revision of the old and faulty edition by Alessandro Torri of the commentary to Dante's *Comedy* known as the *Ottimo Commento* [*Best Commentary*] (1827–1829), for instance, an occurrence of the rarely attested long form of the Italian definite article, *ello* instead of *lo*, found its way into the online OVI *Early Italian Corpus* and was recorded in an important article by Vittorio Formentin (2002). In fact, the OVI corpus offers the original reading "per ello dosso" ["over his back"] (MS Laurenziano XL.19, f. 125r2, l. 49), which Torri (1827–1829, 3: 103, l. 3) corrected to "per lo dosso". The second solution is for lexicographers to inform readers of the characteristics of their sources and to alert them to their reliability. In *TLIO*, all suspicious quotations are clearly flagged up and are often accompanied by textual notes that contextualize the problem.

The following examples may serve to illustrate *TLIO*'s procedures: (1) Under the entry for *inantire*, a gloss for the form *inanto*, meaning "I turn my attention to (somebody), as a lover", tells users that this is a conjectural emendation by Bruno Panvini in his edition of *Le rime della scuola siciliana* (Panvini 1962-1964); both extant manuscripts read "intendo" (which has the same meaning, but which is derived from the verb *intendere*), but this form is faulty because the word is supposed to rhyme with "tanto") (Figure 1).

The entry also mentions d'Arco Silvio Avalle's *Concordanze della Lingua Poetica Italiana delle Origini* (*CLPIO*) which argues in favour of *intend* in his edition of the oldest Italian lyrical manuscripts (Avalle 1992: CCXLIIa).[2] The comment that follows quotation [2] indicates that in his edition of the same text Avalle does not agree with Panvini's emendation. Because *TLIO* is no edition, it only highlights textual problems; in this case, the reader is alerted to the fact the quotation may belong under *inantire* according to how one solves the philological problem (even though a preference in favour of Panvini is implicitly expressed).

Also from Panvini's edition comes the unique attestation of *avamparliere*, or *avamparlieri*, "advocate, defender" (see Figure 2).

As the note explains, this is again an emendation, for the only extant manuscript reads "avantiparlieri", which is also the reading adopted in M. Spampinato Beretta's edition ("Già non m'era mestiere" ["it was not good for me"], see Di Girolamo 2008, 905), but which renders the verse hypermetrical.[3] These examples show that editorial choices based on poetic form and metrics change the vocabulary, which has significant impact on the lexicographer's work. Lexicographical evidence does not consist of brute facts, at least not insofar as the makers of dictionaries must deal with mediated texts that did not originate directly with the

---

[2]   Incidentally, A. Fratta, in his new edition of Iacopo Mostacci's *Umile core e fino e amoroso* (included in Di Girolamo 2008, 412 and 415) prints *intend* according to the manuscript and emends *tanto*, v. 24, to *tando*, a supposed alternative form of the same word. This could be an instance of the so-called "French rhyme", *–an* sometimes rhyming with *–en* in old Italian poetry.

[3]   In my review (Beltrami 2010a) I criticized Di Girolamo's edition (Di Girolamo 2008) for its stance on metrics.

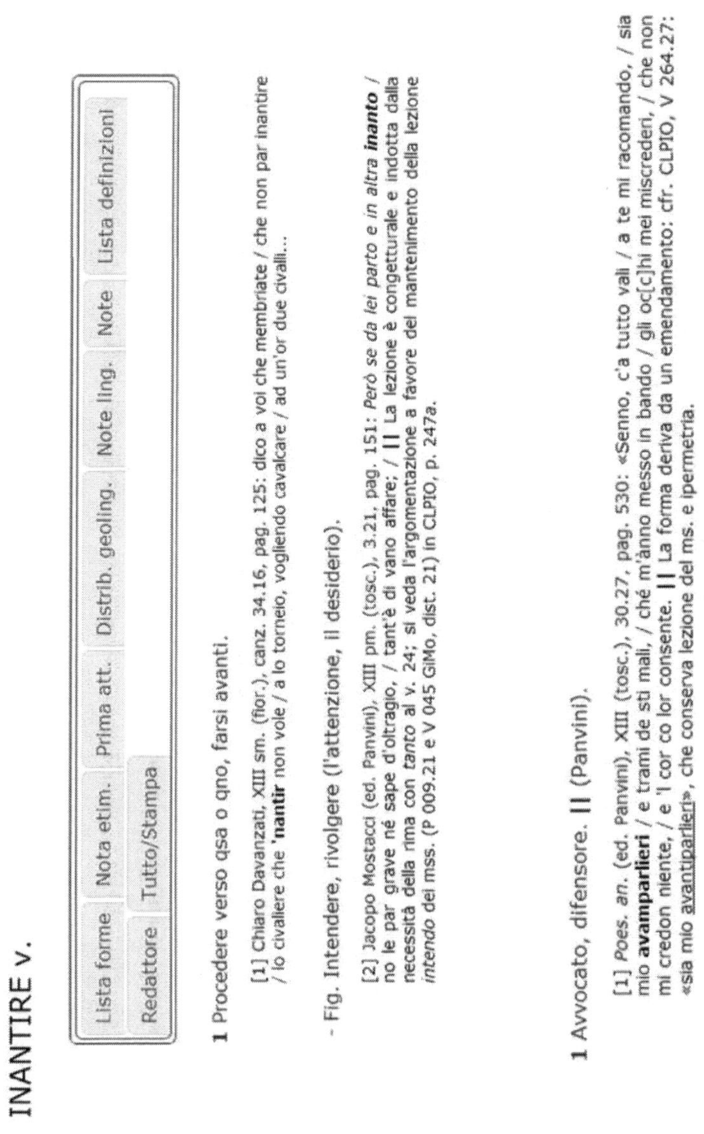

INANTIRE v.

Lista forme | Nota etim. | Prima att. | Distrib. geoling. | Note ling. | Note | Lista definizioni

Redattore | Tutto/Stampa

1 Procedere verso qsa o qno, farsi avanti.

[1] Chiaro Davanzati, XIII sm. (fior.), canz. 34.16, pag. 125: dico a voi che membriate / che non par inantire / lo civaliere che **'nantir** non vole / a lo torneio, vogliendo cavalcare / ad un'or due civalli...

- Fig. Intendere, rivolgere (l'attenzione, il desiderio).

[2] Jacopo Mostacci (ed. Panvini), XIII pm. (tosc.), 3.21, pag. 151: *Però se da lei parto e in altra* **inanto** / no le par grave né sape d'oltragio, / tant'è di vano affare; / || La lezione è congetturale e indotta dalla necessità della rima con *tanto* al v. 24; si veda l'argomentazione a favore del mantenimento della lezione *intendo* dei mss. (P 009.21 e V 045 GiMo, dist. 21) in CLPIO, p. 247a.

1 Avvocato, difensore. || (Panvini).

[1] *Poes. an.* (ed. Panvini), XIII (tosc.), 30.27, pag. 530: «Senno, c'a tutto vali / a te mi racomando, / sia mio **avamparlieri** / e trami de sti mali, / ché m'ànno messo in bando / gli oc[c]hi mei miscrederi, / che non mi credon niente, / e 'l cor co lor consente. || La forma deriva da un emendamento: cfr. CLPIO, V 264.27: «sia mio avantiparlieri», che conserva lezione del ms. e ipermetria.

Figure 1: *TLIO,* main entry for "inantire" and Figure 2: *TLIO,* main entry for "avamparliere".

1 Insieme di ciò che rende qno o qsa più bello, più decoroso, di aspetto più importante.

[1] Uguccione da Lodi, *Libro*, XIII in. (crem.), 185, pag. 606: ave con grand rapinamento, / le rique vestimente e l'autr'**adornamento**, / destrieri e palafreni, vassieg d'or e d'arçento.

[2] Restoro d'Arezzo, 1282 (aret.), L. II, dist. 2, cap. 5, pag. 87.32: Adonqua è mestieri per forza de rascione che questa donna, la quale noi chiamamo Venere [[...]] vegna colle corone e con tutte le gioie, e cum li **adornamenti** d'auro e d'argento...

[3] Jacopone, *Laud. Urbinate*, XIII ui.di. (tod.), 10.137, pag. 523: De la viltate fa' lo vestemento, / tale ke tte nne copri in onne parte; / e ·dde la povertate **adornamento**.

[4] Jacopone, *Laud. Urbinate*, XIII ui.di. (tod.), 10.150, pag. 524: Le parole de Deo te siano pasto / e le santi virtuti guarnemento, / e sse ttu vivi puro, necto e ·ccasto, / avarai parte nell'**adornamento**.

[5] *Fiore*, XIII u.q. (fior.), 165.4, pag. 332: Or sì.tti vo' parlar del guernimento, / Come ciascuna dé andar parata, / Che per sua falta non fosse lasciata / Sì ch'ella fosse sanza **adornamento**. || Il ms. ha inte(n)dime(n)to. 'Adornamento' è congettura di Contini necessitata dal contesto e dalla rima altrimenti identica con il v. 5, nonché dalla fonte (*Roman de la Rose* v. 13530: «bien atiree»).

[6] *Distr. Troia*, XIII ex. (fior.), pag. 167.9: e lla chiesa era ornata di nobili **adornamenti** e ricchi tesori.

4 Signif. incerto.

[1] Bonvesin, *Volgari*, XIII tu.d. (mil.), *Disputatio mensium*, 104, pag. 6: Indug a penitentia tug i fedhi cristian / E g'aregord ke i serviano al nostro rex sopran, / Perzò ke la quaresma ne ven a man a man, / E tal **adornamento** sí plax al rex sopran. || Probabilmente da emendare in 'adoramento'.

[2] *Diretano bando*, XIV (tosc.), cap. 25, pag. 19.19: Et del dormire d'amore vien tucti li pericoli; et a tucti li **adornamenti** seguiscie la morte, sì come al liocorno che s'adormenta alla pulcella, et de l'huomo che s'adormenta alla serena che poi l'uccide. || E' traduzione dal fr. «les endormis». Si può dunque supporre che sia errore (forse per aplografia) o forma hapax col valore di 'addormentamenti'.

Figure 3a and 3b: *TLIO*, main entry for, "adornamento".

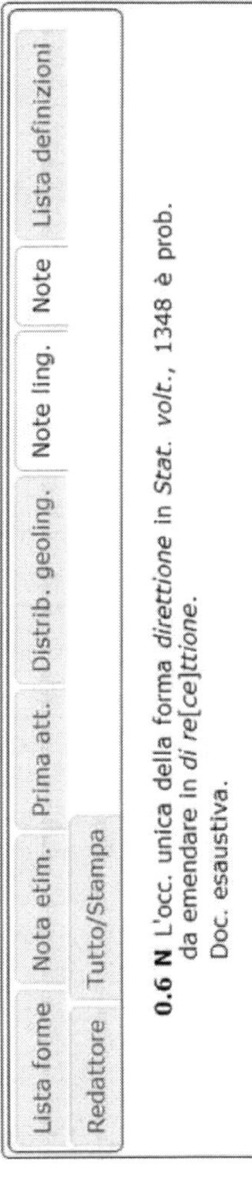

Figure 4a and 4b: *TLIO*, main entry for "direzione".

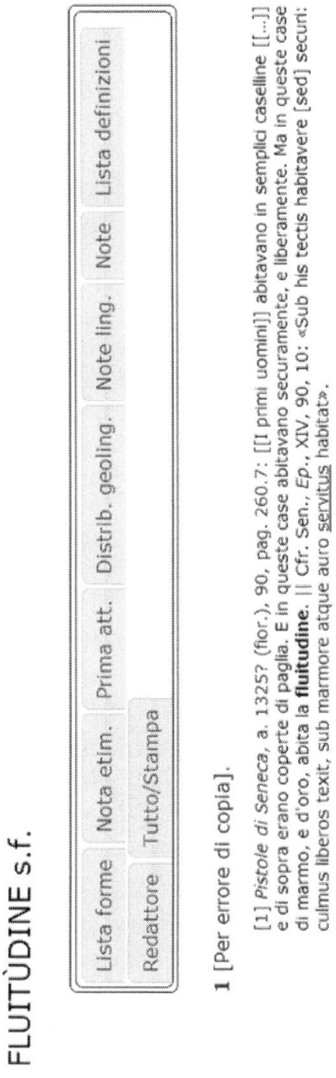

Figure 5: *TLIO*, main entry for "fluitudine".

author. How one interprets the attestation of a particular word in the manuscript as an error or not is a matter of judgment. In this example, the original form should be *avamparliere* (or *avamparlieri*) if we believe that the verse was not meant to be hypermetrical, or *avantiparlieri* if we believe that the verse was meant to be hypermetrical. The matter is one of interpretation and choice.

(2) In the entry for *adornamento* ["adornment"] at least three instances of the word required textual notes (Figure 3).

In the excerpt from the *Fiore* (sub-entry [5]), *adornamento* is a conjectural emendation made by Gianfranco Contini to the manuscript reading "intendimento" ["intelligence"] for three reasons: *intendimento* does not fit the context; it would otherwise occur twice as a rhyme in the same sonnet; and, finally, at this point the source, the *Roman de la Rose*, reads "bien atiree", ["well adorned"] (Contini 1984: 332–33). Conversely, two instances of *adornamento* quoted in the same *TLIO* entry seem to be scribal errors. In the excerpt from Bonvesin da la Riva's *Disputatio mensium* [*Debate of the Months against Each Other*] (1941), the context strongly suggests that *adornamento* should be emended to "adoramento" ["worship"]. In the quotation from the *Diretano bando* [*Last Call*] (1997), *adornamenti* should certainly be emended to "addormentamenti" ["the act of falling asleep (plural)"], as the original French text, the *Bestiaire d'Amors* [*Bestiary of Love*] by Richard de Fornival, has "les endormis" ["the sleepers"], and the manuscript reading makes little sense. Since neither editor emended — as they should have done — the text, both excerpts are given in a separate rubric headed "significato incerto" ["doubtful meaning"], and followed by a gloss explaining the crux at issue.

(3) In the following example, the *TLIO* does not take into account an occurrence of *direzione* ["management, direction"] found in the statutes of a religious congregation, the Disciplinati of San Giovanni di Pomarance (Vigo 1889), because, as a note states, the context makes it clear that one must read "di re[ce]ttione" ["of receiving, welcoming"] (Figure 4).

In the database this occurrence is lemmatized as "direzione" because this form is present, once, in the manuscript text. This type of lemma shows, again, that the dictionary participates in the interpretation of the textual evidence and may suggest emendations.

In instances like these, we are really talking about "parole fantasma" ["ghost words"]; these are words that do not exist in the language, but which *TLIO* assigns individual entries to inform readers of their occurrence in the corpus. For instance, the meaningless *fluitudine*, in the old edition of the early fourteenth-century Tuscan translation of Seneca's *Epistulae* (1717) is a copying error occasioned by the misreading of the abbreviation for "Ser" (with a long "s") as "fl"; the correct reading should be *servitudine* ["slavery"].

Entries such as this one will eventually be deleted as new readings from improved editions are incorporated into the corpus.

Reliable editions and what to expect from them

What makes editions "unreliable" is the presence of editorial interventions that are made without any apparent method or reason, such as questionable emendations, the supply of misleading punctuation supplied and plain misreadings. Far more challenging, however, is to ask what it is we expect from a "good" critical edition, not in the least because perceptions of value reflect on both methods and expectations.

My point is that an edition must establish a text that is as close as possible to that written by its author.[4] This raises a number of questions. Was there an original text that its author considered perfectly finished and not to be changed? Did medieval Romance texts have "authors" in the modern sense? How, or in what measure, can we be sure that what we reconstruct is close to what the author wrote? Is the reconstruction of an original text worth attempting?

To answer these questions, editors must harvest as much evidence as possible about a text's growth, transmission, and publication; and they must explain, justify and consistently apply their editorial policies. To a certain extent, a text-oriented edition — an edition that tries to establish what existed *before* the extant manuscripts were produced — is always reconstructive, even if the text survives in only one manuscript. I fully agree with Gianfranco Contini's statement that "anche la conservazione è una tuzioristica ipotesi di lavoro" (Contini 2007, 20) ["to stick to the reading in the manuscripts is a rigorous working hypothesis"].

Even if, in text-oriented editions, "originality" is a questionable concept, not easy to define (see Beltrami 2010b, 153–57), it must

---

[4]   See Beltrami 2010b where I explain thoroughly my views on the subject of critical editions.

be addressed, regardless of the practical difficulties and theoretical problems that it raises. After all, most medieval literary manuscripts are, to a certain extent, *editions*; they are more than mere (and, at times, faulty) reproductions resulting from copyists' general concern — as we are — with reproducing a "good" text, that is, a text suited, in their opinion, to the expectations of their readership. Thus, their interventions in the texts they were copying militate against later stemmatic interpretations and generally complicate our tracing of a text's transmission.

In addition to the choice of method, the reliability of a text-oriented edition is predicated also on the editor's understanding of the text and its tradition, and, of course, on a clear presentation of the sources and of his presentation of other kinds of evidence in the introduction, the critical apparatus and the commentary. Editors who shy away from reconstructing a text close to the original, or who challenge the idea that an original ever existed (like, for instance, Cerquiglini 1989; see Varvaro 1999) may choose to publish the text of a single manuscript. This method was famously championed by Joseph Bédier, whose "best text" method favoured the selection of a *documentary* text over the construction of a *critical* one, on the grounds that documents embody the texts that were available to past readers who lived closer to the time of original composition.

In classical philology, by contrast, the *codex optimus* was a critical reconstruction of a text that approximated as well as possible the original. For Bédier, the "original" text was unattainable and therefore remained outside of the purview of the editor's view. Moreover, it is not consistent with Bédier's method to publish a text according to a base manuscript, or "copy-text", and to incorporate into it "better readings" from other sources at points where the base text is unsatisfactory. Such a method is almost identical to the pre-scientific method that was in use before the development of new methodologies, during the nineteenth century. According to these outworn methods, to reconstruct an original text, editors would emend an authoritative printed edition (the so-called *vulgata*), or a manuscript, by reference to other manuscripts available to them bearing "better readings". (The only significant difference between that method and the new is that modern editors are much less inclined to emend [see Leonardi 2011b].)

Polycarpe Chabaille's edition of Brunetto Latini's *Tresor* (Latini 1863) offers a good illustration of this nineteenth-century method in Romance philology. Chabaille selected as his base manuscript the document fr. 12581 (MS F), held at the Bibliothèque nationale in Paris, for the following reasons: it was very old, and, in the editor's opinion, required fewer emendations than the others. Chabaille incorporated into his base text readings drawn from other manuscripts and placed a selection of the *varia lectio* in his critical apparatus.

The second critical edition of Brunetto Latini's *Tresor* by Francis J. Carmody (Latini 1948) is, by contrast, a Bédierist edition. The editor constructs a *stemma codicum*, then chooses a manuscript (BnF, fr. 1110, MS T) containing what he believes to be the final revised version of the *Tresor*, whose text appears to be grammatically correct and logical in itself. Carmody makes very few emendations (generally, manifest linguistic errors or referential inconsistencies) by reference to other manuscripts and through conjecture.

The more recent edition of the *Tresor*, by Baldwin and Barrete (Latini 2003), also based on a single manuscript (Madrid, Biblioteca del Escorial, L.II.3), is somewhat atypical in that the editors mostly emend the manuscript text on the basis of readings from Chabaille's and Carmody's texts and critical apparatuses, and do not mention minor alterations.[5]

An outcome of Bédier's method is that a manuscript may be considered worth editing for its own sake; rather than considering it as a witness within a textual tradition, the manuscript is seen as a unique, historical document which had its own readership and reception. This is the guiding concept of Avalle's edition of the corpus of Italian verse texts which includes all manuscript verse up to the end of the thirteenth century (Avalle 1992), the most important section of the corpus being constituted by three well-known manuscript anthologies of early Italian lyric poetry (Biblioteca Apostolica Vaticana, Vat. Lat. 3793 = V; Biblioteca Medicea Laurenziana [Florence], Redi 9 = L; and Biblioteca Nazionale Centrale di Firenze, Banco Rari 217 [formerly Palatino 418] = P) (see Leonardi 2011a).

---

[5] Another recent example of an edition based on a single manuscript, emended with readings taken from other manuscripts, is Sharman's edition of Giraut de Borneil's poems (Borneil 1989).

Avalle's edition does not attempt to recover an "original" text, but sets out to reconstruct the text that the copyists wished to write. Crediting the compiler of the manuscript with a desire to make a perfect copy, Avalle only removes copying errors. Where different versions of one poem exist, they are edited separately as if they were individual works. Over the last decades, this view of manuscript books as independent books has gained new importance in literary-historical studies, albeit mostly with regards to books of lyric poetry, which are typically anthologies.[6]

Avalle's editorial method has much in common with that of a semi-diplomatic edition, but it must not be confused with it. Avalle's edition is "manuscript-oriented" or, rather, "witness-oriented", in that it aims to interpret not only the meaning of the manuscript text, but also the manuscript itself as an individual work of art. The primary purpose of Avalle's edition is of course the creation of a corpus of early Italian poetic language.[7] Avalle's edition recalls other, strictly manuscript-oriented editions, designed to present reliable evidence of linguistic facts, whether this evidence survives in only one manuscript (typically an original in the case of notary deeds, wills, contracts of sale, account books and so on) or more, in which case one manuscript is selected and edited for its linguistic significance (editions of this type also usually include a linguistic commentary).

Manuscript-oriented editions are good sources of lexicographical evidence, because owing to the way they preserve the integrity of the manuscripts they provide reliable information about language use. In OVI's textual databases a special tag is attached to texts (available in such editions) that represent certain regional linguistic varieties (for instance, Florentine) in the manuscripts. This tag allows the user to select sub-corpora for study, which in combination with the dates of the manuscript sources, allows for a refined analysis of lexicographical change. For instance, the Pisan translation of Albertano da Brescia's treatises quoted above (Faleri 2009) enables us to record and date to the period 1287–1288 the earliest occurrences, and the only occurrences for the thirteenth century, of *disutilità* ["disutility"] and *dubitativo* ["doubtful" (a person) or "dubious" (a thing)]. These

---

[6]   See the study on the Vatican Codex Lat. 3793, one of the three manuscripts I mentioned, by Roberto Antonelli (Antonelli 1992).

[7]   The lemmatized concordance to the corpus still awaits publication due to technical difficulties.

treatises also record the only instance of the verb *disvilare* ["not to give importance to"].

However, one must guard against dating earliest usage on the basis of the dates of surviving manuscripts. For instance, Brunetto Latini wrote his *Rettorica* around the years 1260–1261, surely before 1266, yet the earliest surviving manuscript dates from the late-thirteenth or early fourteenth century. Likewise, the only occurrence of the word *badaggio* ["waiting"] (from old Occitan "badatge") appears in a sonnet by the thirteenth-century poet Dante da Maiano, whose poetic corpus, however, was published by the Florentine Filippo Giunti more than two-and-a-half centuries later, in 1527. To be more precise, the form *badaggio* looks like a thirteenth-century word, but this may not be more than an impression that has no grounding in fact. Cases like this, where the authorship of a certain form is in doubt, show how one must treat unusual forms in the transmitted text (and their authorship) critically. When the text of a thirteenth-century author is transmitted *only* in a source dating from the sixteenth century (regardless of whether this is a manuscript or a printed source), we must refrain from dating the lexicographical evidence to the thirteenth century because the authorship attribution is wrong or doubtful, or the transmission unreliable; however, if neither the authorship nor the transmission is questionable, we must date the attestation to thirteenth century even if the actual source is from the sixteenth century. Such chronological aberrations argue in fact for the continued use and relevance of text-oriented editions as sources of lexicographical evidence.

Brunetto Latini's *Rettorica* offers another interesting example, explained in a recent paper by Elisa Guadagnini (2010). In his *De inventione*, from which Brunetto translates, Cicero speaks of the *constitutio iuridicialis*, i.e., the final point in a legal argument that determines whether the points at issue are right or wrong. The Latin word *iuridicialis* is trivialized into *iudiciale* (modern Italian *giudiziale* ["relating to the judgement"]) in the texts of the branch that Francesco Maggini used for his edition in 1968 (M= Florence Biblioteca Nazionale Centrale, II.IV.124, 13th cent. ex-14th cent. in., and m = II.IV.73, 14th cent. ex.). But the texts in the other branch (including M1 = the MS of the same Library II.IV.127, 2[d] quarter, 14th cent., L = the MS Firenze, Biblioteca Laurenziana, Plut. XLIII.19, 15th cent., and S = the *editio princeps* by Serfranceschi [1546]) turn up "iuridiciale" in most occurrences. While the *Grande Dizionario della Lingua Italiana* includes an entry for *giuridiciale*, quoting the *Rettorica* indirectly from the *editio princeps* (through the editions of Zambrini and Lenzoni [1850] and Nannucci [1837–1839]), there is no occurrence of *iuridiciale / giuridiciale* in the *Corpus OVI dell'Italiano antico*, which uses Maggini's text. Guadagnini suggests that possibly the original reading was *iudiciale* in the first occurrence in the text, *iuridiciale* in the following ones. In sum, those who favour Maggini's edition will base their dating of *iuridiciale* on the age of the earliest manuscript in which the term appears; conversely, those who endorse Guadagnini's claim that Brunetto used *iuridiciale* will trace the word's origin to the middle of the thirteenth century.

Modern text-oriented editions generally share with manuscript-oriented editions a concern for the accurate reproduction of all the linguistic features of manuscripts, and in particular their spellings. For instance, the base manuscript (V^2 = Verona, Biblioteca Capitolare, 508) for the text-oriented edition of the *Tresor* by Beltrami et al. (Latini 2007) was selected for the edition's formal consistency, and emended by reference to other manuscripts, rarely through conjecture, on the basis of what we know about the textual tradition (see Beltrami 1988 and 1993), and with all rejected readings reported in the critical apparatus. Where no emendation was necessary, the edition preserved the manuscript readings in every detail.

Although I did not enforce this editorial policy in my edition of the *Tresor*, I believe that variant spellings are worth preserving in editions made for the sake of historical linguistics and, generally, in manuscript-oriented editions.[8] The case, for instance, can also be made in respect of another manuscript in the *Tresor* tradition: Raimondo da Bergamo's translation in eastern Lombard, preserved in a manuscript whose text was considerably altered by a copyist from Veneto (late fourteenth century?; Venezia, Biblioteca Nazionale Marciana, 4910, end of 14th–beginning of 15th cent.; see Beltrami 1993: 178–90); the translation is a valuable linguistic document and it would be worth having an edition that preserves the variant spellings as a witness to the *Tresor*'s reception in Northern Italy.

---

[8]   The reason why my co-editors and I decided to preserve variant spellings in our edition of the *Tresor* was because a substantial bit of work still needs to be done on the manuscript tradition; we felt that for the time being it was safer not to go against prevalent editorial policies and standardize the spelling.

In text-oriented editions of literary works, Italian philologists used to modernize spelling. The reason was the perception that the entire body of Italian literature, including works (or at least the works of the most prominent authors) written in early Italian, were all part of living Italian. Nowadays early Italian is usually considered as a dead language, as are the other Medieval Romance languages, and editors tend to leave spelling variants unaltered. Lexicographers plead in favour of this solution. In his review of the new edition of the poetry of the Sicilian School by Max Pfister (2010), the editor in chief of the *Lessico Etimologico Italiano* strongly claims that

> ormai è chiaro come conti anche il peso della variante e della sua esatta grafia. La scienza filologica esige uno sforzo in questa direzione e non deve cercare di adattarsi alla supposta comodità del lettore moderno (che spesso esiste solo nel desiderio degli editori) e alle sue pretese esigenze livellatrici. (Pfister 2010, 424)

> [the importance of the variant readings and of their exact spelling has become clear. Philological science necessitates an effort in this direction, and must not try to adapt to the alleged convenience of the modern readers (which often is but an editor's wishful thinking) and to their alleged demand of normalization.]

Here again, perceptions of value impact on methodological choices. That said, and by contrast with what seems to have become the dominant trend in recent Italian philology, I believe that it is useless to record variant spellings as lexicographical evidence — for instance, of *consiglio* spelled with /l'/, <gli>, <gl>, <lgli>, <lgl>, with an initial <ch> instead of <c>, with <m> instead of <n>, and so on. For to do so means that these minor variants in orthography were of similar importance to variant phonetic forms such as *conseglio* and *gonsiglio* (spelled <gonsilglio>). To remove such minor differences in spelling from a literary text is one of the tasks that editors must perform for the reader.

Modern (written) Italian still is very similar to the language of thirteenth-century Florence; in a certain sense it still is the same language (or was until recently, though of course the matter is much more complex), and therefore to print a text suitable for general readers means in most cases to adopt modern spellings instead of the old (and variable) spellings.[9] A modern reader expects that the same word is spelled the same way throughout the text. One solution therefore is for the editor to select the most frequently-used spelling from the manuscript and use it for all spelling variants of the base manuscript, but also for readings admitted into the text from other manuscripts.

However, no edition can meet the needs of all users: just as there may be various answers to the question What texts are worth editing?, there are various ways, determined by various goals, to answer the question of what method to adopt for the editing of a text.

Bibliography

Antonelli, Roberto. 1992. "Canzoniere Vaticano latino 3793". In Alberto Asor Rosa (ed.), *Letteratura italiana: Le opere, 1: Dalle origini al cinquecento.* Turin: Einaudi, pp. 27–44.

Avalle, d'Arco Silvio. 1992. *Concordanze della Lingua Poetica Italiana delle Origini (CLPIO).* Milan and Naples: Ricciardi.

Beltrami, Pietro G. 1988. "Per il testo del *Tresor*: appunti sull'edizione di F. J. Carmody". *Annali della Scuola Normale Superiore di Pisa,* 3rd series, 18, pp. 961–1009.

——. 1993. "Tre schede sul *Tresor*". *Annali della Scuola Normale Superiore di Pisa,* 3rd series, 23, pp. 115–190.

——. 1999. "The Lexicography of Early Italian: Its Evolution and Recent Advances (*Tesoro della Lingua Italiana delle Origini*). In Silvia Bruti, Roberta Cella and Marina Foschi Albert (eds.). *Perspectives on Lexicography in Italy and Europe.* Newcastle upon Tyne: Cambridge Scholars Publishing, pp. 29–53.

——. 2010. "Lessicografia e filologia in un dizionario storico dell'italiano antico". In *Storia della lingua e filologia: Atti del convegno ASLI (Pisa-Firenze, 18–20 dicembre 2008).* Florence: Cesati, pp. 235–48.

——. 2010a. "I poeti siciliani nella nuova edizione (con appunti su testo e metrica)". *Bollettino del Centro di studi filologici e linguistici siciliani,* 22, pp. 425–46.

---

[9] The same does not apply, of course, for other medieval languages which changed so much that there is little correspondance. It is impossible, and it makes no sense, to spell old French and old Occitan texts according to modern usage.

——. 2010b. *A che serve un'edizione critica? Leggere i testi della letteratura romanza medievale.* Bologna: Il Mulino.

Bonvesin da la Riva. 1941. *Le opere volgari.* Ed. Gianfranco Contini. Rome: Società Filologica Romana.

Borneil, Giraut de. 1989. *The Cansos and Sirventes of the Troubadour Giraut de Borneil: a Critical Edition.* Ed. Ruth Verity Sharman. Cambridge: Cambridge University Press.

Lo diretano bando. 1997. Ed. Rosa Casapullo. Florence: Accademia della Crusca.

Cerquiglini, Bernard. 1989. *Éloge de la variante: Histoire critique de la philologie.* Paris: Seuil.

Contini, Gianfranco, ed. 1984. *Il Fiore e il Detto d'Amore attribuibili a Dante Alighieri.* Milan: Mondadori.

Contini, Gianfranco. 2007. *Frammenti di filologia romanza: Scritti di ecdotica e linguistica (1932–1989).* Ed. G. Breschi. Florence: Edizioni del Galluzzo.

Del reggimento de' principi di Egidio Romano: Volgarizzamento trascritto nel MCCLXXXVIII. 1858. Ed. Francesco Corazzini. Florence: Felice le Monnier.

Di Girolamo, Costanzo, ed. 2008. *Poeti della corte di Federico II.* Milan: Mondadori.

Corpus OVI dell'Italiano antico. 2012. Florence: Institute Opera del Vocabolario Italiano. <http://gattoweb.ovi.cnr.it/>.

Corpus TLIO (Tesoro della Lingua Italiana delle Origini). 2000–. Florence: Institute Opera del Vocabolario Italiano. <http://tlioweb.ovi.cnr.it/>.

Faleri, Francesca. 2009. "Il volgarizzamento dei trattati morali di Albertano da Brescia secondo il 'codice Bargiacchi' (BNCF II.III.272)". *Bollettino dell'Opera del Vocabolario Italiano,* 14, pp. 187–368.

Formentin, Vittorio. 2002. "Antico padovano 'gi' da ILLI: condizioni italo-romanze di una forma veneta". *Lingua e Stile,* 37, pp. 3–28.

Gaiter, Luigi, ed. 1878–1883. *Il Tesoro di Brunetto Latini volgarizzato da Bono Giamboni.* Bologna: Romagnoli, I–IV.

Grande Dizionario della Lingua Italiana. 1961–2002. Ed. Salvatore Battaglia and Giorgio Barberi Squarotti. Turin: UTET.

Guadagnini, Elisa. 2010. "Una nuova edizione della *Rettorica* di Brunetto Latini". Paper delivered at the 26th Congrés

Internacional de Lingüistica i Filologia Romàniques, València, 6–11 September 2010).

Latini, Brunetto. 1863. *Li livres dou Tresor*. Ed. Polycarpe Chabaille. Paris: Imprimerie Impériale.

——. 1948. *Li livres dou Tresor*. Ed. Francis J. Carmody. Berkeley and Los Angeles: University of California Press.

——. *1968. La Rettorica*. Ed. Maggini, Francesco. Florence: Felice le Monnier.

——. 2003. *Li Livres dou Tresor*. Ed. Spurgeon Baldwin and Paul Barrette. Tempe, Arizona: Arizona Center for Medieval and Renaissance Studies.

——. 2007. *Tresor*. Eds. Pietro G. Beltrami et al. Turin: Einaudi.

Leonardi, Lino, ed. 2011a. *I canzonieri della lirica italiana*. 4 vols. Florence: SISMEL.

——. 2011b. "Il testo come ipotesi (critica del manoscritto base)". *Medioevo romanzo*, 35, pp. 5–34.

Nannucci, Vincenzo. 1837–1839. *Manuale della letteratura del primo secolo della lingua italiana*, 3 vols. Florence: Magheri.

L'Ottimo Commento della Commedia. 1827–1829. Ed. Alessandro Torri. 3 vols. Pisa: Capurro.

Pfister, Max. 2010. "La nuova edizione dei poeti della Scuola siciliana". *Bollettino del Centro di studi filologici e linguistici siciliani*, 22, pp. 421–24.

Le rime della scuola siciliana. 1962–1964. Ed. by Bruno Panvini. Florence: Olschki.

Serfranceschi, Francesco, ed. 1546. *Retorica di ser Brunetto Latini in volgar fiorentino*. Rome: M. Valerio Dorico and Luigi fratelli bresciani.

Squillacioti, Paolo. 2007. "Il bestiario del Tesoro toscano nel ms. Laurenziano Plut. XLII 22". *Bollettino dell'Opera del Vocabolario Italiano*, 12, pp. 265–353.

Varvaro, Alberto. 1999. "The *New Philology* from an Italian Perspective". *Text: An Interdisciplinary Annual of Textual Studies*, 12, pp. 49–58.

Vigo, Pietro, ed. 1889. *Statuto dei Disciplinati di San Giovanni di Pomarance*. Bologna: Romagnoli-Dall'Acqua.

Volgarizzamento delle Pistole di Seneca e del Trattato della Provvidenza di Dio. 1717. Ed. Giovanni Bottari. Florence: Tartini e Franchi.

Zambrini, Francesco and Filipppo Lanzoni, eds. 1850. *Opuscoli di Cicerone volgarizzati nel buon secolo della lingua toscana*. Imola: Galeati.

The Third Way

Philology and Critical Edition in the Digital Age[1]

Tara L. Andrews

In 2006, as I prepared to begin my doctorate, I met with my supervisor-to-be to discuss prospective research topics. It became clear during the meeting that he already had a project in mind: I would produce a critical edition of the Armenian-language *Chronicle* of Matthew of Edessa, and it would be a digital critical edition. Some time later, at the celebration that followed my viva examination, my supervisor cheerfully admitted that he had not had the least idea what a "digital critical edition" might be when he had set me on the path to making one. He simply trusted that I, as a software engineer turned humanist, would figure something out along the way. The fact that I now write this suggests that I did produce something that was accepted by my supervisor and examiners as a digital critical edition. So where is it? What does it look like? And if, as recently as that, a lone doctoral student had to work out for herself what a digital critical edition should be, does it not go some way toward explaining why there are so few of them about?

This paper arises from a round table discussion whose aim was to question whether digital techniques can coexist with traditional critical editing, or whether digital methods make critical editing obsolete. Given the ability to publish faithful digital facsimiles of all our source material, is there any need for the editorial emendation or text reconstruction that is the central activity of the traditional philologist? Is the so-called "new philology" better suited for the digital age than the "old" methods that have their root in classical philology, and does the "old" way have a future? Here I shall address some of these questions from the perspective of a relative philological neophyte to whom the digital realm is second nature. I argue (and I am by no means the first to do so) that digital methods afford opportunities to transcend the distinction between old and new philology,

---

[1]   A version of this paper was originally presented at the LECTIO Round Table "Digital or critical / digital and critical?" held in Leuven on 21 November 2011.

allowing the scholar to adopt the best of both approaches as suits the nature and heritage of each individual text. In order for us to grasp those opportunities, however, the working methods of all philologists must adapt to the realities and capabilities of the digital age.

I will discuss here some of the working methods of the digital philologist as pioneered in the late 1990s and early 2000s and adapted for my own doctoral work, and point to some of the technological progress that has been made since then through initiatives such as the Interedition project (Interedition 2012) to make these digital methods ever more feasible for ever more texts. Finally, I will look at the particular problem of text stemmatology — how it serves neatly to divide philological opinion, and how it might be reinvented when we revisit our assumptions about what is possible to analyze and compute.

Digital editions and digital philology

I would argue that digital critical editions are rare for two reasons. First, very few people have articulated a clear idea of what a digital edition ought to look like. Only two years ago, a session held at the THATCamp "unconference" connected to the Digital Humanities conference in London aimed to re-think the forms that a digital edition might take (Timney et al. 2010). It was widely agreed that most users want a reading text and transcriptions of the source; the idea of a standardized visual vocabulary to represent text features was also supported. Beyond that, there were many potentially useful feature proposals but very little consensus. This is somewhat surprising, given the comprehensive and complementary visions set forth both before and since by Robinson (2004), Buzzetti and McGann (2006), Buzzetti (2009), Bodard and Garcés (2009), and van Zundert and Boot (2011) among others, but the 2010 session made it abundantly clear that consensus is indeed lacking on what exactly a digital critical edition should be. As long as there is no agreement on the end result of digital philology, there can be none on its methods; as long as there is no consensus on method, there will not be widely applicable computational tools available to help produce digital critical texts.

This lack of consensus brings me to the second reason for the dearth of digital critical editions. With rare exceptions, both old and new philology remain fundamentally non-digital in their methods, eschewing the standardization and formal models that computers by their nature enforce. Even the TEI guidelines, which comprise the *de facto* representation standard for textual scholarship, are interpreted differently and routinely customized for each new project; this idiosyncratic interpretation and insistence upon customization, wherein exception becomes the rule, is a misunderstanding of the nature of a digital data model that effectively prohibits large-scale interchange or machine analysis across different projects (Schmidt 2011). If this is the current state of the art of digital scholarship, it goes some way toward explaining the paucity of tools for the task. At the TEI Members' Meeting in October 2011, partially in response to the discussion initiated by Schmidt, a think tank was sponsored by Interedition on the subject of TEI and interoperability. It became clear over the course of the meeting that flexibility and customizability is currently much more important to textual scholars than the sort of standardization that would allow for true progress toward digital critical editions.[2]

Part of the difficulty in defining what a digital edition might be is that the term refers simultaneously to two things. There is the eventual digital publication of a text edition, which may have been prepared using state-of-the-art digital tools for the purpose, specialist software such as Classical Text Editor (Hagel 1997–2012), in a spreadsheet, in a word processor, or even on paper and then transcribed into electronic form. Alternatively, there is what we might call "digital philology", an approach to textual editing that welcomes the aid of technology wherever possible and which will usually, but not necessarily, result in a digital publication. The difference between the traditional approach to philology, whether "old" or "new", and the digital approach lies in their respective willingness to divide labour between human and artificial intelligence; where the former tends to be reluctant to embrace digital possibilities, the latter favours a more efficient division of labour and encourages the production of new methods of presenting texts. The method of production, rather than the published form that the resulting editions take, is the practice wherein lies most of the promised revolution within textual scholarship, but it has attracted considerably less attention than the

---

[2]   Summaries of the participants' conclusions may be found online (Interedition 2011)

question of digital publication. Consequently, as the 2010 session at THATCamp showed, it is only rarely that scholars express a conception of a digital critical edition as anything more than an electronic and hyperlinked version of a book that can accommodate a very large and detailed critical apparatus. Indeed I am aware of only a very few digital critical editions which were produced outside of the conventional, painstakingly manual, framework of twentieth-century philology in either of its forms.

Editions based on the conventional, manual approach are all produced in roughly similar ways, notwithstanding their segregation into products of the "old" and "new" philology. Manuscripts must be transcribed into a computer format; multiple manuscripts of the same text are collated. A critical text is then produced, whether it be a full diplomatic representation of a single manuscript witness, a normalized version of a consensus text with variations noted in an *apparatus criticus*, or an attempt at reconstruction of a lost archetype after the construction of a stemma.

At its core, the difference between old and new philology can be seen as a subtle but crucial shift in purpose. The older practice of philology, whose methods are taken from traditional classical philology, emphasizes the "ideal" text whose authority supersedes that of any surviving witnesses; the specific ideal text in question might be the author's original, the recoverable archetype, or even the emended and conjectured version of a sole surviving witness. Conversely, the emphasis of new philology is on the "real" text as it has been preserved, received, annotated, and used. The distinction between "ideal" and "real" is a simple shift that nevertheless prescribes radically different working methods.

For the "old" philologist seeking to recover the ideal text, an entire series of steps has been prescribed (Maas 1957, West 1973) to use philological principles and editorial intuition to determine the extent to which the surviving manuscripts have fallen into copying error of various sorts. This requires a full collation of all witnesses, almost always reduced to "a full collation of all significant differences between witnesses" in the interests of time and practicality. The new philologist, who is generally more interested in the individuality and the variation in each witness (Cerquiglini 1989) than in a unified *textus receptus*, will often publish an edition of a single manuscript or a very few at most, and will take care to provide as accurate as possible a transcription. Consequently, editions produced according to the principles of new philology only rarely require extensive text collation.

If there are multiple witnesses, their groupings into witness families can be done in a variety of ways. Many old philologists use Lachmannian or neo-Lachmannian principles to construct a stemma hypothesis of the copying relationships between the manuscripts based on shared copyist error; this stemma becomes the key to the reconstruction of an archetype. Other philologists, whether old or new, might use cladistic analysis based on methods borrowed from phylogenetics to group the manuscripts into statistically probable families based on the variation within the text. Still others rely entirely on observation and intuition in discussing the relationships between texts. The methods for stemma construction or manuscript groupings, digitally assisted though they may be, remain grounded in assumptions about what we can and cannot know dating from before the digital age.

The critical text may now be produced according to the principles of the philologist, along with the *apparatus criticus*.[3] It is immediately obvious to almost all editors that digital publication removes the practical limitations on the size of the apparatus, and thus on the granularity of variation that may be displayed. This insight has nevertheless had little practical effect on most resulting editions, as the fine-grained variation has usually been excluded already at the time of transcription and/or collation.

In essence, then, the old philologist is limited from the outset by the perception that there is too little value in the "insignificant" data provided by the manuscript sources to justify the time it would take to include all of it in a critical edition. The new philologist, while more likely to make this data digitally available in the first place, needs little more than a way to present and annotate the text to be published. Little wonder that the result so often amounts to an electronic and hyperlinked book, and that the practices of new philology might therefore seem at first glance more suited to digital edition than those of the old. In both of these cases, the preparatory work is still largely manual in nature, even where it is computer-assisted with

---

[3]   Greetham (1992, 313–46) gives a good overview of the different schools of thought, particularly with regard to early modern and modern texts, as they emerged throughout the twentieth century.

word processors, spreadsheets for collation, or XML editors for TEI transcription. How may we move beyond this to the sort of "digital edition 2.0" envisioned by van Zundert and Boot (2011)?

A third way: digital philology

Many sceptics of digital technology labour under the illusion that digital editions leave no room for human agency, that they obviate human judgment. To answer this charge, Peter Robinson (2004) put forward a set of working methods for true digital textual criticism; these are largely the methods I used in my own doctoral work (Andrews 2009a), and they owe their origins to both "old" and "new" philological practices. Robinson took pains to point out how manual, exacting, and exhausting his methods are; this was necessary to counter the objection he faced, but was a little unfortunate from the perspective of convincing other philologists that fully digital methods are worth their while.

The most immediate value of digital methods is the ability to assign as much as possible of the work — particularly that which is repetitive, exacting, and error-prone — to the computer (Robinson 1989). It allows us to take advantage of the complementary strengths of man and machine to achieve a result far superior to that produced by either alone. The deeper value of digital philology, however, is that it should allow not only for innovative means of publication and display, but also innovative working methods and unexpected results, when we can cast aside so many of the practical limitations on the management of data that existed through to the end of the twentieth century. With these principles in mind, let us consider a digitally modified workflow for text criticism, and consider what can now be done and what may be possible in the near future.

Transcription. This represents the bulk of the manual work that must unavoidably be done by the editor or by human assistants. Fundamentally, as Robinson (2004) points out, the act of reading (and therefore transcription) of a text is an act of interpretation. There has been some research into the problem of optical character recognition (that is to say, automated transcription) for manuscript texts; although there is work in this direction (Wüthrich et al. 2009), very little generalizable progress has yet been made. Moreover, while OCR and other automated methods might speed the work significantly in the future, might someday even manage perfectly accurate automated transcriptions,the scholar who wishes to critically edit a text has little alternative but to closely read it in all its forms. Transcription remains thus a useful exercise, if a painstaking one.

In fact, witness transcriptions need not take any more time than manual collation of texts, and can usually be made to take considerably less. A full text transcription of any witness may be made simply by copying and altering the transcription of a similar witness, a process that is akin to the creation of a spreadsheet of variants but simpler and easier in execution. There is a small risk that the readings of the similar text might influence the readings of the manuscript being transcribed, but that is more than offset by the fact that a full transcription removes the scholar's temptation to exclude a peculiar reading because it seems not to be worth the effort to set up a new variant location in a spreadsheet.

While transcription work can be (and often is) done directly into a text editor or an XML editor (especially if the scholar is transcribing according to the TEI guidelines), the need for more user-friendly transcription tools has long been recognized. Of the several development initiatives underway to address this need, the T-PEN system developed at Saint Louis University (Ginther et al. 2009–2012) is currently the most promising.[4]

Collation. It is the need to collate the source texts that most often deters editors, particularly old philologists, from transcribing each of them in full. Although they understand the service to posterity that the transcription work represents, it is often not judged feasible to record and compare each non-normalized spelling, each punctuation mark, if the edition is ever to be completed.

As long as the collation must be done manually, the editor has a point. Whether directly into XML markup, into a specialist program such as Classical Text Editor, or (most painstakingly) into a separately maintained spreadsheet of text variants, manual collation is time-consuming, error-prone, and exhausting. If the workflow of

---

[4]   It is ever more widely recognized that digital publication of a manuscript should include a full diplomatic transcription; however, I have omitted here to enter the lively discussion of what a diplomatic transcription can and should entail. See Robinson 2009 and Pierazzo 2011, among others, for more on this topic.

edition is to be truly digital, an automatic collation of the transcribed witnesses with a program such as Juxta (Performant Software n.d.), CollateX (Dekker et al. 2008–2012, itself the successor to Robinson's own COLLATE), or nCritic (Andrews 2009–12) is indispensable. The use of one of these programs frees the scholar to transcribe the sources as precisely as possible, secure in the knowledge that the minute level of detail in a diplomatic transcription will lengthen the collation process by mere minutes. The scholar need then spend only a very few hours checking the results.

Analysis. Once the texts have been fully transcribed and collated, using tools that have minimized the temptation to curtail or "normalize" the data prematurely and have avoided the need to assess the significance of any piece of evidence, the process of analysis may begin. Examples may include phylogenetic analysis of the variant relationships (Baret et al. 2006), any form of stylistic analysis such as authorship attribution (e.g. van Dalen-Oskam and van Zundert 2007), or even inclusion in a corpus for large-scale data mining or the application of distant reading techniques (Moretti 2005). The most common sort of analysis performed at this stage is exactly the stemmatic analysis that is considered central to text edition by those who would reconstruct an archetype, and that tends to be rejected outright by new philologists. I will return to this below.

Edition. Given a full set of diplomatic transcriptions made without prejudice as to "true" or "errant" readings, a detailed collation, and the results of any analysis that has been run, the editor may now begin to construct the critical text, applying the editorial and philological judgment that the text in question calls for. Here too the computer may assist, primarily by ensuring consistency of decision throughout the text and by ensuring that any departure from the given witnesses is marked out and commented upon. Computer-assisted creation of a critical text is a relatively straightforward task, and can be done with a tool that is much simpler in conception than (for example) an automatic collator, but to my knowledge there is not yet any tool widely available for the task. For my own edition I developed a simple command script, which used as input and output an XML-encoded collation using the TEI parallel-segmentation method; that tool remains available for academic curiosity (Andrews 2009b). The early months of 2012 have seen the development of a proof-of-concept tool (Andrews et al. 2012), developed under the aegis of the Interedition project, that has been incorporated into the workflow of the editors of the Greek New Testament at the Institut für neutestamentliche Textforschung (INTF) in Münster.

Publication. We can now see that digital methods can (and should) lend substantial support to critical analysis in the task of preparing an edition, before the reader sees a single published result. It is the published form of the critical edition, however, that most scholars have in mind when they wonder why there are so few digital editions. What then should the finished digital edition look like? Robinson (2004, 420) describes it thus: "The analysis, editorial commentaries derived from the analysis, all texts and all collations are published in electronic form." This is a very open definition, and may be interpreted in a perfectly conservative fashion: the texts are presented individually and through collations, optionally with hyperlinks (or pop-up information) to connect related readings and supply additional commentary. More recently, Rosselli del Turco (2011) has proposed several best practices for the graphical interface components of any digital edition. These discussions are welcome and needed, but how far do they take us beyond our hyperlinked book?

In the case of my own critical edition, the situation was very simple. My university's examination regulations required a printed publication; I duly wrote a script to convert my XML-encoded edition into LaTeX format for rendering to PDF, and thought no more about the matter beyond the occasional reflection that it would be nice to have the texts published online somehow, somewhere, someday. Only in recent months, as the collaboration within Interedition grew and began to produce some exciting tools and techniques, and as the "digital edition 2.0" began to emerge as an idea, have I begun to experiment with these innovative tools using my own critical text. The result (Andrews 2012) remains a work in progress. In accordance with Robinson's description, the full text of each witness is available for display and download; commentary is available for each witness, for individual locations in the text, and for the text as a whole; the analysis is available in the form of the critical text and the stemma. Taking the edition more fully into the digital realm, the individual witness texts are available through a REST-like (REpresentational State Transfer, a simple URL-based mechanism for querying and updating resources on the Web) interface as TEI-encoded XML, as HTML for browser display, and as a series of JSON

(JavaScript Object Notation, a very simple interchange format for any form of data) tokens for use in tools such as automatic collators. The critical apparatus for any variant location may be displayed or dismissed with a mouse click; the text at that location may also be viewed in graph form, in a modified version of the variant graph first described by Schmidt and Colomb (2009). The reader may likewise view the stemma, colour-coded according to witness agreements for that location.

I do not pretend that my own critical edition is the apex of innovation for digital critical editions, or anything approaching that. The visions of Robinson, of Buzzetti and McGann, of Bodard and Garcés, of van Zundert and Boot, remain largely unrealized by this edition as well, and it is so far impossible to say which of these features, if any, may be adopted by other editors or used in further research. In that sense, consensus about what digital editions will become is still missing from our field.

This does at first glance seem disappointing. The inability, as yet, for textual scholarship as a whole to progress substantially beyond the conception of a digital critical edition as a feature-rich electronic book indicates that not enough scholars yet grasp the possibilities of large-scale analysis of texts, or the variety of ways in which their own work might be useful in the research of others. The onus cannot fall entirely on the producers of critical editions, however; production is almost always driven by demand. Until those who might use our editions, beyond printing out a PDF copy of the critical text and citing the page number of an associated printed version, present themselves, our digital editions will continue to offer a convenient PDF version of the critical text with apparatus, and they will continue to have associated print publications to which most of the effort is devoted. It is the practice of deep and/or large-scale text analysis, rather than that of textual criticism itself, which must drive the development of digital editions in all their potential.

Digital philology and its impact on stemmatology

The concept of a stemma can often be used as a handy litmus test to determine the sort of philologist before you. An old philologist will nod and begin discussing *Leitfehler*; a neo-Lachmannian may launch into a discourse about type-2 variant locations (Wattel and van Mulken 1996) and text-genealogical variants (Salemans 2000). A new philologist will reject the entire concept of variation as "error" (Cerquiglini 1989), and in many cases will reject the desirability or existence of a single archetype (e.g. Driscoll [2010]), rendering the entire concept of a stemma somewhat useless for his or her purposes.

This exchange might leave the digital philologist in some confusion. Surely it cannot be a choice between, on the one hand, an idealized and orderly picture of faithful yet fault-ridden copies of an authoritative source, and on the other hand a tangled web of texts whose relations to each other are coincidental and possibly even beside the point? Given the vast quantities of data that can be produced about a set of texts and given the generally accepted axiom that texts were, indeed, copied from other texts, the digital philologist might expect that, with enough aggregate empirical data, a scholar ought to be able to use computational analysis to arrive at an approximate order of copying. We ought moreover to have no fear of contamination, horizontal transmission, multiple archetypal versions, or extra-textual influences having skewed the result. The history of the text lies in its witnesses, and the historian of the text must seek to uncover that history.

In that sense, stemmatology is central to the methods of digital critical edition. It is the form of text analysis that lies at the heart of old philology, and it is the type of analysis that, if done more correctly and sympathetically, could be of great help to mediaeval philologists whether of the old school or the new. Such analysis would necessarily render a "hyperlinked book" edition into something inalienably digital.

From this perspective, stemmatology is a field that desperately requires a new approach. Its shortcomings were first highlighted in the early twentieth century, most famously by Bédier (1928), and certain of those critiques still ring true. Classical stemmata still tend to bifurcate, even more so since the advent of cladistic analysis with its binary trees. The situation where a manuscript text is copied from multiple exemplars or influenced by an oral tradition is still called "contamination", reminiscent of an unfortunate disease, and is still generally regarded as a block to further analysis even when it is suggested as a possible means to explain away puzzling textual evidence. If stemmatology is ever to be accepted as more than an idealized justification for preferring the reading that appeals most to the editor, it must be reinvented, grounded this time in a theoretical framework more rigorous (and more falsifiable, in the sense of the scientific method) than intuition and prejudices.

Even thirty years ago, such a proposal for a "new stemmatology" would have been dismissed as utterly impractical; it would take more than the lifetime of a scholar to consider every piece of evidence, to find a probability and a weighting for each comma shared between multiple witnesses to a text.[5] Even up to the present, as the field of computer-assisted stemmatology has gained momentum, the implicit assumption remains that some variants are more "relation-ship-revealing" than others, and that scholars should restrict their attention to those considered *a priori* to meet some criterion for transmissibility. I would argue now that this approach too looks back into the capabilities of the past, rather than ahead to those of the present and future, and unnecessarily constrains the result to be that which we were already likely to find based on our intuition and prej-udices. We should instead seek to use *all* the information available to us; we should be attempting to find out if some of those commas are significant after all. I do not claim that the attempt will meet with certain success, but given the volume of mediaeval texts that do after all survive, and given the fact that circumstantial and external infor-mation also survives about the manner in which some of them were copied, it can only be a matter of time before a corpus of empirical evidence about text transmission begins to surface.[6]

This is the true strength of digital philology, a strength that nei-ther the old nor the new can match. We can generate an enor-mous quantity of sheer data through digital methods; the level of detail in transcription and collation that was inconceivable during Lachmann's career is now simply tedious, sometimes daunting, but entirely attainable and becoming easier every day. Freed from the constraint of limiting ourselves to a practical level of text variation, we may also begin to free ourselves from the heuristic crutches that

---

[5]   An outright dismissal of the idea can be found in the controversial appendix to Timpanaro's history of Lachmannian method (2005, 182); Sale-mans (2000, 8–10) also justifies his use of deductive reasoning in terms of the impracticality of amassing enough data for inductive reasoning.

[6]   The "Tree of Texts" project at KU Leuven (2010–12), led by Caroline Macé, aims to lay the methodological foundations for just such an accumulation of empirical data and the creation of a model for mediaeval text transmission.

have been a feature of text criticism since its inception, and harness the power of raw computation to ask ourselves "what if?" What if some of our heuristics are wrong? What if a scholar finds a set of features of variants that were previously thought insignificant, and uses these to detect horizontal transmission in certain texts, and radically overturns our ideas of how twelfth-century historical chronicles were adapted for the seventeenth? What if the availability of full transcriptions, lexically tagged and morphologically analyzed, of Syrian, Cypriot and Catalan poetry of the fourteenth century provides evidence of cultural transmission never before imagined?

I truly believe this to be the future of text research, and it is tremendously exciting; but it is also a test for our field. Will we collectively shift from methods that are almost purely manual to embrace the capabilities that the digital world affords us? Will we learn to look at our texts in new ways, free of what we think we already know? Far better that we do, for this is the only way that we can continue to learn from them.

Bibliography

Andrews, Tara L. 2009a. *Prolegomena to a Critical Edition of the Chronicle of Matthew of Edessa, with a Discussion of Computer-Aided Methods Used to Edit the Text.* D.Phil., University of Oxford.

——. 2009b. *Source for do_edit.pl.* <http://cpansearch.perl.org/src/AURUM/Text-TEI-Collate-2.1/scripts/do_edit.pl>. [Accessed 31 March 2012].

——. 2009–12. *nCritic.* <http://byzantini.st/ncritic/collate/>. [Accessed 31 March 2012].

——. 2012. *Excerpts from the Chronicle of Matthew of Edessa.* <http://byzantini.st/ChronicleME/>. [Accessed 31 March 2012].

Andrews, Tara L., et al. 2012. "Shared Tools for Digitized Workflows — a Text Regularization Case Study". Paper presented at Interedition Symposium: Scholarly Digital Editions, Tools and Infrastructure, 19 March 2012, The Hague.

Baret, Philippe, et al. 2006. "Testing Methods on an Artificially Created Textual Tradition". In Caroline Macé, Philippe Baret, Andrea Bozzi, et al. (eds.), *The Evolution of Texts: Confronting Stemmatological and Genetical Methods.* Pisa and Rome: Istituti Editoriali e Poligrafici Internazionali, pp. 255–83.

Bédier, Joseph. 1928. "La tradition manuscrite du Lai de l'Ombre: Réflexions sur l'art d'éditer les anciens textes.". *Romania,* 54, pp. 161–96, 321–56.

Bodard, Gabriel and Juan Garcés. 2009. "Open Source Critical Editions: a rationale". In Marilyn Deegan and Kathryn Sutherland (eds.), *Text Editing, Print and the Digital World.* Farnham: Ashgate, pp. 84–98.

Buzzetti, Dino. 2009. "Digital Editions and Text Processing". In Marilyn Deeganand Kathryn Sutherland (eds.), *Text Editing, Print and the Digital World.* Farnham: Ashgate, pp. 45–61.

Buzzetti, Dino and Jerome J. McGann. 2006. "Electronic Textual Editing: Critical Editing in a Digital Horizon". In Lou Burnard, Katherine. O'Brien O'Keefe and John Unsworth (eds.), *Electronic Textual Editing.* New York: Modern Language Association of America, pp. 53–73.

Cerquiglini, Bernard. 1989. *Éloge de la variante: Histoire critique de la philologie.* Paris: Éditions du Seuil.

Dekker, Ronald Haentjens, et al. 2008–2012. *CollateX.* <http://interedition.github.com/microservices/>. [Accessed 31 March 2012].

Driscoll, Matthew J. 2010. "The Words on the Page: Thoughts on Philology, Old and New". In Judy Quinn and Emily Lethbridge (eds.), *Creating the Medieval Saga: Versions, Variability, and Editorial Interpretations of Old Norse Saga Literature.* Odense: University Press of Southern Denmark, pp. 85–102.

Ginther, Jim, et al. 2009–2012. *T-PEN: Transcription for Paleographical and Editorial Notation.* <http://t-pen.org/TPEN/>. [Accessed 15 May 2012].

Greetham, D. C. 1992. *Textual Scholarship: an Introduction.* New York: Garland Publishing.

Hagel, Stefan. 1997–2012. *Classical Text Editor.* <http://www.oeaw.ac.at/kvk/cte/>. [Accessed 31 March 2012].

Interedition. 2011. *Würzburg TEI 102011 Participants — Interedition Wiki.* <http://www.interedition.eu/wiki/index.php/Würzburg-TEI102011_Participants>. [Accessed 31 March 2012].

——. 2012. *Interedition: Powered by Interoperability.* <http://www.interedition.eu/>. [Accessed 31 March 2012].

Maas, Paul. 1957. *Textkritik.* Leipzig: Teubner.

Moretti, Franco. 2005. *Graphs, Maps, Trees: Abstract Models for a Literary Theory.* New York: Verso.

Performant Software. n.d. *Juxta: Collation Software for Scholars.* <http://www.juxtasoftware.org/>. [Accessed 31 March 2012].

Pierazzo, Elena. 2011. "A Rationale of Digital Documentary Editions". *Literary and Linguistic Computing,* 26, pp. 463–77.

Robinson, Peter. 1989. "The Collation and Textual Criticism of Icelandic Manuscripts (1): Collation". *Literary and Linguistic Computing,* 4, pp. 99–105.

——. 2004. "Making Electronic Editions and the Fascination of What is Difficult". *Linguistica Computazionale,* 20–21, pp. 415–38.

——. 2009. "What Rext Really Is Not, and Why Editors Have to Learn to Swim". *Literary and Linguistic Computing,* 24, pp. 41–52.

Rosselli del Turco, Roberto. 2011. "After the Editing is Done: Designing a Graphic User Interface for Digital Editions". *Digital Medievalist,* 7. <http://digitalmedievalist.org/journal/7/rosselliDelTurco/>. [Accessed 31 March 2012].

Salemans, Ben J. P. 2000. *Building Stemmas with the Computer in a Cladistic, Neo-Lachmannian, Way: The Case of Fourteen Text Versions of Lanseloet van Denemerken.* Ph.D., Katholieke Universiteit Nijmegen.

Schmidt, Desmond. 2011. "TEI: clean, unclean & document interchange?". *Humanist Discussion Group,* 25.190 (26 July). <http://lists.digitalhumanities.org/pipermail/humanist/2011-July/002333.html>. [Accessed 31 March 2012].

Schmidt, Desmond and R. Colomb. 2009. "A Data Structure for Representing Multi-Version Texts Online". *International Journal of Human-Computer Studies,* 67, pp. 497–514.

Timney, Meagan, et al. 2010. "Rethinking the Digital Scholarly Edition". <https://docs.google.com/document/d/1OXflh4AwaCpvwsX1ha8nnGmsHlZmjZAq_t_TaBWWVus/edit>. [Accessed 31 March 2012].

Timpanaro, Sebastiano. 2005. *The Genesis of Lachmann's Method.* Chicago and London: University of Chicago Press.

Van Dalen–Oskam, Karina and Joris van Zundert. 2007. "Delta for Middle Dutch: Author and copyist distinction in 'Walewein'". *Literary and Linguistic Computing,* 22, pp. 345–62.

Van Zundert, Joris and Peter Boot. 2011. "The Digital Edition 2.0 and the Digital Library: Services, not Resources". *Digitale Edition und*

Forschungsbibliothek (Bibliothek und Wissenschaft), 44, pp. 141–52.

Wattel, Evert and Margot van Mulken. 1996. "Weighted Formal Support of a Pedigree". In Pieter Th. van Reenen, Margot van Mulken and J. W. Dyk (eds.), *Studies in Stemmatology*. Amsterdam; Philadelphia: Benjamins, pp. 135–68.

West, Martin L. 1973. *Textual Criticism and Editorial Technique: Applicable to Greek and Latin Texts*. Stuttgart: B. G. Teubner.

Wüthrich, Markus, et al. 2009. "Language Model Integration for the Recognition of Handwritten Medieval Documents". In *IDCAR 2009: Proceedings of the 2009 10th International Conference on Document Analysis and Recognition*. Los Alamitos, Cal.: IEEE Computer Society, pp. 211–15.

All texts are equal, but...

Textual Plurality and the Critical Text in Digital Scholarly Editions[1]

Franz Fischer

IS THERE A FUTURE for the "old philology"? Why are "truly critical" and "truly digital" editions so rare? This article discusses the questions raised at the Leuven round table by showcasing two scholarly editions that claim to be both digital and critical: the edition of William of Auxerre's *Summa de officiis ecclesiasticis*, an early thirteenth-century Latin treatise on liturgy, and the so-called HyperStack edition of Saint Patrick's *Confessio*, a fifth-century open letter by Ireland's patron saint, also written in Latin and the oldest text that has survived from Ireland in any language. In giving a comparative introduction to both of these online editions — to their underlying methodology and theoretical implications — I will make the following arguments: (1) Critical texts matter. The critical reconstruction of an assumed original text version as intended by an author remains of major interest for most textual scholars and historians as well as any person with an interest in historical texts. (2) Critical texts have the same legitimacy as various and different manifestations of a text. Digital editions enable the presentation of textual plurality. (3) There is no reason intrinsic to the digital medium that makes the idea of a critical text obsolete. Rather, a critical text can serve as the standard reference, as an ideal text to start with and as a portal to access the variety of textual manifestations of a particular work.

---

[1]   The title of the present article (alluding to the famous slogan in Orwell's *Animal Farm*) was not ingeniously coined by myself on the occasion of the the LECTIO Round Table discussion on "Digital or critical / digital and critical?" held in Leuven on 21 November 2011, but (as I learned only subsequently) had been used already by Paul Morgan [quoted in Sahle forthcoming]). I am grateful to Patrick Sahle, Anthony Harvey and Philipp Steinkrüger for their support in developing this paper.

Definitions

The primary purpose of scholarly editions is to make texts from the past available. Through editions textual scholars access, assess, prepare and present primary data for research. A scholarly edition is the critical representation of historical documents and texts (Sahle 2008). But what does "critical" mean? And, even more fundamentally, what is a text?

According to the pluralistic text theory of Patrick Sahle a definition of what text actually is depends on the perspective on a particular text and on the individual perception of this text.[2] Text, or textual identity, can be understood according to six features. Firstly, texts need to be understood in terms of their *idea*, its content or intention: texts are intentional. And: text are what they mean. Applied to editorial practice, this is the realm of interpretation, exegesis, commentaries and the justification for the most noble of all editorial interventions: emendation — a correction of the text as present in the witnesses, based on the editor's understanding of the author's intentions. Traditional philology according to the Lachmannian paradigm has always been seeking to transcend the material contingencies and corruptions of textual transmission by aiming at reconstructing an assumed original version or archetype — whatever the definition of this might be.

But text of course is also understood, secondly, as a *work* with a clearly defined narrative structure; thus, for example, the opening paragraph of Saint Patrick's *Confessio* is always *Confessio* 1, be it in the original Latin or in the German translation; it is always the same text. This is not the case when text is dealt with, thirdly, as a specific expression, a *linguistic code*, a certain series of words. A translation is entirely different from the original under the perspective of text as a linguistic code. But the original Latin of the *Confessio*, which was first published in a scholarly edition in 1950-51, reprinted in 1993 and now digitized and made available online, is still the same text, with exactly the same words. However, these texts, fourthly, are all different *versions*, so that, for example, in a seminar situation, though everybody may be consulting "the same text", not everyone will find

---

[2]   Sahle forthcoming; see Fischer 2008. For a similar concept in the field of bibliography see the Functional Requirements for Bibliographic Records as issued by the International Federation of Library Associations and Institutions (IFLA 1998, 12-29).

that (say) "page 12" contains the same thing — and some will not be working with pages at all.

But even if everyone has the same version, they still have, fifthly, different *documents* in their hands. And this distinction is even more obvious when we talk about handwritten copies, manuscripts or even charters. We can describe these documents topographically ("here is text, there is text") and as regards the chronology of its creation ("this has been corrected or added at a later stage, that at an earlier stage"). And this is why we have so-called genetic editions, recording and representing the genesis of a text in time and space. Also, we can analyse and describe the script and the writing materials, the colour or the chemical components of the ink, the parchment, the paper, the script or font size, and other visual features. And this is why we have so-called diplomatic editions that claim to represent, sixthly, the visual features and signs of a particular document — because they are significant. The physical appearance of medieval charters or, most notably, of the Bible as a book (e.g., in a liturgical context, or in court when you swear on it) is highly meaningful. The "text itself" does not matter here at all — the book might even contain blank pages — yet the text is identified by means of its physical appearance and, as such, points to a certain idea or truth. This brings us back to the text understood as idea or intention: platonic, eternal and true, and transcending any particular physical manifestation.

Arranged in a circle these aspects of textuality build the so-called text wheel according to Sahle — visualizing a pluralistic understanding of what text actually is (Figure 2). Any sort of text is all this at once, at least potentially, *in posse* if not necessarily *in esse*. Indeed, one should always be able to ask: where is the text, when all documents, all witnesses are corrupted, full of mistakes, incomplete? And where is the text when all documents are lost? And then, of course, if we accept a somehow ideal or intentional existence of texts, then which is the text when an author has changed or revised his or her intentions during the course of time?

On the other hand, there has always been a certain mistrust towards the written word, as manifest for example in Saint Paul's famous statement in his second letter to the Corinthians: *The letter kills, but the spirit gives life.*[3] However, textual scholars and historians

---

[3]   2 Cor 3,6. Another well-known example is Socrates telling the anec-
dote of the king of Upper Egypt criticizing the invention of script because it

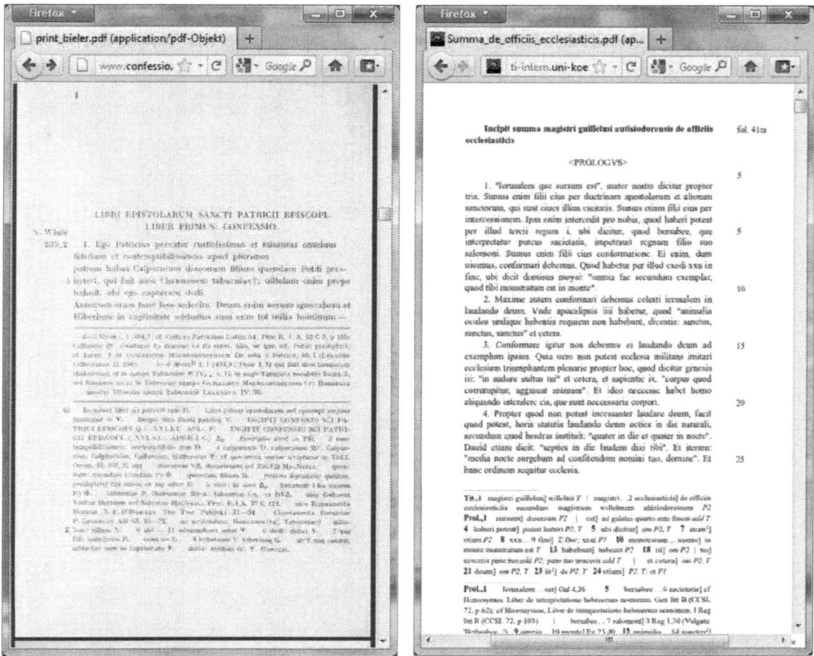

Figure 1: PDF versions of a critical text online — *Confessio* (Bieler 1950-51) on the left, *Summa* (2007) on the right.

rely completely on textual evidence in a very pragmatic way: there is no textual evidence without its material manifestation. But also, there is no text without an abstract meaning. By the means and techniques of textual criticism (*recensio, collatio*, etc.) traditional editors try to bring both perspectives as far as possible into accordance.

---

creates pseudo-knowledge instead of true knowledge (Plato, Phaidros 274B ff, esp. 275D-E): "Writing, Phaedrus, has this strange quality, and is very much like painting. For the creatures of painting stand like living beings, but if one asks them a question, they preserve a solemn silence. And it is the same with written words; you might think they spoke as if they had intelligence, but if you question them, wishing to learn about their sayings, they always tell you one and the same thing. And every word, when once it is written, is tossed about, alike among those who understand and those to whom it does not belong, and it knows not to whom to speak or not to speak; and when ill-treated or unjustly reviled it always needs its father to help it; for it has no power to protect or help itself" (trans. Fowler, with changes by Philipp Steinkrüger). The editor in that sense is the godfather of the text. In his exegetic capacity the critical editor proclaims to know and execute the author's intention when emending and commenting the written word accordingly.

Either way, textual perspectives and respective research interests are much more diverse. The text wheel might help to distinguish these specific notions of texts as realized in an edition. And the value of a scholarly edition might be measured and assessed by asking how far all of the textual aspects stated above are covered or, at least, how consistent is an editor's choice in representing just some or even just one of these textual aspects.

Two digital critical editions, two methodologies

Both editions shown in Figure 1 are digital *and* critical, but methodologically they have been created using completely different approaches (from opposite directions, as it were). On the one hand (Figure 1, left), the work of Saint Patrick's *Confessio* had already been published in an excellent print edition by the Austrian scholar Ludwig Bieler in 1950-51. On the other hand (right), the *Summa* by William of Auxerre had never been printed or published before. Here the point of departure was the text as witnessed by fifteen manuscript copies dispersed in fourteen libraries and archives across Europe.

Both of these editions are critical editions according to the Lachmannian paradigm (Maas 1927, West 1973; see Andrews in this volume); that is, both editions establish a text that is based on a meticulous comparison of the physical evidence as furnished by the manuscripts. They claim to present "*the* text", or "the *best* text", the text as intended by the author, a reconstruction of an assumed archetype, emended, structured and annotated. Variant readings of the manuscript testimonies are recorded in the *apparatus criticus*. Inter-textual references are recorded in the *apparatus fontium*, in the *apparatus biblicus* and (as a special feature of the edition of the *Summa*) in an *apparatus* indicating the use of text passages by authors of later times. All *apparatus* entries are referenced by means of *lemmata* and line numbers. Each text is introduced with a description of the textual material and the methodology applied for re-creating "the actual text".

And these texts are, as they stand, also digital texts (which is already a considerable achievement in itself): they are accessible online, as PDF; they can easily be copied and shared; they are searchable and printable; and any passage can be copied and pasted to any other electronic document. Yet "digital" is also supposed to entail "more" — more than just creating an electronic duplicate of the printed page of the printed page (Robinson 2002, Gabler 2010). Both editions offer many more features and functionalities than just "copy and paste" etc. And both editions cover a much wider range of textual manifestations of the respective works.

Ideally, a scholarly edition that is "truly digital" should be an edition that aims at covering all or, at least, as many of the textual aspects as possible of a particular work in the best possible way, by exploiting the full potential of the digital medium while maintaining the highest possible academic standards.

The HyperStack edition

The Saint Patrick's *Confessio* Hypertext Stack is a virtual stack of closely interlinked text layers representing all relevant versions of the text, as well as translations into several modern languages, manuscript facsimiles and descriptions, existing print editions and transcriptions, and a series of special features such as electronic text versions of Patrick's earliest biographies, a bibliography, a novel, audio files, scholarly articles, source files and background information (*Saint Patrick's Confessio* 2011). Methodologically, most fundamental for the realization of a digital edition providing such a broad variety of textual layers is not "the text itself", whatever this might be, but an abstract and persistent structure of books, of chapters (or, here, of words and paragraphs) in order to align and interlink all different versions and documents — without privileging or subordinating the specific characteristics of any particular text version.

This structure, along with a reliable critical text version considered to be canonical by the academic community, has been taken from Bieler's scholarly print edition, published in 1950-51, which itself is based on the foundational edition by Newport J. D. White (1904). (The latter is also provided in the Stack in the form of PDF scans from a "clean" copy and, most interestingly, from a unique copy with handwritten annotations by Ludwig Bieler, dating from the time when he was preparing his own "definitive" edition in the 1940s.)

The text of the critical edition was electronically available in the Royal Irish Academy's *Archive of Celtic-Latin Literature (ACLL)*. But this text version was, as it were, flat, or two-dimensional; that is, the text is devoid of its academic framework (apparatuses etc.) in order to fit it into a database that aims to incorporate the whole corpus of Latin texts from Celtic sources into a searchable but single-layered expanse of text. This expanse may be thought of as very wide, but very thin. In contrast, and as a kind of case study, the HyperStack intended to cover just one single — if the most iconic — text from the entire corpus, but in full depth. A tower has been built at one point on the flat plain of text; a third dimension has been added. In order to achieve this, the existing electronic text version has been complemented and enriched with all the relevant textual information that lies beyond, beside or beneath it — both metaphorically, as regards the textual tradition, and literally, as regards the features and functionalities of the printed edition, since these indicate the contextual characteristics of the reconstructed text (the "text itself") according to the conventions of philology in the Lachmannian tradition of textual criticism.

To achieve this, the three-part apparatus, extensive commentary, and some addenda and corrigenda published in 1966, were scanned and converted automatically via optical character recognition (OCR) into electronic form along with the critical text itself. The result — particularly messy in the apparatus and commentary because of the use of different languages (Latin, English), mixed fonts (Greek, Latin and Hebrew) and formats (superscripts, subscripts, italics etc.) — was proofread, and the basic structure of the text marked up with reference to paragraphs, line numbers, and page breaks. Each word was given a unique ID in order to be able to give clear, machine-readable references, and to provide links to any word or range of words, especially with a view to cross-referencing entries in the apparatus with the relevant passages in the text. Sigla and other references to manuscripts, to biblical, source and parallel texts, to abbreviations etc. — in fact all forms of textual information, implicit and explicit — were encoded in TEI.

For the online presentation of the critical text this information was converted and realized by (1) coordinating all parallel text versions (manuscript facsimiles, earlier editions, and translations); (2) causing relevant passages in the text to be highlighted when

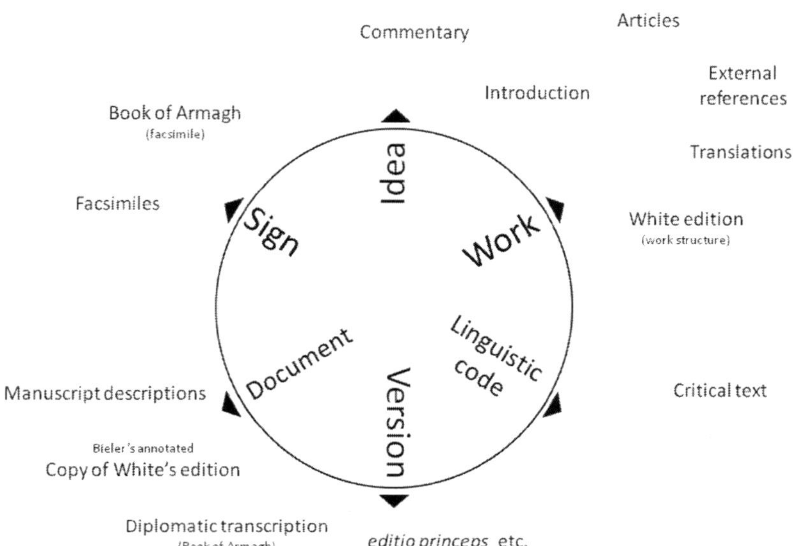

Figure 2: Text Wheel according to Sahle – applied to the HyperStack resources.

corresponding apparatus notes were moused over; (3) embedding hyperlinks to referenced manuscript witnesses, passages and editions; (4) resolving sigla and abbreviations by mouse-over; (5) integrating addenda notes and corrections; (6) linking bibliographical references to the bibliography; (7) linking keys and symbols to an auxiliary list with relevant information, etc.

All in all, this has not only made the information given in the critical print edition (often in an idiosyncratic manner) more accessible, understandable and usable in its digital guise, but has also added valuable information or given additional value to it — not just by so-called "retro-digitization", but by (in effect) creating a new edition in its own right, aiming at superseding all previous editions.

The critical text thus covers various aspects of Saint Patrick's writings; primarily, however, it establishes a single authoritative linguistic code, based on the manuscript witnesses, and establishes an abstract work structure that can be referenced. Furthermore, the digital critical text gives access and directs one to a variety of further textual layers within the Stack. These resources can also be assigned to specific notions of texts as defined above and as tentatively portrayed by Figure 2: translations, for example, primarily reflect the text as a work by conveying its meaning into a new linguistic code; the introduction as well as the commentary provide information on all textual aspects that are necessary to understand "the text itself" and the context of the work; scholarly articles place the text in an even wider context (as do external references). Facsimiles and descriptions give all relevant information about the manuscripts, both as witnesses for the text in terms of content and visually as material objects of history. For instance, the famous Book of Armagh contains the oldest copy of the *Confessio* known to exist, but in a version that deliberately omits significant passages in order to promote Saint Patrick as a most successful missionary and glorious founder of monasteries in Ireland without failure — and to validate Armagh's claims to ecclesiastical primacy in Ireland in the Middle Ages.

The Summa edition

In the case of William's *Summa* the print version of a critical text stood at the very end of the editorial process (*Summa* 2007; see Fischer 2010). There was no previous edition to rely on, only manuscripts. So where does one begin creating a digital scholarly edition? How does one create a pluralistic edition that includes a critical text? Methodologically it does not seem to be elegant to begin with digital tools such as the Classical Text Editor (CTE) that are designed to create print editions, for these editions then need to be marked up and enriched to transform them into truly digital editions (i.e., editions that offer as much textual information as possible and that have the largest feasible number of user features and functionalities).

On the other hand, there is no out-of-the-box software available for creating truly critical and truly digital editions at the same time. The ability of collation tools to support editorial decisions is improving all the time (CollateX, Juxta; see Andrews in this volume); virtual research environments and laboratories are being built to facilitate editorial work (TextGrid, MOM, DARE); the TEI standard for textual criticism is constantly being refined. Yet the entire editorial process of producing a scholarly edition that reaches both traditional (print) and modern (digital) standards remains a complex task only very few projects aim to fulfil.

The point of departure for the creation of the *Summa* edition was the transcription of a manuscript. This is common practice. But which manuscript to choose? Under the pluralistic approach a transcription is not just a temporary state in the (re)construction of a critical and definitive version. Rather a transcription represents an original document in its own right. Furthermore, it assures editorial transparency and serves as a basis for multiple text presentations. It thus should be executed in as detailed and faithful a manner as possible.

The worst that a critical editor can encounter is an intelligent scribe: understanding what he is copying, an intelligent scribe will have subtly transformed and modified the original and introduced his reading to the text. But as a matter of fact, the intelligent scribe tends to attract our attention more than the unintelligent one. And the copy itself is the result and a manifestation of an intellectual exchange, a transfer of thoughts. The very fact that an intellectual, high-profile individual has considered it worthwhile to create a copy of a particular work adds value to the work itself. In the case of William of Auxerre's *Summa de officiis ecclesiasticis,* from fifteen extant witnesses a manuscript from the Bibliothèque nationale de France was chosen that at a first and superficial glance looked very much the same as the handwriting of Albert the Great: Albertus Magnus — what a find! Albert, the great philosopher, had deemed this text worthy of spending hours and hours copying 35 folios, 70 pages, 140 columns during his time at the university in Paris. Unfortunately, a closer view could not verify this hypothesis. Some scribal and graphic characteristics turned out to be too different.

Nonetheless the writing of this Parisian manuscript, a very small and highly abbreviated *Semitextualis libraria,* was executed by the hand of a distinguished thirteenth-century scholar. That much, at least, is suggested by internal evidence too: the work structure is consistently marked up in line by rubrics and paragraph marks as well as in the margins (e.g. by *questio-solutio* titles), the order of words and the record of biblical quotations is often slightly changed, etc. Given these considerations the manuscript witness was deemed worthy of a detailed transcription. The decision on what scribal characteristics to encode while transcribing was based on the principle of covering as many details as possible subject to a reasonable investment of time. The following codicological and palaeographical features were recorded: column and line breaks, margins, rubrics, initials, original spelling, abbreviations, punctuation, allographic distinctions between *u* and *v*, etc. The distinction, however, between the Tironian *et*–abbreviation with and without strike-through was dropped because it seemed too tedious to record this all the way through — a practical decision, but one that has rendered the data inconsistent and therefore useless as regards a systematic analysis of this feature.

Still, the transcription, or rather diplomatic edition, bears a rich set of digital palaeographical data to be exploited, for instance, by quantitative research. Significant characteristics of the scribe, the scriptorium or region of provenance could be compared to similar data from other documents to be recorded by future scholars.

Yet scholars interested in either the person and the thinking of William of Auxerre, the highly distinguished philosopher and theologian who was actively involved in the foundation of the University of Paris, or in understanding medieval liturgy and how it was perceived and understood by their contemporaries want a text that is somehow critical, corrected, structured, normalized. They are not interested in contingent features of a medieval manuscript copy. And many among the most distinguished scholars will hesitate to acknowledge the superiority of digital philology over traditional editing for as long as the former does not deliver what they expect.

Considering again the amount of time and resources available a full collation of all fifteen extant manuscript witnesses would have been too laborious: the text was too long and time too short. For this reason only two further manuscripts were chosen. Test collations of all manuscripts at the beginning, in the middle, and at the end of the text led to a first approximate stemma, and proved that both of these manuscripts had "good readings" and that each of them represented one of a total of two manuscript families. Of these witnesses each and every reading constituting a variant from the Parisian MS was recorded — consistently and without exception, apart from variant spellings — in order to avoid as far as possible any arbitrariness in the recording of variants and in the collection of data.

To mark the difference between, on the one hand, readings that are commonly regarded as insignificant and not worth mentioning and, on the other hand, those that are commonly regarded as being of interest for the reader, an attribute value was added in the markup of each of the variant readings. Such readings were variously flagged as (1) "not important", that is, not worth being displayed in a default view of an *apparatus criticus*; as (2) "important", that is, worth being displayed in a default view of an *apparatus criticus*; and, most importantly, as (3) "better readings", that is, as readings that will replace those recorded in the Parisian principal manuscript witness in the critical version of the text.

The transformation of raw textual data into a standardized presentation of the critical text, whether in print or in digital form, is not supported by any software tool or editor, nor is the TEI encoding standard in itself sufficient to achieve the critical text. In addition to that, serious problems arise that are both theoretical and practical. On the theoretical side, beside the criticism of critical texts as being highly speculative and ahistorical (a criticism worthy of being called traditional in its own right), the question of normalization, spelling (especially of "better readings") and suppression of the most characteristic variants and features of the principal manuscript testimony can hardly be answered in a way that is satisfactory for all user scenarios. On the practical side, creating a lemmatized apparatus for a text that has not yet been created proved to be a challenging task since, for each type and sub-type of editorial intervention, a standardized process had to be defined and implemented to transform the source data into a form readable according to the conventions of textual criticism.

Despite these difficulties, a critical text was created and presented, in both a print and a digital version, that displays the "best readings", is clearly structured, is slightly normalized, and has a modern punctuation. The three-part apparatus is referenced by lemmata and diacritics. The user of the digital edition navigates via a dropdown menu, via the table of contents, or by browsing chapter by chapter. Each chapter is closely interlinked with the respective passage in the diplomatic transcription of the principal manuscript witness from Paris and with the transcription (or rather reading text) of a variant version as present in an expansively and artistically illuminated thirteenth-century miscellany from Cambrai. All edited texts as well as extensive manuscript descriptions are interlinked with digital facsimiles of the respective documents located within an integrated virtual archive. Thus any record and observation can be viewed and verified. Various indexes generated from the source document give yet another means of access to the text. Philological introduction, manuscript descriptions and edited texts are also available as PDF downloads and will be published in print as soon as a revision of the entire edition is completed.[4]

Conclusions

There is nothing in print that cannot be realized in digital form as well. In contrast, there is quite a lot one can do digitally that cannot be realized in print. Most strikingly, the digital medium supports an egalitarian presentation of text versions, including facsimiles and transcriptions. There is, therefore, no theoretical justification for creating critical editions exclusively in print — though there might be practical reasons such as scholarly tradition and prestige or reliable publication workflows to name just a few.

A further advantage of the digital form over print is that editions can be updated: editorial mistakes, typos and misinterpretations can easily be corrected; information can be added at some later stage, etc. This general improvability of digital scholarly editions gives justification for the publication of preliminary or beta-versions in order to make the valuable resources created accessible to the community as soon as possible. But in fact this might turn into a disadvantage because, in practice, a resulting decline in the quality and accuracy of scholarly editions has become noticeable — it is quiet telling that both of the editions presented here are to some extent still "unfinished". The *Summa* edition has been "preliminary" since its first publication in May 2007.

Each medium has its favourite or natural or most compliant perspective on texts. Print of course very much favours "the one text", the final version of a reconstructed archetype (whether or not such a thing ever actually existed); facsimiles are too expensive; transcriptions are seldom encountered in print, to say nothing of multiple transcriptions of the same text.

The digital medium very much favours flat texts and images that can be easily replaced and updated. In practice, digital editions tend to privilege texts that have a minimum of editorial intervention,

---

[4]   For a graphic tentatively illustrating the extent to which various textual aspects are covered by the *Summa* edition see Fischer 2010, 159–61 (corresponding to §§ 27–38 in the online version).

plain texts and (meticulously) transcribed or digitally converted text versions — albeit at times extensively marked up and annotated. But there is no reason intrinsic to the digital medium that would make the idea of a "truly critical text" obsolete. On the contrary, the plurality of equally legitimate texts makes even more obvious the need for a critical text and for the guidance it furnishes by offering a suggested reading based on expert analysis of the textual material and on editorial decisiveness (Robinson 2000). Moreover, as regards editorial decisions the digital medium is particularly suited to providing the transparency that is so fundamental for scholarly research and so imperfectly realized by the apparatus in scholarly print editions.

Critical texts do matter — for the reader's sake and especially in the context of multi-textual editions — and one is tempted to say: all texts are equal, but critical texts are more equal than others.

Bibliography

Archive of Celtic-Latin Literature (ACLL-2). Comp. Anthony Harvey and Angela Malthouse. Turnhout: Brepols.

Bieler, Ludwig, ed. 1950-51. "Libri Epistolarum Sancti Patricii Episcopi". *Classica et Mediaevalia*, 11, pp. 5–150, and 12, pp.79–214; reprinted Dublin: Stationary Office, 1952.

——. 1966. "Libri Epistolarum Sancti Patricii Episcopi: Addenda". *Analecta Hibernica*, 23, pp. 313-315. [Reprinted in Bieler 1993.]

——. 1993. *Clavis Patricii II; Libri Epistolarum Sancti Patricii Episcopi.* Dublin: Royal Irish Academy.

Fischer, Franz. 2010. "The Pluralistic Approach — The First Scholarly Edition of William of Auxerre's Treatise on Liturgy". *Jahrbuch für Computerphilologie*, 10, pp. 151–168, <http://computerphilologie.tu-darmstadt.de/jg08/fischer.html>. [Accessed 24 April 2012].

Gabler, Hans Walter. 2010. "Theorizing the Digital Scholarly Edition". *Literature Compass*, 7(2), pp. 43–56, <http://onlinelibrary.wiley.com/doi/10.1111/j.1741-4113.2009.00675.x/abstract>. [Accessed 24 April 2012].)

IFLA. 1998. *Functional Requirements for Bibliographic Records: Final Report.* München: K. G. Kraus; reprinted in *International Federation of Library Associations and Institutions (IFLA)*, 1998 and 2009, Den Haag: IFLA, <http://www.ifla.org/publications/

functional-requirements-for-bibliographic-records>.   [Accessed 24 April 2012].

Libri Sancti Patricii: The Latin Writings of Saint Patrick. 1905. Ed. Newport J. D. White. *Proceedings of the Royal Irish Academy*, 25 (Section C) Dublin: Hodges Figgis & Co., pp. 201–326.

Maas, Paul. 1927. *Textkritik*. Leipzig: B.G. Teubner.

MOM-CA. 2011. *Monasterium Collaborative Archive*. Köln: Universität zu Köln, <http://www.mom-ca.uni-koeln.de/>. [Accessed 24 April 2012].

Morgan, Paul. 1991. "Hypertext and the Literary Document". *Journal of Documentation*, 47, pp. 373–88.

Robinson, Peter. 2000. "The One Text and the Many Texts". *Literary and Linguistic Computing*, 15(1), pp. 5–14.

——. 2002. "What is an Electronic Critical Edition?" *Variants*, 1, pp. 51–57.

Sahle, Patrick, comp. 2008. *A Catalog of Digital Scholarly Editions*. Köln: Universität zu Köln, <http://www.uni-koeln.de/~ahz26/vlet/>. [Accessed 24 April 2012].

——. Forthcoming. *Digitale Editionsformen: Zum Umgang mit der Überlieferung unter den Bedingungen des Medienwandels*. Schriften des Instituts für Dokumentologie und Editorik 7. Norderstedt: Books on Demand, <http://www.i-d-e.de/schriften>.

Saint Patrick's Confessio. 2011. Eds. Anthony Harvey and Franz Fischer. Dublin: Royal Irish Academy, <http://confessio.ie>. [Accessed 24 April 2012]..

"TEI Guidelines". 2007. In *TEI: Text Encoding Initiative*. Charlottesville: Text Encoding Initiative, <http://www.tei-c.org/Guidelines>. [Accessed 24 April 2012].

West, Martin L., 1973. *Textual Criticism and Editorial Technique Applicable to Greek and Latin Texts*. Teubner Studienbücher. Stuttgart: B. G. Teubner.

William of Auxerre. 2007. *Magistri Guillelmi Autissiodorensis Summa de officiis ecclesiasticis: Kritisch-digitale Erstausgabe*. Ed. Franz Fischer. PhD, University of Cologne. <http://www.thomasinst.uni-koeln.de/sdoe> (preliminary version). [Accessed 24 April 2012].

Texts Worth Editing

Polyperspectival Corpora of Letters

Annemarie Kets

WHAT TEXTS ARE WORTH editing? In the case of Dutch collections of letters written between 1800 and 1900, the answer to this question can be found in a report compiled in 1996 on the basis of a questionnaire circulated among literary historians (Maas and de Man 1996). Forty-four years earlier, the Rijkscommissie voor Vaderlandse Geschiedenis (National Committee for Dutch History) had pondered the same question (Rijkscommissie voor Vaderlandse Geschiedenis 1952). It is unsurprising that many of the collections listed in the 1952 report should also feature in the 1996 report, for "belangrijke personen en instellingen — en dus ook de bronnen die met hen in betrekking staan — [behouden] over het algemeen hun status te midden van de 'paradigma-wisselingen'" (Maas and de Man 1996, 7) ["significant individuals and institutions — and thus also the sources connected with them — tend to retain their status amid all the 'paradigm shifts'"]. Thus, only a small proportion of the goals set in the 1952 report were met in four decades following.

A similar fate may befall the archives mentioned in the 1996 report. The highest priority was here accorded to the correspondences of key figures in the cultural and social life of the nineteenth century whose activities often covered a wide range of disciplines (literature, philosophy, the visual arts, politics and history) (Maas and de Man 1996, 13). These correspondences tend to be extensive. Aware that a thoroughly annotated scholarly edition of letters militated against prompt publication, Maas and de Man pleaded not to annotate the texts, and they also put forward the possibility of using floppy discs or CD-ROMs instead of books (Maas and de Man 1996, 14). What they failed to consider, however, was that preparing a work for publication is less time-consuming than the preparatory editorial work that goes into facilitating access to the sources. And it is precisely in this latter area that, thanks to technological developments, we have made much headway in recent years. The realization, within manageable time-frames, of editions of extensive collections of letters is now within our reach.

One of the central figures whose correspondence was mentioned in both reports is Albert Verwey (1865–1937). Verwey was part of what is known as "De Tachtigers" [the "Eighties Movement"], one of the most influential cultural-historical movements in Dutch history. The intellectual and artistic output of the Tachtigers is characterized by its interdisciplinary and international nature. Collections of letters dating from around 1900 show that there was a lively national and international exchange not only between the various artistic domains (such as literature, the visual arts, and music), but also with non-artistic domains, such as philosophy, the exact sciences, politics, and several social movements. Verwey considered himself to be chiefly a poet, but he was also an essayist, an editor of several influential journals, a critic and an academic. From 1880 until his death in 1937, he exchanged some 30,000 letters with over 2,000 correspondents, both at home and abroad. His correspondents included not only prominent literary authors but also the leading historians, politicians, philosophers, composers and musicians, architects, visual artists, and scholars of his day, as well as numerous influential intermediaries in literary circles, such as publishers and journal editors. In 1982, a group of researchers launched the "Albert Verwey-Brievenproject" ["Albert Verwey Letters Project"], designed to produce a complete, chronologically ordered edition of the letters written by and to Verwey, with an introduction and annotations. The researchers had ambitious and interesting plans for what they called a "computer edition", but unfortunately the project had to be abandoned prematurely (Stapert-Eggen 1991). However, the importance of the Tachtigers and of Verwey's role within it did not abate, and this undiminished interest prompted the Huygens Institute for the History of the Netherlands to revive the project in 2008. For the moment, the scope of the edition is limited to covering the early years (1880–1895) of the Tachtigers, during which Verwey exchanged some 3,000 letters with more than 300 correspondents (Kets-Vree 2008). Two thirds of these have not been edited before. The remaining letters appeared in three scholarly editions (Van Deyssel and Verwey 1981–1986; Verwey 1995; Kloos and Verwey 2008). The new edition is being prepared using *eLaborate*, a collaborative editing tool developed by the Huygens Institute that enables

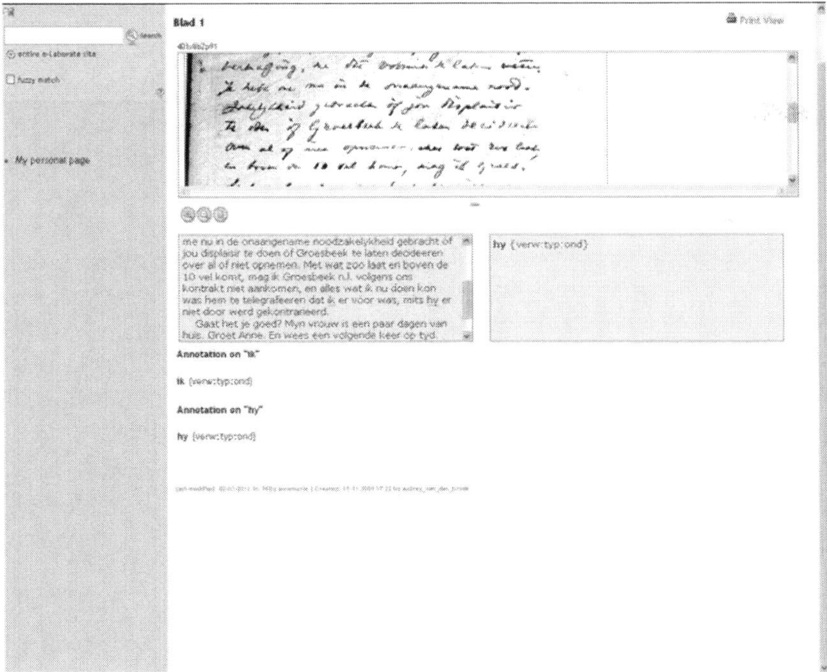

Figure 1: *eLaborate* working environment for editors, with a separate window for facsimiles, for transcriptions and for annotations.

editors to transcribe and to annotate texts from digital facsimiles that have been uploaded into the programme (Figure 1).[1]

The editors of the Huygens project are encouraged — at times forced — to seek collaboration with other individuals and with institutions (archives or libraries) housing the relevant collections, such as the Amsterdam University Library, which holds the archive of Verwey's private papers, and which digitized them and made available high-quality digital colour facsimiles of them. Here, the advantages of partnership are evident: the editors of the Verwey project can produce their transcriptions at any time — on any computer with an internet connection — from faithful copies of the original. Because they enable high magnification, these digital copies are, at points, easier to decipher than the originals. The facsimiles will ultimately form part of the online publication of the edition. The Amsterdam University Library has also compiled a detailed

---

[1]   See https://www.e-laborate.nl/en/. [Accessed 18 June 2012].

catalogue of the Verwey collection, which is currently available online. For each letter, which has been allocated a unique identifier, the catalogue lists information about the sender, the recipient, the place from which the letter was sent, etc. (Figures 2a and 2b).[2] The compilation of this catalogue and the provision of facsimiles fulfill the first steps of the editorial project — to delimit the corpus and to make the originals available.

In addition to institutional collaboration, the establishment of informal working groups also opens up new prospects. Two recent developments in the field of editorial studies have been successfully combined in the Verwey project: "crowd sourcing" and the formation of a "community". What is special about the Verwey community is that it is operative even in the preliminary phases of the work.[3] Researchers, trained volunteers, and students of various universities collaborate with the editorial team on the transcription of the letters — through seminars, in undergraduate dissertations, or through traineeships.

Working with non-professional editors calls for strict organization. Five detailed instruction manuals have been produced. The first deals with the structure of the online edition (a hierarchical system of folders and subfolders). The second explains how to create folders and how to upload scans. The third focuses on feeding transcriptions and annotations into the *eLaborate* tool. The last two manuals deal with the recording of metadata and the transcription of manuscripts. This systematic approach has greatly facilitated and accelerated transcription. By now all letters written between 1880 and 1894, as well as a considerable number of those from 1895, have been transcribed and checked. Once the defined corpus has been transcribed, proofed and corrected, the editor responsible for the edition will undertake a final quality check; compare the transcriptions with the scans and, if necessary, with the originals; and adjudicate on conflicting readings (between the transcriber and the proofreader).

Several researchers wishing to make use of our provisional results have joined the Verwey community. Among them are, for instance,

---

[2]   See http://opc.uva.nl. The inventory is based on the results of the first phase of the "Albert Verwey-Brievenproject", launched in 1982.

[3]   For the possibilities and — as far as the Dutch language area is concerned — the limitations of the concept of "community", see Van Raemdonck 2009, 296.

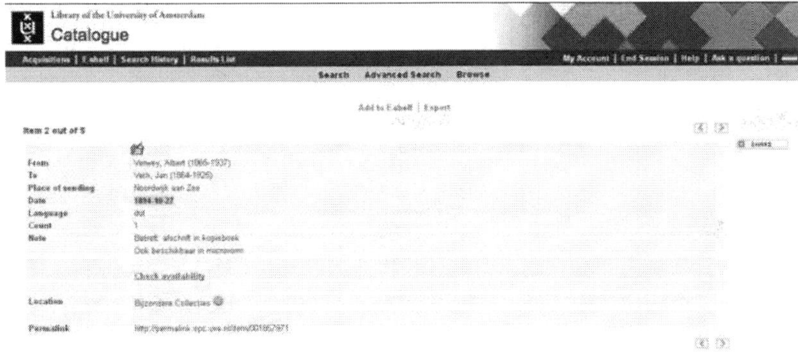

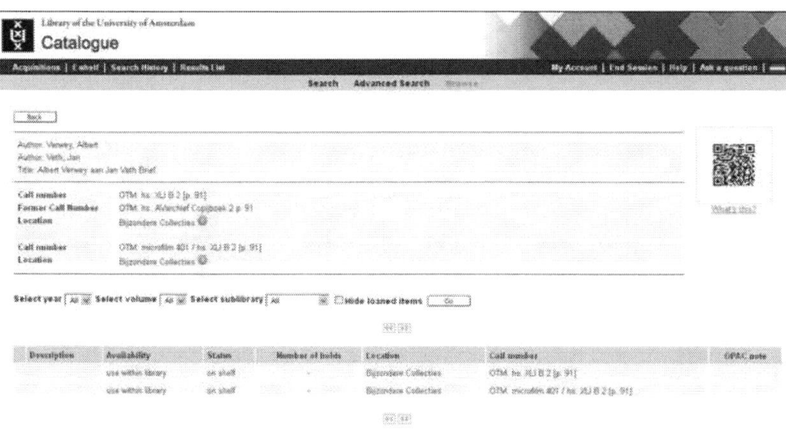

Figures 2a and 2b: Amsterdam University Library Online Publieks Catalogus [Online Public Catalogue].

the biographers of Verwey and of Willem Kloos (1859–1938, the most important poet of the Tachtigers movement). That our transcriptions are not yet final at this early stage is not really a problem for the researchers can consult the digital facsimiles. Moreover, they need not travel to the relevant archives to consult the original documents; they can peruse the transcriptions at any moment at their desk. They can also search within this voluminous corpus thanks to electronic search functions. Finally, collaboration is advantageous for us editors too: we can benefit from the researchers' feedback.

The approach chosen for the editing of Verwey's correspondence has uncovered fascinating webs of relationships and provides information on other people gravitating around Verwey. One of Verwey's correspondents was Willem Arnold Witsen (1860–1923), a famous Dutch painter, etcher, and photographer. Just as Verwey was at the centre of literary circles, or, as the Dutch expression goes, was like "the spider in the web", Witsen was a key figure in the world of the visual arts. From 1877 until his death in 1923, he exchanged some 2,000 letters with approximately 150 correspondents. These letters have now been edited and published online (Witsen 2007). A collation of Witsen's and Verwey's respective correspondents for the same period shows that they had forty-five correspondents in common. (This number would doubtless increase if one included the letters written by and to Verwey between 1895 and 1923.) In many cases the matters that exercised the great minds of the day are discussed in both Verwey's and Witsen's networks, sometimes from diverging viewpoints — divergences that militate for the grouping together of their respective correspondences.

Even so, the combination can only in part do justice to the whole epistolary network. Other members of the networks to which Verwey and Witsen belonged of course exchanged letters among themselves. There are also letters from individuals who did not belong to either of these networks, but who nonetheless played an important role in the cultural and social life of the day. Some of these letters have already been published in book form or online; others are currently being edited. A rough count yields approximately 20,000 edited letters from members of the Tachtigers and their contemporaries. Apart from the painter, engraver and photographer Willem Witsen (1860–1923), there are letters by the composer Alphons Diepenbrock (1862–1921; Diepenbrock 1962–1998), by

the actor Arnold Ising, Jr. (1857–1904; Van Deyssel and Ising 1968),
by the author and psychiatrist Frederik van Eeden (1860–1932; Van
Eeden and Van Deyssel 1964), and by the painter Jacobus van Looy
(1855–1930; Van Looy 1975). Our goal is to combine as many the-
matically connected sources as possible from *c.* 1900 within one
searchable system to be known as the "Web van Tachtig" ["Eighties
Web"]. The expansion of the "Web van Tachtig" will eventuate in
a wider and clearer picture of the diversity and spread of the opin-
ions, ideas, and ideals of the social and cultural elite of the time.
Grouping these letters together will also enable users to examine the
events and developments of this period from various viewpoints. The
researchers involved in this project believe that such a "polyperspectival" corpus of letters will constitute an extremely rich research tool:

> Een doorzoekbare, digitale brieveneditie waarin verschillende
> (parallelle) correspondenties zijn opgenomen, zou het onderzoek
> naar "knooppunten" in de literatuurgeschiedenis — de Beweging
> van Tachtig [...] — of centrale figuren op het literaire veld [...]
> krachtig bevorderen. Tegelijkertijd zou zo'n elektronische databank
> met correspondenties een vollediger overzicht geven van de verschil-
> lende posities die een schrijver in onderscheiden correspondenties
> inneemt, en hoe die posities in de loop van de tijd veranderen. (Van
> de Schoor 2008, 225–26)

> [A searchable, digital edition in which a number of parallel collec-
> tions of letters have been included, would strongly encourage the
> research on "nodes" in literary history — the Eighties Movement
> [...] — or on the main players in the literary field [...]. At the same
> time such a database of letter collections would provide a more com-
> plete overview of the different roles taken by an author in the various
> correspondences, and how these roles change in time.]

The nucleus of the "Web van Tachtig" is formed by the edition
of Verwey's letters (1880–1895). The primary audience for this
edition (and also for the "Web van Tachtig") is the scholarly community. What matters most, therefore, is not the aesthetic nature
of the letters, but their significance for documenting the life and
ideas of these figures. The emphasis, therefore, is on accuracy. All
hitherto unpublished letters by and to Verwey are to be transcribed
diplomatically, with all their peculiarities, inconsistencies, and slips
of the pen. This approach differs from that used by the editors of

the letters previously published (Van Deyssel and Verwey 1981–
1986; Verwey 1995; Kloos and Verwey 2008),[4] whose editions were
intended not only for scholars but also for a broader readership,
and whose transcriptions were amended with a view to greater "read-
ability". Moreover, the differing rationales for the establishments of
these three digitized editions prompted us to ask ourselves the following question: Should we go back to the sources and edit them
again diplomatically, or should we incorporate the transcriptions as
presented without changes? We chose the latter option and decided
to invest our limited resources to expand the corpus rather than to
emend existing editions. Our decision is even more justifiable when
it comes to dealing with the "Web van Tachtig".

The presentation of the metadata of the hitherto digitized
editions was also inconsistent. For instance, names and dates were
variously represented (sometimes even within a single edition), and
the repositories and shelf-marks of the documents were not always
given. Because the digital data is fed automatically into *eLaborate* and
the linking of metadata, transcriptions, facsimiles and annotations
can be done only partially, painstaking and time-consuming input by
hand was also necessary. Moreover, additions and adjustments were
required to bring the metadata of the three digitized editions in
line with that of the born-digital part of the project (Figure 3). Such
painstaking work is indispensable; without complete and consistent
metadata, it is impossible to search within the whole corpus.

To conclude, the ongoing work I described above fulfils and
exceeds the goals set in 1952 and 1996. In 1952, the report of the
National Committee for Dutch History focused, in the realms of art
and literature, specifically on the archives of Willem Kloos, Willem
Witsen, Jacobus van Looy, Albert Verwey, Frederik van Eeden and
Alphons Diepenbrock — all members of, or closely connected with,
the Tachtigers (Rijkscommissie voor Vaderlandse Geschiedenis
1952, 48–49). Forty-four years later, Maas and de Man mentioned
many of the same figures and, in addition, suggested publishing all
the correspondences that one could trace within a specific, limited
period (Maas and de Man 1996, 13). They thus pleaded *avant la
lettre* for a polyperspectival corpus of letters. Recent technological

---

[4]   These letters have been digitized by the Digitale Bibliotheek voor de
Nederlandse Letteren (Digital Library of Dutch Literature), which is also a part-
ner in the Verwey project.

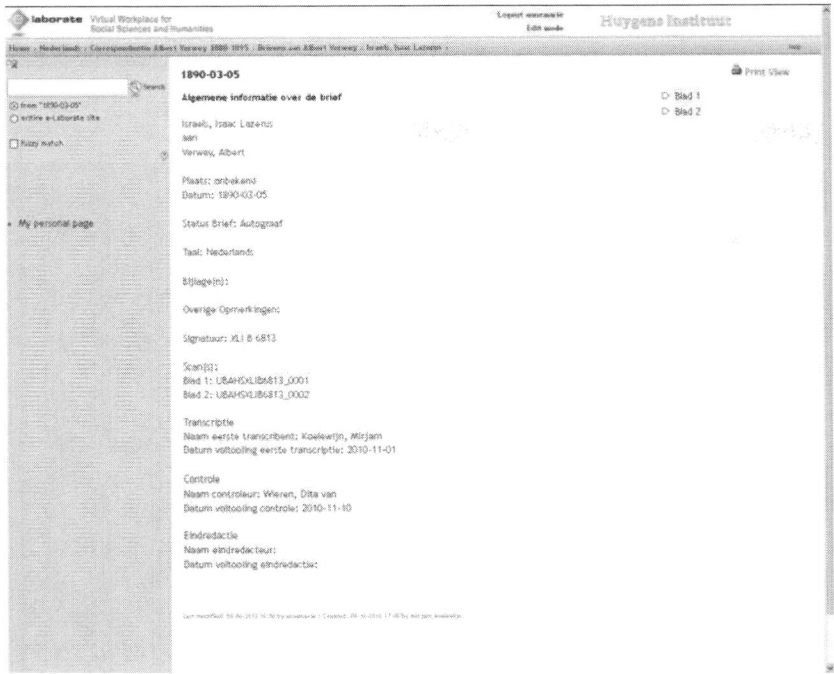

Figure 3: Metadata listed per letter in the *eLaborate* working environment for editors.

developments allow us to claim that Maas and de Man's proposal — repeated in a digital context by Van de Schoor (2008, 225–226) — is a realistic goal.

Bibliography

Diepenbrock, Alphons. 1962–1998. *Brieven en documenten*. Ed. Eduard Reeser. 11 vols. Den Haag: Vereniging voor Nederlandse Muziekgeschiedenis and Amsterdam: (Koninklijke) Vereniging voor Nederlandse Muziekgeschiedenis.

Kets-Vree, A. 2008. *Oude bronnen, nieuwe vragen. Ontwikkelingen in de editiewetenschap. Rede uitgesproken bij de aanvaarding van het ambt van bijzonder hoogleraar Editiewetenschap [...] bij de Faculteit der Letteren van de Vrije Universiteit Amsterdam op 20 november 2008.* [Amsterdam]: Vrije Universiteit. <http://dare.ubvu.vu.nl//handle/1871/13145>.

Kloos, Willem and Albert Verwey. 2008. *Van de liefde die vriendschap heet: briefwisseling Willem Kloos — Albert Verwey 1881–1925*. Ed. Rob van de Schoor and Ilona Brinkman. Nijmegen: Vantilt

Van Looy, Jacobus. 1975. *"Wie dronk toen water!": Bloemlezing uit de briefwisseling met August Allebé gedurende zijn Prix de Rome-reis, 1885–1887*. Ed. F. P. Huygens. Amsterdam: Meulenhoff.

Maas, Nop and Jacqueline de Man. 1996. *Rapport van het Project Nederlandse literaire brievencollecties en- edities, 1800–1900*. [Den Haag]: Constantijn Huygens Instituut voor tekstedities en intellectuele geschiedenis.

Rijkscommissie voor Vaderlandse Geschiedenis. 1952. *Drie rapporten over de uitgave van bronnen voor de Nederlandse geschiedenis*. Den Haag: Martinus Nijhoff.

Stapert-Eggen, M. 1991. "Op weg naar een computereditie van de correspondentie van Albert Verwey". *Gezelliana: Kroniek van de Gezellestudie*, 1991(2), pp. 45–68.

Van de Schoor, Rob. 2008. "Zelfrepresentatie in brieven: epistolair ik en lyrisch ik". *Tijdschrift voor Nederlandse Taal- en Letterkunde*, 124, pp. 219–226.

Van Deyssel, Lodewijk and Arnold Ising. 1968. *De briefwisseling tussen Lodewijk van Deyssel en Arnold Ising jr., 1883–1904*. Ed. Harry G. M. Prick. 2 vols. Den Haag: Nederlands Letterkundig Museum en Documentatiecentrum. Repr. Den Haag: DNBL, 2007. <http://www.dbnl.org/tekst/deys001hgmp08_01/>.

Van Deyssel, Lodewijk and Albert Verwey. 1981–1986. *De briefwisseling tussen Lodewijk van Deyssel en Albert Verwey*. Ed. Harry G. M. Prick. 3 vols. Den Haag: Nederlands Letterkundig Museum en Documentatiecentrum. Repr. Den Haag: DNBL, 2007. <http://www.dbnl. org/tekst/deys001hgmp09_01/>.

Van Eeden, Frederik and Lodewijk van Deyssel. 1964. *De briefwisseling tussen Frederik van Eeden en Lodewijk van Deyssel*. Ed. H. W. van Tricht and Harry G. M. Prick. Zwolle: W.E.J. Tjeenk Willink.

Van Raemdonck, Bert. 2009. "De definitieve teksteditie: definitief achterhaald?" In Peter de Bruijn et al. (eds.), *Trends en thema's in de editiewetenschap*. Special issue of *Verslagen en mededelingen van de Koninklijke Academie voor Nederlandse Taal- en Letterkunde* 119, pp. 283–299.

Verwey, Albert. 1995. *Briefwisseling 1 juli 1885 tot december 1888*. Ed. Margaretha H. Schenkeveld and Rein van der Wiel. Amsterdam:

Querido. Repr. Den Haag: DNBL, 2008. <http://www.dbnl.org/tekst/verw008brie01_01/>.

Witsen, Willem. 2007. *Volledige briefwisseling.* Ed. Leo Jansen et al. Den Haag: DNBL, 2007. <http://www.dbnl.org/tekst/wits009brie01_01/>.

Towards a Theory of Digital Editions

Peter Robinson

A THEORY OF SCHOLARLY editions should offer a set of principles to guide practice.[1] What is a scholarly edition? how should a scholarly edition be made? who should make it?[2] By appeal to principles, a theory may then explain why one way of thinking, one way of acting, one form of edition, is preferable to another — or, at least, better explain how our views and our editions differ. Debates have emerged in the last decades among scholarly editors, around questions of intention, of the weight to be accorded the material documents, of the meaning of key terms such as "document", "text", "work", "original", of the contingency of editions upon the community and circumstances in which they are made.

All these issues are as pressing and relevant for digital editions as they are for print editions. However, the title of this article presumes that there is an emergent theory of digital editions, distinct from the theory of print editions. It took some time for the need for such a theory to manifest itself. One can find, in the first years of production of digital editions, numerous descriptions of what individual digital editions might contain, in terms of content and facilities.[3] Often these descriptions glance at their print predecessors, usually with expressions of how much more these digital editions can contain

---

[1]   This essay has been shaped by a series of discussions with Paul Eggert, to the degree that I could not be sure which ideas are his, which mine: except that the misunderstandings and errors are mine alone. I am grateful to him also for his comments on successive drafts of this paper.

[2]   See the definitions of "theory" offered by the Oxford English Dictionary: "a set of principles on which the practice of an activity is based" (http://oxforddictionaries.com/definition/english/theory); Merriam-Webster "the general or abstract principles of a body of fact, a science, or an art" (http://www.merriam-webster.com/dictionary/theory) [accessed 14 September 2012].

[3]   Among many articles which have focused on what digital editions might contain are Deegan and Robinson 1994; Jerome McGann's article "The rationale of hypertext", first disseminated as a conference paper and on the web in 1994 and 1995, with selections published in 1995 (McGann 1995) and finally published in full as chapter 2 of his *Radiant Textuality* (McGann 2001, 53–74); and the essays collected in Burnard, O'Brien O'Keeffe and Unsworth 2007.

than ever could be included in print editions, and how much more
the reader can do with them. A description is not a theory. We have
seen enough examples of digital editions in the last decade, indeed,
to know what they may be.[4] Unavoidably, perhaps, we had to explore
the medium and test its limits, to establish what we as editors could
and could not achieve, before asking: what should we do? We could
even justify this course, along the lines of declarations that practice
must precede theory: that by doing, we would learn what we should
do. For the first heady years, we who made digital editions told ourselves we did not need to make choices. We could include everything; we could enable every way of using everything we included.
There were no limitations beyond our imaginations: resources alone
bounded what we could and could not do. There was no need for
theory. Practical possibility alone was our guide.

Now, however, the time for theoretical innocence is over. Partly,
this is because our resources are finite, and require us to choose
where we place our effort. Theory, even of the most rudimentary
kind, can help us choose, and help us justify our choices. But most
significantly, it is because several scholars who had previously concentrated on the theoretical underpinnings of traditional print editions have become engaged with the possibilities of digital editions
(Eggert 2009, Shillingsburg 2006, and Gabler 2007, 2010, 2012).
The continuity of their thinking about digital editions with their
previous contemplation of print editions is significant. We cannot
suppose that digital editions are so revolutionary that all previous
discussions about scholarly editing are irrelevant. Quite the reverse.
Digital editions confront us with the same fundamental problems
as do print editions, transposed to a new medium. Further, debates
about scholarly editing in the last decades have themselves been part
of larger discussions within the humanities (and in the wider world)
about concepts of authority, agency, text and meaning, which have in
turn shaped scholarly editing. In the decades before digital editions
became possible, positivist editing, associated in the anglophone
world with Greg and Bowers, gave way to more anxious and self-
aware modes of editing through the seventies and eighties. Over the

---

    4   Thus, my own edition of the Chaucer's *Wife of Bath's Prologue* (1996);
McDermott's edition of *Johnson's Dictionary* (1996); the Blake and Rosetti
Archives (1997; 1993), and the electronic editions discussed in Burnard,
O'Brien O'Keeffe and Unsworth 2007.

same period, many scholars — Shillingsburg, Greetham, McGann to name just three — argued that scholarly editing is much more than provision of an edited text, following well-established procedures. Rather, editing comprises a series of acts heavy with implications: texts are embedded in complex webs of discourse, with multidimensional relations between author, text, everyone involved in the making and reception of a text, editor and audience (McGann 1991, Shillingsburg 1996, Greetham 1999).

A theory of digital editions, then, must be rooted in the debates about scholarly editing which have unrolled over the last decades. Three terms lie at the heart of any theory of scholarly editions: document, work, text. What does it mean to edit a document, a work, a text? What does it mean to read a document, a work, a text? How is our thinking about these questions changed in the digital environment? Behind these questions, lie yet others: how do we relate documents, works and texts to narratives of authorship, publication, production, dissemination, reception, authority, agency and meaning? What, precisely, is a "text"?

The justification for the claim in the title of this essay, that a distinct theory of digital editions is required, is this: the digital realm offers different answers to the questions asked in the last paragraph than does the print realm. Document; work; text: classically, editors from the age of print saw their task as creating an edition of the work. It is not that they regarded documents as unimportant, just that they saw the editions they made as representing something other than the documents: the edition represents the work. But two decades of making digital editions, and recent papers about digital editions, have moved the needle away from the "work" to the "document", to the point where we might need only think of "documents". Because a digital edition can present facsimiles of every form a text ever had — every copy of every Shakespeare folio or quarto, every copy of every Chaucer manuscript or incunable — then, we can do just that. Indeed, this is what the great majority of "digital editions" so far created have done, to the point that a debate has arisen about whether such objects should be called archives or editions.[5] We might declare

---

[5]   See, for example, the careful discussion of the terms "digital archive" and "digital edition" by Kenneth M. Price (2008): "In fact, electronic editorial undertakings are only imperfectly described by any of the terms currently in use: edition, project, archive, thematic research collection" and "In an electronic

that this frees the documents from all the difficult questions invoked by the terms "text" and "work", and so allows the reader a completely transparent view of the documents, untainted by all the prejudices which might otherwise constrain an open and fresh encounter with the documents. One could invoke substantial arguments in favour of this way of thinking. Leah Marcus, for example, argues in favour of reading renaissance documents containing versions of texts stigmatized as "bad", yet highly revealing of discourses otherwise lost (1996). One could also read various of Randall McCleod's writings, with their emphasis on study of the most fundamental material forms of the document, to support the exclusive focus of digital editing on the document alone (2004). This would be consistent, too, with the marked shift towards study of the "material text" (which one could identify as the document, and the document alone) in the writings of many recent thinkers about textual editing (Bornstein 2001, O'Brien O'Keeffe 2006, the essays collected in Van Mierlo 2009) — and, of course, McGann's foregrounding of bibliographic codes (1991).

There is an attractive simplicity in this narrow focus in digital editing on documents alone. It plays well with the advances in digital imaging in the last decades, which have made it feasible to gather and distribute vast numbers of digital images at low cost. One might produce an edition of a document containing high-resolution, full-colour images, capable of magnification so that the tiniest detail of the page may be analysed, which would be very useful for the kinds of document-centred analysis advocated by the writers mentioned in the last paragraph. Nor, indeed, does this mean that one need regard questions of text and work as unimportant: just that consideration of these could be deferred. It means too that the editor can concentrate on the document alone, and (if he or she chooses) leave other questions to others. It should be observed too that such editions are almost impossible in the print world. One can produce high-quality print facsimile editions of individual documents, but one could certainly not do so for every document in the Blake Archive, or every manuscript of *The Canterbury Tales*.

Two recent articles by Hans Walter Gabler present a lucid rationale for this view of scholarly editing as document-based: "The

---

environment, archive has gradually come to mean a purposeful collection of digital surrogates".

primacy of the document in editing" (2007) and "Theorizing the Digital Scholarly Edition" (2010). In the first of these he focusses on the words "document" and "text". In the light of his experience working with digital tools on James Joyce and other manuscript materials, Gabler is led to assert the primacy of "document" over "text". As he describes it, he now wants to put "the horse of the document properly before the cart of its eventually emerging text" (2007, 201). To those of us used to decades of talk about material texts and such like, this may not sound very exciting. However, Gabler's densely argued article is far more than a simple plea for editors to pay more attention to the documents. He proposes a complete refocusing of editorial perspective: away from a concentration on the finished product, the editorial text which is supported by reference to various documents, towards a concentration on the documents themselves, from which an editorial text may (or may not) emerge. This is an immense shift. Gabler proposes that the intense editorial effort which for centuries has seen as its goal the construction of an editorial text, should now focus on the construction of the text of the documents. To put this another way: for centuries we have thought of the scholar editor as distant from the documents. He or she constructs an editorial text and apparatus, often on the base of an existing editorial text, diving now and then into the documents to find or deny a reading. In place of that, we are now to imagine the scholar gazing intently at a single document, pondering exactly what is happening, what messages we can extract from this page.

Gabler's insistence on the primacy of the document is, we may argue, a key characteristic of digital editions, not print editions. For three reasons: first, in his discourse, it appears that the confrontation of material document with immaterial digital media has problematized the notions of text and document, leading to the reversal of their positioning in the editorial gaze fundamental to his argument. Secondly, due to the omnipresence of digital images, what the editor sees, the reader can see too. Thirdly, and I think most importantly (though Gabler does not touch on this), the digital medium permits a level of involvement by reader and editor with the document which is not possible in the print medium. Gabler notes (2007, 200) that typically "critique génétique" presents a narrative analysis of the document. The digital medium can do something very different: it can allow the reader to see the text of the document construct itself, layer by layer, from blank page to fully written text.

Gabler's argument that the editorial gaze should focus on the single document may surprise readers familiar with his edition of Joyce's *Ulysses*, which famously presents a text based not on any one single document, but on Gabler's own extraordinarily careful examination of all the documents: not, indeed, the text of one document, but of Joyce's work *Ulysses* as realized by Gabler from the documentary evidence. One can trace a tension between the two editorial perspectives, on text as document and on text as work, in various Gabler articles, composed close to the time of his edition of *Ulysses*. His 1981 address to the Society for Textual Scholarship (Gabler 1984) plays on the tension between "synchronous" and "diachronic" texts, a dichotomy which looks towards document and work; a later article (1990) worries at the problems of the different versions of *King Lear*, with text and work shadowing the proposition (which he neither rejects nor approves) "that even a single revision constituted a new version of a text" (1990, 162). A clear shift towards his recent emphasis on the document appears, however, in a 2002 article published in the first number of *Variants*, in which he discussed, in intricate detail, Joyce's writing of a single page of the "Circe" episode of *Ulysses* (several of his later articles reference this same page).

Over the same period as Gabler was developing these arguments, roughly from 2001 on, other scholars were also working their way towards a theory of digital editing focused on the document, but from a different starting point to that of Gabler and others. For Kevin Kiernan and Elena Pierazzo the starting point was the making of digital editions of unique documents. For Kiernan, the document was the manuscript of the Old English poem *Beowulf*, and his creation of an edition of the manuscript based around the remarkable digital images created in the early 1990s: the first such digital edition of any single document for any English work. In the following years, he developed a theory of the "image-based scholarly edition", in which editorial work was predicated on the availability of high-quality digital images of the document (2006). Pierazzo follows Kiernan, but centres the edition on the creation of a precise and information-rich transcription of the document: hence, a "digital documentary edition" (2011). For Pierazzo, the possibilities of the digital medium have created new possibilities, which enable the making of detailed digital representations of the document using complex encoding, which in turn permit multiple perspectives on the edited document.

Thus, we now have a convergence of opinion. For both Gabler and Pierazzo, digital editing is rooted in the document: it is difficult to imagine a more articulate and forceful exposition of a theory of digital editing as focused on documents than that given by Gabler. However, Gabler sees an editor as far more than a collector of documents, and a digital edition as much more than an archive. In this document-centred editing, Gabler argues that the central responsibility of the editor is to explain to the reader the tale told by the documents. This is the theme of his second article, "Theorizing the Digital Scholarly Edition" (2010). In this he emphasizes, repeatedly, that it is the editor who creates the "web of discourses" which is, to him, the scholarly edition (2010, 44). Indeed, just as his first article foregrounded "document" over "text", in this article he foregrounds the "editor" over "author" and "text". The editor (who might be a team of editors) is "pivotal to an edition"; the text of an edition — and by this he means the entire "web of discourses" which compose the edition — is "the editor's text of the text or work cited".

However, there are areas where his arguments are incomplete. Consider Gabler's formulation cited in the last sentence of the last paragraph: the edition is the "editor's text of the text or work cited". Suddenly, Gabler has introduced the concept of the "work" into his discussion. Further, he identifies the "text of the work" with the text of the "web of discourses" created by the editor. But this "web of discourses", as he insists throughout his articles, must be the text of the document as carefully laid-out by the editor. Does this mean that the "work" is completely represented by the "document"? Now, we can see that for many works, and many documents, it can indeed be argued (as do Marcus and McLeod) that the work may be completely represented by a single document. This is particularly true for authorial manuscripts and papers. Indeed, one may read Gabler's edition of *Ulysses* as built on a direct equation between work and document. Gabler asserts that in *Ulysses* document and work are together "the totality of the Work in Progress" (1984, 325); hence, the work is the totality of all the documents, conceptually collapsed into a single document as Gabler traces the record of Joyce's writing as it winds through all the typescripts, scraps, galleys which constitute what he calls the "continuous manuscript text" (1984, 318).

One might in these cases argue that the work is best edited and best read from a single document, edited as Gabler advocates. But how could we do this in the case, for example, of the Greek New Testament, or of Dante's *Commedia,* or of Shakespeare's *King Lear,* or of any work which exists in many versions, in many documents, none of which can claim pre-eminently, completely and singly to represent the work?

In a later article, Gabler distances the document-based editions he envisages from the "work" (2012). He distinguishes between what he sees as "endogenous" to the document — essentially, what can be deduced directly from the document itself — and what he sees as "exogenous" to it. For him, everything which cannot be deduced directly from the document, including all knowledge of the author, of the circumstances of the document's creation and transmission, of other versions of the work understood as present in the document, indeed everything normally understood by "work", is "exogenous". Gabler acknowledges that this "exogenous" information is important, but he specifically and categorically excludes it all from the editorial act, as applied to the document. "Text-critical investigations would continue to be directed towards them, and these would continue to be accounted for in introduction and commentary discourses of editions": thus, not in the edition of the documents which lies at the heart of these editions (Gabler 2012, 32). In particular, this leads Gabler to distinguish sharply between the author as present "endogenously" in the text of the document, and as he or she may be conceived "exogenously": the actual historical personage who wrote the document. To effect this distinction, Gabler adapts Foucault's famous "author function" (1984). In his formulation, the "author function" can be deduced by the editor from the evidence of variation in the document alone: "their variability is an expression of the author function which is inscribed into them, and thus contributes to constituting texts as texts" (2012, 24). That is: the editor scrutinizes the document, and from the traces of the writing processes there found constructs a narrative of its writing, and hence an expression of the "author function" posited as responsible for the writing acts which the document presents.

The advantage of Gabler's formulation is that it keeps the text created by the editor very close to the document. Only what the editor sees as directly attested by the document is to be included in its edition. As Eggert (forthcoming) points out, this places his thinking directly in line with the arguments of Zeller and others from the German text-editing tradition, with their aspiration to an "objectification of editing", free from necessarily speculative matters such as "authorial intention" (Zeller 1995, 54). Thus, Gabler separates the "author function", which can be shown as materially and actually present in the physical document (thus, "endogenous"), from "authorial intention", which must be conceived on the basis of (say) biography, letters, articles all outside the document (thus, "exogenous").

There is, indeed, a self-contained perfection about this model of document-based editing. But the problem with a self-contained model is that it achieves an impeccable consistency by rigorous exclusion of everything which does not fit into it: in this case, everything which Gabler regards as "exogenous" to the document and its text. This means that almost everything which interests us about a literary work — what it means, who wrote it, how it was distributed and received, how it is differently expressed — is excluded from Gabler's model. Gabler certainly does not say that these are not important, just that they are irrelevant to the editor's work with the document. The effect of this is to separate entirely what we do as editors with a document, and what we do as readers trying to understand the work which this document presents. Thus, we have to separate completely the "author function" responsible for the marks on the page from the historical individual who actually wrote these marks. We have to do this even if we know, as certainly as anything can be known, that all the marks on this paper were made by (say) James Joyce, and that the document can be precisely related to a series of other documents which together show how Joyce was shaping the novel we know as *Ulysses*. Gabler requires that we completely disassociate the "author function" implicit in the editor's analysis of the document from the James Joyce who we know actually made these marks, in the course of writing the work *Ulysses*. This seems counter-intuitive.

Indeed, there is a deeper problem in Gabler's formulation, which lies at the root of the difficulties it has with the concept of document and text as work. The problem is this: exactly what is the text which the editor represents as present in the document? Gabler presents the text of the document as an object in a hermetically sealed universe, distinct from anything else: an object in and of itself, which the editorial subject discovers and presents. But it is not. Gabler's own use of the term "the author function" betrays it. Any attempt to account for variation in a text must implicate editor and reader in a series of judgements about intention, about agency, about authority, about meaning. There is a stroke though a word: as soon as we say "this indicates that this word is to be deleted" we are declaring that, in our judgement, the person who put the stroke through the word intended that the text here should be read without that word: intention. We are saying that this stroke was made by someone: agency. We are saying that this stroke is not to be ignored (as we might ignore much else on the document surface): authority. We are saying that this stroke through this word has an impact on what we read: meaning. Intention, agency, authority, meaning: the four terms an editor, a critic, a reader must grapple with when trying to understand the work *Ulysses*. Gabler would move all consideration of these four terms out of the "endogenous" editing of the document, to the "exogenous" commentaries we might erect around the work of which this document is a witness: thus, the wall he places between "the text of the document", considered as editorial object, and the "work", considered as an object of readerly contemplation. But there is no such wall. Exactly the same issues of intention, agency, authority and meaning which engage us on the broadest plane, when considering (say) Joyce's design for *Ulysses* engage us on the most narrow plane: what did Joyce mean when he made this mark on this page; did he make it; how does it affect what we read? It might appear that by hewing close to the document, we can avoid the difficult questions of intention, agency, authority, and meaning. But we cannot.

In place of Gabler's attempt to divide document from work, it can be argued that document, text and work exist in a continuum, and that the questions of intention, agency, authority, and meaning exert pressure at every level of reading. Indeed, the fundamental editorial act of document-based editing, transcription of the text, involves a complex sequence of editorial acts, intimately intertwined with these four questions. The account that follows draws on experience of transcription of the manuscripts of Dante's *Commedia*. If the documents with which Gabler works are at one end of a continuum (single authorial manuscripts, which might stand for the work itself) the documents in the *Commedia* tradition are at the other: multiple versions of a work, none of which can claim to stand for the work itself. There are other differences. The manuscripts are the product of distinct and rich iconographic histories; the linguistic and semiotic systems underlying the writing of the text itself were in flux, and every page contains many signs of no clear textual significance. Accordingly, the transcription of these documents passes through two distinct stages. I describe here the practice of the *Commedia* transcription, as performed for Shaw's edition of the *Commedia* and as developed and described by Barbara Bordalejo in her appendix C ("The Encoding System") to the edition (Bordalejo 2010). Bordalejo distinguishes between two separate stages of transcription. In the first of these, "the text of the document" is transcribed; in the second, the "variant states of the text" are recorded:

> In this article, I use the phrase the "text of the document" to refer to the sequence of marks present in the document, independently of whether these represent a complete, meaningful text. That is: the reader sees a sequence of letters, occurring in various places in relation to each other (perhaps between the lines or within the margins) and carrying various markings (perhaps underdottings or strikethroughs). These make up what I here refer to as the text of the document.

> The reader understands the marks present in the text of the document as meaningful and constructs one or more specific senses from them. Where more than one sense can be constructed from the text of the document, I refer to these as the "variant states of the text", or as the "constructed" texts.

Bordalejo illustrates this with the example of a single word from *Inferno* iii.9, in Ms Riccardiana 1005 ("Rb"). This appears in the manuscript as

The sequence of potentially textually meaningful marks here is identified by the transcriber as "d u r a-with-an-underdot o". Using the characters available to the transcribers, this is transcribed as:

durao

In Bordalejo's terms, this is "the text of the document". It is a sequence of marks in the document identified as potentially meaningful by the editor. Note that even at this first stage the transcriber has made a series of decisions. The first is that this is a text in Italian, written by an Italian scribe around 1340 and so using letter forms and conventions characteristic of Italian vernacular manuscripts of that period. This determines the decision that the first letter be transcribed as "d" (and not an "o", as it might have been in some scripts), the second as "u" (although in other contexts the same two minims might be transcribed as "n"), the third letter as "r" (even though the stroke to the right top, without which this letter is identical to a single minim, and hence either could be "i" or part of "m" with the preceding minims), the fourth letter as "a" with a dot beneath it, the fifth as "o". Note that once the first letter is identified as "d", in Italian the second letter must be "u", not "n", and the third letter must be "r". Note too that the transcriber does not ignore the dot under the "a". In many contexts, dots on the manuscript serve non-textual, apparently calligraphic, functions and are ignored. But here, the dot is identified by the transcriber as textually meaningful and is transcribed.

One might seek to identify this first stage of transcription with Gabler's "document-centred" edition, including only "endogenous" information derived from the document alone. But this account shows that even at this level, we may not exclude intention, agency, authority and meaning. The first three letters are transcribed as "dur" because this is the only sequence of these marks which makes sense in Italian. The dot under the "a" has meaning because we think it shows that the scribe intended this letter to be read in a particular way. In the next stage of transcription, the transcriber "constructs one or more specific senses" from the transcribed text of the document. The sequence

durạo

actually means nothing in Italian. Here, the transcriber constructs two variant states of the text: "dura" and "duro". Further, the transcriber places them in sequence. The scribe first wrote "dura", realized this was mistaken, marked the "a" for deletion by underdotting it, and then wrote a final "o", so transforming the "dura" to "duro".

Bordalejo observes that these are two distinct activities:

> Firstly, the reader realizes that there is a set of marks on the page that are text. Secondly, the reader constructs meaning out of those marks on the page. The first is an act combining perception and interpretation, the second is an act purely of interpretation.

As Bordalejo notes, in normal reading the two acts occur so closely together that we do not distinguish them. We see marks; we immediately identify these as letters; we read these as a sequence of words. The process is so natural to us, and in well-printed modern books so unproblematic, that we think we are reading a text which is actually present in the book we are reading, independent of our reading of it. But we are not. When we read, we construct a text from marks on the page. We give that text meaning according to our knowledge of what has come earlier; who wrote it; what work it is part of, and what other works were written by that author; even, what other versions exist of this work and of this particular passage. In this case, the transcriber knows (as did the scribe, and as does any likely reader) that this word is part of the *Inferno* by Dante and that it occurs in the context of Dante's description of the gates of Hell, concluding with the famous line "Abandon all hope, you who enter":

> Dinanzi a me non fuor cose create
> se non etterne, e io etterno duro.
> Lasciate ogne speranza, voi ch' intrate'

Further, the reader knows that the terza rima scheme used throughout the *Commedia* requires that the reading is "duro", rhyming with "oscuro" and "duro" in the next three lines, and may deduce that the scribe too knew this, recognized that "dura" was incorrect, and changed this to "duro".

We see here that as we move along the scale of reading, from deciphering the marks on the page to considering how they contribute to our understanding of Dante's *Commedia*, we pass between minute scrutiny of the document to contemplation of the work. We can now begin to answer the question: what, exactly, is the "text" which we, as editors, extract from the document? First, we can say what it is not. It is not a fixed object existing independently of the reader, awaiting

only the editor who will discover it and pass it on to the reader. It is
an object we as editors and readers create, first from our recognition
of the potentially meaningful marks we see on the page, and second
from our construction of one or more texts from these marks, a construction influenced by our knowledge of the work of which these
words are part, our knowledge of its author, indeed by everything we
know about intention, agency, authority and meaning. We use our
understanding of the work whose text we identify as present in the
document to help us interpret that document, just as we must use
our knowledge of the documents towards our understanding of the
work. The movement from document to work is not a one-way process: we look backwards and forwards, as we read from document to
work and back again.

The "work" is part of our reading of the document: what do we
mean by "work"? While Gabler and others have focused on text
as document, Paul Eggert has been examining the concept of the
"work". In *Securing the Past* (2009), he extends the concept of the
work beyond textual productions, however conceived (the "works"
of Shakespeare, his *Hamlet*, Sonnet 100), to buildings and works of
art, taking in along the way issues of forgery, authenticity, conservation and presentation. Indeed, while Eggert confines his discussion
to art, architecture and literature, his arguments may apply to any
object created by human agency: anything we make is a "work".
Anything we make, his last chapter argues, is subject to questions of
intention, agency, authority and meaning. Across all these domains,
we who read books, look at paintings, walk through historic buildings, must ask ourselves the same questions: what is it I see here; who
made it and how does what I see relate to its original making; what
has happened to it since its first making; how does this affect what
I see? These questions, Eggert shows, take us into philosophy, into
concepts of being, epistemology and semiotics, and the first part of
Eggert's key chapter "The Editorial Gaze and the Nature of the Work"
summarizes how philosophical moves through the twentieth-century,
from Husserl's phenomenology to Adorno's negative dialectic, have
changed our understanding of the "work". Eggert maps out, firstly,
how the work has ceased to be seen as an object independent of
our perception, which editing might present in approximations
increasingly close to a perfect representation, and traces how editorial thinking shifted (often belatedly) in response to the rethinking

of authorship, text, work, discourse and meaning by Heidegger, Saussure, Foucault, Barthes and Blanchot (221–27). In Eggert's analysis, the impact of these ideas has been to problematize in useful ways our thinking about text and work, as we have had to shed misleading assumptions about (for example) originality and intention. In the last part of the chapter, he introduces the thinking of Charles Sanders Peirce and Theodor Adorno, focusing on their presentation of meaning as an ongoing semiosis involving three elements: the object which is known, the subject which knows, and the process of knowing (Eggert 2009, 231). He finds particularly attractive Adorno's "negative dialectic", in which subject and object are locked in a "experiential embrace" in which "[e]ach requires the other's difference in order to secure its own identity". This dialectic, Adorno argues, never achieves resolution. Rather, our knowing is "an ongoing, antithetical but interdependent identity-relationship that unfolds over time" (Eggert 2009, 234). Thus, what we know changes as we change; and we change as what we know changes. Eggert applies this to the formation of texts, as an intricately unfolding process implicating document, work, and reader in a continuing generation of meanings. His conclusion is worthy of full quotation:

> The document, whether hand-written or printed, is the textual site where the agents of textuality meet: author, copyist, editor, typesetter and reader. In the acts of writing, copying or reading, the work's documentary and textual dimensions dynamically interrelate: they can be seen as a translation or performance of one another. They are, in this sense, one another's negative constituting principle. Document, taken as the material basis of text, has a continuing history in relation to its productions and its readings. Any new manifestation of the negative dialectic necessarily generates new sets of meanings. (Eggert 2009, 234–235)

Eggert goes on to define "work", in this environment, as "a regulative idea that immediately dissolves, in reading, into the negative dialectic of document and text" (235). I believe that we can put this differently, in a way which offers a stronger, more positive definition of "work" than does Eggert.[6] In accordance with the

---

[6]   As this phrasing implies, my formulation of the document-text-work triad is not a departure from Eggert's perception, but rather a rephrasing, or at most an extension.

subject-meaning-object triad, the "work" is the object we seek to know. This operates at many levels. As we explore the document we seek to discover the work in the text we draw from the document. At every point, questions of agency, authority, intention press upon us as we seek the meaningful object which is the work. For a work which exists in just a single page (or less) of a document — a letter, an authorial manuscript, a unique copy of a poem, even anonymous materials with no title — we find ourselves asking: who wrote this? What did the writer intend; what meaning can I extract? As we look across many documents, all offering different versions of a work, with the work made of many parts, extending over many pages of many documents, the same core questions of intention, agency, authority and meaning recur, complicated as we puzzle our way through variation heaped on variation. The process never ends. The work is not a fixed object, apprehended in some marvellous epiphany by a reader, so that forever after the unchanging reader holds an unchanging image of the work in mind. Rather the work changes as we know it, and we change too as we know. We see this most easily when we return to a well-loved book and read it again. Suddenly meanings we had not seen before crowd upon us. We think: the book has not changed. But the meaning of the book, the work we apprehend, has changed, and this is all the book that we know. We know too that the change is in us, that while we were not looking, we changed, and in each instant of apprehension, we change again.

We can now arrive at a definition of text. The text is the site of meaning which links the document and the work. The work can never have a fixed physical expression. It can only be apprehended (and ever only incompletely) in the text we construct from the document. The document without the text of the work we construct from it is mute, simply marks on a surface. Our construction of the text of the work, from one document, from a thousand documents, demands all our attention, all our knowledge, all we know of intention, agency, authority. There is no end to this knowing. At the very beginning of our work on *The Canterbury Tales*, Elizabeth Solopova and I defined transcription thus:

> [T]ranscription of a primary textual source cannot be regarded as an act of substitution, but as a series of acts of translation from one semiotic system (that of the primary source) to another semiotic

system (that of the computer). Like all acts of translation, it must be seen as fundamentally incomplete and fundamentally interpretative (Robinson and Solopova 1993, 21).[7]

Now, we can see that what this describes is not just transcription; it is an instance of how we know, so that the many acts of transcription are each separate forays into meaning, as our gaze moves from the marks on the paper, to the text we seek to construct from these marks, to the work we seek to know from this text, then back again through text and to the document. We know now too that the work we seek is not just instanced in a linguistic text: how the marks are arranged on the page, images on the page, these too may be part of the work we seek. Indeed, as Eggert demonstrates, what we seek may not be linguistic at all: it might be a painting or a building.

Evidently, this conceptualization of document, text and work is not unique to digital editions. It is not even unique to linguistic objects, but might apply to any meaningful object created by human agency. Its roots in the thinking of (especially) Peirce and Adorno, who died in 1914 and 1969 respectively, date it well before the digital age. However, one can see how the thinking of Peirce and Adorno resonates with the radical instability of the digital medium. The time for this idea has come. While Eggert makes few references to digital editions in his discussion, one suspects that his long acquaintance with digital editions has influenced his intellectual trajectory. Further, digital editions, which may remake themselves from instant to instant in response to the reader's ever-changing requests, are perfectly adapted to this manner of thinking. They are objects in need of this theory. In contrast, the plausible fixity of print editions may be seen to have encouraged the view which this theory counters, that the work can achieve a knowable fixed form and be expressed forever within the covers of a book. In addition, digital editions may include tools which allow the reader to engage with the work by creating new texts, for example through the emergent use of phylogenetic methods to generate visualizations of the relationships between different texts in different documents (Robinson and O'Hara 1992, Van Reenen 2004). We may explore as we read, and read as we explore.

---

[7]   The core of this formulation, placing semiosis at the heart of a never-ending process, was suggested by Solopova.

While applicable to any form editions might take, this theory is specially amenable to digital editions.[8]

There is one area where a theory of digital editions may have to advance where a theory of print editions need not. The rise of social media in the last decade has led to the contemplation of a new kind of edition: the "social edition", discussed extensively by Siemens and his co-authors (forthcoming).[9] Siemens' article concentrates on the technical achievement of social editions, leaving no doubt that editions made by many people freely co-operating with one another are now feasible. While Siemens deliberately eschews theoretical discussion (asserting rather that "the *social* edition is something that we will articulate and define, through theory and functional prototyping, together") the core elements of the social edition — its fluidity, its ever-continuing reshaping as new materials are added, new perceptions generated — sits perfectly with the view of document, text and work here set out, without extending it. However, in one area the social edition appears to require an extension of the theory here expressed. In Peirce and Adorno's formulations, and in Eggert's representation of their arguments, the subject which seeks to know is, we presume, an individual. But what if it is not an individual, but a group, a community? Siemens specifically invokes the developing concept of "communities of practice" as agents and creators of knowledge: meaning may be made not just by an individual, but by a group. Of course, even when I read as an individual, I am aware of the readings of others. I am aware that when I see a vertical stroke with a dot over it, after a mark which I interpret as "h" and before another which I interpret as "t", that my reading of this mark as "i" and hence part of the word "hit" is likely to be the interpretation of everyone who looks at these marks on this page, and accordingly I can write about these marks, confident that others will understand what I say.[10] At another level, I know when I speak of

---

[8]   Thus, the digital "work-sites" which Shillingsburg (2006) conceives as the places where readers encounter the documents which witness a work.

[9]   I am grateful to Ray Siemens for giving me access to a pre-publication draft of this article.

[10]   Compare Robinson 2009, 44: "An 'i' is not an 'i' because it is a stroke with a dot over it. An 'i' is an 'i' because we all agree that it is an 'i'". Pierazzo (2011) agrees with this assertion, that the text created by any transcription is not "objective"; the declaration in her article (466) that "if scholars as competent readers agree on something, then by this definition that thing is objective" is out of step

the work *The Canterbury Tales* I am basing my understanding of the work ultimately on the same documents (a few manuscripts and a few modern editions) upon which others base their understanding, and that the meanings we attach to this work will be sufficiently close for us to be able to speak to each other, not past each other. We can imagine individuals within a community discovering a work together, through the texts they construct from the documents, and discovering both where they agree and disagree, in an ever-continuing shared semiosis. In the print world, this shaping of shared knowledge takes place in a kind of slow motion, as a book is published and generates a counter-argument, resulting in another book, another argument. In the digital world, it can take place as fast as we can think, write what we think, and read what others write.

A theory of scholarly editions is a set of principles to guide practice. The preceding analysis suggests a defining principle, upon which our editions in the digital age might be built: that "text is the site of meaning which links the document and the work". Thus "text" in scholarly editing has a dual aspect. It is both "text-as-document" and "text-as-work". The two are indissolubly linked. We may only know the text through the documents we read, and may only communicate any text we make through documents we create. But every time we look from one document to another, or look away from the document to consider what we have read, or try to express what we think we are reading, we look to the work, shadowy but omnipresent. One cannot know the work without the documents — equally, one cannot understand the documents without a comprehension of the work they instance. From this, a principle appears: a scholarly edition must, so far as it can, illuminate both aspects of the text, both text-as-work and text-as-document. Traditional print editions have focused more on the first. An evident advantage of digital editions is that they might redress this balance, by including much richer materials for the study of text-as-document than can be achieved in the print medium.

However, the view of digital editions offered by Gabler, Pierazzo and Kiernan (among others) appears indifferent to this principle of the two-fold nature of text. Instead, the model of editions they offer focusses on the documents, to the point where the concept of

---

with the argument she expresses elsewhere.

"work" disappears altogether. This has real-world implications in the practice of digital editions. It means that encoding the text of the document may concentrate (and, according to Gabler, must concentrate) only on the document itself: offering a "recording of as many features of the original document as are considered meaningful by the editors" (Pierazzo 2011, 475). Accordingly, the Text Encoding Initative workgroup on Genetic Editing (Burnard et al., n.d.) specifies a system for representing a text of in terms of a single document containing it: thus, the text is dispersed through "document", "writing surface", "zone" and "line". In terms of its own aims, this is extraordinarily successful: one may easily link the transcribed words of the text to their place in the physical document, making possible such effects as the text "floating" over the image. It is extremely well suited to the making of "genetic editions", where the aim is to present, in the greatest possible detail, the text of a single document of extraordinary significance: usually, an author's own draft (thus, the Joyce manuscripts of which Gabler writes). But what of the case where the text is not present in a single document; when it exists in thousands of manuscripts and print editions? Indeed, this is true even for genetic editions: what Joyce wrote in this one page of the "Circe" manuscript made its way through a series of proofs and galleys into the 1922 edition, and then through all the editions down to this day, including Gabler's own. An edition which ignores all this would be a pale thing indeed. One might reasonably expect that a digital edition would allow the reader not just to see the text of any one page alongside an image of the page; the reader would like to see how the words changed through the proofs on their way to the first printed edition, and then all the later printed editions. To do this, one needs to encode not the divisions of the document, as "surface", "writing area", "zone"; one needs to encode the divisions of the work, as "chapter" and "paragraph", or "verse" and "line", so that one can locate the different parts of the work within the particular documents containing them. Indeed, the Text Encoding Initiative guidelines have long offered comprehensive means of encoding text-as-work (line one of the General Prologue of *The Canterbury Tales*), as well as the recently developed system for encoding text-as-document offered by Burnard and others.

On the face of it, the answer is simple: one should encode both text-as-document and text-as-work. But there is a problem with this.

The model of text encoding prevailing in the digital community at this time is that each text may be organized according to a single hierarchy of "ordered content objects" (DeRose 1990; Renear 1996). One may define a text as a set of logical structures, with each book containing chapters, each chapter containing paragraphs, each paragraph containing sentences: text-as-work. Or one may define a text as it appears in a particular document: as composed of a volume, containing a sequence of quires, each quire containing a sequence of pages, each page made up of a sequence of writing spaces. The current digital tools for scholarly editing make it easy to encode either view of the text. However, it is much more difficult to do both to the same degree of detail in the one encoding. It is usual to encode one view as the primary structure (say, the text-as-work view, organizing the text into sentences contained in paragraphs contained in chapters), with information on the other view recorded in the document (say, the locations of page-breaks, and perhaps line-breaks), but not used to structure the content.[11]

In the early days of digital editions, it was common for encoders to privilege the text-as-work view: thus, my own editions of Chaucer (1996, 2004), and those of *Piers Plowman* initiated by Hoyt Duggan (1994, 2005). In recent years, this has been exactly reversed. Indeed, while the earliest digital editions did at least include information on the text-as-document in their encoding of the text-as-work, the pendulum has now swung so far that many encodings of texts now present only the text-as-document. The online edition of Jane Austen's manuscripts at http://www.janeausten.ac.uk (Austen 2010), for which Pierazzo was the technical research associate, and which uses a form of the "genetic edition" encoding described in Burnard et al. (n.d.) and developed by a team in which Pierazzo was a key member, provides an extraordinarily rich representation of each written page. Yet the transcription offers no information whatever about the text-as-work. We are given full page-by-page transcriptions of (for example) three volumes of Austen juvenilia, containing

---

[11] This is a version of the long-known "overlapping hierarchies" (or "concurrent hierarchies") problem: that "content objects" may nest, but not overlap. In other words, text may be contained within a paragraph, or contained within a page, but it cannot be contained in both if page and paragraph overlap. There are ways about this problem, typically ingenious and demanding to implement (e.g. DeRose 2004; see the ongoing discussion in Porter 2005).

some twenty-seven works by her, in various genres. But we are offered no way into any of the manuscripts, except page-by-page. There is no table of contents of the work; no way, for example, of locating her playlet "The Mystery" except by going through the whole transcription a page at a time (it begins on page 141 of the first volume). Nor is there any encoding of structural divisions in the text. Austen provides "The Mystery" with a list of *dramatis personae* and diligently sets out the play as a single Act divided into three scenes. None of this is reflected in the encoding of the edition. A reader might want to extract the first scene of this play and compare it to various printed versions: in this edition, he or she cannot. Nor is this an isolated example. As I write, there is a ferment of activity in the creation of transcription tools: Brumfield (2012) lists twenty-eight online collaborative transcription editing systems. Every one of these is designed to record text-as-document. Not one of these offers the possibility of recording text-as-work.[12]

Principles may define practice. But practice may become so accepted, so ingrained, that principles are determined by practice, and not the other way about. The dominance of the document model of textual editing in the digital realm suggests that a theory of digital editions is emerging, based on page-by-page transcription of individual documents, which asserts that a digital edition should concentrate on the documents alone. Gabler's articles explicitly formulate this: scholarly editing must perforce concentrate on the text of the document alone. Gabler is writing of modern documents. Matthew Driscoll (2010) would extend this focus to medieval documents, even to editions of works existing in many manuscripts, as he argues that traditional stemmatic attempts to investigate whole manuscript traditions are flawed, and that instead one should focus on the edition of individual documents. Some of his language echoes Gabler's search for an objective mode of editing, as he argues that a transcription should make clear "what is actually written in the source, as distinct from however the editor has decided this is to be interpreted" (Driscoll 2010, 103).

---

[12]   One tool, T-PEN (Ginther n.d.), did appear to permit embedding of limited text-as-work information (in the form of paragraph information) when accessed in May 2012; I was unable to find this facility when accessing the site again in September 2012.

One can welcome this attention to documents as a long overdue correction to the millennia-long concentration of scholarly editors on the work rather than the document. But there are dangers here. Should this model of the digital edition prevail, we will see a flood of facsimile editions in digital form ("digital documentary editions", to use Pierazzo's term), such as those of the Austen Manuscripts project. Notoriously, facsimile editions in print form are of very little use to the reader, or even to scholars, whose interest (so far as it touches on the documents) is likely to be in questions of how the received text changed over time, how it was received, how it was altered, transformed, passed into different currencies. If we make only digital documentary editions, we will distance ourselves and our editions from the readers.

Of course, there will be a place for digital documentary editions, as there long has been for facsimile editions. But such editions, with their narrow focus on editor and document, fall far short of achieving the potential of editions in the digital world. The digital medium is perfectly adapted to enactment of editions as an ever-continuing negotiation between editors, readers, documents, texts and works. The involvement of whole communities of practice — indeed, everyone who reads documents in pursuit of the work, and so every reader — in the making of editions may lead us to a completely new kind of edition, made by many people. Documents may not change. But the advent of the digital medium has changed the texts we construct from them, and the works whose meaning we seek change too, and will change endlessly with every new reader, every new document, every new text. Finally, the theory we attempt to make for digital editions, itself a work whose meaning is shaped and reshaped by readers, will itself change.

Bibliography

Austen, Jane. 2010. *Jane Austen's Fictional Manuscripts: A Digital Edition*. Ed. Kathryn Sutherland. <http://www.janeausten.ac.uk/index.html>. [Accessed 17 September 2012].

Blake, William. 1996–2012. *The William Blake Archive*. Eds. Morris Eaves, Robert N. Essick, and Joseph Viscomi. <http://www.blakearchive.org/blake/>. [Accessed 30 March 2012].

Bordalejo, Barbara. 2010. "The Encoding System". In Prue Shaw (ed.), *The Commedia of Dante Alighieri: A Digital Edition*. Saskatoon: Scholarly Digital Editions.

Bornstein, George. 2001. *Material Modernism: The Politics of the Page*. Cambridge: Cambridge University Press.

Brumfield, Ben W. 2012. "Crowdsourced Transcription Tool List". In *Collaborative Manuscript Transcription,* <http://manuscripttranscription.blogspot.co.uk/2012/04/crowdsourced-transcription-tool-list.html>. [Accessed 18 September 2012].

Burnard, Lou, Fotis Iannidis, Elena Pierazzo and Malte Rehbein. n.d. "An Encoding Model for Genetic Editions". In *TEI: Text Encoding Initiative*. Charlottesville: Text Encoding Initiative, <http://www.tei-c.org/Activities/Council/Working/tcw19.html>. [Accessed 14 September 2012].

Burnard, Lou, Katherine O'Brien O'Keeffe, and John Unsworth, eds. 2007. *Electronic Textual Editing*. New York: Modern Language Association of America.

Chaucer, Geoffrey. 1996. *The Wife of Bath's Prologue on CD-ROM*. Ed. Peter M. W. Robinson. Cambridge: Cambridge University Press.

―――. 2004. *The Miller's Tale on CD-ROM*. Ed. Peter M. W. Robinson. Birmingham: Scholarly Digital Editions.

Coombs, James H., Allen H. Renear and Steven J. DeRose. 1987. "Markup Systems and the Future of Scholarly Text Processing". *Communications of the Association for Computing Machinery*, 30: 933–47.

Deegan, Marilyn and Peter M. W. Robinson. 1994. "The Electronic Edition". In D. G. Scragg and P. E. Szarmach (eds.), *Editing Old English Texts*. Woodbridge, Suffolk: Boydell and Brewer, pp. 27–37.

DeRose, Steven J., David G. Durand, Elli Mylonas and Allen H. Renear. 1990. "What is Text, Really?" *Journal of Computing in Higher Education*, 1(2): 3–26.

DeRose, Steven J. 2004. "Markup Overlap: A Review and a Horse". In *Proceedings of Extreme Markup Languages*. n.p: Extreme Markup Languages, <http://conferences.idealliance.org/extreme/html/2004/DeRose01/EML2004DeRose01.html>. [Accessed 18 September 2012].

Driscoll, Matthew J. 2010. "The Words on the Page: Thoughts on Philology, Old and New". In Judith Quinn and Emily Lethbridge (eds.), *Creating the Medieval Saga: Versions, Variability and Editorial Interpretations of Old Norse Saga Literature.* Odense: Syddansk Universitetsforlag, pp. 85–104.

Duggan, Hoyt N. 1994. "1994 Prospectus: Archive Goals". In *The Piers Plowman Electronic Archive.* Ed. Hoyt N. Duggan et al. n.p.: Society for Early English and Norse Electronic Texts (SEENET), <http://www3.iath.virginia.edu/seenet/piers/archivegoals.htm>. [Accessed 18 September 2012].

———. 2005. "Transcriptional Protocols: Piers Plowman Electronic Archive and SEENET". In *The Piers Plowman Electronic Archive.* Ed. Hoyt N. Duggan et al. n.p.: Society for Early English and Norse Electronic Texts (SEENET), <http://www3.iath.virginia.edu/seenet/piers/protocoltran.html>. [Accessed 18 September 2012].

Eggert, Paul. 2009. *Securing the Past: Conservation in Art, Architecture and Literature.* Cambridge: Cambridge University Press.

———. Forthcoming. "Anglo-American Critical Editing: Concepts, Terms and Methodologies". *Ecdotica* 10

Foucault, Michel. 1984. "What is an Author?" In Paul Rabinow (ed.), *The Foucault Reader.* New York: Pantheon, pp. 101–20.

Gabler, Hans Walter. 1984. "The Synchrony and Diachrony of Texts: Practice and Theory of the Critical Edition of James Joyce's *Ulysses*". *Text*, 1, pp. 305–26.

———. 1990. "Textual Studies and Criticism". *The Library Chronicle.* The University of Texas at Austin, pp. 151–65.

———. 2002. "For *Ulysses*: a Once and Future Edition". *Variants*, 1. pp. 85–105.

———. 2007. "The Primacy of the Document in Editing". *Ecdotica*, 4, pp. 197–207.

———. 2010. "Theorizing the Digital Scholarly Edition". *Literature Compass*, 7, pp. 43–56.

———. 2012. "Beyond Author-Centricity in Scholarly Editing". *Journal of Early Modern Studies,* 1, pp. 15–35, <http://www.fupress.net/index.php/bsfm-jems/article/view/10691>. [Accessed 30 March 2012].

Ginther, James, n.d. "T-PEN: Transcription for Palaeographic and Editorial Notation". <http://t-pen.org/TPEN/>. [Accessed 18 September 2012].

Greetham, D. C. 1992. *Textual Scholarship: An Introduction.* London and New York: Routledge.

———. 1999. *Theories of the Text.* Oxford: Oxford University Press.

Kiernan, Kevin. 2006. "Digital facsimiles in Editing". In Lou Burnard, Katherine O'Brien O'Keeffe and John Unsworth (eds.) *Electronic Textual Editing.* New York: Modern Language Association of America, pp. 262–68.

McDermott, Anne, ed. 1996. *Johnson's Dictionary on CD-ROM.* Cambridge: Cambridge University Press.

McGann, Jerome J. 1983. *A Critique of Modern Textual Criticism.* Chicago: University of Chicago Press.

———. 1991. *The Textual Condition.* Princeton: Princeton University Press.

———. 1995. "The Rationale of HyperText (selections)". *The European English Messenger,* 4, pp. 34–40.

———. 2001. *Radiant Textuality: Literature after the World Wide Web.* New York: Palgrave Macmillan.

McLeod, Randall. 2004. "Gerard Hopkins and the Shapes of Sonnets". In Raimonda Modiano, Leroy F. Searle, and Peter L. Shillingsburg (eds.), *Text and Hypertext: Emerging Practices in Textual Studies.* Seattle: University of Washington Press, pp. 177–297.

Marcus, Leah. 1996. *Unediting the Renaissance: Shakespeare, Marlowe and Milton.* London and New York: Routledge.

O'Brien O'Keeffe, Katherine. 2006. *Visible Song.* Cambridge: Cambridge University Press.

Pierazzo, Elena. 2011. "A Rationale of Digital Documentary editions". *Literary and Linguistic Computing,* 26, pp. 463–77.

Porter, Dorothy, et al. 2005. "TEI. SIG Overlap". In *TEIWiki.* Charlottesville: Text Encoding Initiative, <http://wiki.tei-c.org/index.php/SIG:Overlap>. [Accessed 18 September 2012].

Price, Kenneth M. 2008. "Electronic Scholarly Editions". In Susan Schreibman and Ray Siemens (eds.), *A Companion to Digital Literary Studies.* Oxford: Blackwell, <http://www.whitmanarchive.org/about/articles/anc.00267.html>. [Accessed 12 March 2012].

Renear, Allen H., David G. Durand and Elli Mylonas. 1996. "Refining our Notion of What Text Really Is: The Problem of Overlapping Hierarchies" In S. Hockey and N. Ide (eds.), *Research in Humanities Computing 4: Selected Papers from the ALLC/ACH Conference, Christ Church, Oxford, April, 1992.* Oxford: Oxford University

Press, pp. 263–80. Reprinted Providence, RI: Center for Digital Scholarship, Brown University Library, <http://www.stg.brown.edu/resources/stg/monographs/ohco.html>. [Accessed 17 September 2012].

Robinson, Peter M. W. and Robert J. O'Hara, 1992. "Report on the Textual Criticism Challenge 1991". *Bryn Mawr Classical Review*, 3, pp. 331–37.

———. 2009. "What Text Really is not, and Why Editors have to Learn to Swim". *Literary and Linguistic Computing*, 24, pp. 41–52.

——— and Solopova, E. 1993. *Guidelines for transcription of the manuscripts of the Wife of Bath's Prologue.* In Norman F. Blake and Peter M. W. Robinson (eds.), *The Canterbury Tales Project: Occasional Papers.* Vol. 1. London: Office for Humanities Communication, pp. 19–52.

Rossetti, D. G. 1993. *The Complete Writings and Pictures of Dante Gabriel Rossetti: A Hypermedia Archive.* Ed. Jerome McGann. Charlottesville: Institute for Advanced Technology in the Humanities. <http://www.rossettiarchive.org/>. [Accessed 30 March 2012].

Siemens, Ray, Meagan Timney, Cara Leitch et al. Forthcoming. "Toward Modeling the Social Edition: An Approach to Understanding the Electronic Scholarly Edition in the Context of New and Emerging Social Media". *Literary and Linguistic Computing.*

Shillingsburg, Peter L.. 1996. *Scholarly Editing in the Computer Age: Theory and Practice.* Third Edition. Ann Arbor: University of Michigan Press.

———. 2006. *From Gutenberg to Google: Electronic Representations of Literary Texts.* Cambridge: Cambridge University Press.

Van Mierlo, Wim, ed. *Textual Scholarship and the Material Book.* Special Issue of *Variants* 6.

Van Reenen, Pieter, August den Hollander and Margot van Mulken, eds. 2004. *Studies in Stemmatology II.* Amsterdam, John Benjamins.

Zeller, Hans. 1995. "Record and Interpretation: Analysis and Documentation as Goal and Method of Editing". In Hans Walter Gabler, George Bornstein and Gillian Borland Pierce (eds.), *Contemporary German Editorial Theory.* Ann Arbor: University of Michigan Press, pp. 17–58.

Reflections on Textual Editing in the Time of the History of the Book

Wim Van Mierlo

A FUNDAMENTAL ISSUE frequently discussed in textual scholarship is the relationship between "text" and "work". Since the emergence of the History of the Book, a third term must be taken into consideration too: the "book". As a field of inquiry that is by its own admission incredibly diverse, the History of the Book encompasses multi-disciplinary and multi-cultural approaches to the study of the book and of the production and dissemination of all written and recorded knowledge. According to David Finkelstein and Alistair McCleery, book history aims "to study all aspects of the creation of books" whether as "physical artefacts" or objects with "unique cultural symbols" (2005, 5), an undertaking that has its roots firmly in the traditional bibliographical disciplines such as descriptive and analytical bibliography and textual criticism.

To these forms of study, book history added a new layer of social and socio-economic history that began with the paradigm-shifting work of D. F. McKenzie in the ground-breaking essay "The Printers of the Mind" (1969) and culminated in his Panizzi lectures collected in *Bibliography and the Sociology of Texts* (1999).[1] In that early essay McKenzie not so much challenged traditional analytical bibliography as expanded it, when he showed how knowledge of printing-house practices in seventeenth- and eighteenth-century England by using quantifiable evidence from printing catalogues, accounts' ledgers and business correspondence could significantly improve our bibliographical understanding. His emphasis on the conditions of book production, moreover, indicated a breaking away from the study of the individual book or text to *books* plural. With that not just the production of literature, but the production of all books and their dissemination fall within the purview of the history of the book.

---

[1] "The Printers of the Mind", originally published in *Studies in Bibliography*, is reprinted in McKenzie 2002, 13–85. The Panizzi Lectures were delivered at The British Library in 1985.

In the first instance, book history investigates the economic support structures that existed to bring these commodities to the reader — from book designs to marketing tools, from pricing mechanisms to the means of transportation. But books are also cultural products that help with the exchange of knowledge and ideas across time and space, and thus the production and reception of books play an essential role in shaping (as well as being shaped by) historical *mentalités* (Willison 2006, 2–3). The book, in other words, is no longer only the subject of bibliographical analysis, but sits at the nexus of a broad spectrum of economic, intellectual, social and cultural investigations.

In my introduction to *Textual Scholarship and the Material Book*, I pointed out that textual scholarship and book history share the book as an object of study but look at it from different perspectives, and attempted a broad characterization of the relationships between the two fields (Van Mierlo 2007, 4–5). In the present essay, I wish to deepen my inquiry into this relationship by looking at the directions textual editing has taken since the sociological turn in Anglo-American textual scholarship introduced by D. F. McKenzie and Jerome McGann and the emergence of book history.[2] What potential there is for further cross-fertilization rests in particular on the concepts that McKenzie and McGann introduced in their work. Each in his own way placed the "book" alongside the "text". McGann did this conceptually when he distinguished between the linguistic code of a work and its bibliographical code (McGann 1991, 13 and *passim*). McKenzie more directly linked the "integrity of the text", which the textual editor seeks to preserve or restore, with "the formal unity of the book" which embodies that text (McKenzie 1999,

---

[2]   Insofar as this essay is concerned with the history of the book in textual scholarship, its counterpart — the importance of textual scholarship, and particularly textual editing, for the history of the book — deserves consideration as well. Ian Willison has argued that if the importance of book history to the development of the humanities is to continue further, book historians must consolidate their research procedures and scholarly practices, which include "technical" practices such as textual editing and archival research (2006, 13–15). To achieve this it must become necessary to reorient the importance of textual and bibliographical analysis and, rather than seeing them as origins from which book history developed, give them new pertinence. Given the complexities of this exercise, not in the least because textual scholars tend to focus on individual texts and works, I reserve dealing with this matter for another occasion.

35). One outcome of their thinking in my view is that the same work — the same text even — can exist with differing degrees of granularity. The sort of text that you find in Project Gutenberg, for example, has a very low granularity, while that same text in its original first edition or in a *de luxe* format especially produced for the book collector has a high granularity. I contend that this granularity of the text is an aspect of bibliographical investigation that editors have not yet quite reckoned with.

For many scholars, rather, the question remains as to how the sociological turn, despite the obvious and inherent value of the insights it has produced, is at all relevant to the textual editor's work.[3] How does one edit socially? To answer this question we must revisit some of the underlying assumptions at work in textual editing, which is tantamount to asking again what editions purport to do and who they are for, an issue I will return to towards the end of this essay. The Anglo-American editorial tradition, aiming to produce authoritative editions that ideally reflection authorial intention, produces scholarly editions in which the edited text is foregrounded over the transmission history of that text. When it comes to social editing, In other words, it is not that this approach is logically impossible, but that it is considered incompatible with accepted author-centred theories. I will argue that this need not be so; in fact, McKenzie's own practice in his posthumous edition of William Congreve proves otherwise. What is needed, therefore, is a consideration of the nature of work, text and book that realigns the sociological turn with the business of editing. As such, this essay is both about editing and editions, about the scholarly practice of textual criticism and the intellectual endeavour that makes our literary heritage available to the reading public.

---

[3]   Tanselle, for example, for the most part resists the relevance of a sociological approach in editing. While the the socially produced text may be of considerable historical relevance, textual scholarship cannot avoid concerning itself with the authorially intended text precisely because of the difference between the author's conception of his work and how that work evolved in production. Editing socially is permissible as an option, but for Tanselle the stakes of recovering an authorially intended text are simply higher: the one is matter of minor intervention in specific historical instantiations of the work; the other "requires acts of informed critical judgment" (2005, 171, 214).

The sociological turn in textual scholarship

To bring about this realignment, I will draw on recent discussions in the area of digital text and scholarly digital editions about the notion of the interface. These discussions take place in the wake of the sociological turn in textual scholarship and the new ways of thinking about text it has brought about.

As textual scholarship became more interdisciplinary in the 1980s, it was also moving, so it seemed, beyond the core business of correcting texts according to well-established scholarly principles. The history of the Society for Textual Scholarship in the United States reflects this evolution. New theoretical perspectives meant there was a decrease interest in pure analytical and descriptive bibliography and a rising concern with questioning what "text" was in the first place. At the same time, the notion of final authorial intention was being slowly displaced. The outcome of this evolution was that textual scholarship became something of a broad church where the study of textual phenomena flourished as a goal in its own right.

Out of these new developments, and in reaction to the abstract notions of "texts" bandied about loosely in critical theory, emerged an increased interest for textual materiality. Terms like "material text", "material philology", and "textual culture" all indicated that texts are more than disembodied vehicles of meaning, but that instead they exist in specific socio-economic contexts and possess physical attributes, and that they come into being through the action of various agencies that include not only the author but also the publisher, typesetter, editor, marketing director, censor and so on.[4]

---

[4]   In the UK alone no less than three research centres devoted to material text have sprung up in recent years. Between 2005 and 2007 the then Centre for Publishing Studies at the University of Stirling ran a short series of conference and an M. Res degree in textual cultures (see http://www.textual-culture.stir.ac.uk/index.html). In Cambridge the Centre for Material Texts was founded in 2009 (see their blog at http://www.english.cam.ac.uk/cmt/). In 2011 the Material Texts Network was set up at Birkbeck College, University of London (http://www.bbk.ac.uk/arts/our-research/centres/the-material-texts-network). Others like exist around the world, such the Electronic Textual Cultures Lab (Victoria, Canada established in 2008), the centre for Materiale Textkulturen at Heidelberg (established in 2012, see http://www.materiale-textkulturen.de) and the Textual Cultures group of the Research Institute for History and Culture at the University of Utrecht. In the United States even the Society for Textual Scholarship followed suit when in 2004–5 it broadened its

The variety of approaches and research agendas that have emerged are almost always interdisciplinary. New research advocates "new perspectives, practices and technologies, which will transform our understanding of the way that texts of many kinds have been embodied and circulated" ("Welcome to the Cambridge Centre for Material Texts") and endeavour to frame the materiality of the text in new theoretical understandings at the junction where history, culture and literature come together (*Material Texts Network*). The influence of book history is evident, because "book historians are increasingly framing their work in terms of 'mediation', shifting the emphasis from recovering exact meanings in text to understanding the place of texts within contemporary society" (Finkelstein and McCleery 2005, 27).

Not infrequently, however, these new approaches are being framed in direct opposition to the perceived normative functions of traditional philology and textual editing. Textual editing, far from being on the wane, is undergoing some significant changes too. The idea of a "definitive" edition now seems long behind us (at least in certain quarters). For a while it was replaced by an enthusiasm for the everyone-his-own-editor movement inspired by the power of hypertext. But that wave too has now fortunately passed. The most radical change, however, is coming from the digital humanities. Scholarly digital editions, far from having made editing obsolete, are leading us into exciting new directions, while respectfully keeping an eye on the traditions that they inherited from printed scholarly editions. Indeed, digital editions require scholars to think again about what is at stake in textual editing (Galey 2010, 100–101). New technological possibilities are creating new ways of understanding what text is,

Rethinking the relationship of form to content in digital humanities — a relationship that was almost completely bypassed in theories about hypertext — Alan Galey considers the function of the interface as having a "granularity" that places itself between "material form" and "idealized content" (Galey 2010, 93–94; see also Kirschenbaum 2002, 20–27). Galey's remarks about the design of digital tools equally apply to printed books, whose granularity is what separates them from "plain" text. Just as with the digital medium, the "interface" of the book — its design, layout and typography — uses an

---

remit to all inquiries into the nature of "textuality" and changed its journal's title from *Text* to *Textual Cultures* (Storey 2006, 3–4).

aesthetic form to enable effective communication between writer and reader. For the most part, scholarly editing has ignored this granularity. The textual idealism that underpins the Anglo-American tradition in particular, in which the scholarly edition is meant to represent (or approximate) the ideal incarnation of the work, pushes the non-textual aspects of the book to one side and supplants the original bibliographic code with a new one.

Of course one must acknowledge that critical editing intervenes in the original text, which is deemed imperfect; a reconstruction of the text as the author intended it cannot take place without altering the material nature of that text. This paradox poses a serious difficulty for the social edition. Nonetheless, in order to imagine such editions we may need to temper the old idealism about text and think more strictly — as German textual editors do — along historical-critical lines.[5] What is text without the thing that supports it? If scholarly editions are to be grounded in the history of textual transmission, they ought not to avoid the historical manifestations of the text. Editing in the time of the history of the book requires editors to acknowledge at the very least that texts do not exist on their own.[6]

Texts are not books[7]

Assuming for the moment that texts are material (as is the common view), what is text actually made of? Why is it that we cannot hold text in our hands? What in other words is the material text made of? There seems no satisfactory answer that does not go back to critical theory.[8] For some commentators the expression "material text" is

---

[5]   Tanselle also implicitly aligns social editing with editing documents, as in the German tradition, rather than with editing works (2005, 212–13).

[6]   Roger Chartier makes the point that "it is essential to remember that no text exists outside of the support that enables it to be read; any comprehension of a writing, no matter what kind it is, depends on the forms in which it reaches the reader" (1989, 161).

[7]   For the following discussion, I am grateful to @ETreharne (Elaine Treharne), @nickmimic (Nicholas Morris) and @praymurray (Padmini Ray Murray) for an informative conversation on Twitter on the im/materiality of text, all of whom have suggested further areas where matters get complicated, as in the case of oral text, the functionality of text and the difference between common use and scholarly terminology.

[8]   The notion that text is material itself relies on the notion that language

simply a tautology (Chaudhury 2010, 2). However, I contend that the materiality of the text is not that self-evident. The belief that it is begins to unravel when we turn to the digital realm. Countering arguments that digital text, unlike normal text, is not material, Matthew Kirschenbaum rejects what he calls the "tactile fallacy", the supposition that digital text is not material because "you cannot reach out and touch them", and argues instead that physicality in the digital environment is as real as in the printed environment; just because digital text cannot be touched does not mean that its "computational variables" do not contain any bibliographic codes (Kirschenbaum 2002, 43). Yet rather than make a case for the physicality of digital text one can easily turn this argument upside down and argue against the physicality of all text. The tactile dimension does not lie in the text, but in the paper, the binding of the book or the indentation left by the metal type. Likewise, the bibliographical aspects do not exist in the text, but in such variables as the layout, imposition or gatherings. Material text, therefore, may well be an oxymoron rather than a tautology.[9]

To be fair to Kirschenbaum, he actually does not use the adjective "physical" at all. It still remains to be seen, therefore, how the immateriality of texts works. On the one hand, things need not have physical form in order to be real. Certainly, from a phenomenological as well as from a literary-critical point of view readers experience texts without necessarily being aware of the material features that surround them. On the other hand, texts are more than lexical codifications. If nothing else, texts are visual. They are substantialized by the application of ink to the page (or pixels on the screen, or inscriptions on the writing support), a materialization that allows the writer's message to be stored and conveyed to the reader across time and space . The point in other words is that texts are packaged in ways that may appear transparent to most readers, but that in fact

---

is material, something that can be seen and heard. The idea has its origins in Saussurian structuralist linguistics, whose binomial concept of language bisects the sign into signifier (form) and signified (meaning). As David Chandler remarks, however, the signifier for de Saussure was a sound-image rather than a form; the signifier was not a physical, but a psychological entity. Later theorists reclaimed its materiality (Chandler 2007, 16, 51–52).

[9]   Thus Shillingsburg: "[The text] is something that, although it exists in physical forms, is in some sense capable of existing in more than one form, and is, therefore, not itself physical but must be conceptual or symbolic" (2006, 14).

they are not. One can define bibliographical codes — which are not textual in the sense that they are not meaning-bearing — as layers that support and structure the text.[10] It is possible to strip away some of those layers, which does not at first sight affect the integrity of the text and its meaning, but reduces the granularity of the bibliographic codes. Imagine a black-and-white newspaper photograph of the Mona Lisa next to the original painting; then think of *Hamlet* in the First Folio and *Hamlet* on the Kindle, and the differences in granularity will become apparent.

Peter Shillingsburg helpfully reminds us that there is no universal agreement on what texts are: "By *texts*, for example, some scholars mean physical objects, some mean a series of signs or symbols (the lexical text), and some mean conceptualizations only" (2006, 12). In *Resisting Texts*, Shillingsburg differentiates between the "material text" and the "reception text"; the latter is not quite the "work" (for which he reserves the term "conceptual text") but the abstract mental construction the reader creates in the act of reading, whereas the former is the "union of *linguistic text* and *document*: a *sign sequence* held in a medium of display" (1997, 51–52, 81–82, 101).[11] Text and document are thus different yet wholly interdependent. The text, in other words, is mediated through the book, which functions as its interface and from which it is inseparable. Like a tattoo it sits, as it were, underneath the skin.

The current e-Reader revolution makes the importance of interface and mediation clear. The term "e-Book" is of course a misnomer. As Christian Vandendorpe suggests, the metaphorical application of such words like "page" and "book" in the digital medium represent the strong and lasting legacy of the codex, though the parallel with the scroll may be more appropriate (Vandendorpe 2009, 138–39, 164). More to the point for our argument, the texts Kindles and similar devices display have few of the bibliographical features — paratexts, typographical design and layout — that we normally associate with books. Kindles do not offer pure text — that is in fact

---

[10]   It may be *à propos* to think of the etymological connection between "code" and "codex" as well as the precise meaning of the verb *codify*, which the *OED* defines as "to reduce (laws) to a code; to digest" and "to reduce to a general system; to systematize".

[11]   German editors in this respect talk about "Textgestalt" [literally, text form] and "Textträger" [textual carrier].

impossible — but the layout of their texts certainly represents the lowest common denominator of page design.

That the Kindle is more text than book is demonstrated by a central aspect of the functionality of e-Readers: the capacity of text to reflow. Unlike the text in a pdf say, which is locked into place, the iterative text has no formatting constraints and its flexibility assures that the content adjusts itself to fit the size of the screen. Content creators can still to some extent control the formatting of the text using html and css, but the text is not restricted to one specific layout.[12] Text flow is an important feature of any form of reading on screen. Web browsers allow users to change the layout to suit their needs: they can increase or decrease the font size, overrule stylesheets, and change other settings. The "Readality" extension for Firefox, for example, offers a tool that de-clutters the web page and reformats the text rendering it easier on the eye. Besides the display of text on the screen, digital devices primarily rely on text to reflow when content is exchanged between devices or platforms. The iterability of text is what makes operations like importing content into your Kindle, clipping text to Evernote or copying and pasting in Microsoft Word possible.

Of course, this iterative function of texts existed with earlier forms of copying too (by hand or by print). However, whereas these earlier forms required human agency and, consequently, risked corruption, digital reflow is automatic and error-free. Furthermore, the question of what is a copy in the digital world is an interesting issue. What distinguishes one copy of a text from another is the metadata, i.e., something linked with but separate from the text. Like all paratexts, metadata exist on the margins of the text. In the analog world, the metadata extend and include to the physical medium that carries the text. A copy of a text, errors notwithstanding, does not create a new text, but it does create a new a new document. Peter Shillingsburg therefore sees the property of iterability as a form reincarnation. The copy of a manuscript results in "two material objects each occupying a different space, though each purports to bear the same text" (2006, 13, 14). In particular, Shillingsburg associates the reincarnation of the text with the editorial act.

---

[12]   With this freedom also come limitations. On the web, html is mostly inadequate to represent some finer aspects of typography (e.g., ligatures, tables) and devices like the Kindle are better suited to displaying prose than poetry.

I do not want to push the argument about the im/materiality of texts any further, except to say that often people use the phrase "material text" when they actually mean "book", whose physical attributes are of course not in doubt. The book, therefore, has no iterative properties. Its physical form is unique and stable, and therefore cannot be "edited" in the normal sense of the word. Hence, there remains a challenge to define what role they play in textual editing.

The granularity of the text

McKenzie, more than anyone else in the field, has made the leap from text to book, advocating that we should amplify "our sensitivity to the printed book as physical form in order to refine our notions of the historicity of printed texts and our function in editing them" (1984, 334).[13] A discussion of the nature of text and book cannot take place without reference to McKenzie's seminal idea that "forms effect meaning", a subtle but profound adjustment of the old structuralist idea that form and content are inseparable.[14] What he means is not that bibliographical forms *have* meaning, but that they bring about meaning.

Certainly forms can also *affect* meaning, as Jerome McGann has argued in respect of his bibliographical codes. However, I am somewhat skeptical as to the ability of the bibliographical codes to bring about "shifts and changes" in meaning (1991, 59). The examples that McGann himself and other scholars have cited strongly support his arguments, but in each case the circumstances are exceptional and a general theory is more difficult to validate. What may be obvious for Byron's "Fare Thee Well", for instance, may not be so obvious with other works. James Joyce's *Ulysses*, for instance, which was serialized

---

[13] Still, even McKenzie uses "text" as a shorthand for any kind of carrier of verbal and non-verbal communication (1999, 13). In common English usage, the words "text" and "work" are of course practically interchangeable, but without a doubt the pervasive use of "text" in literary scholarship, which has experienced a dramatic increase since the 1980s, has left its mark too.

[14] The depth of McKenzie's statement is adumbrated when we consider its misprint in the Routledge *Book History Reader*: "forms *affect* meaning", with an "a" rather than an "e" (Finkelstein and McCLeery 2006, 37; the error was first spotted by Galey 2010, 113–14). In English the words "effect" and "affect" are often confused. Obviously close to each other in sense and orthography, the first means to bring about something; the second to have an influence on.

in two little magazines, *The Egoist* in England and *The Little Review* at the other side of the Atlantic, both from 1918 onwards, before it was published in book form by Sylvia Beach's Shakespeare & Co (1922). The similarities of these two publications are probably greater than their differences. Despite looking very different, the two magazines were both aimed at the individualist, discerning and conscientiously modern reader. Both were partly orchestrated by the impresario of literary modernism, Ezra Pound, and occupied a niche in the literary market in England and the United States. They also shared a do-it-yourself attitude towards publishing that was later fulfilled by Beach when she offered, even though she had never ventured into publishing before, to bring out *Ulysses.*

McGann's conceptualization, appealing though it is, perhaps overdetermines the power of form. The circumstances in which Byron's poem was published — privately printed, twice pirated, and finally canonized in the 1816 *Poems* — show that not just the "look" of the printings but also their function and audience were different. The conditions in which other works were published may not have created such marked differences. I agree that different bibliographical codes *may* result in differentiation in meaning, but we should also ascertain whether these differences indeed registered in the minds of readers. To check this is a matter for reception history.[15]

I find McKenzie's point, therefore, more discerning. His argument is less about hermeneutics than about facilitating the transmission of texts and their meaning; it is about understanding that transmission from the evidence in the books themselves as well as from "conceptions of the book", the way printers expected readers to interpret the forms of their book designs. (McKenzie 2002, 207). Running headers, type size and other paratextual features of the book do not have any meaning in their own right; to appropriate a term from Roland Barthes, they are a zero degree of printing, unburdened by the need to communicate themselves. Nevertheless, they facilitate communication and the production of meaning. The aims of book design and typography thus involve "aesthetic sensibility, technically informed, serving the communication of meaning, the creation of the distinct experience of reading the work" (McKenzie 2002, 214). Functionality combined with aesthetics determine for McKenzie the

---

[15]   Evidence in the case of Byron's "Fare Thee Well" certainly suggests that the four versions were received differently.

"book's total form", but the effect on meaning really depends on what "expressive resources" were "available to an author through his printer" (2002, 215–16). While it is the case that decisions about format were generally motivated by business practices (2002, 220–21), McKenzie does not exclude agency and intention from book production, which is a very important point when it comes to textual editing.

The distinctive "typographic vocabulary" (McKenzie 2002, 218) of James Joyce's *Ulysses* may serve to illustrate the complexities of the book's "expressive resources". The only areas of the book's get-up in which Joyce was involved were the now famous pale blue colour of the cover and the white lettering of the title. Joyce requested several samples before he was satisfied that the tone of blue was right and evoked the colours of the Greek flag. Readers may have missed this vexillologic allusion, but they could not have failed to see (and heft) the book's bulk: the large-sized edition (state B) printed on *vergé d'arches* handmade paper ran to 732 pages and was approximately 46 mm thick. It was also a very fragile item as its weight easily caused the inner hinges to crack. On the inside, the layout was rather unusual. On the one hand, the classic Elzevir typeface, although it was probably chosen for its compactness, adds gravitas. The layout of the text, on the other hand, does not conform to the so-called Van de Graaf canon, which stipulates that the text area be proportional to the page size; the result is an imbalance between the position of the text area and the margins.[16] The physical composition of the page thus almost acts as an impediment, creating a sense, compounded with the inherent difficulty of the novel itself, that this is a book that is difficult to digest, and prompting critical derision. George Slocombe in his Paris column in the *Daily Herald* of 17 March 1922 exclaimed: "And here it is at last, as large as telephone directory or a family Bible, and with many of the literary and social characteristics

---

[16]   *Ulysses* in "state B", printed on large-sized paper, measures 195 x 225 mm and the text area 122 x 164 mm, with an inner margin of 30mm and an outer margin of 46mm. To conform to the Van de Graaf canon, the triangle A-C in Figure 1 should pass through the bottom-left and top-right corner of the text area on the verso and the top-left and bottom-right corner of the recto; the cross formed by lines D-E and F-G should pass through the top left and top right corner of the text area; finally when line H-I passes through the top-left corner of the text area on the recto, then the line I-J should finish where B-C and F-G intersect.

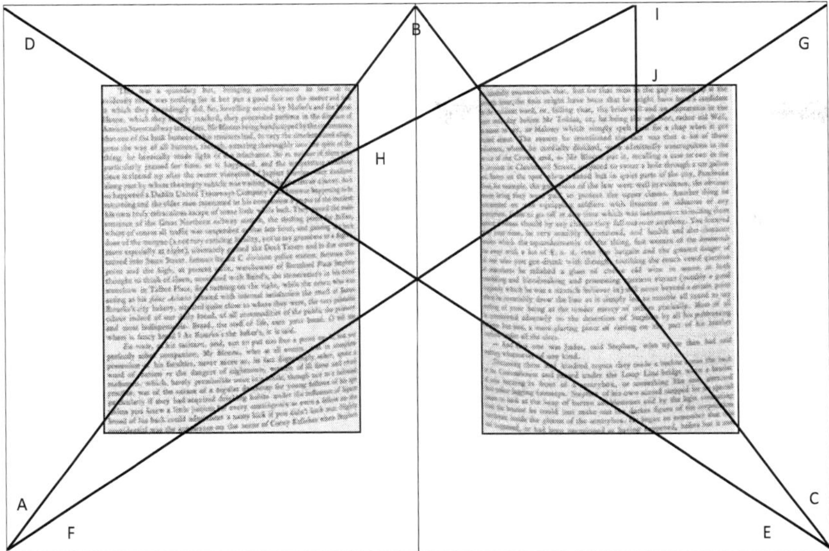

Figure 1: Van de Graaf canon. Mock-up of James Joyce, *Ulysses* (1922; state "B").

of each" (quoted in Deming 1997, 217). The format, however, was not intentional, but resulted from the challenges posed by Joyce's lengthy work.

For the textual editor, the challenge then lies in what to do with the bibliographical information, particularly in cases where typography itself has gone wrong. T. S. Eliot's *The Waste Land* is a case in point. Eliot's poem was published no less than four times as an individual poem: in October 1922 the poem appeared in the first issue of Eliot's new magazine *The Criterion*, followed a month later by publication in the American magazine *The Dial*; on 15 December Boni and Liveright of New York issued the first book publication with a print run of 1,000 copies; Virginia and Leonard Woolf's The Hogarth Press finished their hand-set edition of 460 copies almost a year later, on 13 September 1923. Citing Eliot's approval, most editors consider the text of the American edition to be the most reliable, and it has been used as copy-text in Lawrence Rainey's critical edition (Eliot 2006; see 46–48 for details). *The Criterion* text and the Boni text were almost certainly set around the same time from two different typescripts.[17] Concerned about the form of the poem and other details, he warned Boni and Liveright upon sending the typescript: "I only hope the printers are not allowed to bitch the punctuation and the spacing, as that is very important for the sense" (2009, 1: 707). His worries, however, had been unwarranted, for when the proofs came back he thought they were "excellent" (2009, 1: 746). The same was not true for the proofs of *The Criterion*, which arrived a week later from the English printers. Clearly agitated, he complained to the magazine's publisher that the printer had had made a number of "undesired alterations". What these undesired alterations were is unknown, but one may assume that they consisted of changes to the punctuation and spacing. With considerable effort, Eliot reversed the errors and managed, in spite of a few misprints that remained, to create a text that principally matched his intentions. The affair, however, may have left him with a lingering dissatisfaction over *The Criterion* text, even though in the end it was the better version.

The reason is that while the Boni and Liveright text carries authority, its layout does not. Feeling that a poem of a mere 430 lines was not enough to fill a book, Horace Liveright, one of the firm's directors, had asked Eliot whether he could not add a few extra poems to pad out the book. Eliot objected, but produced instead the famous notes. The publishers, no doubt deliberately, chose a small, octavo format and printed the poem in large type with ample leading so that the whole in the end ran to a reasonable book of 64 pages. Owing to the reduced size, the printers had to turn most of Eliot's long lines, lending the poem, with the original spacing and line divisions almost completely lost, an air of even greater disjointedness than is actually the case. The *Criterion* text, by comparison, comprised only 15 pages of a larger format (height *c.* 23 cm). Eliot's poetry, uninterrupted by line division, really comes into its own in this more spacious environment and has an orderly, almost classic

---

[17] Whether the American typescript is among the four typescripts still extant is not yet known (see McCue 2006, 25). The *Criterion* typescript (a carbon copy with some autograph corrections) may be the one in the Hayward Collection at King's College Cambridge; it contains a handwritten note by Eliot in which he says that it was possibly used by the printer for *The Criterion* (MS CAM/ HB/TSE/V4a). However, about 10 lines were accidentally omitted as a result of an eye skip and remain uncorrected.

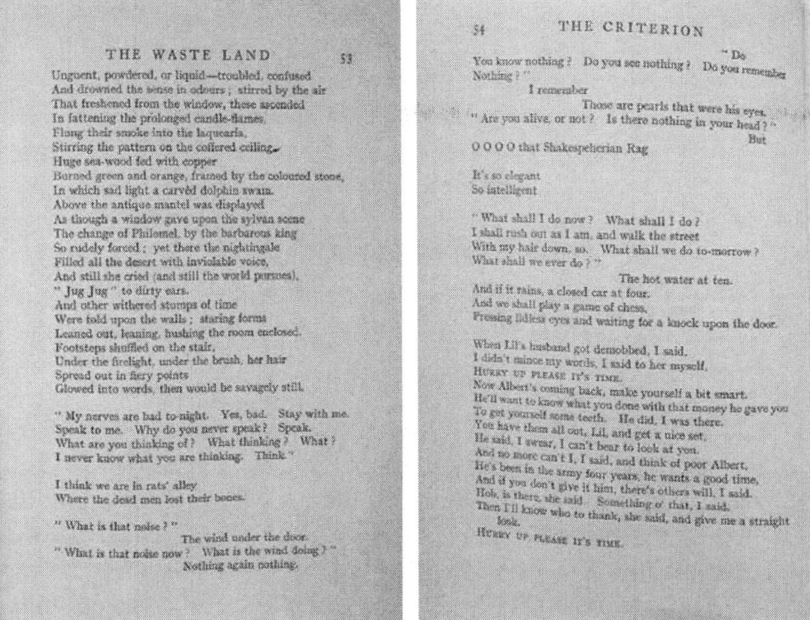

Figure 2: The Waste Land, "What is that noise", *The Criterion* I (1922), pp. 53 and 54.

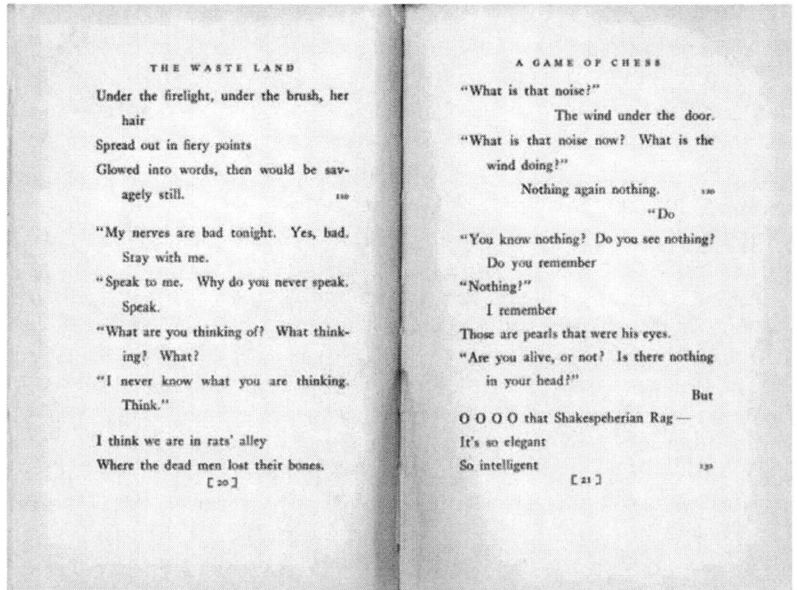

Figure 3: The Waste Land, "What is that noise", Boni and Liveright (1922), pp. 20–21.

feel to it.[18] The spacing, moreover, follows more closely the spacing in the typescript preserved at King's College Cambridge. In one particularly difficult passage, the text literally cascades down the page, a feature meant to convey typographically the anxiety of the speaker; *The Criterion* manages to replicate the intended shape, although it does not get it exactly perfect (Figure 2). None of the other early editions — *the Dial* and the Hogarth Press — does so either (and nor for that matter any of the later Faber editions of Eliot's *Collected* and *Selected Poems*). But in the Boni and Liveright the feature is lost entirely, and with the layout's expressive form (Figure 3).[19]

Editions, their aims and audience

The argument that books as carriers of texts are important for textual scholarship is largely self-evident. But how should it change our practice? Is the aim merely to produce scholarly editions with additional content, as Bodo Plachta (2007) has suggested? The case Plachta puts forward uses examples of "politically charged" paratexts to demonstrate the importance of book forms to the study of the production, dissemination (to stay under the radar of censorship, for example) and reception of printed texts (2006, 96, 99). His recommendation to include facsimile materials in (digital) editions is not meant to replace textual criticism, but rather to add to it, so that the edition may also serve as an archive" while "offer[ing]

---

[18] When almost a year Eliot thanked Virginia Woolf for the Hogarth Press edition, the first English book edition, he told her that he was "delighted": "Spacing and paging are beautifully planned to make it the right length, far better than the American edition" (2009, 2: 202).

[19] Rainey further claims that the Boni and Liveright edition was used as copy-text for the Hogarth Press edition because Eliot considered it the best text (Eliot 2006, 47). This is, however, not the case. The famous Notes apart, which had only appeared in the Boni edition, a small number of substantive variants make it obvious that the Woolfs did not set their text from the American edition, but presumably from a typescript that was related to the typescript that was sent to New York. (The number of readings where the Hogarth text is not in agreement with the Boni text and that are not clearly the result of non-authorial intervention is very small.) The marked dissimilarity of the Hogarth edition's layout to that of the Boni and Liveright makes it quite obvious that the Woolfs did not use the American edition as their model. It would have been impossible for them to reconstitute the layout of the poem in accordance with Eliot's intention.

urgently needed starting points for the use of editorial products in literary studies" (2006, 103). Of course, the practical implications of bringing the physical features of the book into the edition remain considerable, even in the electronic environment, no matter how better suited it may be to completist editions.

Textual editing in the time of the history of the book should, however, not simply be a matter of producing editions that have more content, but rather of editions that do more things. Such a reconceptualization of scholarly editions should go beyond the bipolarization created by the digital era: of having digital critical editions on the one hand and digital archives on the other. Shillingsburg has stated repeatedly that in order to fulfil his responsibility to the reader the task of the editor is to edit; editors "whose work stops at archiving perform valuable work, but they offer no more than starting places" (1997, 224). One might object that Shillingsburg takes a rather narrow view when he sees the digital archive only as a toolkit for making editions and not as a repository for the process of textual transmission; he certainly does not see the critical apparatus that way: rather than being "a dumping ground for superseded textual forms", the apparatus is "a guide to the progression of composition and production processes creating a succession of versions" (1997, 212).[20] Digital archives are no doubt better adapted at providing this guidance than are the printed edition whose apparatus — mockingly dubbed a *Variantenfriedhof* [cemetery of variants] (see Gabler 2008, 14) — is often difficult to repurpose. Regardless of the painstaking accuracy with which apparatuses are put together, to reconstruct particular states from the welter of detail in them is laborious, if not impossible. Digital editions, by contrast, being both edition and archive, offer the potential for digging more deeply into the textual data.

Once it was enough for editions to present an accurate text and to provide a rationale for its emendations as well as a record of the textual history and transmission. But the objectives from the past no longer satisfy the editors of the digital era, whose scholarly editions

---

[20]   Shillingsburg of course is no adversary of digital archives, as long as they are both "an archive of historical documents whose iconography is intact" and "edited texts [. . .] produced to reflect the work of a historian [i.e,. critical editor]" that should be "introduced historically, critically, and textually" (1997, 24).

are becoming richer, more ambitious and more diverse. One way that digital editions are moving beyond the print edition is that they no longer simply offer access to the textual data, but present "ways of filtering" that data that enable readers to interrogate the text's transmission history (Lavagnino 2009, 72).[21] Furthermore, if we now agree that editions have only a limited life cycle before new theoretical perspectives and new research questions prompt us to remake our editions, then we must also acknowledge that not all editorial aims can be served by one edition alone. Even though we currently accept that having rival editions is good (since no edition can claim to be "definitive"), we still tend to see them as rivals for truth rather than as editions occupying different shares of the scholarly and readerly market .

Textual pluralism is good — as long as it furthers our understanding of the nature of text, work and book; it cannot simply be good for its own sake, or to make it fit a liberal humanist agenda. The point is that textual pluralism only becomes really insightful when we recognize the differences in *purpose* that editions serve and that different editions may have different users.

In some cases, it would seem that differences in purpose are better reflected in public controversies over editorial practice rather than in explanations about editorial rationales in the editions themselves. There are two rival critical editions of W. B. Yeats's poems: that by Richard Finneran, originally published in 1983, revised in 1989 and available in the *Collected Works* issued by Scribners in New York; and that by A. Norman Jeffares, published by Macmillan (but available only in the UK) (Yeats 1989 and 1997). Both editions apply the principle of final authorial intention, and as a result both editions agree on most readings. The editors agree on the meaning of the words "final" and "intention", but they disagree on the meaning of the word "authorial". For Finneran, Yeats is the author; his edition accepts only the final readings that Yeats authorized during his lifetime. The same is not true in the Jeffares edition. Warwick Gould,

---

[21]   For Lavagnino, the scholarly editions of the past were too concerned with access to information, rather than understanding that information; he feels that by focusing on the "activity of the editor", rather than that of the "user", too many editions "offered access to the wrong thing" (2009, 66). Not only was the apparatus side-lined, leading it to be overlooked by readers, but its function and workings were not adequately explained.

who was Jeffares' collaborator, categorically rejects Finneran's view (Gould 1989). Yeats was of course the author of his poems for Gould too, but not so to speak the sole author. Using letters and other archival evidence, Gould demonstrates that Yeats delegated certain "final" decisions about his texts to other people, in particular to his editor at Macmillan, Thomas Mark, and to his wife, George Yeats. After Yeats's death, Mark worked closely together with Yeats's widow, who implemented revisions that Yeats had indicated he wanted but had never carried out (Gould 1994, 110–11). Gould, in other words, sees Yeats as a "social" author who was at the heart of a small network of people who all had some authorial input.

Apart from generating a handful of variant readings, this different conception of authorship has had significant impact on the order of the poems in Yeats's canon. When in 1933 Macmillan issued the *Collected Poems* containing all of Yeats's work to date in two volumes, Mark suggested a departure from the normal chronological order (an order which had already been established for the *Edition de Luxe*) in favour of a division between "Lyrical Poems" in volume one and "Narrative and Dramatic Poems" in volume two. Mark proposed this arrangement primarily for commercial reasons. To arrange the poems chronologically would have meant opening the volume with a long narrative poem called *The Wanderings of Oisin*, which Mark felt might put off potential buyers; placing the narrative poems in the second volume meant that volume one could open with the better-known lyrics from *Crossways* (1889) and *The Rose* (1893), including the immensely popular "The Lake Isle of Innisfree". Yeats warmly welcomed Mark's suggestion (Gould 1989, 714–15). Since no other collected edition appeared during Yeats's lifetime, the order of the *Collected Poems* became, *de facto*, the poet's final intention and was thus followed by Finneran.

However, this is not the full story. As Gould argues, *Collected Poems* represents Yeats's canon for a particular time and audience: it served its purpose wonderfully as a trade edition, satisfying both old and new audiences while aiming for a sense of completion; but it deviated from Yeats's own vision of his canon, which did not marginalize the longer poems. During the 1930s, he was making preparations for no less than two *de luxe* editions of his collected works, one to be published by Macmillan in the UK and Ireland, the other by Scribner's in the United States. At no point was the new arrangement of

Collected Poems, separating lyrical from narrative poems, considered for these editions (see, e.g., Gould 1989, 725). Unfortunately, neither edition ever appeared. Although they were not published, they exist in numerous runs of page proofs and draft contents, and therefore their authority supersedes that of the texts in the 1933 *Complete Poems*.

Yeats's poems are not just separate aesthetic entities, but exist within the larger constellation of his œuvre; as such, they cannot be separated from the book as physical object, to the extent that design and layout form an integral part of the symbolic structure of the poetry (though this dimension has not yet been realized in any existing edition). Yeats, moreover, not only frequently and obsessively revised his poems, he was apt to reconceive the total form of his body of work whenever a new publishing opportunity presented itself. More is at stake, therefore, than simply the words that constitute the text. Yeats's intentions are embedded in the social conditions that that supported the coming into being of his œuvre — a process that invites us to recognize the dynamic interplay between text and work — whose realization involved agencies other than the poet himself.

What this example illustrates is not simply that different rationales lead to different editions, but that editors deal with more than just text. (While Finneran's edition is defensible in its application of accepted editorial principles, it is narrowly author-centred and does not encompass the full history of the textual transmission. Jeffares' edition uses a broader conception of authorial agency as well as a more complete textual history that gives credit to Yeats's collaborators in the creation of his text. Moreover, in arguing *against* Finneran, Jeffares' edition manages to clarify its own editorial purpose within the editorial landscape. Not only do different rationales lead to different editions; they also lead to different uses and fulfill different research needs.

While critical editions normally have a statement about editorial rationales, they generally do not show great self-awareness about the ideological value and impact of these aims. Eclecticism in the Anglo-American world still all-too often produces editions allegedly suited to the needs of all readers. The norm still seems to be to accept "texts as given" (Gabler 2008, 14). The textual idealism that exists within the editorial tradition, whose aim it is to establish a text as the author would have wished it, also suffuses the discourse about scholarly editing. The term authoritative edition seems attached not to the soundness of the scholarship that went into its making but to the edition itself. It appears to suggest that its established text is authoritative, and therefore timeless, while the format of the edition and the way it presents the text, and the evidence for its critical emendation, is portrayed to be objective, transparent and neutral. The academic book market is complicit in this. Not only are popular series like the Norton Critical Editions and Oxford World Classics uncritical when they boast about offering the most "authoritative texts" (a nomenclature that is ambivalent at best, because most are simply reprints of what is considered the "best" text), but most academic publishers of scholarly editions also see their editions as offering 2-for-1: "an error-free, authorial, clear-text edition for the general reader and a repository of textual information for the specialist reader" (Egger 2009, 163). This attitude allows them subsequently to issue "light" versions that greatly condense or downright suppress the edition's paraphernalia (i.e., textual introduction and critical apparatus) on the grounds that students of literature have no interest in this. A self-fulfilling prophecy if ever there was one.

Yet it is evident that the "interface" of the scholarly edition and the textual information it conveys is interpretive and highly mediated. According to Hans Walter Gabler, editions present "editorial arguments" and their design is "an achievement [...] of networking texts and knowledge" (Gabler 2008, 6). Interestingly, the language that Gabler uses is borrowed from the digital edition (although ostensibly it recalls the medieval tradition of marginal scholia), but he recognizes a problem as well: despite the "stringent formalisation" of the edition's "intellectual substance", the apparatus and commentary are relegated to the back of the edition.[22] Editors nowadays generally accept that no edition can be definitive, and they acknowledge that their emendations are reasoned choices from the evidence available to them. But the editorial choices, even when they are appreciated in the spirit of textual pluralism, are too often seen

---

[22]   This displacement prompts John Lavagnino's criticism that the apparatus is too much a store-house for data, and not enough a tool for critical analysis; in his view, the emphasis of the scholarly edition should shift away "from the data to ways of filtering it, so as to put readers in the position not of asking for more but rather of finding ways to get just what they want" (2009, 70, 72).

as the product of scholarship, not as part of an on-going intellectual investigation into textual history.

At first sight, even McKenzie in his posthumous edition of the works of William Congreve did not fully implement his own conceptualization of the sociology of the text. Opting for the 1710 Folio edition of Congreve's *Works* as his copy-text instead of the first Quarto editions of the individual plays, McKenzie produced, by his own admission, an eclectic text based on final authorial intention.[23] His preference for an authorially revised text over the historical context of its original production, however, was not simply motivated by editorial orthodoxy. In fact, the choice of copy-text was far from obvious given that *Works* was not without problems. Congreve in some cases relied on corrupted reprints for his own base text; he seems to have revised his texts in a rush (2011, xxxiii); and not all his revisions can be considered improvements, particularly not because, following increased pressure from Queen Anne's Court to quell licentiousness, Congreve submitted himself to self-censorship (2002, 224–25; 2011, xxi-xxii). What motivated McKenzie's choices, however, was the fact that *Works* was consciously fabricated as an *œuvre*. While its "historical form and concept" are just as valid as the "textual structures" of the original Quarto design, Congreve gave his plays a whole new intent. Congreve did more than just revise his texts; he regenerated their "textual structures" as he lifted them, as McKenzie puts it somewhat lyrically, "from the soil of [their] first growth" and replanted them "in new relationships". The Folio differs from the Quartos in that the individual plays have been given a new "display" [that] is more likely to favour the design of the whole than the diverse forms of the earliest state of each item" (2011, xviii). The neo-classical design that he gave to this plays was not only an innovation for the time, the result of a close collaboration between Congreve, the bookseller and publisher Jacob Tonson, and Tonson's

---

[23]   Scholars have expressed surprise at McKenzie's seemingly conservative approach, but this is no doubt due to a misapprehension of what the sociology of texts means. Even Tanselle points out that "a socially edited text can contain unintended errors just as easily as can a text constructed by one person. Unless one wishes to refrain from all emendation of documentary texts, one is admitting the concept of intention" (2005, 288). Thus while McKenzie's editorial practice adheres to the editorial tradition of Greg, Bowers and Tanselle, this is not an argument against social editing; as my example from Yeats the social edition is possible and, in many cases, desirable.

printer John Watts; it also approximates the "distinct unitary form" that Congreve used for scene divisions and stage groupings in some of his extant manuscripts (2011, xxiii; see also McKenzie 2002, 123–24). McKenzie, therefore, believed that for Congreve the Folio edition meant a typographical translation of the play text into the form of the book with the intent to create a "hand-held theatre" (2002, 201).

In an unexpected twist, however, McKenzie argues that the eclectic edition itself constitutes a "sensitive response to social [and historical] context" that "serve[s] the play to the fullest" (2002, 226).[24] Explicitly positioning himself against Hans Zeller, who sees eclecticism as a violation against the integrity of the text, he states: "Conflation is inevitable. But it is also critically and historically responsible only in so far as the causes of the variant readings have been explained, in this case by that peculiar complex of attitudes — personal, social and trade — which obtained for Congreve [. . .] in the first decade of the 18th century" (2002, 225). One can quibble with McKenzie's insistence that the eclectic text does justice to rather than violates the historicity of the text. Zeller and McKenzie are at odds here in that McKenzie, somewhat unexpectedly, defends the historicity of the variants in the text, whereas Zeller argues for the historicity or "Befund" ["record"] of the authorized versions of the text (see Zeller 1995).

The history of books and texts

The fact remains that specific texts, existing in specific books, have a specific history which begins with their composition and revision, continues with their printing, publication and dissemination, and ends with their reception. In the first instance, editing in the time of the history of the book is "keeping the documentary in touch with the textual" (Eggert 2009, 157). But even when texts are faulty, they have a life of their own. Rather than simply removing errors, we may also want to ask, as Peter Shillingsburg advises, why a reader's responses to one text are — or are not — different from the his responses to another version of the same work (2006, 77). If the virtue of all bibliographical studies is, to quote again from

---

[24]   Again, Tanselle is in agreement with McKenzie: "[I]ntentionalist eclecticism is itself a manifestation of the historical drift of texts" (2005, 294).

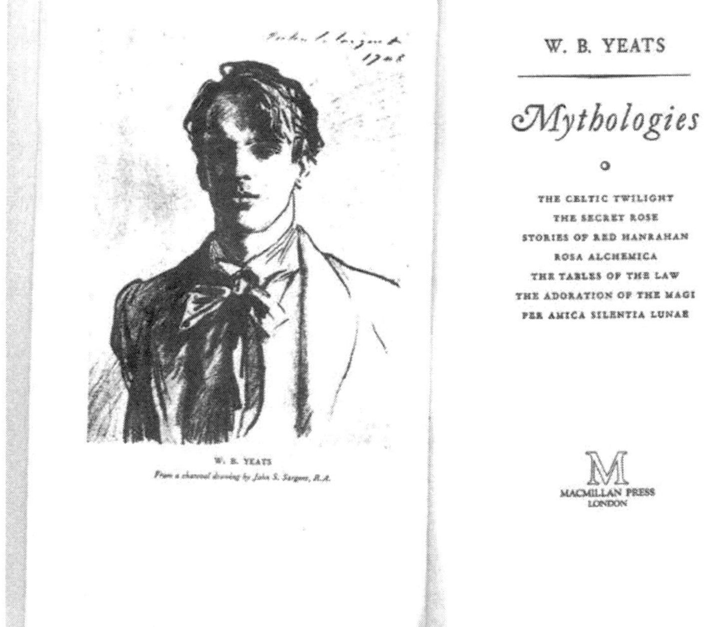

Figure 4: W. B. Yeats, *Mythologies*, Macmillan (1959; reprinted 1984).

McKenzie's theoretical work, "to show the human presence in any recorded text" (1999, 29), then we must do this indeed for *any* text, not just for those closest to the top of the stemma. Critical editions should incorporate "the making of" of literary works more comprehensively than they currently do — and also, self-reflexively, their own making of. In the digital arena, several scholars have already put forward new ideas for this new type of edition. Ray Siemens' social edition, which envisages a new model of researcher engagement involving the user community in the construction of the digital edition to replace the old model, in which the final word rests exclusively with a small editorial team; Siemens and his colleagues see editions as a processs and editors as facilitators (Siemens at al., forthcoming). Edward Vanhoutte has repeatedly argued for the diversification of the functionality of digital editions: they should suit different audiences (e.g., Vanhoutte 2010; see also Lavagnino 2009, 65). That Vanhoutte's wish is not simply a return to textual pluriformity is made clear by Elena Pierazzo (2011), who distinguishes between the

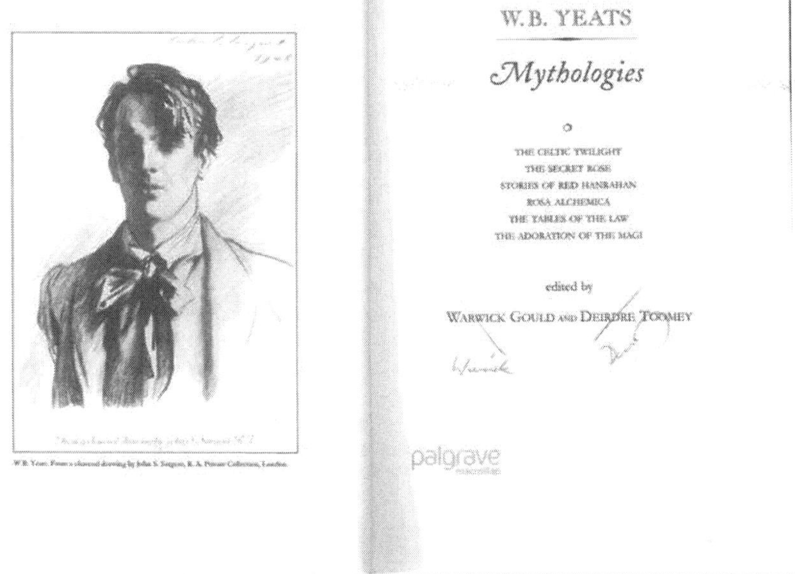

Figure 5: W. B. Yeats, *Mythologies*, edited by Warwick Gould and Deirdre Toomey, Palgrave Macmillan (2005).

display text and the embedded source files: variant editions exist *in potentia* within the TEI encoding and can be activated at will.

What critical editions in the time of the history of the book will look like is not a question I can answer specifically, but that it will build on the new directions in digital editing is certain. One can already see that the creation of new digital tools is also bringing about changes in editorial practice: it is apparent that in five or ten years we will be editing differently.

This prediction brings me, by way of conclusion, back to the issues of the granularity of editions and of McKenzie's sociology of the text. For McKenzie, textual scholarship was insufficiently concerned with the "material concerns of historical bibliography" considered from the "economic and social dimensions of production and Readership" (McKenzie 2002, 200). For generations, critical editors have performed a vital role and more often than not have performed it well. But what they have done is simply to produce editions — and texts — that are *new* and different from the old. By the very nature of what editors do, they push to a greater or lesser degree the old texts to the side. What they have not reckoned with, however, is the pastness of these texts, and that these texts do not exist independently from the books that contain them. Books look the way they do because of the involvement of other agents, such as the typesetters and designers that helped them into print. The non-textual elements of books, then, have expressive form, and we need to factor in these forms of expression, whether or not they came about with the author's sanction. It is time we learned how to read their language (McKenzie 2002, 207). I firmly agree with Paul Eggert when he advocates that "[e]ditorial experiments are needed" (2009, 152). To my knowledge only one print critical edition exists apart from McKenzie's own that has the characteristics of a social edition and that is the edition of Yeats's *Mythologies* prepared by Warwick Gould and Deirdre Toomey. This edition of Yeats's early prose stories tries to do justice not only to Yeats's final intention, but also to the intentions of his collaborators. Moreover, *Mythologies* is not just a collection of texts, but a book project that existed in ever-changing forms and incarnations; *Mythologies* grew over time as stories were collected and then re-collected in separate volumes, sometimes under different titles. Gould and Toomey represent the text of the *Edition de Luxe* that was in preparation with the Macmillan press in London but never realized on the grounds that this edition was to be, in Yeats's mind, the expression of his permanent self. To top it all, the layout of the new edition, published by Palgrave Macmillan, pays homage to the original Macmillan format by replicating Yeats's favourite typeface, Caslon Old Style, in the text and running headers and by its imitation of the title page from the standard edition (Figures 4 and 5).

This example shows that the material aspects of texts and books must not by necessity be suppressed in a scholarly edition. Although the edition of *Mythologies* by Gould and Toomey is a new book, its design references the time and place of the work's original production. An edition like this mediates its text differently than the ordinary scholarly edition. It does not purport to exist outside of its own interface.

The digital environment, rather than diminishing the granularity of the text, increases it. This statement is becoming self-evident in those areas of textual transmission in which the physical form of the book is as important as the text that it contains. Digital editions of medieval manuscripts or of modernist magazines cannot really avoid the forms of their original design. One can only hope that scholarly editions of texts and books that have a less spectacular design will nonetheless follow suit in rendering some of their original historical forms.

Bibliography

Chandler, Daniel. 2007. *Semiotics: The Basics*. 2nd ed. Oxford, New York: Routledge.

Chartier, Roger. 1989. "Texts, Printing, Readings". In Lynn Hunt (ed.), *The New Cultural History*. Berkeley and Los Angeles: University of Berkeley Press, pp. 154–175

Chaudhury, Sukanta. 2010. *The Metaphysics of Text*. Cambridge: Cambridge University Press.

Deming, Robert H. 1997. *James Joyce: The Critical Heritage*. Vol. 1: 1907–27. London: Routledge.

Eggert, Paul. 2009. *Securing the Past: Conservation in Art, Architecture and Literature*. Cambridge: Cambridge University Press.

Eliot, T. S. 2006. *The Annotated Waste Land with Eliot's Contemporary Prose*, 2nd ed. New Haven and London: Yale University Press.

——. 2009. *The Letters of T. S. Eliot*. 2 vols. Eds. Valerie Eliot and Hugh Haughton. London: Faber and Faber.

Finkelstein, David and Alistair McCleery. 2005. *An Introduction to Book History*. New York and London: Routledge.

——, eds. 2006. *The Book History Reader*. 2nd ed. London: Routledge.

Gabler, Hans Walter. 2008. *Argument into Design: Editions as a Sub-Species of the Printed Book*. London: School of Advanced Study, University of London. <http://www.ies.sas.ac.uk/sites/default/files/files/Publications/Coffin%20lectures/HWG%20Coffin%20 2008.pdf>. [Accessed 12 April 2012].

Galey, Alan. 2010. "The Human Presence in Digital Artefacts". In Willard McCarty (ed.) *Text and Genre in Reconstruction: Effects of Digitalization on Ideas, Behaviours, Products and Institutions*. Cambridge: Open Book Publishers, pp. 93–117.

Gould, Warwick. 1989. "The Definitive Edition: A History of the Final Arrangements of Yeats's Work". In A. Norman Jeffares (ed.), *Yeats's Poems*. London and Basingstoke: Macmillan Papermac, pp. 706–749.

———. 1994. "W. B. Yeats and the Resurrection of the Author". *The Library*, 6th ser., 16, pp. 101–134.

Kirschenbaum, Matthew G. 2002. "Editing the Interface: Textual Studies and First Generation Electronic Objects". *Text*, 14, pp. 15–51.

Lavagnino, John. 2009. "Access". *Literary and Linguistic Computing*, 24, 63–76.

Material Texts Network. London: Birkbeck College, University of London, 2011. <http://www.bbk.ac.uk/arts/our-research/centres/the-material-texts-network>. [Accessed 12 March 2012].

McCue, Jim. 2006. "Editing Eliot". *Essays in Criticism*, 56, pp. 1–27.

McGann, J. J. 1991. *The Textual Condition.* Princeton: Princeton University Press.

McKenzie, D. F. 1984. "The Sociology of a Text: Orality, Literacy and Print in Early New Zealand". *The Library*, 6th ser., 6, pp. 333–65.

———. 1999. *Bibliography and the Sociology of Texts.* 2nd ed. Cambridge: Cambridge University Press.

———. 2002. *Making Meaning: "Printers of the Mind" and Other Essays.* Eds. Peter D. MacDonald and Michael Suarez. Amherst, Boston: University of Massachusetts Press.

———. 2011. "Textual Introduction". In D. F. Mckenzie and C. Y. Ferdinand (eds.). *The Works of William Congreve.* Vol. 1. Oxford: Oxford University Press, pp. xvii-xxxiii.

Nutt-Kofoth, Rüdiger. 2004. "Author's Reading—Author's Literary Production: Some Reflections on the Editing of Reading Notes in German Critical Editions". In Dirk Van Hulle and Wim Van Mierlo (eds.), *Reading Notes.* Special issue of *Variants*, 2/3, pp. 293–302.

Pierazzo, Elena. 2011. "A Rationale of Digital Documentary Editions". *Literary and Linguistic Computing*, 26, pp. 463–47.

Plachta, Bodo. 2007. "More Than Mise-en-Page: Book Design and German Editing". In Wim Van Mierlo (ed.), *Textual Scholarship and the Material Book.* Special issue of *Variants*, 6, pp. 85–105.

Shillingsburg, Peter L. 1997. *Resisting Texts: Authority and Submission in Constructions of Meaning.* Ann Arbor, Mich.: University of Michigan Press.

———. 2006. *From Gutenberg to Google: Electronic Representations of Literary Texts.* Cambridge: Cambridge University Press.

Siemens, Raymond, et al. Forthcoming. "Toward Modeling the Social Edition: An Approach to Understanding the Electronic Scholarly Edition in the Context of New and Emerging Social Media". *Literary and Linguistic Computing*.

Storey, H. Wayne. 2006. "Dirty Manuscripts and Textual Cultures: Introduction to Textual Cultures 1.1". *Textual Cultures*, 1(1), pp. 1–4.

Tanselle, G. Thomas. 2005. *Textual Criticism since Greg: A Chronicle, 1950–2000*. Charlottesville: The Bibliographical Society of the University of Virginia.

Vandendorpe, Christian. 2009. *From Papyrus to Hypertext: Toward the Universal Digital Library*. Trans. Phyllis Aronoff and Howard Scott. Chicago: University of Illinois Press.

Vanhoutte, Edward. 2010. "Defining Electronic Editions: A Historical and Functional Perspective". In Willard McCarty (ed.), *Text and Genre in Reconstruction: Effects of Digitalization on Ideas, Behaviours, Products and Institutions*. Cambridge: Open Book Publishers, pp. 119–144.

Van Mierlo, Wim. 2007. "Introduction". In Wim Van Mierlo (ed.), *Textual Scholarship and the Material Book*. Special issue of *Variants*, 6, pp. 1–12.

"Welcome to the Cambridge Centre for Material Texts". In *Centre for Material Texts: A New Forum for the Study of the Word in the World*. Cambridge: Cambridge University, 2009. <http://www.english.cam.ac.uk/cmt/>. [Accessed 12 March 2012].

Willison, I. R., 2006. "The History of the Book as a Field of Study within the Humanities". *SAS-Space e-Repository*. London: School of Advanced Study. <http://sas-space.sas.ac.uk/8/>. [Accessed 9 March 2012].

Yeats, W. B. 1989. *Yeats's Poems*. Ed. A. Norman Jeffares. London and Basingstoke: Macmillan Papermac.

——. 1997. *The Poems*. Ed. Richard J. Finneran. 2nd ed. New York: Scribner.

——. 2005. *Mythologies*. Eds. Warwick Gould and Deirdre Toomey. Houndmills, Basingstoke: Palgrave Macmillan.

Zeller, Hans. 1995. "Record and Interpretation: Analysis and Documentation as Goal and Method of Editing". Hans Walter Gabler et al. (eds.) *Contemporary German Editorial Theory*. Ann Arbor: University of Michigan Press, pp. 17–58.

A Genetic and Semiotic Approach to the Bibliographical Code Exemplified by the Typography of Aaro Hellaakoski's "Dolce far Niente"

Veijo Pulkkinen

THE FIRST TIME I faced the manuscript and proofs of Aaro Hellaakoski's (1893–1952) poem "Dolce far Niente", I was struck by the sense of handiwork that emanated especially from one peculiar document (Figure 1).[1] This document consists of two sheets glued together.

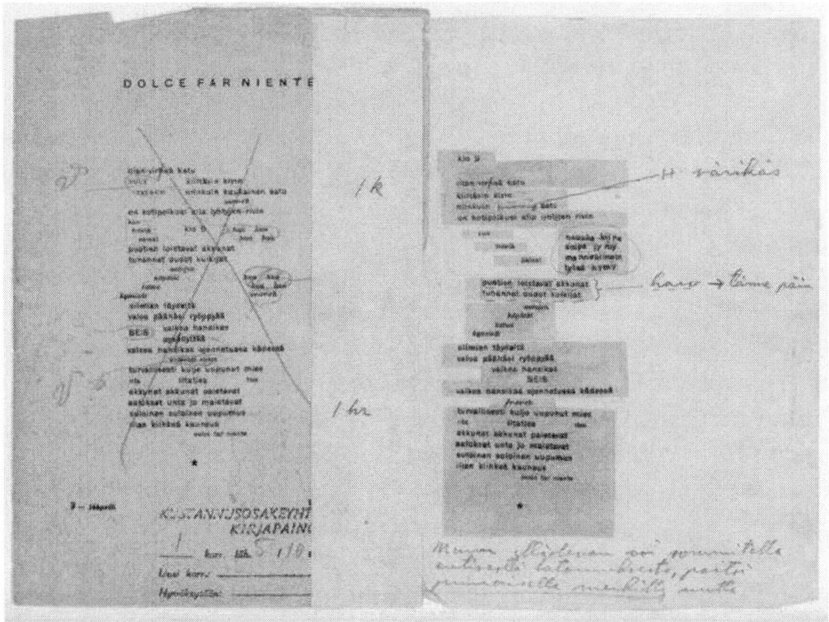

Figure 1: The first proof of "Dolce far Niente". The Literary Archives of the Finnish Literature Society, Aaro Hellaakoski Archive, *Jääpeili*, Manuscripts and Proofs, Laatikko 1.

---

[1]   The manuscript and proofs of "Dolce far Niente" are deposited in the Literary Archive of the Finnish Literature Society, SKS. Aaro Hellaakoski Archive, *Jääpeili*, Manuscripts and Proofs, Laatikko 1. For a translation of the published version of the poem, see Figure 3.

The part on the left looks like a typical page proof, but the one on the right has different slips of paper pasted on it, some of which contain several lines of printed text, others only one word or a single letter. What fascinates me in this document is not so much the aura that manuscripts, especially holograph manuscripts, have in common with autographic works of art like paintings and sculptures, but rather its unusual, hybrid nature. This document is not a manuscript in the strict sense, nor does it unequivocally belong to the mechanically reproducible realm of print, but straddles between the two. As such, it appears to challenge common conceptions about the division between manuscript and print, private and public, fluid and fixed, unfinished and finished, process and product, and so on.

"Dolce far Niente" is a visual poem that experiments with typography. Its manuscript and proofs in particular invite us to rethink the nature of the bibliographical code. This concept, coined by Jerome J. McGann, refers to the socio-historical context and material means of production of a work, such as the binding of a book, its size, quality of ink and paper, typeface, typography, illustration, advertising, distribution venues and price (McGann 1991, 12–15, 56–62). In literary criticism typography has usually been studied as a rather closed entity fixed on the printed page. Although it is a more general concept, the bibliographical code usually refers to a relatively stable set of properties. However, it certainly is not the case that the bibliographical code of a work cannot change. It very clearly does so with every new edition of the work. This observation in turn leads to the question as to how the bibliographical code comes into existence in the first place. It does not seem untoward to posit that the bibliographical code, like the text itself, may develop organically. The change from one set of properties into another set of properties is exactly the sort of development one finds in the archival record of "Dolce far Niente": the process that shows Hellaakoski collaborating with the typesetter to create the poem's final layout. The documents show the bibliographical code, especially the typography, in the process of becoming rather than as a fixed product. In the following discussion I will propose a genetic approach to the bibliographical code of "Dolce far Niente".

This kind of approach is, of course, not without its difficulties. The main problem is that the concept of the bibliographical code does not distinguish clearly between the material and a more abstract

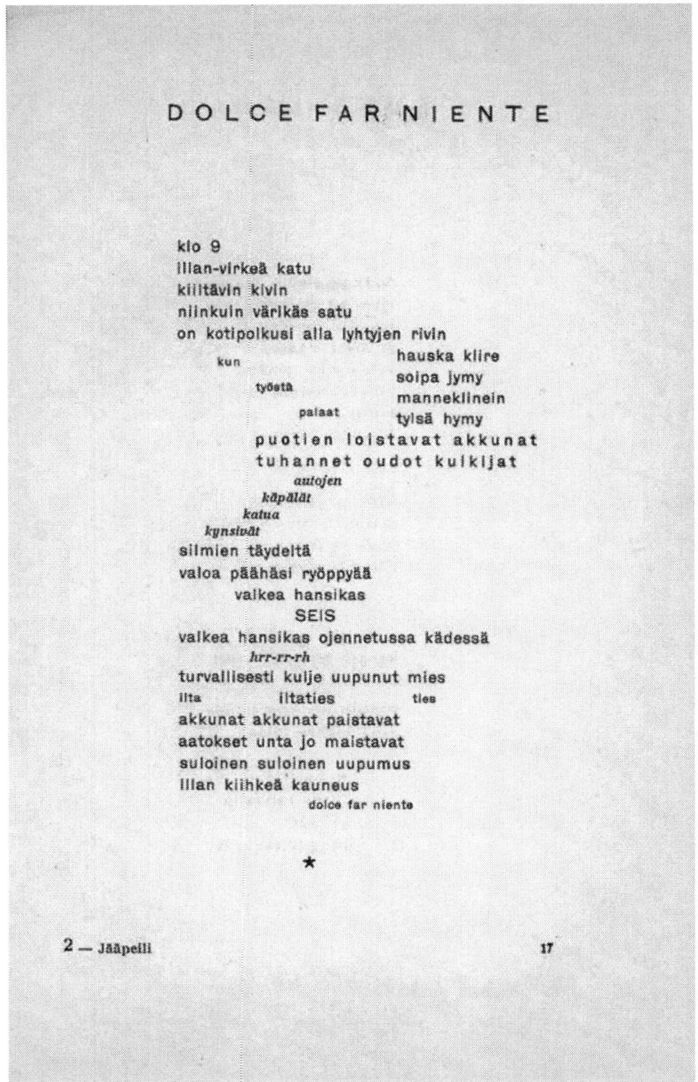

Figure 2: "Dolce far Niente", in Aaro Hellaakoski, *Jääpeili*. Helsinki: Otava, 1928.

dimension of typography. The primary object of study in *critique génétique* is not the material documents themselves, but the genetic processes that they contain, and thus both the work and the documents of the work are seen as by-products (Ferrer 1998a, 12–18). A genetic approach to the bibliographical code, therefore, necessitates

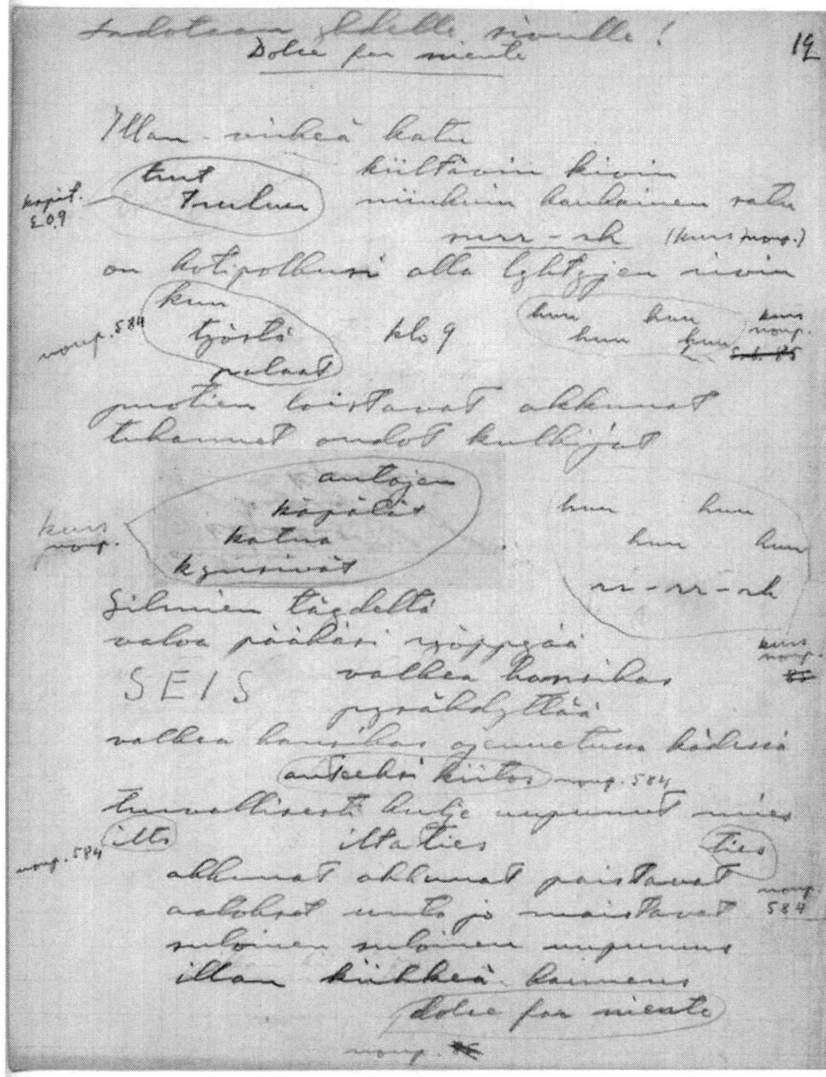

Figure 3: The manuscript of "Dolce far Niente". The Literary Archives of the Finnish Literature Society, Aaro Hellaakoski Archive, *Jääpeili*, Manuscripts and Proofs, Laatikko 1.

that we distinguish the bibliographical code of the documents from the bibliographical code as a process of becoming.

My suggestion is that we apply the theory of the sign developed by Charles Sanders Peirce and analyse the bibliographical code as a complex semiotic object that can have several different representative functions at the same time. This will not only reveal a more abstract dimension of the bibliographical code, but will also give us a more precise description of its historical and material nature and thus enable a genetic approach to the bibliographical code.

Bibliographical genetics

"Dolce far Niente" was first published in Aaro Hellaakoski's *Jääpeili* [*Mirror of Ice*] in 1928 (Figure 2). The poem describes a tired worker walking home at night through a lively city full of distractions. It makes use of various avant-gardist devices such as omitted punctuation and upper case initials, parallel stanzas and onomatopoeia; typographically, it is one of the most complex poems in the collection. Together with a poem called "Sade" ["Rain"], "Dolce far Niente" is usually classified as visual poetry (Grüntahl 1999, 208; Laitinen 1997, 389), even though other poems in the collection contain iconic typography too. *Jääpeili* uses different typefaces and type sizes throughout and can thus be considered an example of typographical experimentation in its entirety. Its author was interested in the visual arts. Hellaakoski wrote art criticism and even did some painting of his own. His thinking on the visual arts was influenced by his brother-in-law, Wäinö Aaltonen (1894–1966), a respected Finnish sculptor who is known for his cubist experiments (Kupiainen 1953, 199–200; Huuhtanen 1977, 46). Hellaakoski's awareness of contemporary avant-garde movements are especially apparent in "Sade", which resembles Guillaume Apollinaire's "Il Pleut" not only in its title, but also with its iconic typography by using diagonally printed letters to suggest rain.

Unfortunately almost all of the documents from the early genetic stages of Hellaakoski's works are lost. Mostly what survive are fair copies and a good number of page proofs. For "Dolce far Niente", the documents that exist are the following. The earliest extant document is a fair copy, which also served as printer's copy (Figure 3) — perhaps unusually so, for a typed copy might have been more efficient to convey the idea for the experimental typography of the poem. It is also worth noting that, at this stage, the poem has more stanzas than in the final version. The most fascinating document of "Dolce far Niente" is the first proof already mentioned (Figure 1),

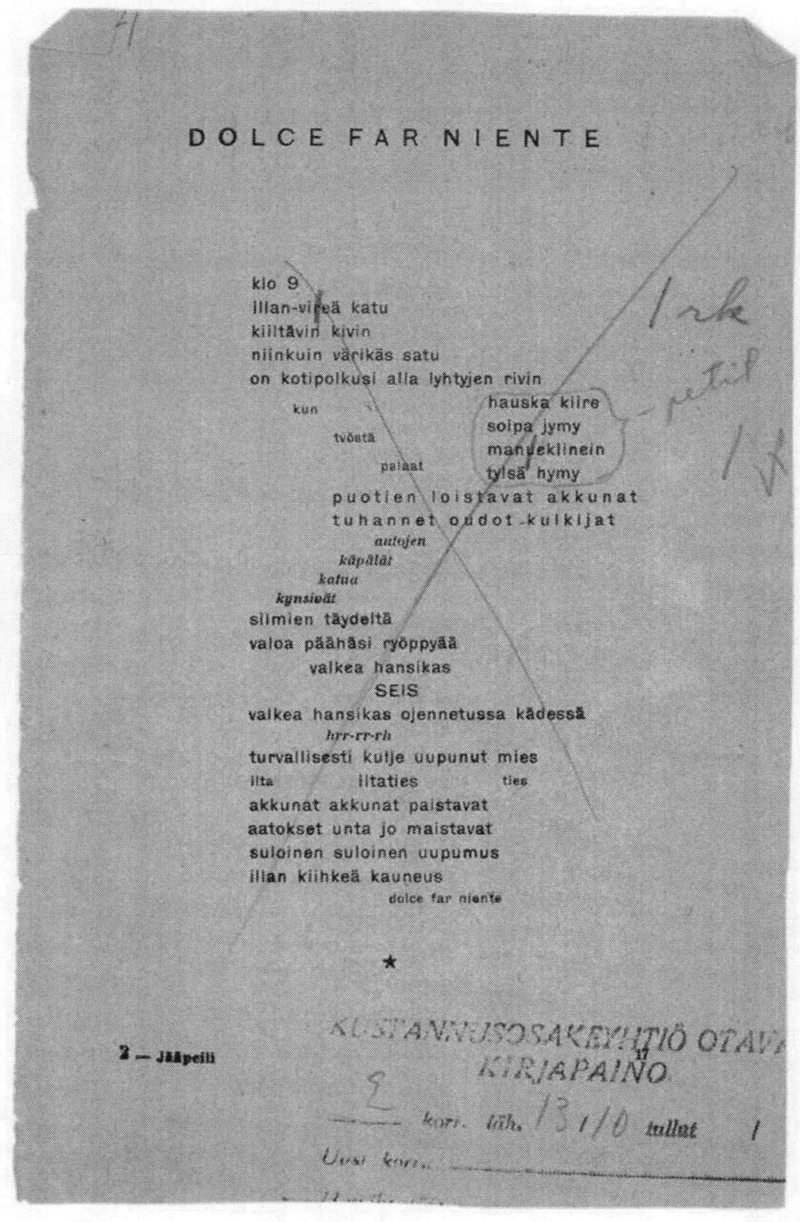

Figure 4: The second proof of "Dolce far Niente". The Literary Archives of the Finnish Literature Society, Aaro Hellaakoski Archive, *Jääpeili*, Manuscripts and Proofs, Laatikko 1.

which contains the proofed text on the left and a model for the layout that Hellaakoski had cut and pasted from a duplicate copy of the proof. During this stage Hellaakoski also revised the poem considerably. The second proof (Figure 4) differs very little from the published version (Figure 2). Some corrections that Hellaakoski made on this proof were not realized in the final text.

Obviously, without outlines, scenarios, sketches, rough drafts, there seems little room for a genetic study. This is true insofar as genetics focuses on the study of the fluid *avant-texte*. However, it may be argued that by prioritizing process *critique génétique* associates the notions of "text" and "work" with the finished, stable and polished text (Debray-Genette 1979, 48; Hay 1986, 13; 1996, 206; de Biasi 2004, 37–38). Not only the printed book falls outside of its purview but also, for example, final manuscript versions or printers' proofs. Thus, according to Pierre-Marc de Biasi, "the definitive manuscript, the one that the author recopied at the end of the writing process in order to provide a readable version for the copyist or the printer" is not usually interesting from a genetic perspective (de Biasi 2004, 39). But in spite of this rejection in principle of such final documents, the genetic approach leaves room to consider evidence, and documents, that are not normally central to the process of writing. Almuth Grésillon, for one, admits the study of authorial revisions and corrections of published works, albeit that she demands that these changes be recorded in the author's hand (Grésillon 1994, 97).

Notwithstanding the importance of the genetic dossier as an object of intellectual investigation, *critique génétique* also characterizes itself as a discipline through its particular approach to that object. Not the manuscripts as such are of interest as much as the traces of the creative process that produced them. The *avant-texte* is not equal to the genetic dossier, but is a critical construction and an inter-pretation of the writing practices that produced the material and ultimately exceed it (Hay 1985, 152; Contat 1991, 23; Grésillon 1994, 7; Ferrer 1998a, 15; Hay 2002, 103; de Biasi 2004, 43). This hypo-thetical reconstruction of the writing process can easily be extended to include the entire mechanism of the text's production when we move from textual genetics to a consideration of the construction of the bibliographical codes in what we may perhaps call a biblio-graphical genetics.

Hellaakoski's proofs, in other words, are interesting not only for their corrections, revisions and other markings, but also for providing us with a record of the development of the layout of *Jääpeili.* The proofs for "Dolce far Niente" in particular are the most enlightening for my purposes. They allow us to see the typographic layout of "Dolce far Niente" as a creative act developing out of an on-going dialogue between poet and typesetter.

The materiality of the bibliographical code

In fathoming the genesis of the typographic layout, we ought to, crucially, be able to differentiate between the material level of the documents and the genetic process that we abstract from it. But this prerequisite throws up a difficulty. A brief review of a few central theoretical issues concerning the bibliographical code reveals a somewhat ambiguous use of the concept of materiality. The usual consideration that the bibliographical is simply the material level of a text or work may not in fact be so straightforwardly simple.

The notion of materiality in the humanities came to the fore with the rise of structuralism and post-structuralism, which advocated a materialistic view of language. The production of meaning moved from the language user to language itself. Language was conceived of a system of signs consisting of a signified (*meaning*) and a signifier (*form*). Despite it being frequently treated that way, the materiality of the sign does not in fact refer to any sort of materiality at all. Ferdinand de Saussure in the *Cours de linguistique générale* clearly states that the characterization of the signifier as material should only be understood in a metaphoric sense.

> The linguistic sign unites, not a thing and a name, but a concept and a sound-image. The latter is not the material sound, a purely physical thing, but the psychological imprint of the sound, the impression that it makes on our senses. The sound-image is sensory, and if I happen to call it "material," it is only in that sense, and by way of opposing it to the other term of the association, the concept, which is generally more abstract. [...] I propose to retain the word sign [*signe*] to designate the whole and to replace concept and sound-image respectively by signified [*signifié*] and signifier [*signifiant*]. (de Saussure 1960, 66–67)

Besides Saussure's position, there are also logical reasons why the signifier should not be treated as a material object in the strict sense. If the signifier were material, the sign would be bound to one spatio-temporal object and it could not be iterated in different contexts in the way that words are used all the time. Therefore, it is the repeatable abstract form or sound-image that we recognize in the material objects that is the signifier, not the objects themselves (de Saussure 1960, 11–12).

In Jerome J. McGann's descriptions of the bibliographical code we find a similar notion of the signifier at work. Not only does he refer to the linguistic code as "linguistic signifiers", he also calls the bibliographical code "bibliographical signifiers" (McGann 1991, 57). McGann's characterization of the bibliographical code as material follows a binary logic similar to that which Saussure uses in his meta-phorical description of the signifier. McGann determines the biblio-graphical code as the material level of the text and the physical form of the book, in opposition to the linguistic code. Furthermore, the nature of the linguistic code is thought to be more abstract because it is the locus where the production of meaning is usually situated (McGann 1991, 12, 56–57). The linguistic code exceeds materiality in the sense that a text can exist in several manifestations simultan-eously (for instance, in all copies of a particular edition of a book). However, it is not at all clear whether McGann thinks that the biblio-graphical code is really material, or whether he uses the term more or less metaphorically, like Saussure.

If we take a closer look at McGann's list of the features of the bibliographical code, some of them do not seem to be material in the strict sense. Obviously, the socio-historical context of book production is a more abstract object in comparison with, say, a brick or a piece of wood. Likewise, it is questionable whether all aspects involved in the recording and transmission of a text — like the bind-ing of a book, its size, quality of ink and paper, typefaces, etc. — are unequivocally material (McGann 1991, 12–13). All of these features are reproducible in the sense that they can be produced in multiple copies. Take, for example, an edition of a literary work: its copies, of course, more or less share the same linguistic text, but they also more or less share the same typography, ornamentation, quality of ink and paper, etc. If these features can be shared by several copies of a book, is not their ontological nature closer to the abstract linguistic code than the materiality of a singular manuscript, for instance?

The same ambiguity between the materiality of a singular document and a more abstract set of properties that can be shared by several objects is present in Peter L. Shillingsburg's and George Bornstein's descriptions of the bibliographical code. In *Resisting Texts* (1998), Shillingsburg describes the relationship between the linguistic and the bibliographical code with reference to the concepts of sentence and utterance from speech act theory (see, among others, Austin 1966; Searle 1969). A sentence is an abstraction separated from context and perceived in a void. In reality, all sentences appear in speech situations, all of which are singular by definition. These situations give the sentence a specific meaning. An utterance is this realization of the sentence in a particular context. Thus, by associating the linguistic code with the abstract and repeatable sentence and the bibliographical code with the context-dependent utterance, Shillingsburg stresses the singular nature of the bibliographical code. Unlike a sentence or a linguistic code that can be repeated from context to context, the bibliographical code is unique (Shillingsburg 1998, 155).

In "Text as Matter, Concept, and Action" (1991) Shillingsburg also seems to stress the singularity of the bibliographical code, even though he does not use the term as such. Instead he uses the concept of "Material Text" (a combination of a linguistic code and a singular document) to refer to a similar set of features as the bibliographical code (quality of ink and paper, typography, weight, size, length, binding, date, origin, provenance) (Shillingsburg 1991, 54). Thus it seems that for Shillingsburg the bibliographical code is more or less identical with the singular material document. Still, most of the features that Shillingsburg mentions are not strictly speaking material or bound to a particular document, as they can be mechanically reproduced.

George Bornstein, for his part, draws an analogy between the bibliographical code and the concept of aura coined by Walter Benjamin. The aura refers to the singularity of the kinds of artwork such as paintings or sculptures that are identical with just one material object that is a product of an artist's handicraft. In Benjamin's view, however, printed books do not have an aura, because they are mechanically reproduced objects (Benjamin 1992, 214–15).

Countering Benjamin, Bornstein insists that especially first editions of literary works do indeed have a certain aura that connects the work to its historical context in which publication first happened. The idea is to show how subsequent editions tend to dissociate the text of the work from its original socio-historical context as a result of which the aura of the first edition, so to speak, withers away (Bornstein 1998, 223–248; 2001, 6–7). Bornstein's adaptation blurs the distinction between works of art that are identical with one material object and works that can be reproduced without a loss of authenticity. This distinction between singularity and reproducibility is also at the heart of the question of the materiality of the bibliographical code.

Although the characterization of the bibliographical code as material has been rather ambiguous, this is not a bad thing from a genetic perspective. On the contrary, it shows potential: if the bibliographical code is not strictly identical with the singular material document but seems also to exist on a more abstract level, it might very well be possible to think of the genetic process of a bibliographical code.

The bibliographical code as a complex semiotic object

At this juncture I want to bring the semiotic theory of Charles Sanders Peirce into play. Peirce's name is not altogether a new presence in the context of the bibliographical code nor in that of *critique génétique*. Mary Keeler has already presented Peirce's philosophy and semiotics (which for a significant part are still only available in manuscript) in her contribution to *The Iconic Page in Manuscript, Print, and Digital Culture* (1998). However, she does not adopt Peirce's theory to rethink the concept of the bibliographical code. Daniel Ferrer in the same volume refers to Peirce's concept of the icon only to denounce it as being too simple for analyzing genetic documents. According to Ferrer, the manuscript page is a complex semiotic object that is better perceived from the indexical nature of genetic criticism (Ferrer 1998b, 251, 253; see also Ferrer 1998a, 16–17, 22).[2] I completely agree with the view of the manuscript page as a complex

---

[2]   Ferrer's rejection of the icon is based on Umberto Eco's critique of the concept (Eco 1976, 190–217). However, I think that Thomas A. Sebeok has presented quite convincing arguments on behalf of the concept of the icon (Sebeok 1989, 107–127).

semiotic object, and I am even inclined to extend this characterization to the printed page. But I am not so convinced about the futility of the concept of the icon. Alain Rey, for example, has quite successfully used all three functions of the Peircean sign to describe the peculiar nature of the manuscript page (Rey 1989). Moreover, as John J. White has demonstrated, the icon, index and symbol are better considered as complementary aspects of the sign rather than distinct entities (White 1999).

Peirce defines the sign as "something which stands to somebody for something in some respect or capacity" (Peirce 1931–1958, 2: 228). Thus the sign has three elements: the sign itself, the thing the sign refers and the user for whom the sign stands for something. Peirce calls these the *representamen*, the *object* and the *interpretant*. Because each of these elements determines one another, a sign has to have all three elements in order to be a sign. Moreover, a sign is never a sign solely by itself. It involves an active participant that uses the sign to signify something and produce meaning. Therefore, the sign is better understood as a process of semiosis rather than a fixed object. It is always already linked into a chain of other signs that precede and come after it. The concept of the *interpretant* takes into account the way in which the sign is used. But in the chain of semiosis the *interpretant* also turns into an object for another sign that in turn produces a new *interpretant*, and so on (Peirce 1931–1958, 2.228; Liszka, 18–20). This is an important point considering the complexity of the bibliographical code. When the same document can be used to signify different things, it is necessary to take into account the user of the sign. In Peircean terms, the same *representamen* can be used to refer to different *objects* in order to produce different *interpretants*. The same document may for one be just another piece of paper, while for someone else it may have a special meaning. Consider, for example, the recent Koran burning episode at the US military base in Bagram, Afghanistan, where the "improper disposal" of religious material led to protests and people being killed and injured (Miakhel 2012).

With regard to the bibliographical code, it is particularly useful that the sign can be examined from the perspective of three different representative functions: symbolic, indexical and iconic. The representative function of the sign is the relationship between the *representamen* and the *object* it represents (Peirce 1931–1958, 1.313,

8.378). In other words, the function describes how the sign refers to the *object*. It is possible that one and the same sign participates in all of these categories. There are no pure or absolute signs that have a clear-cut representative function (Peirce 1931–1958, 2.265; Liszka 1996, 36, 47; White 1999, 84). This is also the case with the bibliographical code that can be analysed from the perspective of all three representative functions.

The symbol is probably the most familiar aspect for textual scholars as it is basically the same thing as the linguistic code. A symbolic sign is determined by a rule, convention or habit. Letters, words, numbers, proofreading marks and so on are instances of symbols (Peirce 1931–1958, 4: 447; Liszka 1996, 39–40). If we now examine the fair copy of "Dolce far Niente" from a symbolic perspective we are interested in its text, i.e., the letters, words and sentences (Figure 3). Besides the text of the poem, the manuscript also includes Hellaakoski's directions to the typesetter. Above the title Hellaakoski instructs that the text should be set in one page ("Ladotaan yhdelle sivulle!"). There are also several notes on the typefaces and sizes in which the circled text passages should be set, such as "kapit. 209", "nonp. 584", "kurs. nonp."

So, what we actually have here, besides the text, is a symbolic description of the bibliographical code that Hellaakoski wants for his poem. Thus the bibliographical code is present in two different senses. First, in the sense in which I think McGann, Bornstein and Shillingsburg define the term: the manuscript itself has bibliographical properties as a material document; it is written in pencil, on such and such paper, etc. Second, the manuscript represents on a symbolic level the bibliographical code of the poem. In this sense, the bibliographical code is not simply here and now, fixed on the material page, but is in the making, in a state of becoming.

To fully appreciate the material and historical aspect of the bibliographical code the index is a really useful tool. There are three basic forms of indexical signs. The deictic index is a sign that establishes a direct perceptive link between the sign and the *object*, such as when pointing at something with a finger generates an imaginary line between the finger and the object it points at. A label is another form of index that is generated, for instance, when a proper name is assigned to someone. For our purposes, the causal index is the most interesting. A common example of this kind of index is the relation of smoke to fire. So, in contrast to the symbolic function, the relation of the index to its *object* is determined by contiguity. Fire generates smoke, therefore smoke is a sign of fire (Peirce 1931–1958, 2.248, 4.447; Liszka 1996, 38–39).

To hark back to Daniel Ferrer's view of *critique génétique* as an indexical field of study, the actual object of *critique génétique* is not the material manuscript but the genetic process that is in part manifested in it. Thus, manuscripts are not studied for themselves as individual documents, but as indexical traces of the genetic process that emanates from them (Ferrer 1998a, 12–18). In a similar fashion, as I have said, the bibliographical code can also exist as a work in progress, as in the case of Hellaakoski's fair copy that symbolically describes the bibliographical code. In this sense the document also functions as an indexical trace of one stage or phase of the bibliographical code in the making. To put it in Peircean terms: the fair copy is the *representamen*, the genetic process of the bibliographical code is the *object*, and the *interpretant* is the use of the sign that makes the fair copy stand as a partial manifestation of the genesis of the bibliographical code.

Another important aspect of the index is the document's relation to its own history of production. Earlier I referred to Bornstein who associates the bibliographical code with the concept of aura in order to stress the significance of the original publication context of a work. However, a mechanically reproduced book existing in several copies does not possess this aura in the Benjaminian sense, because reproductions do not have what he calls a "presence in time and space" or a "unique existence at the place where it happens to be" (Benjamin 1992, 214), whereas a holograph manuscript does have this quality of authenticity. Like a painting or a sculpture, it is a product of its author's handicraft. As such, it is an index of the author's actual involvement in the object's production. As James Jakób Liszka describes the index, "[i]t is the sign's singularity, its spatial or temporal location, its 'here and now' vis-à-vis the object, rather than any qualities that it has, which contributes to making it an index" (Liszka 1996, 38; see also, Peirce 1931–1958, 4: 56). There is a causal relation connecting the manuscript and its bibliographical code to a certain historical time and place.

The ingenious aspect of the index is the fact that it is not restricted to singular objects like Benjamin's concept of aura. The index determines a relation between the *representamen* and its *object*. Thus nothing prevents the possibility that there exist several *representamen*s that have the same contiguous relation to one and the same *object*. This is exactly the case with impressions and editions of literary works. All copies of one impression are singular material objects, but they share a common production history. As indices they are all products of the same printing process. They may even significantly differ from each other, and therefore appear unique, especially when the copies age and deteriorate. But even if a copy of an edition is so severely damaged to the extent that it has become unreadable, it still is a copy of that edition. In my mind this is precisely what the materiality and historicity of the bibliographical code are about. The indexicality of the bibliographical code is what determines its authenticity, or its aura, if you like. It includes all aspects of the bibliographical code that relate to the material and the socio-historical context of the production of the text.

Just as in *critique génétique*, the index plays a crucial role in the study of the bibliographical code. It is the connection between Peircean semiotics and the social and historical dimension of the concept of the bibliographical code. From the semiotic point of view the study of the socio-historical context of a document or an edition is the establishment of an indexical relation. It is production of meaning by reconstructing an *object* (the socio-historical context) for a *representamen* (a book), for example, by tracing the material and technical procedures and the cultural context of a book: how it was made, by whom, for what purposes, and how it was distributed and received.

The significance of the icon is easy to demonstrate with reference to facsimile editions. In an icon the *representamen* resembles its *object* in one way or another. It may share some of the perceptible qualities of the *object*, similar to the way a facsimile visually reproduces the bibliographical codes of its original. An icon may also resemble the *object* diagrammatically when, for instance, the relations among the elements of the *representamen* correspond to the relations among the *object*'s elements. The relationship between a map and a terrain is an example of an icon of this kind. A metaphor is also an iconic relation. It shows a parallel between some of the features of the sign and the *object* (Peirce 1931–1958, 2.247, 2.276, 4.447; Liszka 1996, 37–38).

From the iconic perspective there are at least theoretically no essential differences between an original copy of an edition and a facsimile. In principle all the iconic features of the bibliographical code, such as size, the quality of ink and paper, typography, typefaces and sizes, binding, etc., are reproducible. The difference lies in the indexical properties. Even if they should look exactly the same, they do not share the same production history. This becomes apparent when we compare a facsimile edition with a counterfeit copy of an original edition. The idea of a facsimile is to produce an icon of a particular document by imitating its bibliographical code. The idea of a counterfeit, however, is to produce a fake index of a particular production history by imitating the bibliographical code of a document.

If we take another look at the first proof (Figure 1, left page) of "Dolce far Niente" and compare it with the fair copy (Figure 3), we get a glimpse of the semiotic complexity of the bibliographical code that includes all three representative functions of the sign. First, the typesetter has reproduced the symbolic text of the fair copy. Second, the typesetter has partially used the fair copy as an iconic model for the bibliographical code, in particular for the spatial arrangement of the text. Third, he has also taken notice of Hellaakoski's symbolic directions concerning the bibliographical code, such as the typefaces and type sizes. In this way, the typesetter has not imitated the iconic bibliographical code of the manuscript but has interpreted it as an index of the genesis of the bibliographical code. The first proof is, therefore, an active interpretation that tries to realize Hellaakoski's vision of the bibliographical code instead of a simple reproduction of the iconic or symbolic features of the fair copy.

The first proof on the right-hand page is the next genetic stage of the bibliographical code of "Dolce far Niente" (Figure 1, right page). As I mentioned earlier, the linguistic text has been significantly altered. For example, Hellaakoski has omitted most of the onomatopoetic parallel stanzas mimicking the sound of traffic. But as with the fair copy, this document also provides the symbolic directions for the realization of the bibliographical code. Below the poem is an instruction to the typesetter: "Muun ylläolevan voi sommitella entisestä latomuksesta, paitsi punaisella merkitty uutta" ["The rest of the above can be reset from the earlier setting except that marked with red which is new"]. It is likely that Hellaakoski did not submit a final typed copy to the printers because he knew that the proofs, a crucial stage in the graphical composition of the text, would furnish them with a better opportunity to arrange the layout using the actual printed words, letters, typefaces and sizes. To use Peirce's terminology, Hellaakoski used words and letters not only as symbols, but also as icons and indices. In doing so, he managed to produce a more accurate and detailed model of the envisioned bibliographical code by using all of the sign's three elements. It is interesting to note, however, that Hellaakoski accepted most the typesetter's rendition, or interpretation, of the manuscript in print. So one can argue that the layout of the poem is at least partly the creation of the typesetter, although it is ultimately authorized by Hellaakoski.

From the second proof (Figure 4) we see that the new layout corresponds quite accurately to the model provided by Hellaakoski. Compared with the first edition of *Jääpeili* the bibliographical code is already largely finished in the second proof. Hellaakoski still wanted the second of the two parallel stanzas should to be set in smaller, "petit", type size. But for some reason this change was not realized in the published version of the poem.

A thematic reading of textual and bibliographical changes

As a literary critic, I am interested in how genetic and textual criticism can be applied to the interpretation of literary works. I am especially fascinated by the possibility of a thematic reading of textual and bibliographical changes that in one way or another knit the transformations of the work together with its contents. Peirce's semiotics can be useful in such an intermedial endeavour as it was not primarily devised for linguistic analysis but as a general theory of signs. For a thematic reading of the genesis of the work, we need some luck in finding a feature or figure in the text that can somehow be associated with the textual and bibliographical changes of the work. Such a feature can be found in one small detail a little below the centre of the page of the published version of "Dolce far Niente" (Figure 2). The one-word line "SEIS" ["STOP"] arrests our attention as it puts a halt to the narrative and almost cuts the poem in half. By coincidence this sign, a traffic sign, also happens to be on a road — or a crossroads, to be precise.

"SEIS" is a sort of culmination point where the advance of the poem's protagonist, the tired worker, is interrupted for a moment, as well as the traffic and the poem itself. "SEIS" stands out from the text as it is the only word, apart from the title, that has been set in upper case characters. One reason for the use of upper case is that there is no punctuation in the poem. The use of upper case is therefore a way to achieve a similar effect as an exclamation mark. Furthermore, "SEIS" is an imperative. It is an order from the traffic policeman whose presence is indexically suggested by the white glove in the preceding and following lines. By using upper case characters instead of an exclamation mark, Hellaakoski actually replaces a symbolic expression with an iconic one. When we compare the published version of the poem with its manuscript and proofs we notice a similar kind of movement towards a more visual expression.

"Dolce far Niente" is structured as an opposition between the tired, homeward-bound walker and the liveliness of the city, especially the rumbling of the traffic. In the published version, this opposition is suggested visually in parallel stanzas: "kun | työstä | palaat" ["when you return from work"] and "hauska kiire | soipa jymy | mannekiinien | tylsä hymy" ["jolly rush | what a vibrant rumble | mannequins' | dull smiles"]. In the manuscript and first proof, the onomatopoetic parallel stanzas (not present in the published version) that imitate the sounds of the traffic — "TUUT | TRULUU", "surr-rh", and "huu huu | huu huu" — make the contrast even stronger, both visually and aurally (Figures 1 and 3). It almost looks as if the pedestrian is zigzagging through a gridlock. The simple means by which Hellaakoski builds up suspense are remarkable in the way he depicts the motorcars making them resemble a hostile animal that claws the street and their beaming headlights that violently burst into the eyes of the worn-out man. The imminent conflict is interrupted by the traffic policeman who stops the traffic and lets the pedestrian cross the street and then with his outstretched hand directs the cars to continue on their way. The rest of the poem is more relaxed. The less complicated typographical layout of the ending suggests that the way home is clear now.

From a genetic perspective, it is interesting to note that the word "SEIS" did not find its place in the centre of the page until later. In the manuscript and the first proof, "SEIS" appears in the left margin. Although it already takes up its own line, the word does not yet divide the poem in half. Instead there is another one-word line, "pysähdyttää" ["halts"]. This verb syntactically connects with the previous line, "valkea hansikas" ["white glove"], and amplifies its signification as a stop sign: "a white glove | halts". "Pysähdyttää" fulfils the same function as the imperative "SEIS" in the published version of the poem. Furthermore, in the manuscript and the first proof, the word "SEIS" is presented as a parallel stanza, which associates it with the onomatopoetic parallel stanzas — especially the "TUUT | TRULUU" of the car horns. To further call attention to the aural nature of the policeman's command and the beeping of the cars, the words are set in upper case letters. At this stage of composition, Hellaakoski probably thought of "SEIS" as being part of the traffic noises and as an aural correlative to the white glove. However, when subsequently "SEIS" is used instead of "pysähdyttää" for the central axis around which the poem hinges, the verb loses its connection with the onomatopoetic expressions and its aural quality diminishes. Shifting its function, "SEIS" now amplifies the meaning of the white glove, and, in Peircean terms, it is transformed from being an *object* (a shout) to an *interpretant* (the interpretation of and reaction to a stop sign).

A similar kind of semiotic transformation happens to the onomatopoetic parallel stanzas between the manuscript and the first proof. Just one out of five onomatopoetic expressions survives in the printed version. It is significant that this poetic change takes place precisely when the text's medium changes from manuscript to print. The onomatopoetic stanzas dominate the visual appearance of the manuscript page, which is partly due to the fact that they also get most of the attention in the symbolic description of the bibliographical codes. However, when Hellaakoski starts to work with the printed page, the visual takes over from the aural. All the diverse noises of the traffic are reduced to a single onomatopoetic expression contained in one line in the new parallel stanza that Hellaakoski introduces: "soipa jymy" ["what a vibrant rumble"]. The word "jymy" still has onomatopoetic connotations, but, unlike the omitted parallel stanzas, it is an existing word that can be found in a dictionary. Thus the aural icons are compressed into a symbolic expression.

The semiotic transformation of the poetical devices serves the visual reorganization of the poem. In particular, the manuscript looks chaotic in comparison with the more focused and structured layout of the published version. This is, of course, because of the difference in medium and the fact that the manuscript is laden with symbolic descriptions of the bibliographical code. However, the visual appearance of the first proof is still quite disorienting. In particular, the parallel stanzas seem to be somewhat dislocated. The use of both noisy onomatopoetic and arresting visual elements further complicates the aesthetic experience of the poem. Interestingly, as I have said, it is at the "crossroads" of two different media that the visual form of the poem begins to take shape. Hellaakoski has also found himself between two "Dolce far Nientes", just like the tired pedestrian in the poem. At the manuscript stage, the bibliographical code of the poem is only planned and imagined. It is something that Hellaakoski has in mind and is looking forward to its materialization. The first proof is already a realization of the bibliographical code. It is a compromise between the plan of the manuscript and the realities of the printed page and reveals the elements that do not work on the printed page.

Conclusion

It is remarkable that Peirce's theory of the sign has not been applied more often in textual scholarship. In the study of experimental typography, for example, theories based on the Saussurian sign have been more popular (see, for instance, Bohn 1986, 5; Drucker 1994, 9–47; Van Leeuwen 2005, 139). Saussure's sign is primarily a linguistic sign. Therefore, non-verbal entities have to be adjusted to the signifier/signified pair that is formulated according to the structure peculiar to words. Moreover, the Saussurian sign is based on a synchronic theory of language as a static and ahistorical sign system.

The above overview of the theories of the bibliographical code revealed a similar kind of binary logic to the Saussurian sign. The opposition between the bibliographical and linguistic codes tends to assign only the linguistic code to the abstract dimension of a document and push all the features of the bibliographical code onto the same material level, regardless of their possible differences. This difference made the bibliographical code of an edition of a work, for instance, look like a stable unchanging entity. This is problematic especially if one wishes to study bibliographical codes from a genetic perspective.

Peirce's semiotics is not based on any particular sign system such as language, which makes it apt for intermedial fields of study such as genetic criticism. It is more convenient to analyse signifying processes that cross borders of different kinds of media and mediums without the burden of translating everything into an analogy of the linguistic sign. In my interpretation of "Dolce far Niente", for instance, I could use the same concepts of symbol, icon and index in describing the content of the text, the bibliographical code, and their interaction in producing meaning through the genetic changes.

From the perspective of Peircean semiotics the bibliographical code proved to be more complex than just the material dimension of text. Peirce's theory of the sign enabled us to refine the concept of the bibliographical code by dividing it into the subcategories of indexical, iconic and symbolic bibliographical codes, which makes it possible to study the bibliographical code on several different levels of materiality and abstraction. Although the conceptual framework of linguistic and bibliographical code remains useful, among others in characterizing the historical attitudes towards bibliographical codes, it would perhaps be better to give up its simplistic and restricting description as the abstract and material dimensions of text.

Although all the three functions are essential to the sign, the indexical function turned out to be the most rewarding feature of Peirce's semiotics for both genetic criticism and the theory of the bibliographical code. Indexicality has already been recognized to belong to the core of a genetic practice that studies documents as traces of a genetic process. Unlike the Saussurean theory of the sign, isolated from time and place, Peirce's semiotics offers a general theoretical framework that is able to take into account the signification of the material and historical production processes of signs. It also relieves the theory of the bibliographical code from problematic analogies drawn from other theories that are devised for different purposes. Finally, the index made it possible to distinguish the concept of the bibliographical code from the material document and study it as a process rather than a fixed object.

Bibliography

Austin, J. L. 1966. *How to Do Things With Words: The William James Lectures Delivered at Harvard University in 1955*. J. O. Urtison and Marina Sbisà (eds.). Oxford: Oxford University Press.

Benjamin, Walter. 1992. *Illuminations*. Ed. Hanna Arendt. London: Fontana Press.

Bohn, Willard. 1986. *The Aesthetics of Visual Poetry 1914–1928*. Cambridge: Cambridge University Press.

Bornstein, George. 1998. "Yeats and Textual Reincarnation: 'When You Are Old' and 'September 1913'". In George Bornstein and Theresa Tinkle (eds.), *The Iconic Page in Manuscript, Print, and Digital Culture*. Ann Arbor: The University of Michigan Press, pp. 223–48.

———. 2001. *Material Modernism: The Poetics of the Page*. Cambridge: Cambridge University Press.

Contat, Michel. 1991. "Introduction: La Question de l'Auteur au Regard des Manuscrits". In Michel Contat (ed.), *L'Auteur et le Manuscrit*. Paris: Presses Universitaires de France, pp. 7–34.

de Biasi, Pierre-Marc. 2004. "Toward a Science of Literature: Manuscript Analysis". In Jed Deppman, Daniel Ferrer and Michael Groden (eds.), *Genetic Criticism: Texts and Avant-textes*. Philadelphia: University of Pennsylvania Press, pp. 36–68.

Debray-Genette, Raymonde. 1979. "Génétique et Poétique: Le Cas Flaubert". In Louis Hay (ed.), *Essais de Critique Génétique*. Paris: Flammarion, pp. 21–67.

de Saussure, Ferdinand. 1960. *Course in General Linguistics*. Ed. Charles Bally, Albert Sechehaye and Albert Reidlinger. Trans. Wade Baskin. London: Peter Owen.

Drucker, Johanna. 1994. *The Visible Word: Experimental Typography and Modern Art, 1909–1923*. Chicago: University of Chicago Press.

Eco, Umberto. 1976. *A Theory of Semiotics*. Bloomington: Indiana University Press.

Ferrer, Daniel. 1998a. "Le Matériel et le Virtuel: Du Paradigme Indiciaire à la Logique des Mondes Possibles". In Michel Contat and Daniel Ferrer (eds.), *Pourquoi la Critique Génétique? Méthodes, Théories*. Paris: CNRS Éditions, pp. 11–30.

———. 1998b. "The Open Space of the Draft Page: James Joyce and Modern Manuscripts". In George Bornstein and Theresa Tinkle (eds.), *The Iconic Page in Manuscript, Print, and Digital Culture*. Ann Arbor: The University of Michigan Press, pp. 249–67.

Grésillon, Almuth. 1994. *Éléments de Critique Génétique: Lire les Manuscrits Modernes*. Paris: Presses Universitaires de France.

Grüntahl, Satu. 1999. "Vapautuva Runokieli". In Lea Rojola (ed.), *Suomen Kirjallisuushistoria 2: Järkiuskosta Vaistojen Kapinan.* Helsinki: Suomalaisen Kirjallisuuden Seura, pp. 202–209.

Hay, Louis. 1985. "'Le Texte n'Existe pas': Réflexions sur la Critique Génétique". *Poétique*, 62, pp. 147–58.

———. 1986. "Écrire ou Communiquer? Quelques Remarques pour Commencer". In Louis Hay (ed.), *Le Manuscrit Inachevé: Écriture, Création, Communication.* Paris: Éditions du CNRS, pp.7–14.

———. 1996. "History or Genesis?". Trans. Ingrid Wassenaar. In Michel Contat, Denis Hollier and Jacques Neefs (eds.), *Drafts.* Special issue of *Yale French Studies* 89, pp. 191–207.

———. 2002. *La Littérature des Écrivains: Questions de Critique Génétique.* Paris: Jose Corti.

Hellaakoski, Aaro. 1928. *Jääpeili.* Helsinki: Otava.

Huuhtanen, Päivi. 1977. "Hellaakosken Modernistista Estetiikkaa". *Kirjallisuudentutkijain Seuran Vuosikirja*, 30, pp. 45–69.

McGann, Jerome J. 1991. *The Textual Condition.* Princeton: Princeton University Press.

———. 1993. *Black Riders: The Visible Language of Modernism.* Princeton: Princeton University Press.

Keeler, Mary. 1998. "Iconic Indeterminacy and Human Creativity in C. S. Peirce's Manuscripts". In George Bornstein and Theresa Tinkle (eds.), *The Iconic Page in Manuscript, Print, and Digital Culture.* Ann Arbor: University of Michigan Press, pp. 157–93.

Kupiainen, Unto. 1953. *Aaro Hellaakoski: Ihminen ja Runoilija.* Helsinki: WSOY.

Laitinen, Kai. 1997. *Suomen Kirjallisuuden Historia.* Helsinki: Otava.

Liszka, James Jakób. 1996. *A General Introduction to the Semeiotic of Charles Sanders Peirce.* Indianapolis: Indiana University Press.

Miakhel, Babrak. 2012. "Six Dead in Afghanistan Koran Burning Protests". In *BBC News.* <http://www.bbc.co.uk/news/world-asia-17123464>. [Accessed 28 February 2012].

Peirce, Charles. 1931–1958. *Collected Papers of Charles Sanders Peirce.* 8 vols. Eds. Charles Hartshorne, Paul Weiss and Arthur W. Burks. Cambridge: Harvard University Press.

Rey, Alain. 1989. "Tracés". In Louis Hay (ed.), *De la Lettre au Livre: Sémiotique des Manuscrits Littéraires.* Paris: CNRS, pp. 35–55.

Searle, John. 1969. *Speech Acts: An Essay in the Philosophy of Language.* Cambridge: Cambridge University Press.

Sebeok, Thomas A. 1989. *The Sign and its Masters.* Boston: University Press of America.

Shillingsburg, Peter L. 1991. "Text as Matter, Concept, and Action". *Studies in Bibliography*, 44, pp. 31–82.

———. 1998. *Resisting Texts: Authority and Submission in Constructions of Meaning.* Ann Arbor: University of Michigan Press.

Van Leeuwen, Theo. 2005. "Typographic Meaning". *Visual Communication*, 4, pp. 137–43.

White, John J. 1999. "On Semiotic Interplay: Forms of Creative Interaction Between Iconicity and Indexicality in Twentieth-Century Literature". In Max Nänny and Olga Fischer (eds.), *Form Miming Meaning: Iconicity in Language and Literature.* Amsterdam: John Benjamins, pp. 83–108.

Gunnar Ekelöf and the Rustle of Language

Genetic Readings of a Modernist Poetic Œuvre

Jon Viklund[1]

ALTHOUGH THE ADVENT of literary theories of social materiality and genetic criticism has drawn increasing attention to the issues of textual growth and transmission, literary scholars, by and large, seldom trouble themselves with the authority and stability of their working texts. This indifference to textual considerations is regrettable because it impoverishes textual interpretation as well as one's understanding of an author's relationship to his or her works. In putting the theories of social materiality and genetic criticism into practice in my analysis of a number of poems by one of Sweden's most celebrated twentieth-century authors, Gunnar Ekelöf (1907-1968), I wish to demonstrate how a combined use of these theories enriches our interpretations of literary texts. A Modernist writer obsessed with poetic renewal as "en ständig omprövning av ett och detsamma" ["a constant reconsideration of one and the same thing"] (Ekelöf 1971, 177) and with a sense — borne out by the numerous concurrent surviving drafts of his works — that his poems were never finished, Ekelöf invites a genetic and material reading of his writings. I wish to propose one such reading of his oeuvre, with particular emphasis on a genetic reading of his late poem "Tesbih", from the collection *Sagan om Fatumeh* [*The Tale of Fatumeh*] (1966b).

Drafts as processes

Ekelöf's consideration for, and constant reworking of, his own drafts fly in the face of the presumption, prevalent among literary scholars, that texts are stable and that pre-print textual states are valueless. An examination of the growth of his poem "En ros från Allmag" ["A Rose from Allmag"] shows the absurdity of this assumption. Ekelöf began

---

[1]   I am grateful to Wim Van Mierlo, Bengt Landgren, and Pernille Harsting for their comments on earlier drafts of this article and to Pernille Harsting for improving my English.

"En ros från Allmag" in the summer of 1941 but kept rewriting and revising it over the next ten years (Sommar 1989, 250-51), producing versions of it so dissimilar from one another that they can almost be regarded as different poems. In 1942, the liberal Swedish newspaper *Göteborgs Handels- och Sjöfartstidning* [*Göteborg Trade and Shipping Times*], known for its firm opposition to the German Nazi regime, published Ekelöf's single-stanza poem "Ökenvandring" ["Wandering in the Desert"], a solemn allegory on love and loneliness that uses as a backdrop Xenophon's *Anabasis*, which narrates the story of the retreat of the Ten Thousand from Persia through the deserts of the Middle East. This stanza was excerpted from a poem still in progress that would eventually become "En ros från Allmag". Two years later, in 1944, the Swedish literary magazine *Joker* published another excerpt, under the title "UR BALLADEN om Mannen från havet" ["From the Ballad about the Man from the Sea"]. Headed "Joker på parnassparad" ["A Joker at the Parade of Parnassus"] and extracted from a revised version of the poem's first part, this is a much lighter piece, illustrated, printed in italics, and with Ekelöf's signature in facsimile. Alongside the poem stands a portrait of the young poet-genius — one of Sweden's finest and most remarkable poets, we are told, and one who has abandoned "surrealismens djunglar" ["the jungles of surrealism"] in favour of "den nordiska sommarnattens svala dunkel" ["the cool Nordic summer night"] (1944, 28). In 1946, the final part of the poem, entitled "Envoi", was extracted from yet another revised version and published as "Ballad om Mannen från Havet" ["The Ballad about the Man from the Sea"] in *Vintergatan* [*The Milky Way*], the Christmas calendar of the Swedish Writers Association. By the time the complete poem was printed in the collection *Om hösten* [*In the Autumn*] (1951), under the title "En ros från Allmag", Ekelöf had revised it once again, deleting two previously published stanzas and dividing it into sections. Ekelöf's poem, then, exists in various states embodied in various material supports: magazine form, book form, and even an audio recording, if we add Ekelöf's own stunning reading recorded at his home, which represents yet another distinct version of the poem. A transcription of the recording was published after his death (Ekelöf 2001).

Drafts exemplify the unstable nature of works of art and show, more crudely than polished printed texts, the dialectic nature of invention, which is torn between the poet's boundless imagination and various artistic and physical constraints, such as the exigencies of meter, tempo, rhyme as well as the size of the page. As Dirk Van Hulle notes, an author's drafts reveal the great number of possible — different — poetical solutions to an idea. Modernist writers were aware of the processual value of drafts, and this awareness may account for the survival of a great many drafts supplementary to their published work (2004, 10–11). Ekelöf was particularly sensitive to the value of drafts. In his 1955 collection of *Strountes* [*Nonsense*], he describes himself as an archeologist turning up loam with a spade, searching for words, and constantly reevaluating their meaning. In his metapoetical poems, words are always described as materials, and the process of working with words is described as perhaps more important than the words themselves. This thought is beautifully expressed in "Absentia animi", from his 1945 collection *Non serviam*:

> Det prasslar i min dikt
> Ord gör sin tjänst och ligger där
> Damm faller över dem, damm eller dagg
> tills vinden virvlar upp och lägger ner (dem)
> (och) annorstädes
> den som partout skall söka alltings mening har
> för längesedan insett
> att meningen med prasslandet är prasslandet (Ekelöf 1945, 94)

> [It rustles in my poem
> Words do their duty and lie there
> Dust falls over them, dust or dew
> till the wind swings up and drops (them) down
> (and) elsewhere
> he who *partout* seeks the meaning of everything
> long ago found
> that the meaning of rustling is rustling (Nathan and Larson 1982, 53)]

"Poetik" and the difference between the written and writing

In "Poetik", Ekelöf urges the reader to listen to "tystnaden i retoriken" ["the silence in the rhetoric"] or, as he writes in the poem's last lines:[2]

---

[2] The poem was printed in the magazine *Vi* (1956), collected in *Opus Incertum* (1959a) and in *Poetik* (1959b), and included in many collected editions, of which the earliest is *Dikter* (1965).

> Och allt vad jag så konstfullt söker dikta
> är kontrastvist någonting konstlöst
> och hela fyllnaden tom
> Vad jag har skrivit
> är skrivet mellan raderna (Ekelöf 1959, 9)
>
> [And all that I so artfully aim to compose
> is conversely something artless
> and the whole fullness empty
> What I have written
> is written between the lines]

Through studied repetitions, inversions and line breaks, the text illustrates, performatively, the idea that there is meaning in what is suggested or left unsaid. This idea is conspicuous in the three extant drafts. One of these drafts contains only two lines: "allt vad jag har skrivit | står mellan raderna" ["all that I have written | is found between the lines"].[3] These two lines seem to serve as a heading to the draft of another poem, which, to my knowledge, has never been printed:

> När som jag var liten
> var jag mycket stor
> snusade i skiten
> gjorde hor
> gjorde i sängen
> drömde om kor
> Nu när jag är stor
> gör jag aldrig mera hor
> snusar inte i skit
> känner mig stor liten
> vet inte var jag bor
> och inte vad jag tror.[4]

---

[3] The chronology of the first two drafts is impossible to determine with confidence, Ekelöf having composed both drafts almost simultaneously. Both drafts are found in a notebook called "Spiralblock No. 13" and are dated "1948→" (Uppsala University Library, The Gunnar Ekelöf Collection, IV b, Notebook X, 40). The longest of the two drafts was moved from the notebook into folder XI:1,1 of The Gunnar Ekelöf Collection.

[4] To the right of these lines Ekelöf noted down a variant rhyme: "visste inte vad jag | bodde | och inte vad jag | trodde (?)" ["didn't know where I | lived | nor what I | believed (?)"].

> [When I was little
> I was very big
> sniffed my shit
> fornicated
> wet my bed
> dreamed about cows
> Now that I'm big
> I don't fornicate anymore
> don't sniff my shit
> I feel very small
> don't know where I live
> nor what I believe]

Ekelöf lifted the first line "När som jag var liten" from a popular Swedish song, which he then proceeded to mock.[5] But what appears at first to be a facile travesty and a facetious play on words and rhymes turns out to be a rich poem whose rhetorical and thematic features — the grotesque, the paradoxes, inversions, reverie, alienation and expressions of doubt — are typical of Ekelöf and could earn it a legitimate place in any of his collections from the 1950s. That said, the circumstances of textual production as well as the contrasts between style and thought, and between art and artlessness, lead me to view this poem as, rather, an illustration of the lines I have just quoted that Ekelöf added at the top of the notebook page: "allt vad jag har skrivit | står mellan raderna". The other extant handwritten draft of "Poetik", from the same notebook, further supports my interpretation:

> Förstår ni då inte
> att det är till tystnaden man måste lyssna
> i detta speciella fall min ^speciella^ tystnad
> tystnaden just i retoriken

---

[5]   Compare the following lines from a revue song performed at a vaudeville in the Folkets Hus theatre in Malmö, 1932: "När som jag var liten var jag ful och lång | ja, jag va så räli man kan | men folk sa, han växer nog till sig en gång | och blir vacker och grann" ("När som jag var liten var jag ful och lång" n.d.) ["When I was little, I was ugly and tall | yes, I was as ghastly as can be, | but they said: he'll grow up at some point | and become handsome and good-looking"]. The Scen och manegemuseet in Malmö holds a copy of this version. The first line of Ekelöf's draft is also, as an anonymous reviewer reminds me, reminiscent of the Fool's song at the end of Shakespeare's *Twelfth Night* ("When that I was | a little tiny boy").

> i det så kallade formellt fulländade*
> omtagningarna, formen, allusionerna
> sökandet efter en meningslöshet i meningsfullheten
> och omvänt
> och att vad jag så konstfullt söker dikta
> är ~~konstlöst~~ **kontrastvis** något konstlöst
> och hela fyllnaden tom
> ~~Så har jag tagit om temat~~. En farlig metod
> Det är omtagningen av huvudtemat.
> Men jag har (The Gunnar Ekelöf Collection, XI:1, 01, Uppsala
> University Library.)[6]

> [But don't you understand
> that it is to silence one has to listen
> In this particular case to my ^particular^ silence
> The silence precisely in the rhetoric
> in the so-called formally perfect*
> The repetitions, the form, the allusions
> and conversely
> The search for the meaningless in the meaningful
> And that what I so artfully aim to compose
> Is ~~artless~~ **by contrast** something artless
> and the whole fullness empty
> ~~Then I have repeated the theme~~. A dangerous method
> It is the repetition of the main theme.
> But I have]

The text of this draft differs from that in *Opus Incertum* (1959). The address in the first line suggests that the poetic "I" is arguing before a group of people. The artless repetitions in lines 3–5 clash with the phrase "det så kallade formellt fulländade" ["so-called formally perfect"] in line 5, which Ekelöf described as "nästan skitfint artistbetonade" ["almost snootily artistic"] at the page's foot (see Hellström 1976, 263).[7] Ekelöf's judgment was probably not meant to form part of the poem; nonetheless, it offers an interesting glimpse into the author's creativity and shows the various possibilities contemplated by him. Among these possibilities are the metapoetic comments in

---

[6] My transcription follows the simplified system of diacritical signs listed in Van Hulle 2004, p. x: ~~cancellations~~, **overwritings** (i.e., words or letters immediately following, and replacing, crossed-out letters or words), ^additions^, [conjectural readings].

[7] In his reading of "Poetik", Pär Hellström stresses Ekelöf's rejection of high poetical style in favour of the artless and the inexpressible.

the final lines — "En farlig metod" ["A dangerous method"], according to Ekelöf — and also, perhaps, traces of a wish, later discarded, to make use of a musical schema.

A later typewritten draft bears a fused and condensed version of the texts present in the handwritten drafts, from which it differs mostly in its transformation of the first line. Ekelöf de-emphasizes the "I" of the poem, first superseding it with the impersonal pronoun "man" ["one"] then with the more poetical and abstract "du" ["you"]: "Det är till tystnaden ~~man måste~~ **du skall** lyssna" ["It is the silence ~~one has to~~ **you should** listen to"] (The Gunnar Ekelöf Collection, XI:1, 02, Uppsala University Library). Running to eleven lines, this typewritten text approximates to that printed in *Opus Incertum.*

A diachronic analysis of the composition/revision of "Poetik" underscores Ekelöf's conception of poetry, as expounded in the poem. For instance, the versions of the poem variously decline the artful *vs.* artless opposition, and Ekelöf's successive tinkerings with pronouns in the opening address reflect his shifting views of the poet's position. Inevitably, the existence of multiple versions of competing authority prompts the following question: were these earlier texts superseded by later versions? I shall return to this issue below, in my reading of "Tesbih."

Reading the draft

Ekelöf's one-page draft of "En ros från Allmag" (see Figure 1), held in the Ekelöf collection (IX:17, 304) of Uppsala University Library and possibly dating from the late summer of 1941, bears out Daniel Ferrer's claim that a draft is "an open space, a field of action where events of writing take place" (2002, 54).[8] Manuscripts are not primarily meaningful in relation to the finished text but rather in the way they document the writing process; to use Ferrer again, a draft strictly speaking "is not a text, or a discourse" but "a protocol for making a text" (1998, 261). The centre of Ekelöf's one-page draft features an early version of one of the concluding stanzas of the printed poem (see the circled stanza ending with an asterisk, Figure

---

8   For the date of composition, I follow Sommar who claims that Ekelöf wrote a first draft of the poem immediately after a visit to a dance pavilion in the village of Allmag, on the western coast of Sweden (1989, 251). This draft, inscribed in blue ink, may postdate the other two pencil drafts.

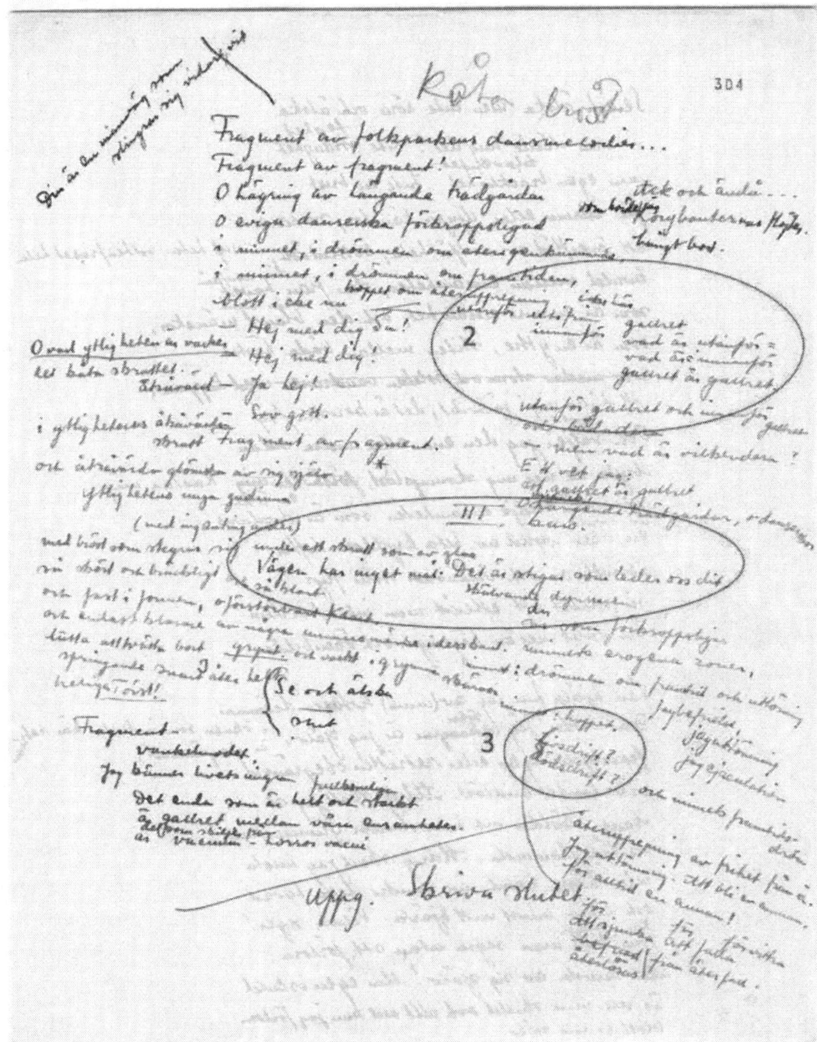

Figure 1: "En ros från Allmag", autograph draft.

1). Below this, Ekelöf inserted the Roman numeral "III", apparently intended to mark a new section beginning with the words "Vägen har inget mål. Det är stigar som leder oss dit" ["The road has no destination. It is the paths that guide us there"]. However, instead of continuing with this stanza — or, perhaps, with a view to illustrating, performatively, the point that it is the small paths that lead us to our destination — Ekelöf fills the page with digressions in which he revisits what he has already written. Ekelöf's manuscript, then, is by no means linear and sequential; rather, the writing runs up and down the page. Moreover, the connections between the various parts of the text are sometimes indicated by arrows and other non-verbal signs, and at the bottom the page also contains metatextual considerations and self-injunctions: "Uppg. Skriva slutet" ["Task: Compose the final part"].

Some of these non-textual comments and signs reflect Ekelöf's attempts to reconcile his inchoate and potentially boundless thoughts with the exigencies of poetry and the spatial limits of a page. Ekelöf appears to be writing and arguing with himself at the same time:

> gallret
> vad är utanför =
> vad är innanför gallret är gallret.
>
> utanför gallret och innanför gallret
> och bådadera
> — men vad är vilketdera?
> Ett vet jag:
> att gallret är gallret.
> O ^minnets^ hängande trädgårdar, o danserskor
>
> [the bars
> what is outside =
> what is inside the bars are the bars.
>
> outside the bars and inside the bar
> and both of these
> but what is which of these?
> One thing I'm sure of:
> that the bars are the bars.
> Oh, the hanging gardens ^of memory^, oh, danseuses]

The words which Ekelöf added to this in the lower right-hand side of the page also evince that writing can be both an act of serious poetic composition and a kind of *jouissance*, a sort of happy concurrence of reading, writing and pleasure:[9]

---

[9]   Here I am, obviously, not using the term "jouissance" in the sense found in Roland Barthes' *Le Plaisir du texte* (1973).

> drömmen om framtid och utlösning
> jagbefrielse
> jaguttömning
> jagejaculation
> och minnets framtidsdröm
> återupprepning av frihet från [ä.]
> Jaguttömning. Att bli en annan.
> för alltid en annan!
> ^för^ Att sjunka ^för^ att falla förvittra
> ~~befriad~~ **återlösas** från återfall.
>
> the dream of future and release
> self-liberation
> self-emptying
> self-ejaculation
> and the memory's dream of the future
> reiteration of freedom from [?]
> Self-emptying.
> Becoming someone else.
> forever someone else!
> ^in order to^ To sink ^in order to^ fall and disintegrate
> ~~liberated~~ **redeemed** from relapse.

This text exemplifies characteristic features of Ekelöf's writing: a gradual veering towards existential issues and, at the same time, an attempt to get down to the meaning of what he is writing about. The text's fragmentariness may be an illustration of the words neatly written at the center of the page: "Vägen har inget mål. Det är stigar som leder oss dit" ["The road has no destination. It is the paths that guide us there"]. Contemplating these metaphorical paths, Ekelöf begins to describe, in fragmented sentences, the "självande dyningar" ["quivering dunes"] that "förkroppsligar minnets erogena zoner" ["embody erogenous zones of memory"]. In connection with these lines, Ekelöf scribbled a note that alludes to Freud's concepts of life- and death-drives: "Livsdrift? | Dödsdrift?" (see Figure 1, circle 3).[10] The draft, then, shows Ekelöf using writing in his search for a meaning, as if he were asking himself: is this it?

A draft, such as that in Figure 1, bears semantic clues that are absent from printed documents. For instance, the draft's various

---

[10]   The drafts of "En ros från Allmag" have never been collated. For an analysis of the version printed in 1951, see Mortensen 2000, 367-71 who comments on Ekelöf's use of Freudian symbolism.

shades of ink may supply information on the poet's state of mind during composition, and the quality of the writing may reflect the order of composition: hastily jotted text betrays new thoughts; carefully inscribed text, recopyings from an earlier draft. Likewise, a ferocious underlining or erasure may reflect the poet's (in)disposition.

Roland Barthes's claim that a text is "un champ méthodologique" ["a methodological field"] and "un travail, une production" (1984, 73) ["an activity, a production" (1977, 157)] ushered in the geneticist's worship of the *avant-texte*, which Pierre-Marc De Biasi defined as a "reconstitution of the genetic operations that precede the text" (2004, 43). Geneticists differ from Barthes, however, in that they attribute greater importance to the material and historical dimensions of a text's growth. Barthes contended that productivity was situated within the reader; geneticists argue that productivity is manifested in the fabric of the documents (see e.g., Jenny 1996, 11–13). Viewed in this genetic light, Ekelöf's *avant-texte* is informative in various ways, furnishing clues on the mechanism of poetic language as well as evidence of Ekelöf's struggles with language.

The remaining part of this article is dedicated to my reading of Ekelöf's late poem "Tesbih". My reading focuses on the poem as an example of writing-in-progress and further illustrates the difference between a text as a finished product and as a continuous process.

"Tesbih" and the author as reader of his own work

The evolution of "Tesbih" is not as drawn out as that of other Ekelöf poems, such as "Djävulspredikan", which Ekelöf began in 1932 and tinkered with until his death in 1968 (Landgren 1992, 89–171). Nonetheless, it offers a representative illustration of an Ekelöfian work in progress. "Tesbih" was first published in 1966 in the Swedish weekly magazine *Vi* and collected in the same year, after some revising, in *Sagan om Fatumeh*. In addition to these two printed versions, a number of drafts survive that enrich our interpretation of Ekelöf's poem and shed light on his writing. Below is the final version of 1966:

tesbiḥ

σορῷ σε μάλιστ᾽ ἐϊκάσδω

Thisbe, ditt namn har ljud av en viskning
och din gestalt har drag av en aning
Fastän den skrovliga muren vill dölja
skepnaden för mig i mörka exilen
kan mina fingrar följa i muren
remnan som tecknar den mjuka profilen
Thisbe, till namnet är du en viskning
och din gestalt är bara en aning

Men när du trevar längs remnan i muren
ser du ett dunkelt Maphorion hölja
den från dig vända, skygga konturen
Liksom ett radband är den att följa
Tesbih! Ditt namn skall vara min viskning.

tesbiḥ

σορῷ σε μάλιστ' ἐϊκάσδω[11]
Thisbe, your name sounds like a whisper
and your figure resembles an inkling
Although the rough wall seeks to hide
the shape from me in the exile of darkness,
my fingers are able to trace in the wall
the crack that draws the soft profile
Thisbe, in name you are a whisper
and your figure is merely an inkling

But when you grope along the crack in the wall
you see a dark veil enveloping
the shy contour that is turned away from you
The fingers tracing it like a rosary
Tesbih! Your name shall be my whisper.

From the earliest draft, the poem focuses on obscurity, uncertainty, and the "inklings" of a poetic "I" addressing his beloved — who appears in his memory when he whispers her name, Thisbe — and seemingly discerning her outline whenever he touches a wall crack. Also present is the association of the name "Thisbe" with *Tesbih*, the Turkish (originally Arabic) word for "a string of prayer beads" ("radband" in Swedish).[12] Fingering prayer beads is connected to

---

[11]   "I can liken you best to an urn", see the discussion below.

[12]   Ekelöf offers this information in the explanatory notes included in *Sagan om Fatumeh*, where he explains that the string of prayer beads symbolizes the aging Fatumeh, the central character in his 1966 collection.

another tactile and meditative act: that of tracing the beloved's contours on the wall. The wall obviously refers to Ovid's *Metamorphoses* and the story of the separated lovers Pyramus and Thisbe who communicate through a crack in the wall (Landgren 1971, 248–50, 258).

The drafts show's Ekelöf's various explorations of intra- and interlinear possibilities. For instance, in the refrain, his near-repetitions of the first line of the poem evince a concern with tense as well as narrative *perspective* (i.e., the question of who is addressing whom). The echo of the first line in the refrain, in slightly altered form, also creates a tension. Below are some of the significant variants within the refrain. The first numbers (e.g., 116) refer to the call number of the Ekelöf Archive at the Uppsala University Library; the digits between parentheses (e.g., 3), to my chronological arrangement of the eleven drafts.[13] In each case, I quote lines 1 and 7 as well as the last line of the poem in progress:

116 (3): Thisbe! Ditt namn tycks mig ~~likna~~ **vara** en viskning
Thisbe, till namnet är du ^< vara^ en viskning
Tesbih, till namnet är du ^ditt namn skall vara^ en viskning

117 (4): Thisbe, ditt namn tycks ~~mig likna en~~ **vara en** ^är svagt som^
viskning
Thisbe, till namnet ~~är~~ **var** du en ~~aning~~ **viskning**
Tesbih! Ditt namn ~~skall vara~~ **är tyst som** en viskning

123 (5): Thisbe, ditt namn ^(^är svagt som^)^ **liknar** en viskning
Thisbe, till namnet var du en viskning

---

[13]   The Swedish literary scholar Reidar Ekner arranged the various manuscript drafts and typescripts of the Ekelöf Collection according to his conjectured chronology of composition. The chronological order of these drafts cannot be ascertained, but my examinations lead me to alter Ekner's order and to suggest the following sequence instead: 115 (1), 114 (2), 116 (3), 117 (4), 123 (5), 122 (6), 121 (7), 119 (8), 120 (9), 118 (10) (which is identical with the *Vi*-version, apart from the handwritten changes), 124 (11). Some problems survive: (a) it is difficult to establish the order of the first three drafts, since they do not contain any clear signs of revision; (b) the chronological order between 122 (6) and 121 (7) can only be determined by the typographical arrangement of the "crack in the text" (see the discussion below); the repetition, in 119 (8), of the variant heading present in 121 (7) — "Sången om Tesbih" ["The Song of Tesbih"] — suggests that 121 (7) is a later typescript; (c) Ekelöf revised 121 (7), and the results of this revision can be found in 119 (8) as well.

> Tesbih! Ditt namn skall vara en viskning

122 (6): Thisbe, ditt namn liknar en viskning
   Thisbe, till namnet var du en viskning
   Tesbih! Ditt namn var bara en viskning

121 (7): Thisbe, ditt namn liknar en viskning
   Thisbe, till namnet var du en viskning
   Tesbih! Ditt namn var bara ~~en~~ **dmin** viskning

119 (8): Thisbe ditt namn har ljud av en viskning
   Thisbe, till namnet var du en viskning
       ~~kanske~~
   Tesbih! ~~Ditt namn var bara min~~ viskning
    ~~Din slöja~~ ~~har ljud~~ ^form^ av min
  ^Tesbih! ~~Min~~ **Din** aning har form av min viskning.^

120 (9): Thisb~~e~~**ah**, ditt namn har ljud av en viskning
   Thisb~~e~~**ah**, till namnet är du en viskning
Tesbih! Di~~tt~~**n** ~~namn~~ **form** har ~~form~~ **namn** av ~~min~~ ~~viskning~~ **en aning**
^Thisbah! Di~~n~~**tt** ~~form~~ **namn** ~~namn~~ **form** av en ~~aning~~ **viskning**^

1966a: Thisbah, ditt namn har ljud av en viskning
   Thisbah, till namnet är du en viskning
   Tesbih! Din form är endast en aning
   Thisbah! Ditt namn är bara en viskning

124 (11): Thisbah, ditt namn är bara en viskning
    Thisbah, till namnet var du en viskning
    Nazm och Tasbīh! Ditt namn är min viskning

1966b: Thisbe, ditt namn har ljud av en viskning
   Thisbe, till namnet är du en viskning
   Tesbih! Ditt namn skall vara min viskning

The above quotations document Ekelöf's cyclical and experimental methods of revision. Ekelöf tinkers with verb tenses in most drafts. In drafts 3 and 9, for instance, he uses only the present tense in the refrains, thus lending to the poem a more static character, an effect also implemented in *Vi* (1966a), the earliest printed version of the poem: till namnet är du" ["in name you are"], "Ditt namn har" ["Your name has"], "Ditt namn är" ["Your name is"]. In drafts 4 and 5 he experiments with three different tenses: the present, the simple past and the future.[14] At times, as during his proofreading of the last pre-print version of the poem for *Sagan om Fatumeh* (1966b), he reinstates readings present in earlier drafts.[15] These reversions are, however, few; most of Ekelöf's alterations introduce new readings.

In the latter part of the poem, Ekelöf tampers with pronouns in an attempt to alter narrative perspective. Draft 7 shows him moving from "Tesbih! Ditt namn var bara *en* viskning" ["Tesbih! Your name was only *a* whisper"] to "*din* viskning" ["*your* whisper"] and then to "*min* viskning" ["*my* whisper"]. In the last line of draft 8, Ekelöf changes, again, the narrative perspective: "*Din* aning har form av min viskning" ["*Your* inkling has the form of *my* whisper"]. A later typescript of the poem (a fair copy of the version that was to be printed in the magazine *Vi*, 118 [10]) proposes an additional perception of the relation between the two lovers:

> men av min aning befolkas exilen
>   mina aningar fyller exilen
> oräkneliga som radbandets kulor
> med fåglar som pickar   smulor
> eller de dricker ur ett springvattnetsens pärlor
> sparvar
> siskor och steglitsor, sparvar och ärlor
> viskning
>   din viskning, var den min viskning,
>   liksom din aning var bara min aning
>
> [but the exile is populated with my inkling
> my inklings fill out the exile
> innumerable like the prayer beads
> with birds that peck   crumbs
> or they drink from the pearls of the fountain
> sparrows
> siskins and goldfinches, sparrows and wagtails
> whisper
> your whisper, was it my whisper,
> like your inkling was nothing but my inkling]

---

[14]   I read "ditt namn skall vara" ["your name will be"] as a future simple; however, the Swedish verb "skall" (like the English "shall") can also be read as a modal verb indicating a command.

[15]   The changes were made in the third round of proofs for the 1966 collection. See the Gunnar Ekelöf Collection, XIV:7, 30.

Such accretions are typical of Ekelöf's late drafts. They show the author placing himself in the reader's shoes to examine his own texts, and setting up a dialogue with himself. Ekelöf returned to these questions of perspective in the third proofs of *Sagan om Fatumeh*, dividing the poem into two stanzas and fiddling again with narrative focus:

> Men när ~~jag~~ **du** trevar längs remnan ~~på~~ i muren
> ser ~~jag~~ **du** ett dunkelt Maphorion hölja
> den från **d**~~m~~ig vända, skygga konturen
> (The Gunnar Ekelöf Collection, XIV:7, 30.)

> [But when ~~I~~ **you** grope along the crack ~~on~~ **in** the wall
> ~~I~~ **you** see a dark veil enveloping
> the shy contour, turned away from ~~me~~ **you**]

A genetic reading of the various drafts of "Tesbih" corroborates what several critics have noted with regards to *Sagan om Fatumeh* as a whole: the lover and the beloved are two sides of the same person, and the destiny of the beloved becomes intertwined with that of the lover — Fatumeh, the protagonist of the collection, is the *fatum* of her lover (Ekner 1967, 144–46). Landgren sees in these themes a typical Ekelöfian erotic mysticism, which is, paradoxically enough, characterized both by alienation and by ecstatic self-effacement (Landgren 1971, 245–49). Another prominent Swedish Ekelöf scholar, Anders Olsson, contends — in his examination of the use of apostrophe and the relation between "you" and "I" in Ekelöf's poetry — that "du" ["you"] often encompasses, especially in the later poetry, everything that the poems want to invoke: "women, cosmos, non-being, and the deeper self of the I" (1983, 282).

A genetic reading of "Tesbih" demonstrates that, at every stage of the writing process, the poem might have become something quite different. Changes in pronouns reorientate our exegeses, as do changes in verb tenses, the latter notably by blurring, in the mind of the poetic "I", the boundaries between past, present, and future. The different intentions discernible at every stage militate against the idea that an overriding "meaning" is to be found in any one variant. A diachronic examination attests that Ekelöf's indefatigable revisions, his experiments with different nuances and connotations, are central to his poetics.

The crack in the text

"Tesbih" is a rondel, a poetical form that arose in Medieval French poetry. Rondels are 13–14 lines in length and restricted to two rhymes. They are often divided into three stanzas, with the first two lines repeated in lines 7–8, and the first line repeated in the last line. If the poem is fourteen lines long, the first two lines are usually repeated again in lines 13–14: for example, ABba abAB abbaA(B), where the capital letters indicate repeated or partly repeated lines. The rondel and its close relative the rondeau — the two terms are sometimes used synonymously — are fairly uncommon in early Modernist poetry, despite some usages by Baudelaire, Mallarmé, and Breton. Ekelöf wrote several rondels, taking liberties with their formal requirements and simply naming each of them "Rondel" (see e.g. Ekelöf 1951, 54 and 56). It is important to consider these formal constraints when analyzing poetry, because they help account for some changes in Ekelöf's drafts; poetical invention results from the dialectic between formal and content-based considerations.

Ekelöf probably had the structure of the rondel in mind when he began composing "Tesbih". The rondel's circular structure ("rondel" comes from the French *rond,* meaning "round") fits well with the poem's main motif: fingers repeatedly going over a string of prayer beads, in a meditative act of remembrance. Two of the early handwritten drafts (115–116) are rhymed, and each of the three drafts (114–116) bears a thirteen-line poem. From the first typescript onwards (117 and ff.), Ekelöf made the rhyme scheme more orderly, creating four or five rhymes.

There are three stages in Ekelöf's composition, each of which represents a peculiar textual or typographic manifestation of "the crack in the wall". The first series of typescripts (Gunnar Ekelöf Collection, XIV:7, 117, 123, 122, and 121, corresponding to nos. 4–7 in my chronological list above) contains a thirteen-line rondel, divided into two quatrains and one quintet, and repeating — with significant variations — the first line of the poem in lines 7 and 13, and the second line in line 8. In going over draft 123 (5) (Figure 2), a fair copy entitled "Sagan om Tesbih" ["The tale of Tesbih"], Ekelöf added a Greek motto: "tó sorón eíkásai ["to liken to an urn"]. Perhaps this addition prompted him to replace, in the opening line, "är svagt som" ["is weak as"] with the word "liknar" ["liken"], a revision

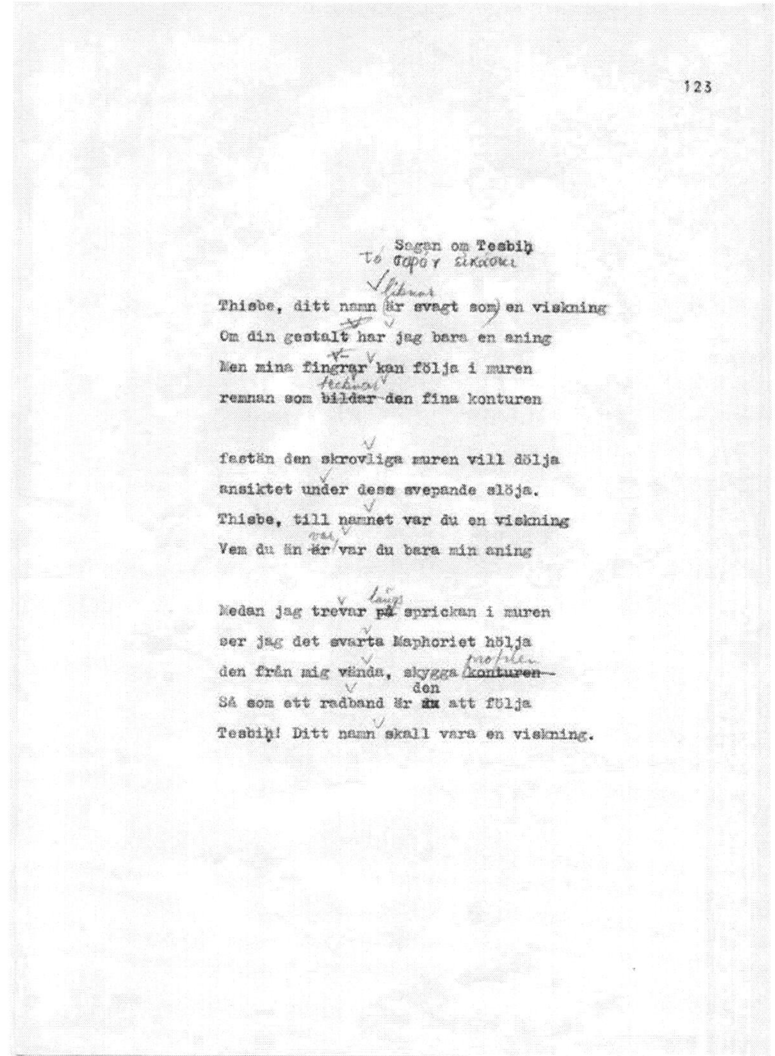

Figure 2: "Sagan om Tesbih", typescript.

that disrupts the earlier version's neat metrical structure. In the fourth line he substituted the word "bildar" ["forms"] (in "remnan som bildar den fina konturen" ["the crack that forms the fine contour"]) with "tecknar" ["draws"], which gives the phrase an almost anthropomorphic meaning, as if the wall itself was drawing the crack.

In two later typescripts, Ekelöf marked out, typographically, interruptions in every line, thereby adding more cracks to the text. In the first typescript the right halves of the lines are lowered, creating an asymmetrical crack that cuts vertically across the horisontal lines; in the second, Ekelöf appears to have used the tabulator or the space key to draw a straight line on one side (see Figure 3). There is another, manually drawn, crack in 121 (7), to the left of which Ekelöf scribbled a description of Thisbe's beauty (see Figure 3). Ekelöf's typographic experiments seem geared towards showing a parallel between cracks in a wall and poetic cracks in an urn; in a letter to Britta Wigforss, Ekelöf mentions that, in the tenth-century Byzantine lexicon *Suidas*, the Greek word *thísbe* is defined as synonymous with the Greek word *sorós*, "urn" (Landgren 1971, 258; Åström 1992, 294).

In his later drafts, Ekelöf abandoned these typographic experiments, perhaps deeming them unsubtle. But does his abandonment entail that we should blot out the existence and implications of these cracks as we read later textual states? I would like to suggest that these cracks convey important messages about the connection between, on the one hand, the objects thematized in the poem — the wall, the string of prayer beads, the urn, the veil, etc. — and, on the other, the poem's form.

The second stage of Ekelöf's revision of "Tisbeh" is documented by three typewritten drafts (119 [8], 120 [9], 118 [10]) and by the magazine version printed in *Vi* (1966a, 24). At this stage, Ekelöf converts the poem into rondel of fourteen lines and one stanza. Gone is the Greek motto, perhaps as a result of magazine requirements, and many revisions are aimed at increasing metrical regularity, with the refrain lines (1–2, 7–8, 13–14) now numbering 10 syllables ($/\breve{}\breve{}/\breve{}/\breve{}\breve{}/\breve{}$) and the other lines 11 syllables ($/\breve{}\breve{}/\breve{}\breve{}/\breve{}\breve{}/\breve{}$). This concern with the tightening of the rhyme scheme reinforces the idea of the poem as a "well-wrought urn", to allude to Cleanth Brooks' famous metaphor. However, one line in the poem (symbolized by "X"), after the first refrain, disrupts the poem's orderly structure: ABcdedABXeceBA. Ekelöf stresses the word "remnan" ["the crack"] by placing it at the end of the line: "Trevar jag åter på muren längs remnan" ["Again, on the wall I grope along the crack"]. Ekelöf creates a rhythmic, phonic break corresponding to the "crack" in the wall described in the poem.

In his third stage of revision, Ekelöf cracked the text yet again. While writing the last version, that which would appear in *Sagan om

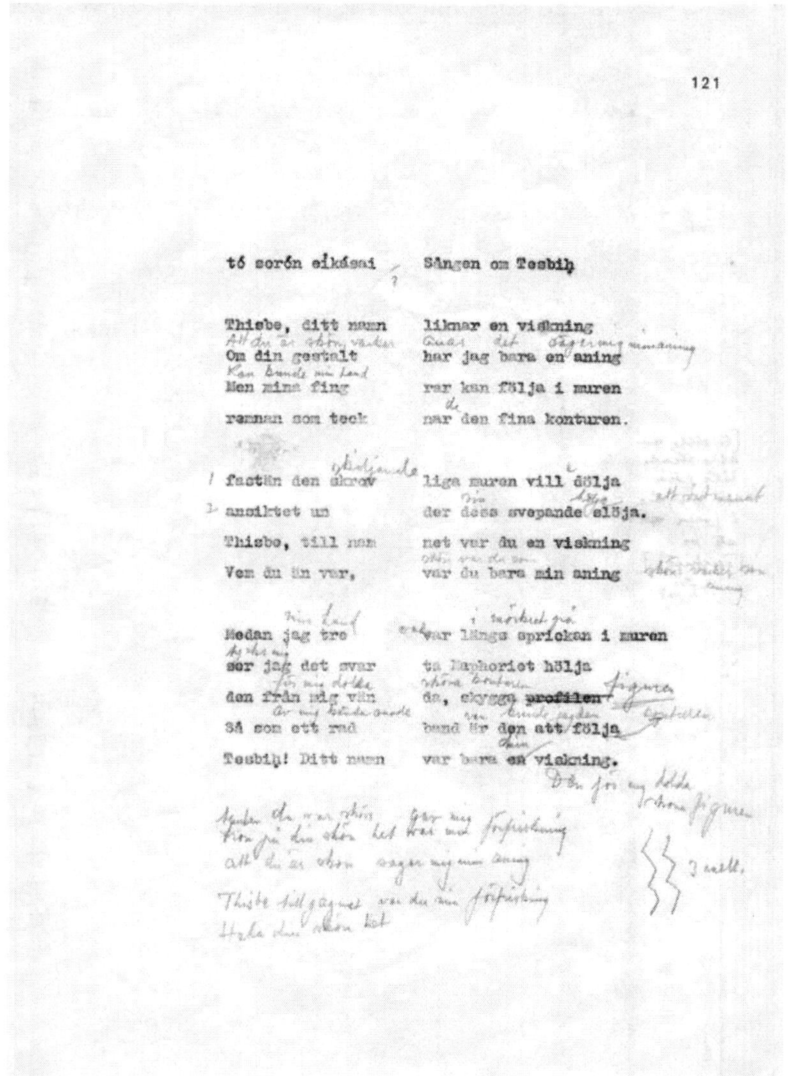

Figure 3: Tesbih, typescript

Fatumeh, he revised, using a blue ballpoint pen, a number of older drafts. He reinstored the Greek motto, transcribing the Greek text in one typescript, erasing it in another, and resuscitating it in a late proof in Greek script. I have already described some of the changes that the text underwent in these last drafts, including Ekelöf's re-implementation of the five-word rhyme scheme, his omission of the penultimate line, and his reversion to the thirteen-line format. In the last version (printed in *Sagan om Fatumeh*), he shatters the metrical regularity of lines 5 and 11 by lopping off one syllable and introducing a caesura, and he divides the poem into two stanzas, the break between them creating a significant pause in the reading, after which the second stanza begins with the word "Men" ["But"]. This adversative conjunction marks a turn in the poem, emphasizing both the change of narrative perspective (discussed above) and the description of the "ett dunkelt Maphorion" ["a dark veil"] enveloping "den från dig vända, skygga konturen" ["the shy contour that is turned away from you"], which the poem's "you" seems to make out in the wall crack.

So what exactly does Ekelöf's crack in the text signify? To answer this question, we need to take into consideration the text from *Sagan om Fatumeh* that I cited at the beginning of the previous section of this article, as well as those drafts of the poem that contain Ekelöf's typographical experiments along with the Greek motto.

Intertextual allusions play an important part in "Tesbih", as they do elsewhere in Ekelöf's poetry. The Greek motto is a variation on Sappho's fragment 104: "Whereunto may I well liken thee, dear bridegroom? | To a soft shoot may I best liken thee" (Thornton Wharton 1895, 143).

In "Tesbih", Ekelöf offers an answer to Sappho's question. The bride in Ekelöf's poem is no longer young and certainly not a virgin. The old Fatumeh is wretched, hungry, and forced to sell her body in exchange for food. Ekelöf tells us that "tesbih" — that is, the string of prayer beads — symbolizes the old woman who is the protagonist in *Sagan om Fatumeh,* and it seems appropriate to view the Thisbe figure of the poem as a representation of Fatumeh. In the printed version of Ekelöf's poem, the Greek motto's comparison of the beloved with an urn — σορῷ σε μάλιστ' ἐϊκάσδω ["I can liken you best to an urn"], that is, to a burial urn — obviously means something quite different from what it means in Sappho's poem. Ekelöf's previous version of the motto — "tó sorón eíkásai" ["to liken to an urn"] — stressed the act of comparison rather than anything else. The added personal pronoun "I" in the later version might relate to the poetic "I" or even to the author. The association between the beloved and the urn is also found in another poem in the collection, as well as on the miniature illustration on the book's cover featuring a prince holding (embracing?) an urn. Obviously, the urn symbolizes the beloved as well as lost love.

But it also makes sense to think of Ekelöf's poem as an urn in itself — an interpretation warranted by the mentioned front-cover illustration.[16] The Greek meter and the Sapphic intertext lead us strongly to suspect that Ekelöf had Keats's Grecian urn in mind. But despite obvious similarities (the comparison between the urn and a woman, the silence and the inaccessibility of the urn), Ekelöf's poem contrasts with Keats's in several ways: Ekelöf's urn is neither an "unravished bride" nor is it "forever young". Keats construed the Grecian urn as a symbol of the artistic ideal; the symbolism of Ekelöf's urn is more complex and less idealistic: if the poem is a well-wrought urn, then this urn is cracked and filled with memories of the dead.

The above genetic reading of "Tesbih" illustrates the open-endedness of Ekelöf's poetic works. The Swedish poet resisted the idea of a finished poem as well as the concept of the "so-called formally perfect". To him the act of creation was part of the meaning of a poem: it formed part of his poetics — a typically Modernist assumption. The reading of a single textual state — the method practiced by most literary scholars — cannot bring to light these Ekelöfian concerns; they can only be disclosed by a genetic-material reading.

Bibliography

Åström, Paul. 1992. *Gunnar Ekelöf och antiken.* Jonsered: Åström.

Barthes, Roland. 1977. *Image, Music, Text.* Trans. Stephen Heath. New York: Hill and Wang.

———. 1984. *Le bruissement de la langue: Essais critiques IV.* Paris: Seuil.

de Biasi, Pierre-Marc. 2004. "Toward a Science of Literature: Manuscript Analysis". In Jed Deppman, Daniel Ferrer and Michael Groden (eds.), *Genetic Criticism: Texts and Avant-textes.* Philadelphia: University of Pennsylvania Press, pp. 36–68.

Ekelöf, Gunnar. 1944. UR BALLADEN om Mannen från havet". *Joker* 2(6), p. 28.

---

[16]   The illustration of the young man with the urn reflects the contents of several of the poems in *Sagan om Fatumeh.* In her 1966 review of Ekelöf's collection, Wigforss suggested that poem no. 29 in the collection is Ekelöf's "Ode on a Persian urn". See also the discussion in Landgren 1971, 259–60.

——. 1945. *Non Serviam*. Stockholm: Bonniers.

——. 1951. *Om hösten*, Stockholm: Bonniers.

——. 1956. "Poetik". *Vi*, 40, p. 20.

——. 1959a. *Opus Incertum*. Stockholm: Bonniers.

——. 1959b. *Poetik*. Sigtuna : Sigtuna bokh.

——. 1965. *Dikter*. Stockholm: Bonniers.

——. 1966a. "Tre dikter av Gunnar Ekelöf", *Vi*, 37, p. 24.

——. 1966b. *Sagan om Fatumeh*, Stockholm: Bonniers, 1966.

——. 1971. *En självbiografi: Efterlämnande brev och anteckningar*. Stockholm: Bonniers.

——. 1982. *Songs of Something Else*. Trans. Leonard Nathan and James Larson. Princeton: Princeton University Press.

——. 1992. *Skrifter 6: Promenader och annan litterär prosa*. Stockholm: Bonniers.

——. 1993. *Skrifter 8: Tankesamling*. Stockholm: Bonniers.

——. 2001. *Heminspelningar*. Stockholm: Gunnar Ekelöf-sällskapet.

Ek, Sverker. 2005. *I dialog med texten: Nio essäer*. Hedemora: Gidlunds.

Ekner, Reidar. 1967. *I den havandes liv: Åtta kapitel om Gunnar Ekelöfs lyrik*. Stockholm: Bonniers.

Ferrer, Daniel. 1998. "The Open Space of the Draft Page: James Joyce and Modern Manuscripts". In George Bornstein and Theresa Tinkle (eds.), *The Iconic Page in Manuscript, Print, and Digital Culture*. Ann Arbor: University of Michigan Press, pp. 249–67.

——. 2002. "Production, Invention, and Reproduction. Genetic vs. Textual Criticism". In Elizabeth Bergmann Loizeaux and Neil Fraistat (eds.), *Reimagining Textuality: Textual Studies in the Late Age of Print*. Madison: University of Wisconsin Press, pp. 48–59.

Hellström, Per. 1976. *Livskänsla och självutplåning*. Uppsala: Litteraturvetenskapliga institutionen, Uppsala universitet.

Jenny, Laurent. 1996. "Genetic Criticism and its Myths". In Michel Contat, Denis Hollier and Jacques Neefs (eds.), *Drafts*. Special issue of *Yale French Studies*, 89, pp. 9–25.

Landgren, Bengt. 1971. *Ensamheten, döden och drömmarna: Studier över ett motivkomplex i Gunnar Ekelöfs diktning*. Stockholm: Scandinavian University Books.

——. 1992. *Odysseus vid masten och Procyons galna hund: Populärvetenskapliga föreläsningar och seminarier*. Uppsala: Litteraturvetenskapliga institutionen, Uppsala universitet.

Mortensen, Anders. 2000. *Tradition och originalitet hos Gunnar Ekelöf.* Stockholm & Stehag: Symposion.

"När som jag var liten var jag ful och lång ". n.d. In *Malmövisor i urval.* <http://skanevisor.se/malmovisor/getagrip/HTML/3index. html>. [Accessed 26 August 2011].

Olsson, Anders. 1983. *Ekelöfs nej.* Stockholm: Bonniers.

Sommar, Carl Olov, 1989. *Gunnar Ekelöf: En biografi.* Stockholm: Bonniers.

Thornton Wharton, Henry, 1895. *Sappho: Memoir, Text, Selected Renderings, and a Literal Translation.* London: Lane.

Van Hulle, Dirk. 2004. *Textual Awareness: A Genetic Study of Late Manuscripts by Joyce, Proust, and Mann.* Ann Arbor: University of Michigan Press.

Wigfors, Brita. 1966. "Skuggan på muren". *Göteborgs Handels- och Sjöfartstidning,* 4 November.

An Omnipotent Tradition

The Illustrations of Kristijonas Donelaitis's Poem *Metai* and the Creation of a Visual Canon

Giedrė Jankevičiūtė and Mikas Vaicekauskas

Kristijonas Donelaitis's poem *Metai* [*The Seasons*] (written *c.* 1765–1775; first published in 1818) is widely regarded as Lithuania's greatest literary work. The poem gained recognition as early as the nineteenth century, but its reputation was not cemented until 1940, a critical time for Lithuania.[1] The author's treatment of peasant culture, which was considered fundamental to the Lithuanian national culture, was then judged to be the major topic of the poem, and any other interpretations were discarded. The present article seeks to examine the historical formation of the interpretive tradition of Donelaitis's poem and its expression in the "material body" of the text, i.e., the editions of the poem in Lithuanian and other languages. Most of our attention is devoted to two editions from 1940 and 1956 which built and established the "bibliographic code" of the work.

Early editions of *Metai*

Donelaitis was born in 1714 in the now-extinct village of Lazdynėliai in Lithuania Minor, in the present-day Kaliningrad region in Russia.[2] From 1731 to 1736 Donelaitis attended Königsberg's (Kaliningrad's) Cathedral College; from 1736 to 1740, he studied theology at Königsberg University. Between 1740 and 1742 he served as cantor at the Stalupėnai village school and became rector of the school in 1742. He held this position until 1743, when he was appointed

---

[1]   On 15 June 1940 Lithuania was occupied by the Red Army, and on 22 June 1941 it was invaded by the German army.

[2]   Lithuania Minor (*Mažoji Lietuva* in Lithuanian, *Preussisch Litauen* in German), in northeast Prussia, was home to a Lithuanian minority. Lithuania Minor never belonged to the Lithuanian state. Almost all Lithuanians in that region were peasants (either free farmers or serfs).

211

pastor of the Lutheran parish of Tolminkiemis.[3] Donelaitis lived
in Tolminkiemis until his death in 1780. In addition to his priestly
duties, which acquainted him with the material and spiritual lives
of his peasant parishioners, he was involved in construction and
mechanical works, and in gardening. He also built scientific and
musical instruments (e.g., barometers and harpsichords) and composed some literary works, writing, apart from *Metai*, six fables in
Lithuanian and three poems in German. None of his writings were
published during his lifetime; they survive only in manuscript
form and in copies made by the German pastor Johann Friedrich
Hohlfeldt (1767–1829).[4]

The most significant work of Lithuanian literature, the didac-
tic and epic poem *Metai* is noted for the originality and mastery of
its language and imagery. In metrotonic hexameters, which Donelaitis adapted to the Lithuanian language (see Girdenis 1993), the
poem offers a realistic description of the daily lives of peasant serfs
in Lithuania Minor. Donelaitis describes, for every season, the peasants' work, their surroundings, their daily activities and celebrations.
Metai also highlights the perfect order of the world, which could not
exist but for the will of God, and depicts earthly joys and hardships,
good and bad behaviours. The peasants' lives are evaluated from
several viewpoints — religious, moral, social, and ethnic. In addition, through his several, detailed descriptions of the circumambi-
ent nature during the four seasons, the poet shows the power and
wisdom of God. The poem was addressed to the peasants of Donelaitis's parish — who must have found its themes, style, and voice
congenial — as well as to his closest friends, who were familiar with
the reality depicted in the poem.

Metai conflates several styles. Its structure, based on the four seasons, is reminiscent of classicism; in it, hyperbole, rustic language,
Enlightenment didacticism and a baroque aesthetic are all mingled
with with realist traits. Its styles and means of expression are determined by the poem's subject matter (the life of the peasantry), the

---

[3]   The jurisdiction of the Tolminkiemis (or Tollmingkehmen) parish covered some 30 villages and 3,000 inhabitants, of whom two thirds were German
and one third Lithuanian.

[4]   For further information on the posthumous publication of Donelaitis's works, see Vaškelis 1964; Lebedys 1977, 194–316; Gineitis 1990, 204–249;
Doveika 1990; Vaicekauskas 2001; and Vaicekauskas 2009.

author's convictions (his Christian world view), the poem's intent (to show episodes from peasant life as well as to give religious, moral, and practical instruction), and, indirectly, literary tradition (classical literature and the prevailing literary tendencies of the period) and specific language features (everyday speech).

Metai was first published, from manuscripts, in 1818, in a bilingual edition ([Donelaitis 1818]) by Martynas Liudvikas Rėza (Martin Ludwig Rhesa, 1776–1840), who was a professor at Königsberg University. Rėza gave the untitled poem its title (in the German translation he named it *Das Jahr*) and divided it into four parts, features that were retained, with some exceptions, in later editions. Rėza's aim, kindled by his romantic idealism, was to portray Donelaitis as the bard of Lithuanian literature and culture. It accounts for some of the radical editorial departures from the original. Rėza eliminated any severe expressions and episodes that represented the Lithuanians negatively; he corrected vocabulary and omitted barbarisms, sometimes inserting new words or entire lines; he changed the names of some of the characters; and he cut out as many as 468 lines (Krištopaitienė 2007, 32–36, 138–141, 258). Rėza's German translation not only introduced Donelaitis's work to German readers but sparked some scholarly interest in it as well: throughout the nineteenth century, German scholars — who viewed the poem as an artefact from one of Germany's national minorities — worked on the poem, analyzing it, editing it, and republishing it.

In 1865, in Saint Petersburg, the German linguistic August Schleicher (1821–1868) published the first, complete scholarly edition of Donelaitis's works, comprising all of Donelaitis's known writings in Lithuanian ([Donelaitis 1865]). Schleicher based his edition on the extant autographs and on Hohlfeldt's copies, as well as on Rėza's edition. He restored most of Rėza's omissions and reinstated Donelaitis's words, but he too departed in some cases from the original. Since Schleicher's interest in Donelaitis's texts was mainly linguistic, he devoted most of his attention to vocabulary, accentuation, and spelling, which he modernized.

Schleicher's edition, consequently, was criticized by the German philologist Georg Heinrich Ferdinand Nesselmann (1811–1881). Seeking to preserve the authority embodied in the autographs, Nesselmann published a critical edition of Donelaitis's works in Koenigsberg in 1869 ([Donelaitis 1869]). Nesselmann sharply criticized

Rėza for his arbitrary distortions of the text, and Schleicher for yielding to Rėza's influence. In his competent edition, grounded in work on the original documents, he rejected his predecessors' cuts and presented the first complete edition of *Metai*, retaining even Donelaitis's accentuation (Krištopaitienė 2007, 258–60). Nesselmann also produced a new German translation of *Metai*.

The first Lithuanian edition of *Metai* was published in Shenandoah, Pennsylvania, in 1897 ([Donelaitis 1897]). Prior to World War II, Donelaitis's poem and his other works were to appear another four times, in 1914, 1918, 1921 and 1927. These editions were not distinguished by scholarly precision or quality of printing, and their physical characteristics (typeface, page layout, cover design and binding) were aesthetically unprepossessing. Some of these editions were, in fact, abridged, poorly edited, and cheaply published schoolbooks, containing mistakes found in earlier editions, and whose sole editorial policy was the standardization of dialect forms (Donelaitis 1914, 1918, 1921, 1927). Contemporary scholars regarded *Metai* as a realistic or classical poem, concerned primarily with nature, peasant life, and other aspects of folk culture. They also devoted much attention to Donelaitis's life and to his social and cultural environment.

The 1940 edition of *Metai*: visualizing the poem's meaning

The first *de luxe* scholarly edition of *Metai* was published by the Lithuanian historian of literature Juozas Ambrazevičius (1903–1974) in Kaunas in 1940 (Donelaitis 1940). Seeking to preserve authorial forms and wishes, Ambrazevičius went back to the autographs and the copies thereof, and to Nesselman's edition. That said, Ambrazevičius's edition was also adapted for the general public and for the schools. He did not formulate editorial principles, but, seeking to make the text accessible to readers lacking philological training, he modernized its forms, syntax and language. He also bowdlerized the text, displaced words, and made other excisions (Krištopaitienė 2005, 101–108). These changes placed Ambrazevičius's text at a further remove from the original than Nesselmann's.

Nonetheless, Ambrazevičius's edition is considered one of the most important because it was the first well-printed and illustrated edition. The illustrations were the work of the printmaker Vytautas Kazimieras Jonynas (1907–1997), whose drawings were greatly superior to those in the earlier editions prepared by Mykolas Biržiška (1882–1962) in the 1910s and 20s. These had featured only modest drawings of shabby peasant huts and a wooden church on the cover. Whereas Biržiška's editions testify to laborious efforts to build a modern Lithuanian culture during the Russian occupation, Jonynas's illustrations suggest a strong admiration for a new national culture that was flourishing in the independent Lithuanian state. Jonynas's drawings gave the edition an elegant and serious appearance that encouraged its readers — mostly rural migrants who had flocked to the country's growing urban centres — to view the poem's representation of peasant life and nature as testimonies of their country's past, and while they themselves had inhabitants of a new and modern Lithuania. The book was addressed to the general public and, above all, to young people. But bibliophiles were interested in it as well. The print run of Ambrazevičius's edition ran to 3,000 copies, of which 300 numbered copies were intended for the rare book market.

The book's success also owed something to contemporary politics. Prepared while Lithuania was independent but published *after* the Soviet occupation of 1940 (Soviet troops invaded Lithuanian territory on 15 June 1940), Ambrazevičius's *de luxe* edition came to symbolize the survival of a national culture. Its cultural significance also helps account for a second edition issued in 1941 under the Nazi regime (Donelaitis 1941). The editor of this second edition, seeking to rectify the damage done by Soviet censorship, reinstated Ambrazevičius's concluding article, "Būrų kultūros poetas" ["The Poet of Peasant Culture"], absent from the 1940 edition. The print run of the second edition was 2,300 copies — quite a large number for Lithuania, especially when those figures are added to those of the previous edition. This once more testifies to the importance of the book for the period.

Both editions were identical in form. They were issued in paper covers so that book collectors could have their copies rebound according to their taste, budget and other books in their collections.[5]

---

[5]   A copy of *Metai*, artfully bound in morocco leather is held in the V. K. Jonynas's House museum in Druskininkai. It was given to Jonynas in 1940 by Tadas Lomsargis, the best bookbinder in Lithuania throughout the 1930s. The book collector Vilhelmas Burkevičius commissioned Lomsargis to bind another copy of *Metai*. On these bindings, see Gudaitis 1995, 34, 38, 57–58.

Figure 1: Cover of the first illustrated edition of *Metai*, by Vytautas Kazimieras Jonynas (Kaunas: Švietimo ministerijos knygų leidimo komisijos leidinys, 1940).

The large format (280 x 220 mm), high quality cream-coloured paper, its richly decorated title page, illustrated chapter headings and tailpieces, and numerous engravings of natural scenes and figures gave the book a luxurious appearance (see Figures 1 and 2). The two editions differ only in three minor points: the initial letter of the title on the cover page was red in the 1940 edition, green in that of 1941; the 1940 edition was published without the concluding article; and the tailpiece of the 1940 edition shows an image of the blessing hand of God (the Soviet censors apparently did not understand the meaning of this symbol), whereas the tailpiece of the 1941 edition depicts God as a half figure. Until the end of the twentieth century, the version of *Metai* edited by Ambrazevičius and illustrated by Jonynas was unquestionably regarded as a *visual* aid for the understanding of the poem.

The publishers' decision to offer an edition of the poem that would be attractive to a wider audience was explained in Ambrazevičius's concluding article. According to the literary historian Viktorija Skrupskelytė, Ambrazevičius understood literature as an artistic or stylized representation of reality that harmoniously related the author's personality to the time in which he lived (Skrupskelytė 2005, 125). Thus, in addition to observing the unity of contents and form, the article examines the origins of Donelaitis's creative work, the social and ethnic dimensions of *Metai*, and the artistic qualities of the poetic text.

Ambrazevičius wrote: "Donelaičio *Metai* yra liudininkas 18 amžiaus lietuvninkų gyvenimo — ekonominio, socialinio, moralinio; liudininkas lietuvių būrų psichinės struktūros, net jų kuriamojo pajėgumo. Juose betgi atsispindi ir apskritai Europos dvasia, kuri buvo užgriebusi patį rašytoją." (Ambrazevičius 1941, 187) ["*Metai* by Donelaitis is a witness to the life of Lithuanians — economic, social, and moral — in Lithuania Minor in the eighteenth century, a witness of the mental structure and even the creative capacity of Lithuanian peasants. Nevertheless, the poem reflected the European spirit in general, which had affected the writer himself"].

Figure 2: Title-page for the first illustrated edition of *Metai*, by Vytautas Kazimieras Jonynas (Kaunas: Švietimo ministerijos knygų leidimo komisijos leidinys, 1940).

The publication of the *de luxe* edition was motivated by the desire to give the poem a special cultural status. This idea first emerged among Lithuanian bibliophiles around 1930 (Andriušytė-Žukienė 2007, 36). Marija Urbšienė (1895–1959) argued that Donelaitis's poem was a monument in the literary canon and that therefore it deserved to be published in a form befitting its stature (Urbšienė 1930, 87). This idea was supported by her colleagues, among whom were teachers who understood the necessity of educating, training, and enlightening their compatriots, above all the younger generation. As a national classic, *Metai* was a core work in the school curriculum after independence, and from 1918 onwards every secondary school student studied, analysed and learnt the poem by heart.

Almost certainly the intervention of the XXVII knygos mėgėjų draugija [Lithuanian Book Lovers Society] had led to Jonynas's involvement with Ambrazevičius's edition. Dissatisfied with the unprepossessing graphic design and print of the editions of the 1910s and 20s, the Society, in 1933, commissioned Jonynas — then a talented young artist studying graphic arts in Paris — to create illustrations and a new layout for a representative edition of *Metai.* Jonynas's chief patron was Paulius Galaunė (1890–1988), an art historian and bibliophile, and the director of the M. K. Čiurlionis Gallery. In 1936 Jonynas was inducted, upon Galaunė's recommendation, into Kaunas's bibliophile society. Presumably, other artists had been sought too to illustrate the poem, for an imagined portrait (no actual portrait of Donelaitis is known to exist) was produced around 1935 by another young and talented printmaker, Telesforas Kulakauskas (1907–1977).[6]

From 1932 onwards, Jonynas was a well-known member of the group of modernist artists *Ars.* Like the group's other members, Jonynas championed the neo-traditionalism typical of Western art in the 1930s. His idea was to create a new hybrid art for young Lithuania that would combine traditional Lithuanian elements with modernist ones. He drew his inspiration from Lithuanian folk sculpture and woodcuts, a tradition that he then sought to represent in post-cubist fashion. In other words, Jonynas's early artwork was influenced by *Art Deco.* Several of Jonynas's early linocuts also show the influence of the German "Neue Sachlichkeit" (see Jankevičiūtė 2008, 66–93). However, Jonynas's work for *Metai* moved into a different direction: neo-classicism. Indeed, it is believed that it was his attempt to portray peasant life in Lithuania Minor and to express the solemnity of the Donelaitis's poetry rhyme and rhythm that prompted him to pay greater attention to realistic details and to embrace the classical tradition.

Searching for new means of expression, Jonynas attentively studied the work of two Soviet printmakers whose artworks were well known and appreciated among Lithuanian professionals in the late 1930s: Vladimir Favorsky (1886–1964) and Aleksey Kravchenko (1889–1940). Jonynas's woodcuts for *Metai* — illustrations of the plot and mood-creating headpieces and tailpieces inserted into the text

---

6   The Lithuanian émigré cultural monthly *Aidai* (1964, No. 3) features a reproduction.

— inspired readers to construe the poem as a narrative of the cyclical lives of peasants set against the background of nature's cycles. Jonynas's prints did much more than simply *illustrate* a classic piece of literature; they acted as a statement about a nation that had its roots in peasant life and that, when faced with the extinction of that life, would recognize and memorialize the images as symbols of an imperilled culture. The illustrations brought out several characteristic themes of the poem, such as peasant life in Lithuania Minor in the second half of the eighteenth century — the peasants' toils, holidays, and natural environment. The crude features of some of Jonynas's illustrations matched the linguistic medium chosen by the author of the poem: colloquial language. The illustrations offered the idealized image of Lithuania Minor and at the same time encouraged readers to view the poem as a realistic work, as an epic of the Lithuanian villages of bygone times. This illusionism prompted readers (and viewers) to connect with the reality of Donelaitis's time, if only briefly.

Village culture and life were celebrated because of their ideological significance in interwar Lithuania. That Jonynas's woodcuts conveyed the aims of the official cultural politics of independent Lithuania was made clear when his work received the national award for art in 1939 — before the prints were even published! This recognition evinces the importance that Lithuanian society attached to Jonynas's work. Jonynas's illustrations were also part of a wider, recently launched programme to illustrate the country's national classics. Jonynas's inclusion in the programme enhanced the cultural significance of his work. The same year the printmaker Domicelė Tarabildienė (1912–1985), who illustrated a collection of Lithuanian folklore, *Šimtas liaudies baladžių* [*A Hundred Folk Ballads*], edited by Jonas Balys (1941), also received a state award.

In the publication of representative editions of classic works, Lithuania lagged behind its neighbours; Latvia, Estonia, and the Scandinavian countries had already produced luxurious and "exemplary" illustrated editions of national literary classics. For example, at the turn of the century, the Finnish artist Akseli Gallen-Kallela (1865–1931) illustrated Finland's national epic *Kalevala* [*The Land of Kaleva*], a work by Elias Lönnrot (1802–1884) based on Finnish and Karelian tales and folk songs. (In 1920–1922 Gallen-Kallela contributed to another representative edition of the poem.) In Estonia there

Figure 3: Dustjacket for the illustrated edition of *Metai*, by Vytautas Jurkūnas (Vilnius: Valstybinė grožinės literatūros leidykla, 1956).

were plans, before World War I, to publish an illustrated edition of the epic poem *Kalevipoeg* [*The Son of Kalevi*], compiled between 1857 and 1861 by the folklorist and poet Friedrich Reinhold Kreutzwald (1803–1882). The Estonian Literary Society also commissioned illustrations from two well-recognized printmakers, Oskar Kallis (1892–1918) and Kristjan Raud (1865–1943), and a representative edition of the epic with Raud's illustrations came out in 1935. In Latvia, an edition of the national epic *Lāčplēsis* [*The Bear-Slayer*] was published in 1936 in a rendition by Emils Melders (1889–1979), with illustrations by Andrejs Pumpurs (1841–1902). Such monumentalizations of national classics during the interwar period not only served to commemorate the literary heritage, but to bolster national identity as well.

To contemporary readers, the representative editions of *Metai* issued during the Soviet (1940) and, later, German (1941) occupations symbolized the nation's resistance to foreign acculturation and were attempts at preserving, intact, the national cultural inheritance for the next generations. The censors of the occupying forces did not see anything dangerous or subversive in the idealized illustrations of peasant life because they believed that the poem and its

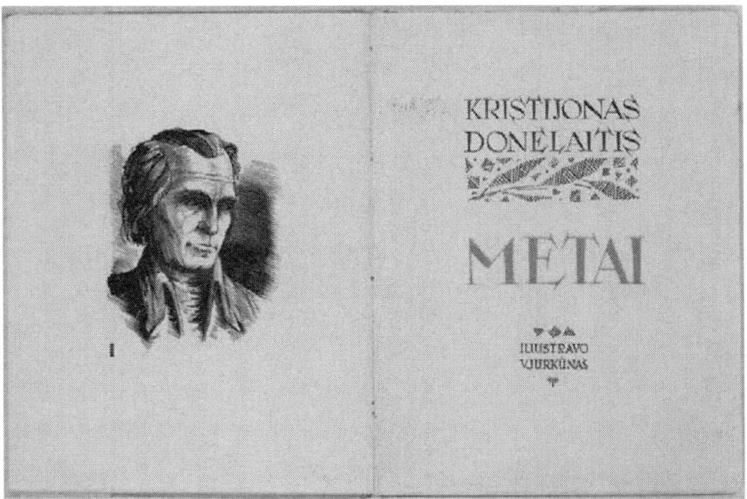

Figure 4: Title-double-page spread designed by Vytautas Jurkūnas for the illustrated edition of *Metai* (Vilnius: Valstybinė grožinės literatūros leidykla, 1956).

illustrations encouraged readers to lose themselves in an idealized past. This attitude was to determine the fate of Jonynas's work after World War II.

Jonynas's realistic — or, rather, neo-classical — stylization of nature and peasant life did not offend the principles of Soviet socialist realism; in fact, Jonynas's work was seen as a successful assimilation of the Lithuanian national heritage into Soviet culture. This explains why his illustrations were used in the Russian translation of the poem by David Brodski (1899–1966), published in Moscow in 1946, in the early days of the post-war Soviet occupation of Lithuania.[7] It is worth noting, however, that Jonynas, who as so many of his compatriots had fled Lithuania at the end of the war and was living in a displaced persons camp in Freiburg im Breisgau, in French-occupied Germany, was not listed as the illustrator in this edition (Донелайтис 1946). The Soviet authorities deemed the artist a traitor and effaced even his initials from the corners of the prints. Jonynas's illustrations were used again, without identification, in the Russian translation

---

[7]   This translation was subsequently revised and improved, and reprinted together with a translation of Donelaitis's fables. Brodski's translation of *Metai* was published in 1951, 1951, 1955, 1960 (this last edition was acclaimed to be the best, and as later re-issued), 1964, 1984, 1990 and 2005.

Figure 5: Chapter head illustration to the first part of *Metai* — "Pavasario linksmybės" ("The Joys of Spring") — by Vytautas Jurkūnas.

published in Vilnius in 1951 (Донелайтис 1951); the edition does list the Soviet Lithuanian printmaker Antanas Kučas (1909–1989) as the cover designer. Jonynas's illustrations became a point of reference, and a model, for all Soviet graphic artists who would illustrate subsequent editions of *Metai*. The popularity of Jonynas's work under the Soviet regime demonstrates, once more, that the neo-traditionalist style favoured by all European states in their attempt to embody the idea of a national identity in visual and decorative art during the 1930s did not differ much from the official art of totalitarian regimes before and after World War II.

The 1956 edition of *Metai*: the establishment of the bibliographic code

A new representative edition of *Metai* was published in Vilnius in 1956 (Donelaitis 1956) (Figures 3 and 4). It was illustrated by Jonynas's contemporary graphic artist Vytautas Jurkūnas (1910–1993). In the 1930s Jurkūnas had made a name for himself with a series of linocuts titled *Žvejai* (*Fishermen*). These prints showed his exceptional talent; they also demonstrated that he had been influenced by the German expressionist artist and printmaker Käthe Kollwitz (1867–1945). This influence was detected by a number of left-wing Lithuanian artists with whose ideas Jurkūnas had been long familiar. This familiarity explains why a social-realist interpretation of Donelaitis's poem, emphasizing the exploitation of peasants and social inequality, appealed to Jurkūnas. Jurkūnas depicted with heartfelt compassion the poverty of the Lithuanian peasantry in the eighteenth century and conveyed the tension between the peasants and the landowners, who despised and physically punished the peasants.

Jurkūnas also relied on Jonynas's interpretation of the poem, employing Jonynas's bibliographic code and following not only his choice of iconographic motifs but also his style,

Figure 6: Chapter head illustration to the third part of *Metai* — "Rudenio gėrybės" ("Autumn Wealth") — by Vytautas Kazimieras Jonynas.

despite the fact that in 1940 Jurkūnas had publicly denounced Jonynas's interpretation of *Metai* in the Soviet Lithuanian press (Jurkūnas 1940). A juxtaposition of the editions' respective head-pieces betrays Jurkūnas's dependence on Jonynas (Figures 5 and 6). Moreover, Jurkūnas's adaptations of the visual canon created by Jonynas reveal the demands of socialist realism. Jurkūnas's illustrations differ from Jonynas's only in their greater emphasis on social criticism with a view to highlighting the class differences between peasants and landowners and revealing the underlying social conflict between the "oppressed" and the "oppressors". Jurkūnas's illustrations poeticize a harmonious nature, but his depictions of human types and characters veer towards caricature (incidentally, not only his landlords, but also his peasants look forbidding) (Figure 7).

The various prizes granted to Jurkūnas by the authorities for his illustrations of *Metai* reveal the significance of the poem, or to be more exact, of its new edition, for Soviet culture: in 1957 the artist

Figure 7: Illustration of *Metai* by Vytautas Jurkūnas.

received the Soviet Lithuanian state award. In 1959 he won silver medal at the Leipzig Book Fair. The award was significant, for it meant that Jurkūnas's visual interpretation of the poem was earning recognition not only in the Soviet Union, but also in other Communist Block countries.

While adhering to Jonynas's original bibliographic codes, Jurkūnas's illustrations nonetheless came to represent the new lens through which to visualize the poem's content. His illustrations were well received and understood by the wider public, and remained so even after the appearance, in 1983, during a time of relative liberalization in Soviet Lithuania, of an edition with Jonynas's original illustrations (Donelaitis 1983). A Russian-language edition published in Vilnius in 1984 also featured Jurkūnas's work (Донелайтис 1984).

Donelaitis's work has received considerable international attention. *Metai* and some of his other works have been translated into twelve languages — English, Armenian, Belarusian, Czech, Georgian, Latvian, Polish, Russian, Swedish, Ukrainian, Hungarian, and German — and excerpts from the poem and other works have been translated into Estonian, Italian, Japanese, Latin, French, Sorbian, Hebrew and Esperanto. In some editions — Polish (1982), Latvian (2006) and Russian (2005, 2011) — the Lithuanian text of the poem was also included. In Soviet Lithuania, discounting the 1940 edition,

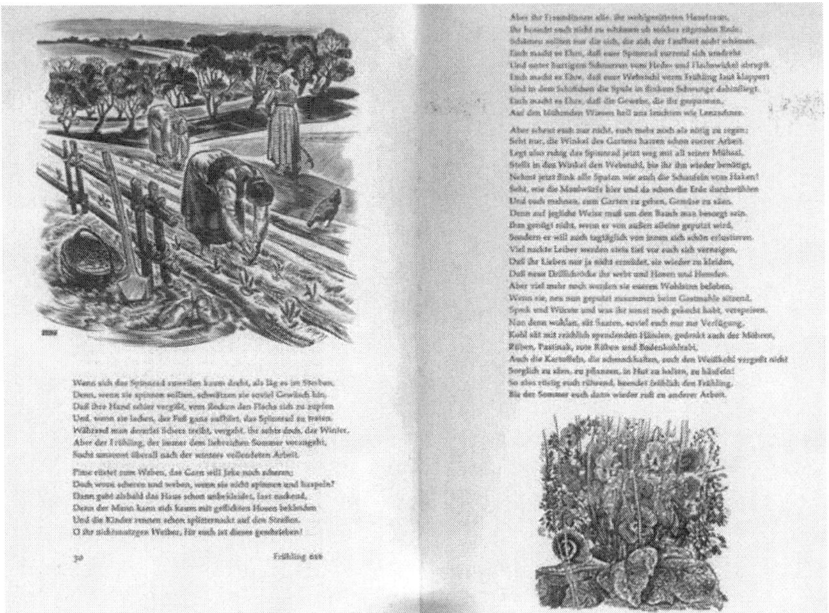

Figure 8: The German edition of *Metai* (*Die Jahreszeiten*, München: Wilhelm Fink Verlag, 1966) combines the illustrations by Vytautas Kazimieras Jonynas with the pictures by Vytautas Jurkūnas; the work of both artists even appears in the same opening.

Metai went through seven editions (1945, 1950, 1956, 1957, 1966, 1977, 1983); in independent Lithuania, there were another seven, in 1994, 2000, 2002, 2004, 2006, 2010, and 2011. Many of these editions appeared with either Jonynas's or Jurkūnas's illustrations. Finally, the publishers of the 1966 German translation (Donelaitis 1966) rejected Jurkūnas's full-page illustrations and replaced them with those by Jonynas, but they kept Jurkūnas's head and tailpieces at the beginning and end of chapters. The book looks stylistically coherent, and the differences between each artist's style are not noticeable at first glance (Figure 8). (Incidentally, this edition disregarded all issues of copyright and artistic rights.) However, the mid-twentieth-century bibliographical code for *Metai* did not spread outside Lithuania. The German edition of 1966 is not an exception to this even though it uses the illustrations of Jonynas and Jurkūnas. The eclectic character of the edition suggests rather that its editors were not sensitive to the Lithuanian bibliographical code in *Metai*. The majority of

Figure 9: Dustjacket for the Hungarian edition of *Metai*, by Gyula Hincz (*Évszakok*, Budapest: Európa könyvkiadó, 1970).

foreign-language editions show that the poem's "message" was variously interpreted by publishers, who adapted it to their respective cultures even when they used Jurkūnas's (or Jonynas's) illustrations. For instance, the Czech edition (designed by Lucia Weisbergova, 1960) presented Jurkūnas's illustrations as a classic of Soviet Lithuanian culture (Donelaitis 1960), but the traditional illustrations were linked to a series of colour squares — a motif typical of the modernist turn to abstract art in the 1960s. Some Russian editions (1955, 1964) featured illustrations by V. Rostovtzev and L. Rostovtzeva that were based on Jonynas's work (Донелайтис 1955; Донелайтис 1964). The Polish version (designed by Barbara Lis-Romańczuk, 1982) used a neutral decorative style (Donelaitis 1982). In Hungary, *Metai* was construed as an expression of carnival culture and illustrated by Gyula Hincz with scenes reminiscent of Picasso's mythological drawings and prints (Donelaitis 1970) (Figure 9). In the Ukraine Bogdan Pikulicki modelled his illustrations on the style of Jonynas and Jurkūnas, the only difference being a preference for decorative imagery over realism (Донелайтіc 1989). The 2006 Latvian edition adapted Jonynas's art to Latvian culture, using an early linocut,

"Piemenėlis" ("The Shepherd Boy", 1932), from Jonynas's Paris period as the cover illustration (Donelaitis 2006). The *art deco* style of the linocut approximates post-cubism — the apex of Latvia's national modernism. The Swedish interpretation (1991) is the most original quite strongly (Donelaitis 1991). The editors used woodcuts from Olaus Magnus's sixteenth century *Historia de Gentibus Septentrional-ibus* (*A Description of the Northern Peoples*, 1555) depicting North Euro-pean peoples, their religions, customs and work, thereby placing

Figure 10: Dustjacket for the Swedish edition of *Metai*, by Susan Dunthorne (*Årstiderna*, Göteborg: Bokförlaget Renässans, 1991).

Donelaitis's poem within that same Nordic tradition (Figure 10). The Swedish reading of *Metai* coincided with the earliest attempts to question the Lithuanian bibliographic code of the poem in Lithu-ania itself.

In the early 1970s scholars started to make out new semantic layers in Donelaitis's poem. They no longer read the poem as a simple depiction of the hardships of peasant life during serfdom but proposed other interpretations. They considered the poem from the viewpoints of Renaissance culture, Baroque literature, literary tradi-tion, and from other angles; they traced the influence of classical lit-erature on the poem as well as its rhetorical strategies and religious aspects. In their research they resorted to various methods, among which were positivism, cultural studies, structuralism, semiotics,

Figure 11: Preparatory drawing by Petras Repšys for the illustrations of *Metai* (1993–2000).

comparativism and anthropology.[8] Although the interpretations of the poem had begun to change, the canon of the bibliographic code — formed by the socio-cultural context of the period of nationalism that flourished in independent Lithuania in the first half of the twentieth century and by the socialist realism that dominated Lithuanian culture in the second half of the twentieth century — have remained virtually unchallenged.

Conclusion: a different interpretation of *Metai* (Petras Repšys)

The first challenge to the hallowed illustrative tradition of *Metai* came from the Lithuanian graphic artist Petras Repšys (b. 1940). He sought to portray Donelaitis's world as a cosmic cycle that constantly

---

[8]   See Venclova 1971; Gineitis 1972, 109–207; Vanagas 1978, 56–83; Žukas 1992; Gineitis and Samulionis 1993; Gineitis 1998; Petkūnas 1998; Vaicekauskas 2001; Dilytė 2005; Petkūnas 2005; Radzevičius 2005.

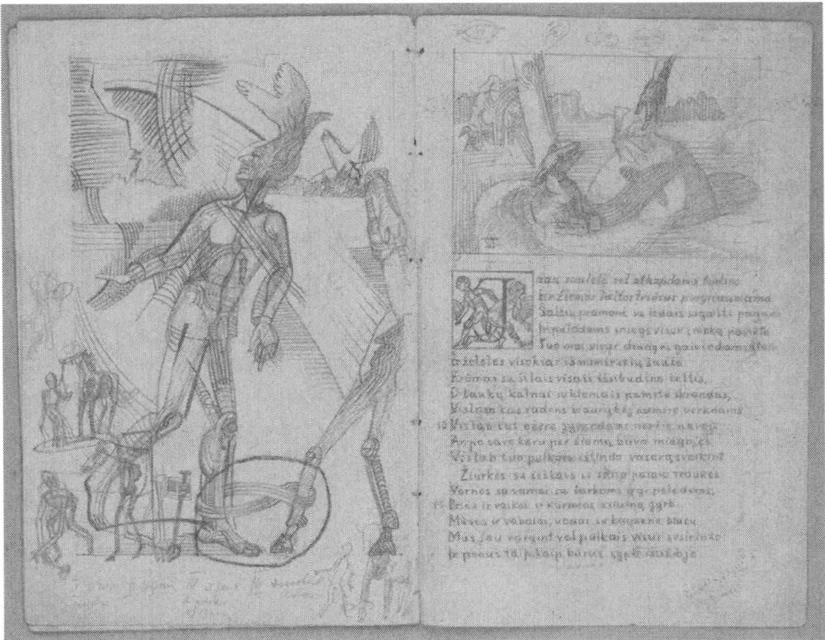

Figure 12: Preparatory drawing by Petras Repšys for the illustrations of *Metai* (1993–2000).

renews itself, a kind of "cosmic symphony". According to Repšys, Donelaitis's poem encompasses all spheres of human life and events. Its central axis being Christian ethics, the poem is conceived as a sermon describing a fragment of God's creation in which concrete details of daily life and the realistic landscape have equal importance. Seeking to break free from the canon of the bibliographical code, established by his predecessors Jonynas and Jurkūnas, Repšys decided to go back to the roots. He visited Tolminkiemis to see the landscape described by Donelaitis, as well as his church and vicarage, which have of course changed since Donelaitis's time. He then put himself in Rėza's shoes and pored over ethnological studies of the daily lives, customs, and religion of peasants in Lithuania Minor. Repšys's scrupulous attention to detail did not distract him from his main goal — to convey the idea that the plot of the poem does not revolve around concrete *realia*, but that it unfolds itself on an altogether different level. The universal ideas about the order of the world that are expressed in *Metai* were very important to Repšys (Repšys 1993, 233, 248–250) (Figures 11 and 12).

Repšys began his illustrations in the late 1980s, but to this day he is still searching for the most suitable way to render his interpretation of Donelaitis's poem. Such a long and painful search for adequate expression is typical of Repšys's creative method, but it also shows how difficult it is to break free from the powerful influence of the canon established by Jonynas and Jurkūnas and from bibliographical codes generally.

This new reading of Donelaitis remains the privilege of only a small circle of specialists. A large portion of Lithuanian readers still read *Metai* as documentary source that evinces the ethnography, anthropology and nature of Lithuania Minor in the late eighteenth century. This tendency shows that the country's rural origins, an ideology that survived the interwar time and Soviet occupation, remain of crucial importance to modern Lithuanian culture. Despite artistic attempts to change the bibliographical code of *Metai*, popular conceptions of national identity prevented its adaptation for a contemporary society. This difficulty is not only limited to Lithuania, but pertains to the modernization of national classics in many other post-Soviet countries as well. It is a problem that might be connected with new attempts to express national identity in a postcolonial phase.

Bibliography

Ambrazevičius, Juozas. 1941. "Būrų kultūros poetas". In Kristijonas Donelaitis, *Metai*. Ed. Juozas Ambrazevičius, illus. Vytautas Kazimieras Jonynas. Kaunas: Valstybinės leidyklos leidinys Nr. 25, spaudė akcinės "Spindulio" bendrovės spaustuvė Kaune, pp. 186–197.

Andriušytė-Žukienė, Rasa. 2007. *Akistatos: Dailininkas Vytautas Kazimieras Jonynas pasaulio meno keliuose.* Vilnius: Lietuvos dailės muziejus.

Dilytė, Dalia. 2005. *Kristijonas Donelaitis ir Antika.* Vilnius: Vilniaus universiteto leidykla.

[Donelaitis, Kristijonas. 1818.] *Das Jahr in vier Gesaengen, ein laendlisches Epos aus dem Litthauischen des Christian Donaleitis, genannt Donalitius. In gleichem Versmass ins Deutsche uebertragen von Dr. L. J. Rehsa, Prof. d. Theol.* Königsberg: gedruckt in der Koenigl. Hartungschen Hofbuchdrukkerei.

[———. 1865.] *Christian Donaleitis Litauische Dichtungen.* Erste vollstän-
dige Ausgabe mit Glossar von Aug. Schleicher. St. Petersburg:
Commissionäre der Kaiserlichen akademie der Wissenschaften,
in St. Petersburg Eggers u. Comp., in Riga N. Kymmel, in Leipzig
Leopold Voss.

[———. 1869.] *Christian Donalitius Littauische Dichtungen.* Nach den
Königsberger Handschriften mit metrischer Uebersetzung,
kritischen Anmerkungen und genauem Glossar herausgegeben
von G. H. F. Nesselmann. Königsberg: Verlag von Hübner & Matz.

[———. 1897.] *Kristijono Donelaiczio Rasztai.* Eds. Aleksandras Burba
and Antanas M. Milukas. Shenandoah, Pa.: Spaustuvėje "Garso
Amerikos Lietuvių".

[———. 1914.] *Kristijono Duonelaičio raštai: 1714–1914. 200 metų
sukaktuvėms nuo autoriaus gimimo paminėti.* Ed. Jurgis Šlapelis.
Vilnius: M. Piaseckaitės-Šlapelienės knygyno leidinys, M. Kuktos
sapaustuvė.

[———. 1918.] *Duonelaičio raštai.* Ed. Mykolas Biržiška. Part 1: *Ištraukos
ir priedai.* Vilnius: Martyno Kuktos spaustuvė, Lietuvių mokslo
draugijos leidinys.

[———. 1921.] *Duonelaičio raštai.* Ed. Mykolas Biržiška. Part 1: *Ištraukos
ir priedai.* Kaunas–Vilnius, Liet. Mokslo D-jos Komisijonieris
„Švyturio" B-vė, Lietuvių Mokslo Draugijos leidinys.

[———. 1927.] M. Biržiškos, *Duonelaičio gyvenimas ir raštai.* Su kalbos
paaiškinimais, 3rd edition. Ed. Mykolas Biržiška. Kaunas: „Vairo"
Bendrovės leidinys.

Donelaitis, Kristijonas. 1940. *Metai.* Ed. Juozas Ambrazevičius, illus.
Vytautas Kazimieras Jonynas. Kaunas: Švietimo Ministerijos
Knygų leidimo komisijos leidinys Nr. 524, spaudė akcinės "Spin-
dulio" bendrovės spaustuvė Kaune.

———. 1941. *Metai.* Ed. Juozas Ambrazevičius, illus. Vytautas Kazimieras Jonynas. Kaunas: Valstybinės leidyklos leidinys Nr. 25, spaudė
akcinės "Spindulio" bendrovės spaustuvė Kaune.

———. 1956. *Metai.* Ed. Aleksandras Žirgulys, illus. by Vytautas
Jurkūnas. Vilnius: Valstybinė grožinės literatūros leidykla.

———. 1960. *Roční doby.* Trans. Hana Jechová, illus. Vytautas Jurkūnas,
design by Lucie Weisbergová. Praha: Svět sovětů.

———. 1966. *Die Jahreszeiten.* Nachdichtung von Hermann Budden-
sieg, illustriert von Vytautas Kazys Jonynas, Vytautas Jurkūnas.
München: Wilhelm Fink Verlag.

———. 1970. *Évszakok*. Trans. Tandori Dezső, illus. Hincz Gyula. Budapest: Európa könyvkiadó.

———. 1982. *Metai* = Krystyn Donelajtis, *Pory roku*. Trans. Zygmunt Ławrynowicz, design by Barbara Lis-Romańczuk. Olsztyn–Białystok: Pojezierze.

———. 1983. *Metai*. Ed. Kazys Ulvydas, illus. Vytautas Kazimieras Jonynas. Vilnius: Vaga.

———. 1991. *Årstiderna*. Trans. Lennart Kjellberg, design by Susan Dunthorne, illustrations from Olaus Magnus' *Historia de Gentibus Septentrionalibus*. Göteborg: Bokförlaget Renässans.

———. 2006. *Gadalaiki* = *Metai*. Trans. Paulis Kalva, ed. Alberts Sarkanis, illus. Vytautas Kazimieras Jonynas. Rīga: Madris.

Doveika, Kostas, ed. 1990. *Kristijonas Donelaitis literatūros moksle ir kritikoje*. Rašytojai literatūros moksle ir kritikoje 10. Vilnius: Vaga.

Gineitis, Leonas. 1972. *Klasicizmo problema lietuvių literatūroje*. Vilnius: Lietuvos TSR Mokslų akademija, Lietuvių kalbos ir literatūros institutas.

———. 1990. *Kristijonas Donelaitis ir jo epocha*. 2nd ed. Vilnius: Vaga, Lietuvos TSR Mokslų akademija, Lietuvių kalbos ir literatūros institutas.

———. 1998. *Kristijono Donelaičio aplinka*. Senoji Lietuvos literatūra 9. Vilnius: Lietuvių literatūros ir tautosakos institutas.

Gineitis, Leonas and Algis Samulionis, eds. 1993. *Darbai apie Kristijoną Donelaitį*. Vilnius: Vaga, Lietuvos Mokslų akademija, Lietuvių literatūros ir tautosakos institutas.

Girdenis, Aleksas. 1993. "'Metų' hegzametras." Leonas Gineitis and Algis Samulionis (eds.), *Darbai apie Kristijoną Donelaitį*. Vilnius: Vaga, Lietuvos Mokslų akademija, Lietuvių literatūros ir tautosakos institutas, pp. 60–96.

Gudaitis, Leonas, ed. 1995. *Tadas Lomsargis: Biografija, kūriniai, dokumentai, laiškai, užrašai*. Vilnius: Mokslo ir enciklopedijų leidykla.

Jankevičiūtė, Giedrė. 2008. *Lietuvos grafika / The Graphic Arts in Lithuania: 1918–1940*. Vilnius: E. Karpavičiaus leidykla.

Jurkūnas, Vytautas. 1940. "K. Donelaičio "Metų" iliustracijos". *Tiesa*, 11 December 1940.

Krištopaitienė, Daiva. 2005. "Juozas Ambrazevičius — Donelaičio "Metų" rengėjas". In Ramutis Karmalavičius (ed.), *Juozas Brazaitis-Ambrazevičius — literatūrologas*. Colloquia 12. Vilnius: Lietuvių literatūros ir tautosakos institutas, pp. 101–108.

——. 2007. *Kristijono Donelaičio raštų leidimai: tekstologinės problemos.* Lietuvių tekstologijos studijos I. Vilnius: Lietuvių literatūros ir tautosakos institutas.

Lebedys, Jurgis. 1977. *Senoji lietuvių literatūra.* Edited by Juozas Girdzijauskas. Vilnius: Mokslas.

Petkūnas, Darius, 1998. "Poema 'Metai' — pamokslų rinkinys?" *Tiltai*, 2–3, pp. 127–34.

——. 2005. "*Kunigo Kristijono Donelaičio ganytojiška veikla, teologiniai motyvai 'Metuose' ir kituose raštuose.*" In Roma Bončkutė (ed.), *Biblija ir literatūra. Tiltai.* Priedas: Mokslo darbai 27. Klaipėda: Klaipėdos universitetas, Humanitarinių mokslų fakultetas, pp. 61–88.

Radzevičius, Algimantas, 2005. *Klasiko kūrybos slėpiniai: Donelaitis ir Renesansas.* Kaunas: Vilniaus universitetas, Kauno humanitarinis fakultetas.

Repšys, Petras, 1993. "K. Donelaitis dailininko akimis". In Leonas Gineitis and Algis Samulionis (eds.), *Darbai apie Kristijoną Donelaitį.* Vilnius: Vaga, Lietuvos mokslų akademija, Lietuvių literatūros ir tautosakos institutas, pp. 233–55.

Skrupskelytė, Viktorija, 2005. "Juozo Brazaičio-Ambrazevičiaus literatūros kritika nūdienos žvilgsniu". In Ramutis Karmalavičius (ed.), *Juozas Brazaitis-Ambrazevičius — literatūrologas.* Colloquia 12. Vilnius: Lietuvių literatūros ir tautosakos institutas, pp. 124–37.

Urbšienė, Marija, 1930. "Bibliofilai". *Gaisai*, 5, pp. 82–87.

Vaicekauskas, Mikas, ed. 2001. *Egzodo Donelaitis: Lietuvių išeivių tekstai apie Kristijoną Donelaitį.* Vilnius: Aidai.

——. 2009. "Donelaitis, Kristijonas". In *300 Baltic Writers: Estonia, Latvia, Lithuania: A Reference Guide to Authors and Their Works.* Vilnius: Institute of Lithuanian Literature and Folklore, Institute of Literature, Folklore and Art, University of Latvia, Under and Tuglas Literature Centre of the Estonian Academy of Sciences, pp. 71–73.

Vanagas, Vytautas. 1978. *Realizmas lietuvių literatūroje.* Vilnius: Vaga, Lietuvos TSR Mokslų akademija, Lietuvių kalbos ir literatūros institutas.

Vaškelis, Aleksas. 1964. "The Life and Age of Kristijonas Donelaitis". *Lituanus*, 10(1), pp. 8–33.

Venclova, Tomas. 1971. "Erdvė ir laikas Kristijono Donelaičio 'Metuose'" In *Poezijos pavasaris.* Vilnius: Vaga, pp. 212–18.

Žukas, Saulius. 1992. "Donelaičio 'Metų' rišlumo klausimu". *Baltos lankos*, 2, pp. 149–63.

Донелайтіс, Крістійонас. 1989. *Літа*. Trans. Dmitro Cherednichenko, illus. Bohdan Pikulitzkij. Київ: Видавництво художньої літератури "Дніпро".

Донелайтис, Кристионас. 1946. *Времена года*. Trans. David Brodskij, design by I. G. Nikolaevtzev. Москва: Огиз, Государственное издательство художественной литературы.

——. 1951. *Сочинения*. Trans. David Brodskij, design by Antanas Kučas. Вильнюс: Государственное издательство художественной литературы Литовской ССР.

——. 1955. *Времена года*. Trans. David Brodskij, illus. V. Rostovtzev and L. Rostovtzeva. Москва: Государственное издательство художественной литературы.

——. 1964. *Времена года*. Trans. David Brodskij, illus. V. Rostovtzev and L. Rostovtzeva. Москва: Художественная литература.

——. 1984. *Времена года*. Trans. David Brodskij, illus. Vytautas Jurkūnas. Вильнюс: Вага.

Are Broadside Ballads Worth Editing?

David Atkinson

IT IS BECOMING increasingly accepted that there is a continuity between the folk songs and ballads collected from singers by the likes of Cecil Sharp in the early years of the twentieth century and copies of the same ballads issued from the broadside press, sometimes over a period of several centuries. Since multiformity or variation is considered an essential and even defining characteristic of "folk" ballads, it has become of interest to analyse the same phenomenon in relation to broadside ballads. The presence of variation then more or less inevitably invites an approach that involves some kind of editing.[1] This article is intended to address some of the issues involved in editing broadsides, and to make the claim that, despite their appearance of ephemerality, these printed ballads are indeed worthy of the attention of the scholarly editor.

The term "broadside" is used to describe a single sheet of paper printed on one side.[2] Broadsides, with texts in verse or prose, started to appear not long after the beginning of printing in England and other parts of Europe, their subject matter ranging widely and including popular fiction, politics and religion, news, topical crimes and scandals, criminals' confessions, domestic and sexual matters, parodies and libels, and so forth. The broadside format was a popular one for printed songs from the sixteenth century onwards, and quite early on narrative songs of this kind came to be known as "ballets" or "ballads". Broadside ballads were still being printed and sold in Britain as late as the early twentieth century.

The earlier broadsides were printed mostly in the old gothic "black-letter" typeface, which was gradually replaced by roman "white-letter" type towards the end of the seventeenth century. They were regularly illustrated with (often quite crude) woodcut images, frequently bearing only a remote connection with the ballad narrative

---

[1]   Some issues in ballad editing at large are addressed in Atkinson (2007).

[2]   Broadside ballads and related literature are described by Collison (1973), Neuburg (1977), Rollins (1919), Shepard (1962; 1973). A good short account is in Simpson and Roud (2000, 34–35).

itself. Although they rarely include music notation, earlier examples often carry an indication such as "To the tune of . . .".[3] This habit died out during the eighteenth century, and it is generally assumed that the tunes for ballads would in any case have been mostly learned by ear. Later broadside sheets often include two songs and could be cut in half to make two so-called slip songs. Other, larger sheets include multiple songs in very small print. Ballads generally sold for a halfpenny or a penny, or the equivalent, and by the eighteenth century broadside production had become increasingly associated with the lower end of the print trade, even while they continued to sell in large numbers. Particularly during the eighteenth and early nineteenth centuries, ballads were also printed in chapbooks, which were small booklets, most commonly of eight to twenty-four pages, often sold by itinerant pedlars or chapmen (the name from which the term chapbook is derived by a back-formation). At this period, chapbooks provided an extremely common format for a very wide range of popular, relatively unsophisticated literature.

It is not unusual to find the same ballad appearing on different broadsides issued by different printers, sometimes over a long period of time. On occasion, different editions can be found issued by the same printer.[4] Databases such as the English Short Title Catalogue (ESTC) and the Roud Broadside and Folksong Indexes are of great assistance in facilitating the identification of the various instances of a ballad. Such things as the imprint (where there is one), the typographical appearance of the sheet, and the accompanying images and decoration, permit each copy to be described and associated with any other extant exemplars of the same printing. Given the current state of knowledge of this area of the print trade, ascribing a date to a broadside can be a very approximate exercise and it is

---

[3]   Simpson (1966) is the prime source for these melodies.

[4]   It is generally thought that type would habitually be distributed following an impression; any subsequent reprinting would require a new setting of type and would therefore qualify as a new edition (there may be exceptions to this general rule in the era of stereotyping). However, printings sometimes differ from one another only in typographical minutiae, often appearing identical when first inspected, so that — at least from a literary historical, as opposed to a strictly bibliographical, perspective — it seems extravagant to describe them as separate editions. Some students of the subject would prefer to describe such instances as separate issues. In the broadside context, there is an argument for speaking simply of different printings.

often possible only to suggest a date range. All this is mostly a matter of descriptive bibliography.

To move further into the field of textual scholarship, although it is widely assumed that different broadside printers would essentially copy from one another, quite possibly sequentially over a long period of time, it is also known that textual variants can and do arise between different printings of the same ballad.[5] This phenomenon, however, has attracted rather little scholarly attention — notwithstanding its very obvious importance for anyone wishing to employ a stemmatic approach to understanding the printing history of such items.[6] Otherwise, it may be that ballad scholars have tended to think of such variants as really no more than typographical errors, without cultural significance, and no more than what would be expected in the context of a largely ephemeral literature — variance effectively ascribed to carelessness. The early folk song collectors tended, on the whole, to regard print of the broadside kind as a corrupting influence on an oral folk song tradition (Baring Gould and Fleetwood Sheppard 1892, viii; Sharp 1907, 101–02). Francis James Child, editor of the standard English-language ballad edition, *The English and Scottish Popular Ballads* (1882–98), held an ambivalent attitude towards broadside ballads, even while they provided some of his oldest examples of the genre (Brown 2010). Yet it is fair to say that the circulation of song texts in broadside and chapbook print was a crucial element in the English-language ballad tradition.

When broadsides are understood as an essential part of the ballad corpus, then they become assimilated to what is widely thought of as the defining characteristic of so-called "folk" or "traditional" art forms: that is, multiformity or variation. This is a key component, for example, of Cecil Sharp's quasi-Darwinian triad of *continuity, variation,* and *selection,* which defined the principles of folk song transmission (Sharp 1907, 16–31). It has, however, been widely assumed that variation is necessarily a consequence of non-written transmission. Laws, for example, in *American Balladry from British Broadsides,*

---

[5] Whether genuine textual variants, other than the mere consequences of mechanical accident, can be identified among different exemplars of the same impression is much less certain.

[6] In the contiguous field of traditional drama research, the work of Smith (2008), studying variation among folk play texts printed in eighteenth-century chapbooks, is worthy of note.

distinguishes ballads that have circulated orally from ballads learned from print on the basis of textual variation present in the former (Laws 1957, 94–100). Therefore, when variation is encountered, even in printed ballads, it must be "oral variation". Laws does not quite go on to say that when variation is absent from ballads that have circulated orally then actually they must somehow be "printed", but the circularity of his reasoning comes pretty close to it.

In fact, variation among printed copies of ballads can be very much the same as among copies collected from singing. Dianne Dugaw observes of two different printings of the female-warrior ballad "Mary Ambree": "Throughout, minor differences in wording and phrasing can be found from one text to the next. At points, stanzas are ordered differently, and a few stanzas are unique to each version. Names and numbers differ, as do details of description and dialogue" (Dugaw 1984, 90). The copies in question are a London broadside of *c.* 1640, and one printed in *The Vocal Magazine*, a miscellany of 1778. It is perhaps unlikely that the late eighteenth-century text was copied directly from the early seventeenth-century broadside, although there are intervening broadside copies that would repay investigation. One question that suggests itself here is whether such instances of printed variation in what is recognizably the same song are primarily a simple product of chronology — that is to say, the longer the time span, the more the anticipated variance. Dugaw went on to compare four texts of another ballad, "The Maid in Sorrow" (Roud 231),[7] including two broadsides from the mid-nineteenth century, one from London and one from Glasgow, and two copies collected from singing in the twentieth century, and drew the conclusion: "all four versions, printed as well as oral, vary the ballad in similar ways" (Dugaw 1984, 102).

For practical purposes, Dugaw necessarily chose examples that could not reasonably be said to be anything other than demonstrably different from one another. Even so, it is immensely difficult when describing the observed differences to avoid falling back on a rather imprecise terminology: "range of continuity and variation", "the same kinds of variations", "minor differences in wording and phrasing", "slight variation in wording", "varies somewhat", and so forth.

---

[7]   Roud numbers provide an identifier for all the exemplars of a particular ballad listed in the Roud Broadside Index and Roud Folksong Index, regardless of variant titles.

In a recent attempt to describe such variation rather more systematically, I examined texts of a number of different broadside copies of
ballads, both across a chronological span of a couple of centuries and
within a narrower chronological range.[8] The following paragraphs
sketch in the various kinds of narrative and verbal variants encountered among four different broadside copies of "The Golden Vanity"
(Child 286),[9] ranging from the end of the seventeenth century to the
end of the nineteenth century, and representing both English and
Scottish provenance. The copies in question are *Sir Walter Raleigh
Sailing in the Low-lands* (printed by Conyers), *Golden Vanity* (printed
by Pitts); *The Golden Vanity* (printed by Such); *Lowlands Low* (printed
by the Dundee Poet's Box).[10] It is not altogether practical to print all
the texts side by side — and the principles are more important here
than the details — but the text of the Such broadside, printed in
London, is given below as a point of reference for the comparative
remarks that follow.

> I have a ship in the North Country,
> And she goes by the name of the Golden Vanity,
> I am afraid she will be taken by some Spanish Galleon,
> As she sails in the Low Lands Low.
>
> Then up starts our little Cabin boy,
> Saying, Master what will you give me, if I do them destroy,
> I'll give you gold and you shall have my daughter also,
> If you sink them in the Low Lands Low.
>
> Undaunted and bold away he jumpt in,
> The boy bent his breast, & most gallant did swim,
> He swam till he came to this Spanish Galleon,
> As she laid on the Low Lands Low.
>
> The boy he had an auger, to bore holes two at once,

---

[8]   The fact that these are all seafaring ballads was determined by other
constraints and, while ensuring a degree of comparison of like with like, is
unlikely to have any bearing on the textual principles under discussion.

[9]   Child numbers provide an identifier for all the exemplars of a particular
ballad in Child (1882–98) and are also searchable in the Roud Broadside Index
and Roud Folksong Index.

[10]   In view of the imprecision over dating, and sometimes the close simi-
larity of titles, the broadsides discussed in this article are most conveniently
identified by reference to their printers throughout.

> While some were playing cards, and some were playing dice,
> He let in the water & it dazzled in their eyes,
> And he sunk them in the Low Lands Low.
>
> The boy he bent his breast and away he swam,
> Saying, Master take me up or I shall be slain,
> For I have effected their total overthrow,
> And have sunk them in the Low Lands Low.
>
> I'll not take you up, the Master he cried,
> I'll not take you up, the Master replied, –
> I will kill you, I will shoot you, I will send you with the tide,
> I will sink you in the Low Lands Low.
>
> The boy he swam, all by the starboard side,
> Until his strength it failed him, then bitteryl [*sic*] he cried,
> Saying, Messmates take me up, for I surely shall be slain,
> For I have sunk them in the Low Lands Low.
>
> His Messmates took him up, but on the deck he died,
> O then they sewed him up, in an old cow's hide,
> And they threw him overboard, to go with the tide,
> And they sunk him in the Low Lands Low.

Finally, it should be noted that these are by no means all the known broadside printings of this particular ballad, which was widely printed in the nineteenth century.

Narrative variation

A first order level of narrative variation has a direct impact on action and outcome (i.e., plot), motivation and characterization, narrative technique and point of view.

The account in the nineteenth-century ballads displays both compression and expansion in comparison with the seventeenth-century ballad. Narrative technique is distinctly tighter than in the Conyers broadside. Sir Walter Raleigh's appeal for a seaman bold, for example, and the enemy sailors' attempt to save the "false Gallaly", which effects a shift in point of view, are absent from the nineteenth-century broadsides:

> Is there never a Seaman bold
> in the Neather-lands:

> Is there never a Seamen [*sic*] bold
>   in the Neather-lands?
> That will go take this false Gallaly,
> And to redeem the sweet Trinity,
>   sailing in the Low-lands.
> (Conyers, stanza 2)

> Some cut their hats, and some cut their caps
>   in the Neather-lands;
> Some cut their hats, and some cut their caps
>   in the Neather-lands,
> For to stop the salt-water gaps,
>   sailing in the Low-lands.
> (Conyers, stanza 8)

On the other hand, the ending is expanded in the nineteenth-century copies with the cabin boy's appeal to his messmates, their bringing him on board ship, and his death and burial at sea. In the Conyers broadside, on the other hand, it is largely just implied that he is simply left to drown. Then a concluding stanza modulates out of the narrative framework, inviting a further point of view, in this case that of the presenter and of the seafaring community at large:

> And thus I shall conclude my Song
>   of the sailing in the Low-lands,
> And, thus I shall conclude my Song
>   of the sailing in the Low-lands;
> Wishing all happiness to all Seamen both
>   old & young in their sailing in the Low-lands.
> (Conyers, stanza 14)

This valedictory technique is not unusual among early modern broadside ballads.

A second order of narrative variation involves devices that affect the tone and the broader connotations of the story, but the presence or absence of which cannot really be said to impact on its course and outcome, rationale, point of view, or technique.

The Conyers broadside identifies the historical character of Sir Walter Raleigh, with all that that might imply — though it should be noted that there is no historical basis for the story — who emerges later on as a "cozening Lord" (Conyers, stanza 13). This is all absent from the later broadsides. Other examples include the cabin boy's reminding his captain of his promise — "Your eldest daughter my wife she must be" — and the latter's refusing to honour it — "my eldest daughter your wife shall never be" (Conyers, stanzas 11–12). In the later broadsides, in contrast, the captain makes an explicit threat: "I will kill you, I will shoot you, I will send you with the tide".

These are all devices that contribute to the particular feel of the story as it is told, but they can also be thought of as slotting in with a pre-existing narrative framework.

Lexical variation

A first order of lexical variation involves substitutions of smaller verbal units that carry semantic weight, affecting the tone of the story or providing extra-narrative connotations, but without impacting the narrative content.

Names and other sorts of descriptors provide good examples: "Neather-lands" versus "North Country"; "sweet Trinity" (Conyers) versus "Golden Vanity";[11] "false Gallaly" (Conyers), "Turkish Galieor" (Pitts),[12] "Spanish Galleon" (Such; Dundee Poet's Box); an auger that can bore fifteen (Conyers) or just two (Pitts; Such; Dundee Poet's Box) holes at once.

A second order of lexical variation comprises substitutions that carry lesser semantic weight, or even none at all, and which are accordingly more closely tied to the comparative methodology.

Examples include "Ship-boy" (Conyers) versus "Cabin boy" (Such); "flash'd in their eyes" (Conyers) versus "dazzled in their eyes" (Such); and "He set his breast, and away he did swim" (Conyers), "The boy bent his breast and away he jumpt in" (Pitts), "The boy bent his breast, & most gallant did swim" (Such), "The boy bent his brest [*sic*] and most gallantly did swim" (Dundee Poet's Box). Variants of this kind can at least arguably be considered semantically neutral, and they are in some degree comparable with the verbal substitutions that occur within more established ballad formulas

---

[11]   But is the ship's name really the *Sweet Trinity*, as Child evidently thought and the use of italics in the Conyers broadside title might indicate, or is it actually just the *Trinity* with the epithet *sweet* attached to it, as the lower-case "s" of the broadside might suggest? The vessel is, of course, fictitious.

[12]   *Galieor* does not appear to be the product of broken type, but the Madden item is the only identified exemplar of the Pitts imprint.

or "commonplaces" (Andersen 1985). Indeed, the phrase "bent his breast" approaches quite closely the condition of the ballad commonplace.

Typographical variation

A third kind of variation that merits classification in the context of the printed ballad is typographical. Just as the sound (timbre, cadence, intonation, accent, etc.) of the ballad when it is sung impacts upon its reception, so does the visual appearance of the printed broadside.

First order variants would certainly include words printed in their Scots as opposed to English forms, which signify culturally, and quite often semantically too.

Because the Dundee Poet's Box broadside is somewhat carelessly printed, it is difficult to be certain to what extent the orthography is deliberate. "Undanted", "brest", "strenth", and "distroy", for example, are attested, if archaic, Scots forms. On the other hand, the equivalent words appear as "Undaunted", "breast", "strength", and "destroy" in a more carefully printed copy of *Lowlands Low* issued by the Glasgow Poet's Box.

Here we need to consider, too, if not necessarily to describe, such matters as typeface, *mise-en-page*, decoration and graphics, paper quality, and so forth. These are all variant characteristics that distinguish different printings and help place them in relation to other cultural markers that coincide in time and place, and in that sense they have semantic significance. For instance, black-letter type, used for the Conyers broadside, signals both a kind of material and a kind of anticipated audience, perhaps most conveniently described by the adjective "popular" (Mish 1953; St Clair 2004, 341). At a later date, the same sort of idea is conveyed by the "Price One Penny" printed at the top of the Dundee Poet's Box and Glasgow Poet's Box broadsides.

Second order typographical variants are those markers that, unlike Scots orthography or a particular style of typography, do not have deliberate semantic significance but that nonetheless help distinguish one printing from another.

These include evident typographical errors, such as "bitteryl" (Such) and "bitterl" (Dundee Poet's Box), and several more in the Dundee Poet's Box broadside. The two Poet's Box ballads are not simply interchangeable; and, however similar their verbal texts, neither is simply an interchangeable copy of the Such ballad.

A third order of typographical variation is perhaps distinguishable, describing the distinguishing marks of specific exemplars of the same imprint.

Examples could include damaged type in the final stanza of the Bodleian copy of the Such broadside, and a worn or broken "e" in "false" in the Pepys copy of the Conyers broadside (stanza 10, line 5) — although it is difficult to be certain of this without examining every extant exemplar. Just as the same ballad sung by two different singers would remain different and singular even in the hypothetical situation that the sequences of words and musical pitches were identical, individual broadside copies, too, have their own feel and occupy their own unique space at any moment in time.

A classification along the lines of these three kinds of variation — narrative, lexical, and typographic — and their subdivisions is, it is to be hoped, more or less intuitive, even if their boundaries are both permeable and debatable. To reiterate, the abstract possibility of a system of measurement that can be applied with some degree of consistency, at least by an individual observer, is much more important than whether or not the specific descriptions offered above command universal assent.

A key point is that these categorizations say nothing about agency. It is perhaps a reasonable assumption that in the nineteenth century the Poet's Box broadsides should have been copied from something along the lines of the Such broadside. But then one might expect the Such ballad to have been copied from something along the lines of the Pitts ballad — they were both London printers after all, one chronologically following the other — but this does not look to have been the case, at least not in an entirely straightforward manner. In practice, virtually any combination of copying from print, intervention from extraneous knowledge, and/or deliberate recomposition could underlie any specific variant reading. By intervention from extraneous knowledge, I mean not just such things as improvements to spelling, grammar, and syntax, but also the possible influence of the individual setting the type already knowing the ballad. Were broadside printers interested in ballads as songs? Did they already know the texts? Might they have "sub-vocalized" as they set up a ballad in print, in the manner posited for the scribes of early medieval manuscript poetry (Chaytor 1945, 10–21), thus bringing the influence of how they might have thought the ballad ought to go to bear on the printed artefact. In the medieval instance, this scenario is sometimes posited as an oral influence on writing, but the terminology seems to perpetuate a dichotomy that might not have been real at all. I am not aware that we know the answers to any of these questions. Neither do any of these options allow for variant readings due simply to accident, carelessness, inattention, extraneous mechanical factors, and what we might call a generally permissive stance towards the copy-text.

A rather more cursory look at some other nineteenth-century English ballads serves to confirm the phenomenon of printed variation. Two of these, "Caroline and her Young Sailor Bold" (Roud 553) and "The Bold Princess Royal" (Roud 528), are among the most popular of English seafaring ballads, judging by the numbers of times they have been collected from singers. "Caroline and her Young Sailor Bold" turns on the common motif of the woman who dresses as a sailor to follow her true love, and is particularly well represented on broadsides, including imprints from Scotland and Ireland. Printed copies run to fifty-six lines and a casual glance through a selection of them discloses perhaps as many as a dozen and a half variant readings. Most would be classified in the schema set out above as no more than second order lexical variants. One that is of possible semantic significance is the sum of money specified in the final stanza: "two hundred thousand in gold" (the more usual figure) versus "[—]ty-five thousand in gold" (a defective copy printed by Birmingham of Dublin). But in any case, perhaps all that it conveys is the sense of a very large sum, regardless of the actual figure.

"The Bold Princess Royal" runs to thirty-two lines in print, and a selection of broadsides reveals perhaps no more than half a dozen variant readings. Nevertheless, at least a couple of them probably classify as first order lexical variants. One is the date cited in the text. Although usually given as the fourteenth of February, other dates are not uncommon among copies collected from singers, and at least one broadside (printed by Pitts) has the sixth of January.[13] Variant forms of the concluding line might also be thought to affect the tone of the story: an immediate sense of relief, "For you have escaped the

---

[13]   There is no known significance for these specific dates, Valentine's Day versus Old Christmas Day.

pirates, my boys, never fear", versus the more long-term optimism of "For while we have sea room, my boys, never fear". One further variant that is perhaps worthy of remark is the rendering in some copies of the line "Our captain being aft, boys, he answered them so" as "Our captain being half, boys, he answered them so". This sounds like a mishearing, and one that an alert compositor might be expected to have corrected, though quite what we should make of that observation remains unclear.

A final instance relates to the fate of HMS *Ramillies*, a ship of the line launched as HMS *Royal Katherine* in 1664 and renamed in honour of the Duke of Marlborough's famous victory at Ramillies in 1706, which was wrecked in a storm on the Devon coast on 14 or 15 February 1760.[14] Details vary slightly in different accounts, but the sinking was a national disaster and out of a crew of more than seven hundred, only just over twenty were saved. At least four different ballads on the fate of the *Ramillies* are known, of which one has remained current among singers into the twentieth century, and it is generally assumed that a *Ramillies* ballad of some kind first came into being fairly close to the time of the catastrophe (Williams 1923, 144).

(*i*) "The Loss of the Ramilies" (Roud 523), collected from singers in the twentieth century and sung to a memorable tune; not known to have been printed on broadsides.

(*ii*) "The Fatal Ramilies" (Roud 1266), well represented in print but collected from oral circulation on no more than a couple of occasions.

(*iii*) "On the Loss of the Ramilies", a broadside ballad of a rather lacklustre literary turn, beginning "Oh the sad and dismal story", not known from oral circulation at all and possibly only printed once.

(*iv*) "The New Ramilies", beginning "You pretty maids where'er you be", printed in Scotland and Ireland.

It is the second of these, "The Fatal Ramilies" (Roud 1266), that is of particular interest here. It has been recovered from oral circulation on two occasions: (*i*) collected by Cecil Sharp from Charles Ash, Crowcombe, Somerset, 16 September 1908 (Sharp MSS, Folk Tunes 1904; Folk Words 1755–1756); (*ii*) collected by Alfred Williams from Mary Sessions, East Hendred, Berkshire, *c.* 1916 (Alfred Williams MS Collection, Bk 9; Williams 1923, 144). A further copy, of uncertain

---

[14] Both the battle site and the ship are correctly spelled *Ramillies*. The broadside spelling is variable but tends towards a single "l".

provenance, is found in a volume of items from the Isle of Wight (Long 1886, 142–43).[15]

"The Fatal Ramilies" is, however, well represented in print. The list of citations in the Bibliography does not purport to be comprehensive, but it does include all the printed copies I have seen.[16] The earliest is in *The British Harmony*, a chapbook anthology of songs from the London pleasure gardens, which might date from fairly close to the origin of the ballad if it was written shortly after the *Ramillies* disaster in 1760 (another item in the same anthology appears to relate to the war against the French in North America; the songs are said to be "new", but such descriptions often have to be treated with caution). A text printed by Such is given below for reference purposes.

> You soldiers and seamen draw near and attend,
> Unto these lines that have lately been penn'd;
> I'll tell you the dangers of the salt seas,
> Of the fatal destruction of the Ramilies.
> Oh, the fatal Ramilies!
>
> Seventeen hundred and seventy brave men had we,
> With ninety good guns to bear her company;
> But as we were sailing, to our great surprise,
> A most terrible storm began for to rise.
>
> The sea looked like fire and rolled mountains high,
> Whilst our seamen did weep, and our captain did cry,
> Boys, mind all your business, do all that you can,
> For if this storm lasts we are lost every man.
>
> We all went to work our lives for to save,
> Whilst all our rigging did beat the salt wave;
> Bear away, says our captain, your skill do not spare,
> So long as we've sea-room the less we've to fear.
>
> In a few moments after with a most dreadful shock,
> The fatal Ramilies she dashed 'gainst a rock;
> Both Jews, Turks, and Christians, might sorely lament,
> To hear the cries when first down she went.

---

[15] For the uncertain provenance, see Long (1886, 125).

[16] Two further entries in the Roud Broadside Index refer to items known only from lists of titles: *Fatal Ramilies* (Edinburgh: Chas. Sanderson), which is likely to be this ballad; *Ramilies* (Bristol: Collard), which is less certain.

> All you that are willing to do a good deed,
> In relieving the widows in their time of need,
> Bear a hand to assist them and God will you bless,
> With happiness greater than I can express.

Among this sample of printed copies there are a substantial number of variant readings, of which just a few are singled out for comment here. At the head of the list are variants that impact on characterization and point of view. While the narrative itself remains essentially stable, a couple of examples of first order lexical variants deserve notice:

(*a*)   The complement of the battleship: "Seven hundred and seventy" or "Seven hundred and twenty", which is close to the actual figure, versus the much greater "Seventeen hundred and seventy".

(*b*)   The final stanza appeal: a direct, first-person address, "All you who have a mind to do a good deed, | Relieve a poor widow in time of her need", versus the more abstract and general formulation, "All you that are willing to do a good deed, | In relieving the widows in their time of need". This contrast relates in turn to the first stanza's "these few lines which I lately have penn'd", versus "these few lines that have lately been penn'd". The first-person address introduces an authorial voice right at the beginning, which is picked up in the voice of the widow at the end. It would be unduly bold to conclude that here we have a ballad actually penned by the widow of a seaman lost with the *Ramillies* (it is known that broadside ballads were sometimes written and sold in order to raise funds for the relief of victims of various kinds of disasters), but it is not inherently impossible.

Lesser turns of phrase, amounting to second order lexical variants, can be picked up throughout the broadsides. Examples include: "soldiers and seamen" versus "soldiers and sailors" (stanza 1); a "most terrible storm" versus a "terrible storm" (stanza 2); "minutes" versus "moments" (stanza 5); "To hear the sad cries when first down she went", "For to hear the sad cries when down first she went", "To hear the cries when first down she went" (stanza 5); and so forth. Here we are dealing with synonyms and paraphrases, changes in word order, and the like.

On the one hand, "The Fatal Ramilies" has a chronological span of a good century in print and the number of different printings suggest that it enjoyed some real currency — perhaps, we might speculate, because of the national, as well as the human, impact of the *Ramillies* catastrophe itself, or perhaps because naval affairs at large remained of current interest throughout the period. On the other hand, the fact that it has been collected only infrequently from singers would seem to indicate rather the opposite, that it was not especially popular — perhaps, we might again speculate, simply because "The Loss of the Ramilies" (Roud 523) was much more popular, on account of its splendid tune. The copy collected by Alfred Williams, which is the most complete of those that can be confidently ascribed to oral circulation (although it lacks stanza 4), contains minor lexical details that can be paralleled in several different broadside copies, as well as a few details of its own that could be considered as additional second order lexical variants. It gives the number of sailors as seven hundred and seventy, and the number of guns as seventy (ninety in the printed copies).

If variation is indeed a defining characteristic of folk literature, then "The Fatal Ramilies" tends to confirm that, as Dugaw posits, it pervades printed broadside ballads as much as those collected from oral circulation. And since the current editorial orthodoxy is to print each collected copy separately, then presumably the same principle should apply to the broadsides. A key piece of thinking behind that orthodoxy is that it acknowledges the agency that individualizes each collected copy — crudely, that would be the impress of the individual ballad singer. The practice has a certain appeal for the handling of printed copies, too, acknowledging the agency of the printer/publisher and others who may have contributed to the finished product. It also serves to cut the Gordian knot of editorial policy. A diplomatic rendering or, more likely, an online digital image of each item would suffice.

Yet if the most interesting observation is that even a broadside ballad such as "The Fatal Ramilies" contains substantial numbers of textual variants, then that dynamic is surely worthy of presentation and representation. There is a sense in which the very idea of variation is relatively meaningless when divorced from some sort of comparative methodology. Simply to print broadside texts alongside one another offers a fairly simple comparative framework. But there are various problems here. The first is the sheer difficulty of tracking down all of the relevant copies and presenting them in the same manner, and then displaying the resulting table in either printed or digital form. Then it is simply not very easy to identify the more detailed variants within such a table.[17] And to repeat: the primary justification for treating ephemeral literature of the broadside kind in this manner — for editing it — is to track variation across the printed copies, and consequently across time and space.

The obvious alternative form of presentation is the conventional list of variants keyed to a base text, which is more or less what Child did with broadside texts in *The English and Scottish Popular Ballads* (although he also had recourse to printing them separately when they differed more greatly). As is well recognized, this can be somewhat inconvenient for the reader, and it necessarily gives the appearance of according precedence to one individual text. Child generally, and quite reasonably, chose the chronologically earliest copy as the base text. Nevertheless, given the wide gaps in our present knowledge of how broadside ballads were prepared for print, it is probably inappropriate to present them in a manner that implies a hierarchy of copies. It is not that one printed ballad was not often simply copied from another — that probably did happen quite frequently. But the perspective derived from considering broadside ballads as an integral part of a corpus of ballads and folk songs, where variation is valued for its own sake, demands that each manifestation be considered as a separate entity and accorded equal textual authority. Because modern ballad scholarship has been heavily influenced by the experience and history of ballad collecting, the immediate agency and context surrounding a ballad are held to outweigh its bibliographical lineage in the ascription of textual authority. Even though each ballad must have had an origin somewhere — and current thinking does favour early broadsides as representing, in many instances, the initial copies — textual genealogy in the guise of conventional stemmatics has fallen out of fashion for application to folk literature texts.

Recently available collation software such as the University of Virginia's Juxta program permits separate text files of broadsides (and collected ballads) to be collated and compared, with the capacity to generate such things as a "heat map" of variance, which visualizes the presence and degree of variation within the texts, along with various other kinds of display and/or a conventional critical

---

[17]   This immediately became apparent when "The Fatal Ramilies" texts were tabulated alongside one another, which was my initial approach for this article.

apparatus. In a sense, it is possible to have one's broadside cake and eat it. Even so, for the purpose of critical discussion of the place of variation in the printed and oral dissemination of ballads, it still seems valuable to have some sort of descriptive framework, such as that outlined above, to hand.

So are broadside ballads really worth editing?

The foregoing account privileges a certain group of broadside ballads: those that have counterparts among songs collected from oral circulation. If we were to consider instead those that were more ephemeral, presumably equating to "popular songs" of their day, it might be harder to make a case for editing. There comes a point at which one decides that a piece may be of interest for what it can tell us (often obliquely) about social and political history, or about the history of printing, or about popular taste at a particular historical juncture, but not because its textual history provides an intellectual and/or aesthetic challenge. In other words, we might want to edit certain broadside ballads because they are thought of as belonging to the canon, but maybe not others that do not enjoy the same status. It is an inconsistency — but only one that is mirrored *de facto* in literary editing at large.

In his chapter on "What Is Critical Editing?" in *The Textual Condition*, Jerome McGann writes that the business of textual criticism, and hence of critical editing and the critical edition, is twofold: "to expose the entire network of transmissive variation in an analytic (as opposed to a purely positivistic) way; and to define and set aside those transmissive variations which can be shown to be corruptions" (McGann 1991, 50). Editing broadside ballads certainly fulfils the first of those criteria, less certainly the second. That is on account of the special value that is accorded to transmissive variation *per se* in the study of folk literature. At first sight, it might seem strange to undertake an extensive comparative analysis without striving towards some sort of synthesis, but it is a necessary consequence of the multiformity that underlies folk literature (and increasingly, in some respects, canonical literature too). This is the context within which current interest in broadside ballads is mostly concentrated, and the scholarly editing of such items provides a further tool for elucidating that multiformity. For that reason, I would contend, broadside ballads are worth editing.

Bibliography

Broadside Ballads

Note. Different printings of the ballad types in this section are listed below in a very approximate chronological order. Exemplars are cited in order to aid identification.

The Bodleian Library Broadside Ballads are online at http:// www.bodley.ox.ac.uk/ballads/ballads.htm. The Madden Collection (Cambridge University Library, Sir Frederic Madden's Collection of Broadside Ballads) is available in a microfilm copy at London, Vaughan Williams Memorial Library. Some of the National Library of Scotland broadside ballads are online at http://digital.nls.uk/ broadsides/. The Pepys Ballads (Cambridge, Magdalene College, Pepys Library, Samuel Pepys Ballad Collection) are online at http:// ebba.english.ucsb.edu/.

"The Bold Princess Royal" (Roud 528)
The Princes [*sic*] *Royal* ([London]: J. Pitts, [1819–44]) [Madden Collection, vol. 8 (London Printers, vol. 2, no. 1188].

"Caroline and her Young Sailor Bold" (Roud 553)
Caroline and her Young Sailor Bold ([Dublin: W. Birmingham, *c.*1867]) [Bodleian Library, 2806 c.15(182), Harding B 19(42)].

"The Fatal Ramilies" (Roud 1266)
"The Ramillies", in *The British Harmony, Part the Second, being a choice collection of most of the new favorite songs sung this and the last seasons at both the Theatres, Vaux-hall, Ranelagh, Sadler's-Wells, &c.* ([London, *c.*1760–80?]), pp. 2–3 [ESTC T300819; Bodleian Library, Harding A 574(8)].
The Ramalies (Manchester: W. Shelmerdine, [1798?–1866?]) [British Library, 1875.d.16.(161.)].
A New Song called The Ramillies (York: J. Kendrew, [1803–41]) [British Library, 74/1870.c.2.(187.)].
The Fatal Ramilies ([London]: J. Catnach, [1813–38]) [British Library, L.R.271.a.2, vol. 4, no. 368; Bodleian Library, Johnson Ballads 187; Madden Collection, vol. 10 (London Printers, vol. 4), no. 557)].

The Fatal Ramilies ([London]: J. Catnach, [1813–38]) [Bodleian
Library, Firth c.13(60), Harding B 16(90b)].

The Ramilies ([London]: J. Pitts, [1819–44]) [Madden Collection,
vol. 8 (London Printers, vol. 2), no. 1192].

The Ramilies ([London]: [J.] Pitts, [1819–44]) [Madden Collection,
vol. 8 (London Printers, vol. 2), no. 1193].

The Fatal Ramilies ([London]: [J.] Pitts, [1819–44]) [Bodleian
Library, Harding B 11(2772); British Library, L.R.271.a.2, vol.
1.1, no. 5; Madden Collection, vol. 9 (London Printers, vol. 3),
no. 284].

The Fatal Ramilies (Portsea: J. Williams, [1823–47]) [Madden Collection, vol. 22 (Country Printers, vol. 7), no. 530].

The Fatal Ramilies (Devonport: Elias Keys, [1830–70]) [Bodleian
Library, Harding B 11(3907)].

The Fatal Ramilies (London: W. S. Fortey, [1860–1885]) [Madden
Collection, vol. 11 (London Printers, vol. 5), no. 914].

The Fatal Ramilies ([London]: H. Such, [1863–1885]) [Bodleian
Library, Firth c.12(80), Harding B 11(1172)].

The Fatal Ramilies ([London]: H. Such, [1863–1885]) [British
Library, 11621.h.11, vol. 5, no. 168].

"The Golden Vanity" (Child 286)
Sir Walter Raleigh Sailing in the Low-lands ([London]: J. Conyers,
[1682–85]) [ESTC R18546; Pepys Ballads, IV, 196].

Golden Vanity; or, The Low Lands Low ([London]: [J.] Pitts, [1819–44])
[Madden Collection, vol. 9 (London Printers, vol. 3), no. 160].

Golden Vanity, The; or, The Low Lands Low (London: H. Such, [1850–
1862]) [Bodleian Library, Harding B 11(1086)].

Lowlands Low ([Glasgow]: Poet's Box, 28 April 1877) [National
Library of Scotland, L.C. Fol.70(122a)].

Lowlands Low (Dundee: Poet's Box, [1880–1900]) [National Library
of Scotland, L.C.Fol.70(103b)].

Manuscript Collections
Alfred Williams MS Collection: Chippenham, Wiltshire & Swindon
History Centre, WSRO: 2598/36, Alfred Williams MS Collection,
http://history.wiltshire.gov.uk/community/folkintro.php.

Sharp MSS: Cambridge, Archive of Clare College, ACC1987/25, Cecil J. Sharp MSS [microfilm copy in London, Vaughan Williams Memorial Library].

Secondary Sources

Andersen, Flemming G. 1985. *Commonplace and Creativity: The Role of Formulaic Diction in Anglo-Scottish Traditional Balladry.* Odense: Odense University Press.

Atkinson, David. 2007. "Editing the Child Ballads: Agency, Intention, and the Problem of Version". *Variants* 6, pp. 123–62.

Baring Gould, S. and H. Fleetwood Sheppard. [1892]. *Songs and Ballads of the West: A collection made from the mouths of the people.* London: Methuen.

Brown, Mary Ellen. 2010. "Child's Ballads and the Broadside Conundrum". In Patricia Fumerton and Anita Guerrini (eds.), *Ballads and Broadsides in Britain, 1500–1800.* Farnham and Burlington, VT: Ashgate, pp. 57–72.

Chaytor, H. J. 1945. *From Script to Print: An Introduction to Medieval Literature.* Cambridge: Cambridge University Press.

Child, Francis James, ed. 1882–98. *The English and Scottish Popular Ballads.* 5 vols. Boston: Houghton, Mifflin.

Collison, Robert. 1973. *The Story of Street Literature: Forerunner of the Popular Press.* London: Dent.

Dugaw, Dianne M. 1984. "Anglo-American Folksong Reconsidered: The Interface of Oral and Written Forms". *Western Folklore*, 43, pp. 83–103.

English Short Title Catalogue (ESTC). London: The British Library, 1980–. <http://estc.bl.uk/>.

Laws, G. Malcolm, Jr. 1957. *American Balladry from British Broadsides: A Guide for Students and Collectors of Traditional Song.* Philadelphia: American Folklore Society.

Long, W. H. 1886. *A Dictionary of the Isle of Wight Dialect.* London: Reeves & Turner; Newport, Isle of Wight: G. A. Brannon.

McGann, Jerome J. 1991. *The Textual Condition.* Princeton: Princeton University Press.

Mish, Charles C. 1953. "Black Letter as a Social Discriminant in the Seventeenth Century". *PMLA*, 68, pp. 627–30.

Neuburg, Victor E. 1977. *Popular Literature: A History and Guide, from the beginning of printing to the year 1897.* London: Woburn Press.

Rollins, Hyder E. 1919. "The Black-Letter Broadside Ballad". *PMLA*, 34, pp. 258–339.

Roud Broadside Index. London: English Folk Dance and Song Society, n.d., <http://library.efdss.org/cgi-bin/query.cgi?cross=off&index_roud=on&access=off>.

Roud Folksong Index. London: English Folk Dance and Song Society, n.d., <http://library.efdss.org/cgi-bin/query.cgi?cross=off&index_roudbroadside=on&access=off>.

St Clair, William, 2004. *The Reading Nation in the Romantic Period.* Cambridge: Cambridge University Press.

Sharp, Cecil J. 1907. *English Folk-Song: Some Conclusions.* London: Simpkin; Novello; Taunton: Barnicott & Pearce.

Shepard, Leslie. 1962. *The Broadside Ballad: A Study in Origins and Meaning.* London: Herbert Jenkins.

——. 1973. *The History of Street Literature: The Story of Broadside Ballads, Chapbooks, Proclamations, News-Sheets, Election Bills, Tracts, Pamphlets, Cocks, Catchpennies, and Other Ephemera.* Newton Abbott: David & Charles.

Simpson, Claude M. 1966. *The British Broadside Ballad and its Music.* New Brunswick, NJ: Rutgers University Press.

Simpson, Jacqueline and Steve Roud. 2000. *A Dictionary of English Folklore.* Oxford: Oxford University Press.

Smith, Paul. 2008. "The Chapbook Mummers Play: Analysing Ephemeral Print Traditions". In John Hinks and Catherine Armstrong (eds.). *Book Trade Connections from the Seventeenth to the Twentieth Centuries.* New Castle, Del.: Oak Knoll Press; London: British Library, pp. 181–202.

Williams, Alfred, ed. 1923. *Folk-Songs of the Upper Thames.* London: Duckworth.

The Functions of *Zenshū* in Japanese Book Culture

Practices and Problems of Modern Textual Editing in Japan[1]

Kiyoko Myojo

IN HIS FAMOUS essay "Qu'est-ce qu'un Auteur?" ["What is an Author"], Michel Foucault asked the question: "Quand on entreprend de publier, par exemple, les œuvres de Nietzsche, où faut-il s'arrêter?" (Foucault 1969, 79) ["When undertaking the publication of Nietzsche's works, for example, where should one stop?" (Foucault 1979, 143)]. Ostensibly a question about the limits of a "work", it is also a question about the value: what parts of an author's work are worth editing? His response, unequivocal at first, was: "Il faut tout publier, bien sûr" ["Surely everything must be published"]. But thereupon, he asks, "mais que veut dire ce 'tout'?" ["but what is 'everything'?"]. After accepting such items as "les brouillons de ses œuvres" ["the rough drafts od his works"] and "les projets d'aphorismes" ["the plans for his aphorisms"], Foucault suggests that unliterary notations be collected as well — "l'indication d'un rendez-vous ou d'une adresse" ["the notation of a meeting or of an address"] and "une note de blanchisserie" ["a laundry list"] — and, thereby, radicalizes the question. Foucault then holds his ground and, instead of proposing a practical solution, points out: "La théorie de l'œuvre n'existe pas, et ceux qui ingénûment entreprennent d'editer des œuvres manquent d'une telle théorie et leur travail empirique s'en trouve bien vite paralysé" (1969, 79) ["A theory of the work does not exist, and the empirical task of those who naively undertake the editing of works often suffer in the absence of such a theory" (1979, 143–44)].

---

[1]   This essay was originally written in 2010. Its ideas contributed substantially to the setting up under my direction of a joint research project in November 2011, which is funded by a five-year government grant on the issues set out in this article funded by the Japan Society for the Promotion of Science (JSPS) under the Grant-in-Aid for Scientific Research (A) [23242016], and which aims to investigation the origins and history of Japanese philology in the light of Western influences and to contribute to the advancement of this field within a global context. I would like to thank Munakata Kazushige (Waseda Univerity), one of the project members, for valuable suggestions for the present article.

In the forty years since Foucault's pronouncement, such issues have been repeatedly discussed in the West, but not so in Japan, where the common, tacit assumption about the limits of a work is that there should be no limit. The Japanese concept of limitlessness, embodied in *zenshū*, may offer some valuable sidelights on Foucault's dilemma, for according to the common assumption *zenshū* should be as inclusive as possible. So for editors the question as to where to stop is answered quite simply: there is no need to stop.

Zenshū and Japanese modernization

The term *zenshū* 全集 consists of two Chinese characters: *zen* 全, which means "everything", and *shū* 集, which means "collection". The word can be translated as "complete works", although with some caveats. In English, "complete works" is always combined with an author's name, as in "the complete works of Shakespeare". *Zenshū* can be used in this way, but it can also designate broader categories: for example, *zenshū* can be combined with *nihon bungaku* 日本文学 ["Japanese literature"] to refer to a comprehensive collection of literary works published in the form of an anthology.

Zenshū is on the whole a modern notion. The first collections labelled *zenshū* were published around the Sino-Japanese War (1894–1895), the first imperialistic war waged by Japan after the Meiji Restoration of 1868, following the overthrow of the Tokugawa Shogunate, which had ruled Japan for over two centuries. These historical changes opened up Japan to the West and accelerated its industrialization. During this time the first *zenshū* appeared, issued in a series named Teikoku–bunko 帝国文庫 ["Imperial Classics"] that ran from 1893 to 1897 and consisted of fifty volumes. "Collected works" and "comprehensive collections" had been in circulation previously during the Tokugawa period, but only under the term *shū*. The neologism *zenshū* intimated a new direction in Japanese culture. According to Munakata Kazushige, the term captured the spirit of the age: 「〈全集〉という発想そのものが、その出発期においては、重厚長大をもってよしとする、力まかせの膨張主義的な性格を帯びていたことも否定できないのではないか」 (Munakata 2004, 156–57) ["it cannot be denied that the very idea of *zenshū* may be tinged with the expansion principle based on the sense of value those days; heavy, thick, long and large was good"].[2] With the rapid progress of modern nation building, the publishing business in Japan grew quickly and the production of *zenshū* increased. It reached its first peak in the 1920s, after successive victories in the Russo-Japanese War (1904–1905) and World War I (1914–1918). Japanese imperialistic expansion had then reached its climax.

Another major event that affected production of *zenshū* was the devastating Great Kantō earthquake of 1923, which made more than 100,000 casualties and caused enormous damage to property in the Tokyo area. Three years later an epochal *zenshū* project was announced by the publishing house of Kaizōsha 改造社, whose premises had been destroyed together with nearly 800,000 books which it had in its stocks. To recoup its losses, Kaizōsha took the risk of issuing a sixty-five-volume *Gendai nihon–bungaku zenshū* 現代日本文学全集 [*A Comprehensive Collection of Modern Japanese Literature*] and to offer each volume at the bargain price of one yen. The bold low-profit / quick-return sales policy was successful: the *zenshū* sold about 250,000 sets. Other publishers promptly followed suit and more than ten similar *zenshū* projects were undertaken in the following three years.

The other type of *zenshū* in the form of anthologies were intended for a general readership and fulfilled an important educational function. These *zenshū* contributed significantly to the country's modernization. The notion of "literature", *bungaku* 文学 in Japanese, did not originally exist as such in Japan, but was a Western import which, along with other "Western" fields of knowledge such as science, philosophy, history and art, came to modify the country's existing arts. Even the concept of "nation", of "Japan" itself, must have been new to a culture that had existed in isolation from the rest of the world for over two centuries. The Japanese people were eager to acquaint themselves with Western thought and culture via literature.

The second *zenshū* boom coincided with a time of high economic growth and the appearance of the modern middle class. The most

---

[2]   In this article all Japanese names, except my own, are given in the conventional Japanese order, with the surname preceding the first name. Where only one name is given, I have followed the Japanese custom to refer to literary authors are referred by their first name; all other individuals, however, are referred to by their surname.

successful *zenshū* was *Gendai nihon bungaku zenshū*, released by the publisher Chikuma–shobō 筑摩書房 between 1953 and 1959. This *zenshū* of modern Japanese literature was vast: it comprised 100 volumes, and 12 million copies were rumoured to have been printed by 1967.[3] These numbers reveal that many literary works were being written and copies of them circulated; the establishment of national identity went hand in hand with the formation of a national, modern literary canon.[4] Moreover, there was a close relationship between the success of contemporary novels (a literary genre recently imported from the West) and the establishment of a standardized national Japanese language (see Mizumura 2008).

The Japanese concept of *zenshū*, then, had two significant functions: canonization and popularization.[5] *Zenshū* taught people which texts to read. And as packaged commodities, *zenshū* were bought not only by the elites but also by the general reading public. It may be added that such voluminous *zenshū* were often unread and used only to decorate the bookcases of living rooms. The books' superb bindings proclaimed westernized high intelligence and cultural prestige.

Zenshū: the Japanese Complete Works

The other type of *zenshū*, i.e., an author's complete works, fulfilled the same functions; moreover, it served to popularize and to canonize authors. Just as miscellaneous *zenshū* taught the Japanese which texts were worth reading, single-author *zenshū* explained what writers were worth following. In addition to creative works, single-author *zenshū* contained an author's casual writings, diaries and letters — almost everything penned by the author. The reason behind this all-encompassing policy is that many Japanese equated a volume's size with its author's greatness.

---

[3]   The publisher Chikuma–shobō drew attention to this number in his advertisement for the revised version issued in 1967: "The authentic *zenshū* for all families, all schools, all libraries, and all offices!" (Toeda 2009, 16).

[4]   In this respect, Japan offers an interesting case study for Benedict Anderson's theory of the association of national identity with "print-capitalism" (Anderson 1983).

[5]   As the Frankfurt School has already expounded, in the modern "cultural industrial" society the canonization of literature can be intricately related to popularization. Even in pre-modern times these two aspects were connected in Japan; see Shirane 2009.

Two of the earliest and most important *zenshū* of this type were the *Sōseki Zenshū* 漱石全集 and the *Ōgai Zenshū* 鷗外全集. The first edition of the complete works of Natsume Sōseki 夏目漱石 (1867–1916), issued in 1917, consisted of thirteen volumes containing his diaries and letters as well as all the novels published during his lifetime. This edition has been revised more than ten times to incorporate freshly discovered writings, including memoranda and even marginalia of books held in Sōseki's library. The current Sōseki zenshū contains 28 volumes, more than double the initial number.[6]

The *Ōgai Zenshū* was also enlarged from its first edition's eighteen volumes to the thirty-eight volumes of the latest edition. More than half of Mori Ōgai's 森鷗外 (1862–1922) complete works contain his translations of Western literary works. Ōgai, who was born six years before the Meiji Restoration, wrote a large number of novels and produced translations Goethe's *Faust* and a 130 works by Kleist, Rilke, Ibsen, Andersen, Flaubert, Wilde, Poe and others.

The distinguishing feature of Japan's modern cultural elites is their leading role as introducers of European literature. Ōgai, a medical officer in the imperial Japanese army who had studied in Germany, fulfilled this role, as did Sōseki. Born in the last year of the Tokugawa shogunate, Sōseki studied in London and later became professor of English literature at Tokyo Imperial University, the first person in Japan to occupy this position. Sōseki can be said to have been more popular with the general public than Ōgai. The main reason for his high popularity is, I think, that, unlike Ōgai, Sōseki, did not conceal his views about Western culture and the tensions that he saw between it and Japanese culture. In his book *Bungaku-ron* 『文学論』 [*Theory of Literature*], he wrote: 「倫敦に住み暮らしたる二年は尤も不愉快の二年なり。余は英国紳士の間にあって狼群に伍する一匹のむく犬の如く、あはれなる生活を営みたり」 (Natsume 1995, 12–13) ["The two years I lived in London were the unhappiest two years of my life. Amongst the English gentlemen, I was like a long shaggy dog mixed in a pack of wolves; I endured a wretched existence" (Natsume 2009, 48)]. Later in his life Sōseki devoted himself to the composition of Chinese poetry, which he had learned during his childhood, as part of his traditional cultural education. Sōseki's internal struggle was shared by most of the reading

---

[6]   The publishing history of the successive *Sōseki zenshū* up to 1984 is given in great detail in Yaguchi 1985.

public in Japan. He became the popular embodiment of the suffering author.

Iwanami Shigeo, a founder of the firm of Iwanami–shoten 岩波書店, which published *Sōseki zenshū* and *Ōgai zenshū*, was one of Sōseki's devoted followers. His company was apparently established to propagate Sōseki's ideas. Since then, Iwanami–shoten has continued to exert a great influence on modern Japan's intelligentsia; in Japan, some publishers, like Iwanami–shoten hold a strong position of authority. Not only has *zenshū* as a form evolved out of mainly industrial or commercial demands, they are, also, authoritative; indeed they are considered the most authoritative even in the scholarly world. Almost all studies in modern Japanese literature rely on *zenshū* texts.

The authority of *zenshū* and the absence of editorial theory

The extent of the authoritativeness of *zenshū* can be inferred from a short essay written in 1969 by Miyoshi Yukio, then a professor in the department of Japanese literature at the University of Tokyo. In "*Zenshū* no ōsoritei" 「全集のオーソリティ」 ["The Authority of *Zenshū*"], Miyoshi points out that the completeness of *zenshū* may give them an air of authority and definitiveness; however, after citing several bibliographical errors in some *zenshū*, he shows that no *zenshū* has, in fact, any authority (Miyoshi 2002, 266–67).

Though this conclusion might sound plausible, one may rightly wonder, insofar as *zenshū* does not provide reliable texts, what other texts ought to be used in Japanese literary studies? This simple question has not been answered yet; in the field of modern Japanese literature, there has been until now almost no discussion about textual editing among scholars. This does not mean, however, that there have been no comments about this absence. Some observations have been made from abroad. For example, in 1981 Masao Miyoshi, then a professor at the University of California at Berkeley, pointed out that there was no scholarly edition of Sōseki's works which containted a critical apparatus, and he wondered why there were no debates about modern textual editing, in Japan, for important works like those of Sōseki (Miyoshi 1982, 394–95).[7]

---

[7] For another example of the same kind of criticism, see Yamashita 1993. Hiroshi Yamashita was a scholar of English literature.

It was not scholars but editorial staff in the publishing houses that attempted to address the issue. Between 1993 and 1999 a new *Sōseki zenshū* was issued by Iwanami–shoten. The editing was attributed to the "Iwanami–shoten henshūbu 岩波書店編集部" ["Iwanami–shoten Editorial Department"]. The afterword explained that the text had been edited so as to be as faithful as possible to the author's manuscript. It was accompanied by a record of variants. There was, however, no justification of the editorial rationale or of the choice of base text. (Considering that Sōseki's works were printed during his lifetime some explanation ought to have been given as to why the manuscripts were selected as copy-text, and not a first or later edition.) Furthermore, the apparatus only listed the variants between existing printed editions, but not the variant readings from the manuscript, even though the edition was based on the manuscript text.

Akiyama Yutaka, a former employee of Iwanami–shoten and one of the editors of the new *Sōseki zenshū*, published a book after his retirement and revealed the inside story. According to him, the scholars who had been involved with the editing of the *zenshū* had only "looked" at the manuscript but had not done any of the actual editorial work. Instead, the editing was carried out by the editorial staff of the publisher. Akiyama adds that, upon embarking on the project of the new *Sōseki zenshū*, Iwanami–shoten had decided no longer to hide the fact that in the earlier edition the names of distinguished scholars and critics had been used only to give it greater legitimacy.

The only exception would be the *zenshū* of Miyazawa Kenji 宮澤 賢治 (1896–1933), *Kōhon Miyazawa Kenji zenshū* 校本宮澤賢治全集, published by Chikuma–shobō between 1973 and 1977. The component *Kō* 校 means "collation" and *hon* 本 "text" or "edition", so *Kōhon* 校本 can be translated as "critical edition". The edition is one of very few editions of modern literary texts that feature a critical apparatus which includes genetic variants.[8] Interestingly, among the eight people involved in its editing were two scholars of French literature and one of German literature. We may assume that these scholars of Western literature must have been familiar with Western scholarly editing. However, as the scholars were not interested, apparently, in

---

[8]   As far as I know, there is only one other example: the complete works of Nakahara Chūya (1907–1937), *Shinpen Nakahara Chūya zenshū*. Issued between 2000 and 2004, this *zenshū* was apparently modelled on *Kōhon Kenji zenshū*.

introducing theoretical issues to Japanese readers, they did not show any sources or references nor did they justify or explain their methodology. Most Japanese literary scholars did not pay attention either to the edition's apparatus or its methodological concerns.

Kenji and Kafka: Contemporaries on different sides of the globe

Miyazawa Kenji, born in 1896, about 30 years after Ōgai and Sōseki, is radically different from them. Whereas Ōgai and Sōseki were of a very high social and repute, Kenji was unknown. He spent most of his life in his hometown in the countryside, never went abroad, concerned himself with agriculture, and transacted mostly with his fellow villagers. At his death of lung disease at the age of thirty-seven, he left behind a large amount of uncompleted and unpublished manuscripts. It is said that on the day before his death, he told his father: 「この原稿はわたくしの迷いの跡ですから、適当に処分して下さい」 (Mori 1974, 242) ["As they [Kenji's papers] are only the trace of my straying, you can freely dispose of them."] Kenji's younger brother, Miyazawa Seiroku, edited them immediately: a *zenshū* was issued a year later that gave Kenji's name as much renown as those of Ōgai and Sōseki.

Most of Kenji's writings that are regarded as "work" today are in fact incomplete drafts. This incompleteness nullifies the distinction between creative works to be read and personal documents not to be read; in other words, there is no reasonable limit to the number of documents to be included in a *zenshū* of Kenji's oeuvre. Consequently, *Kōhon Kenji zenshū* comprises not only fragmentary creative texts, letters and diaries but also various memoranda such as appointments, calculations and so on.

Kenji's situation recalls that of Franz Kafka (1883–1924), whose works were, for the most part, posthumously published by his friend Max Brod.[9] Since these editions contained numerous interventions that were not authorized by the author, Kafka's works were re-edited and republished by the Fisher Verlag from 1982 onwards under the general editorship of Malcolm Pasley from the original manuscripts. In addition, also his private diaries and letters, and even his "Amtliche Schriften" ["Occupational Writings"] have been critically edited

---

[9]   For more on this issue, see Myojo 2003.

(see Kafka 2004), in a spirit of manner that some may consider challenging to received notions of what an author's work includes (for more on this issue, see Wagner 2003).

As with Kafka, the issues of authorization and inclusiveness have sent the editorial work on Miyazawa Kenji into a kind of maze. The revised edition of *Kōhon Kenji zenshū*, published between 1995 and 2009, was according to the editors remarkably original in that it presented for the first time multiple versions of the same texts. For example, *Ginga tetsudō no Yoru* 『銀河鉄道の夜』 [*Night of the Milky Way Railroad*], a prose work uncompleted and unpublished during the author's lifetime, is presented in five different texts that represent different stages in the work's genesis. The collection of poems *Haru to Shura* 『春と修羅』 [*Spring and Evil*], which was published by the author, is given in two different versions because Kenji revised the published text and his handwritten alterations survive.

The editors of *Kōhon Kenji zenshū*, in other words, attempted a form of completion that not only expanded the canon horizontally to include all of Kenji's writings, but also vertically with their inclusion of genetic versions. Their aim, however, was not fully realized, for practical considerations and technological limitations frustrated the editors' all-encompassing policy. As one of them remarked regretfully: 「印刷出版という流通上の制約等から、校本全集では［...］［最終形を］本文として提出するという便宜的形態をとらざるをえなかった」 (Sugiura 1995, 228) ["Under the constraints of printing, publication and distribution, we were sometimes forced to present only [...] [the final version] as an edited text for the sake of convenience"].

What texts are worth editing?

The absence of a rational design might in the near future lead to the introduction of some serious confusion into *zenshū* production, especially now that Japanese scholars have acquired the technology needed to overcome such constraints. Furthermore, since the emergence of digital media has drastically changed the shape of the publishing industry, will it be possible to continue *zenshū* production, which so far has been mostly dependent on private companies, at all? These are important questions that for the moment are difficult to answer as long as literary scholars in Japan remain blind to editorial considerations and blindly reliant on the texts of existing *zenshū*.

I remain committed, and hopeful, however, that scholars will become increasingly involved in discussions on scholarly editing and start emending the texts that their predecessors have accepted unthinkingly. Texts worth editing are texts that are worth reading; more specifically, texts worth studying by literary scholars. During the course of our society's modernization, we Japanese unreflectingly have accepted Western academic frameworks. But from now on we Japanese scholars should start discussing what literary studies are and what they should be like for our own — and for global — culture.

Bibliography

Akiyama, Yutaka. 2006. *Sōseki to iu ikikata.* Tokyo: Transview.

Anderson, Benedict. 1983. *Imagined Communities: Reflections on the Origin and Spread of Nationalism.* London and New York: Verso.

Foucault, Michel. 1969. "Qu'est-ce qu'un Auteur?" *Bulletin de la Société française de Philosophie,* 63(3), pp. 75–104.

——. 1979. "What Is an Author?" In Josué V. Harari (ed.), *Textual Strategies: Perspectives in Post-Structuralist Criticism.* Ithaca: Cornell University Press, pp. 141–60.

Kafka, Franz. 2004. *Amtliche Schriften: Kritische Ausgabe.* Eds. Klaus Hermsdorf and Benno Wagner. Frankfurt: S. Fischer.

Miyoshi, Masao. 1982. "America kara mita Nihon no Sōseki kenkyū. In Miyoshi Yukio et. al. (eds.), *Kouza Natsume Sōseki: Dai go kan. Sōseki no chiteki–kūkan.* Tokyo: Yūhikaku, pp. 394–400.

Miyoshi Yukio. 2002. *Kindai–bungaku kenkyū towa nanika.* Tokyo: Bensei–shuppan.

Mizumura, Minae.　2008. *Nihongo ga horobiru toki.* Tokyo: Chikuma–shobō.

Munakata, Kazushige. 2004. *Tōshoka–jidai no Mori Ōgai.* Tokyo: Iwamami–shoten.

Myojo, Kiyoko. 2003. "Kafka und sein japanischer Zeitgenosse Kenji: Über die nachgelassene 'Schrift' der beiden Dichter". *Saitama University Review,* 39(2), pp. 215–25.

Natsume, Soseki, 1995. *Bungakuron: Soseki zenshu.* Dai 14 kan, Iwanami–shoten.

——. 2009. *Theory of Literature and other Critical Writings.* Ed. Michael K. Bourdaghs, et al. New York: Columbia University Press.

Shirane, Haruo, ed. 2009. *Ekkyōsuru nihon bungaku kenkyū / New Horizons in Japanese Literary Studies.* Tokyo: Bensei–shuppan.

Mori, Sōichi. 1974. *Miyazawa Kenji no shōzō.* Aomori: Tsugaru–shobō

Sugiura, Shizuka. 1995. "'Shin–kōhon Miyazawa Kenji zenshū' henshū–sagyō kara". *Nihon–kindai–bungaku,* 53, pp. 227–29.

Toeda, Hirokazu. 2009. *"Meisaku" wa tsukurareru.* Tokyo: Nihon–hōsō–shuppan–kyōkai.

Wagner, Benno. 2003. "'Beglaubigungsorgen': Zur Problematik von Verfasserschaft, Autorschaft und Werkintegration im Rahmen des *Amtlichen Schriften* Franz Kafkas". *Editio,* 17, pp. 155–69.

Yaguchi, Shinya. 1985. *Sōseki zenshū monogatari.* Tokyo: Seiei–sha.

Yamashita, Hiroshi. 1993. *Honmon no Seitaigaku.* Tokyo: Nihon editā skūru shuppanbu.

WORK IN PROGRESS

Towards an Edition of Edwin John Ellis and William Butler Yeats's *The Works of William Blake: Poetic, Symbolic and Critical*[1]

Arianna Antonielli and Mark Nixon

> You will be surprised to hear what I am at besides the new play — A commentary on the mystical writing of Blake. A friend is helping me or perhaps I should say I am helping him as he shows Blake much better than I do, or any one else perhaps. It should draw notice — be a sort of red flag above the water's oblivion — for there is no clue printed anywhere to the mysterious "Prophetic Books"

> (Letter to Katharine Tynan, 8 March 1889, qtd. in Yeats 1986, 151).

1.

WILLIAM BUTLER YEATS'S WORKS as well as his manuscripts, from major to minor, have all been subject to various scholarly editions and critical scrutiny. There are however exceptions, and one of them is the manuscript material surrounding *The Works of William Blake, Poetic, Symbolic, and Critical. Edited with Lithographs of the Illustrated "Prophetic Books" and a Memoir and Interpretation*, written and edited by William Butler Yeats and Edwin John Ellis, since it has never been published before. In this essay, we want to analyse the extant manuscript corpus and its relation to the published edition, the compositional process, and discuss the most relevant editorial decisions and philological principles we are following in publishing the manuscript material pertaining to the *Works of William Blake*.

The Works of William Blake is a three-volume work on Blake's poetic and pictorial output produced by Ellis and Yeats from 1889 to 1893. The work, published in London by Bernard Quaritch in 1893, was

---

[1]   Images reproduced with kind permission of A. P. Watt Ltd on behalf of Gráinne Yeats and the University of Reading, Special Collections.

unenthusiastically welcomed by major London reviews (Yeats 1986, 355 and 355 n. 2), and widely considered, in Keynes's words in a letter to Joseph Hone of 17 July 1938, "a work of enthusiasm rather than of accurate scholarship" (Adams 1968, 47). The edition's much-debated critical and literary value notwithstanding, Yeats's intense study and interpretation of Blake in this early period of his life profoundly influenced his symbolic and imaginary system, determining its subsequent development up to its codification in the volume of *A Vision* (1925; 1937). As Donald Masterson and Edward O'Shea argued, "Yeats's interest in Blake was life-long, and the themes and aesthetics of both poets are clearly compatible" (1985, 53). With *The Works of William Blake,* Yeats was able to clarify for the first time his own thinking on Yeats, which in turn shaped his literary and existential *Weltanschauung* as well as his poetry. The Quaritch edition represents a clear link between Yeats as a reader and scholar of Blake, and Yeats as a poet and follower of Blake (see Antonielli 2009). As he wrote to Katharine Tynan in May 1890:

> The book must rouse a good deal of interest among literar[y] people & what will please me better influence for good the mystical societies through out Europe. You will like his system of thought it is profoundly Christian — though wrapped up in a queer dress — & certainly amazingly poetical — It has done my own mind a great deal of good — in liberating me from formulas & theories of several kinds. You will find it a difficult book — this Blake interpretation — but one that will open up for you I think as it has for me new kinds of poetic feeling & thought. (Yeats 1986, 218)

The manuscript material pertaining to *The Works of William Blake* will be published in 2013 by Firenze University Press in a one-volume facsimile edition, with critical commentary, entitled "William Butler Yeats' and John Edwin Ellis' *The Works of William Blake: Poetic, Symbolic and Critical.* A Manuscript Edition, with Critical Analysis".

Following a "Preface", and three brief sections, "Historical Apparatus and Overview", "This Edition", and "Editorial Conventions", the volume will reproduce the loose manuscript leaves corresponding to fragments of Books 1, 2, and 3 of the Quaritch Edition, as well as the abandoned sections which were not included in *The Works of William Blake.* The "Preface" is aimed to provide a description of the manuscript cluster and its contents, as well as an immediate classification of its folders and folios into three groups corresponding with the three books of the Quaritch Edition. It also deals with the background of the manuscript corpus, as well as their relation to each other and their source. The "Historical Apparatus and Overview" outlines the historical order of composition of the chapters within the three books of *The Works of William Blake* on the basis of Yeats's correspondence (including some unpublished letters that are part of the manuscript cluster) and the autobiographical *The Trembling of the Veil*. It also focuses on the vicissitudes of publication of the Quaritch Edition, a discussion of its critical reception, and the history of the manuscripts themselves. The two sections headed "This Edition" and "Editorial Conventions" deal with the issue of permissions, and editorial decisions and conventions regarding the classification of folders, folios, and foliation. The second part of the volume then includes a "Critical Apparatus", in which the manuscript material is examined. This section also incorporates a formal and content-related analysis of the discrepancies between the manuscript and *The Works of William Blake*.

2.

A full set of manuscripts and typescripts of the three volumes of *The Works of William Blake* has not survived, but the extant material is of great interest in clarifying the compositional process and context of the edition. As such, a facsimile reproduction of the manuscript corpus informing the Quaritch Edition constitutes the central part of the current volume. The large part of the cluster is held at Special Collections of the University of Reading, within the "Papers of Edwin John Ellis" (UoR MS 293, specifically 2/2). This collection also includes correspondence and typescripts written by both Edwin John Ellis and William Butler Yeats, a number of paintings and drawings, prints and sundry papers, as well as five letters that Yeats wrote to Ellis and three letters addressed to Mrs. Ellis (293/1, ff. 1–40), and volumes of Yeats's poems.

Beside the material held at Reading, other relevant documents pertaining to the Quaritch Edition can be found within the Yeats collection at the National Library in Dublin (NLI MSS 30,289 and 30,584). They amount to merely 28 sheets, and include 22 pages of manuscript notes and three manuscript pages, together with three galley proof pages with corrections, mostly of Blake's illustrations.

Furthermore, within Yeats's library held at the National Library in Dublin there are various books annotated by Ellis and Yeats with the Quaritch edition in mind. The three main books in this context are Blake's *Milton* (NLI MS 40,568 / 19; 14 sheets; envelope no. 1909C; annotated by Ellis), Blake's *The Marriage of Heaven and Hell* (NLI MS 40,568 / 17; 32 sheets; envelope no. 1886; and NLI MS 40,568 / 18; 2 sheets; envelope no. 1894; annotated by Yeats), and William Michael Rossetti's *The Poetical Works of William Blake* (NLI MS 40,568 / 20; 61 sheets; envelope no. 1183). Yeats's annotations of Blake's *The Marriage of Heaven and Hell* are of particular interest as they show Yeats's careful analysis of specific poems by Blake. Finally, Yeats's library contains his own copy of the three-volume 1893 *The Works of William Blake* (NLI MS 40,567/4/1–3), which appears to have been annotated at different moments in time after its publication — a total of 54 pages contain marginalia. This copy is of course of immense interest, as it reveals how Yeats's aesthetics changed in these years, and how he continued to think about Blake's work in terms of his own developing poetics.

In the forthcoming edition, the entire extant manuscript of *The Works of William Blake* is presented in high resolution photo-facsimiles, accompanied on each facing page by a caption giving the folders and folios in chronological numbering. To facilitate a permanent pagination for the entire holograph manuscript, a continuous foliation for each leaf has also been introduced in brackets. The facsimile pages of the 25 holograph leaves of the Dublin material are reproduced together with the 263 holograph leaves of MS 293 at Reading, and combined together as to reproduce the final disposition of *The Works of William Blake*. Alongside the actual manuscript, a selection of facsimiles will be included from the galley proof pages, Ellis's own annotated copy in UoR MS 293/2/20, as well as from Yeats's notes on Blake's *Marriage* and his own annotated copy of *The Works of William Blake*, in order to represent contextual material which illustrate the composition, publication and reception of the work.

3.

The correspondence between Yeats and Ellis, as well as Yeats's other letters and autobiographical writings, give us a rough idea of the genesis, composition process and thematic array of their project, the

MS 293/2/2, Folder 10, f. 91

Deletions and interlinear additions by Yeats (pen) and Ellis (pen and pencil); at top writing by Ellis (pen), deletions and interlinear additions also by Ellis (pencil).

MS 293/2/2, Folder 24, f. 10

Deletions and interlinear additions by Yeats (black and red pen) and Ellis (pencil); addition by Yeats (red pen).

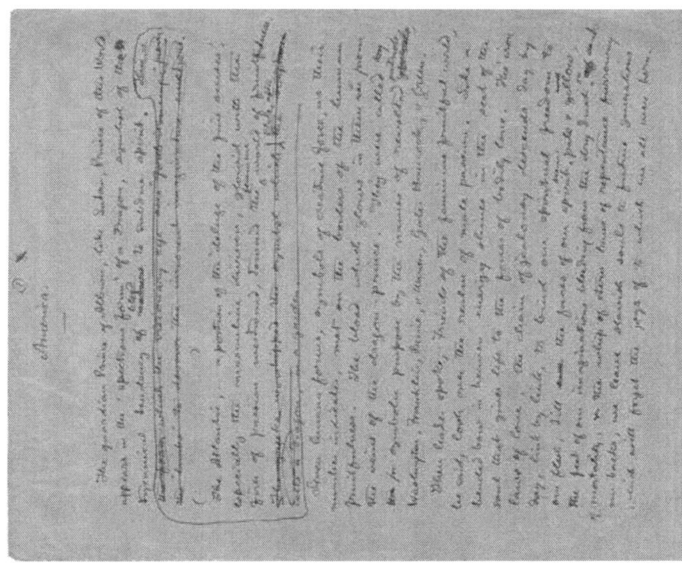

MS 293/2/2, Folder 31, f. 1
Handwritten by Ellis (pen)

MS 293/2/2, Folder 31
Unfoliated. Handwritten by Ellis (pen)

origins of which date back to February 1889 (Yeats 1955, 161). As reported in *The Trembling of the Veil*, it was Ellis's interpretation of Blake's "The Fields from Islington to Marylebone" (Blake 1966, 649) that originally led Yeats to suggest they work together on Blake:

> The four quarters of London represented Blake's four great mythological personages, the Zoas, and also the four elements. These few sentences were the foundation of all study of the philosophy of William Blake, that requires an exact knowledge for its pursuit and that traces the connection between his system and that of Swedenborg or of Boehme. I recognized certain attributions, from what is sometimes called the Christian Cabala, of which Ellis had never heard, and with this proof that his interpretation was more than phantasy he and I began our four years' work. (Yeats 1955, 161)

At the moment, it is unclear how the manuscripts were separated and ended up in two different locations. Yeats's annotated books were obviously part of his library that had remained in the possession of the Yeats family before making its way to the National Library in Dublin, but we do not know why the manuscripts were not kept together. The fact that the bulk of the manuscripts and typescripts were in the hands of the Ellis's heirs rather than Yeats's may confirm the supposition that Ellis was, on the whole, responsible for the publication, or at least was responsible for dealing with Quaritch. We can also assume that he was in charge of its final revision before publication. As a consequence, there was probably no reason for Yeats to have any material back after publication. However, the provenance of the Reading material is relatively well documented. The late Ian Fletcher, who was instrumental in obtaining these manuscripts for the University of Reading, observed in the article "The Ellis-Yeats-Blake Manuscript Cluster" that it "was not until 1961 that manuscript material came to light. In April 1962, 265 leaves, the larger proportion containing Yeats's holograph, were purchased by the University of Reading" (Fletcher 1972, 73).[2] The "Papers of Edwin John Ellis" were acquired for £700 by the University of Reading on 23 March 1963, from Willhelm Keller, Ellis's nephew by marriage, residing

---

[2]   Ian Fletcher's essay in the *Book Collector* constitutes the first and only study entirely focused on the manuscript material. In this essay he announces his ultimately unfulfilled idea of putting together a manuscript edition with the Yeats scholar Robert O'Driscoll in Toronto (Fletcher 1972, 81 n.2).

in Germany (as noted in the Register of Entries of the University of Reading Library). Thirty-eight additional leaves came to the University of Reading as a gift in 1971, after Keller's death in 1966.

4.

The 280 folios forming MS 293/2/2 at the University of Reading, which contain the majority of extant manuscript material pertaining to *The Works of William Blake*, are divided and contained in 39 folders.[3] Each folder is formed of individual or paired folios, sometimes sewn end to end. All the folders' sheets are chronologically numbered, except from ten folders. However, not all folios start from number 1. For example, folders 3 to 13, as well as 15, 16, 25, 27 and 28 do not start from 1, but respectively from 22, 21, 38, 26, 61, 34, 38, 90, 95, 106, 120, 112, 27, 3, and 7. Therefore, we can assume that the aforementioned folders are missing roughly 785 folios, as evidenced by a comparison with the three published volumes. The extant part of MS 293 is composed of MS 293/1/1 with 40 leaves; MS 293/2/1/1–7 with 66 leaves; MS 293/2/2/1–40 includes 300 leaves devoted to *The Works of William Blake* and 2 leaves to Blake's paintings; MS 293/2/3/1–3 with 11 leaves; MS 293/4/1–151 with 151 leaves; and MS 293/6/1–6 includes 7 leaves.

The greatest part of the folders contains foliated pages, written either in pencil in Ellis's hand or red pen in Yeats's hand. They have been ruled both on recto and verso, depending on the folders. Lines to a page range from 9 to 25. Dimensions of the pages vary from a minimum of 15cm wide to a maximum of 35 cm long. Yeats's hand is much bigger and more imprecise and irregular than Ellis's.

In general, the manuscript folios appear to be slightly damaged mostly at the edges and a number of pages have lacunae.

In the first folder of UoR MS 293, an initial scheme is included, so that folia 1–4 already foresee a division into three books — thus implying that MS 293 belongs to a phase later than 1890, when Yeats wrote two letters to Katharine Tynan anticipating that their work on Blake would be composed of two volumes. In the first letter, dated May 1890, he stated: "It will be in two volumes — the first containing the text of the prophetic books the second an interpretation of the

---

3   Folder 20 contains 17 pages photocopied from the Quaritch edition.

philosophy contained in them" (Yeats 1986, 218). In a second letter to Tynan of September 1890, he wrote that "[t]here will be two volumes one containing the mystical poems [...] The other volume will contain our commentary" (Yeats 1986, 227–28).

The initial scheme of MS 293 does not properly correspond to the Quaritch edition chapters, or to the actual textual structure of the manuscript itself. The content and structure of the manuscript thus mirror the final Quaritch version of the volume more closely than the titles outlined in the initial scheme. In the MS scheme, the whole volume appears to be composed of three books, respectively entitled "Symbolism" (Book I), "Explanation of the Poems" (Book 2), and "Psychology" (Book 3). The three books are divided in the MS scheme into 15, 7 and 6 chapters. While each chapter of the first two books is already provided with a title, only the last chapter of the third book is endowed with a title ("Blake and the Celestial Love of Swedenborg"). As a consequence, unlike the third book, books 1 and 2 must have been clear to the authors in terms of topics and corresponding placement within the volume. Nonetheless, titles, order and occurrence of related topics — as well as their description and analysis — in volumes 1 and 2 of *The Works of William Blake* are quite different from books 1 and 2 of the MS scheme. The second volume is composed of three chapters. While the first chapter, "Interpretation and paraphrased Commentary", appears to correspond to the second book in the manuscript, entitled "Explanation of the Poems", the last two chapters of book 2, "Blake the Artist" — on Blake's pictorial production — and "Some References", which "presents a concordance of the characters of the four zoas in *The Prophetic Books*" (Antonielli 2008, 13), are not yet included either in the MS scheme or in the MS text. But it is mostly the third volume of *The Works of William Blake*, "The books", that diverges from the third book as projected in the MS scheme, "Psychology", the latter deviating in its very title from the real argument of this book in the Quaritch edition, which is instead devoted to Yeats's and Ellis's edition of Blake's poetic and pictorial works. Thus this volume actually includes the *Poetical Sketches, Songs, Gates of Paradise*, the handwritten poems taken from the *Pickering MS*, the *Note-book*, the *Notes* to the first poems, *Tiriel, Vala, or the Four Zoas*, the *Lambeth prophecies*, the *Marriage of Heaven and Hell, Thel, Jerusalem*, and *Milton*.

In other words, both the scheme of MS 293 and the text differ to some extent from the final Quaritch edition. The volume of *The Works of William Blake* which appears to be closest to its related draft version in MS 293 is the first volume. In the Quaritch Edition this volume is made up of four sections, respectively entitled "Preface", "Memoir", "The Literary Period", and "The Symbolic System". The "Preface" is called "Introduction" in the scheme of MS 293, but it is not included in the MS text at this stage, as confirmed by Yeats's words on the very first folio of the manuscript, "(may be numbered separately and send not ... until last)". The second section of the first book of *The Works of William Blake*, "Memoir", figures in the scheme as "Life of Blake", while in the manuscript text it is entitled "The Events of the Life of William Blake", which was later erased by Yeats and substituted with "A critical Memoir of William Blake" and eventually simplified to "William Blake". "The Literary Period" is not foreseen in the initial scheme, but it is included in the text of MS 293 (Folder 16, folios 27–29). We know from Yeats's correspondence that it was mostly conceived and written by Ellis (Antonielli 2009, 214). This is also evident from Yeats's note "inscribed in Lady Gregory's copy of *The Works of Blake* (Berg)", dated 14 November 1899:

> The book was written in this way. I wrote a life of Blake about as long as my life of him in "The Muses Library Book", an account of the symbolic system as a whole, & a short interpretative argument of each prophetic book. Ellis expanded, or rather completely rewrote the life into its present form, he accepted with some additions & modifications the chapter on the symbolic system & expanded the short arguments to ten times their original length, & wrote a number of extra chapters. The actual interpretation of the philosophy, which is contained in both his book & mine was made out absolutely together. His mind was far more minute than mine, but less synthetic. I had a tendency to make generalisations on imperfect foundations, & he to remain content with detached discoveries. We worked about four years & our method was to collate every mention of a mythological personage, or symbol. Ellis compiled a concordance to aid us....With the exception of the part called 'The Symbolic System' almost all of the actual writing is by Ellis. (Yeats 1986, 226 n.4)

"The Symbolic System" finally constitutes the fourth Section of the first book of *The Works of William Blake*. It is considered to be the fruit of Yeats's aesthetic and visionary symbolism, as Yeats himself writes in his letters and *Autobiographies*. Both in *The Works of William Blake* and in the MS scheme, where it is called "Symbolism", this section is composed of 14 and 15 chapters. The title of the first chapter is in both cases "The Necessity of Symbolism". Chapter 2 in *The Works of William Blake* is entitled "The Three Persons and the Mirror", while in the MS scheme it appears as "The Three Persons and Throne". Chapter 3 figures in the MS scheme "The Four Zoas. Four Elements", while in *The Works of William Blake* simply "The Four Zoas". All the other titles included in the contents page of MS 293 are slightly different from their final versions in *The Works of William Blake* or do not appear at all.

Focusing attention on the text of MS 293, the fourth section of volume I of *The Works of William Blake* starts in the manuscript from Folder 18, with a chapter entitled "Dual Aspects" (F. 18, ff. 1–14, Yeats's hand) in both the manuscript and the printed work. This chapter corresponds to chapter 12 in *The Works of William Blake* (315–319), but its title is not included in the scheme. Chapter 13 (320–326), "The two Contraries of Humanity", is clearly drawn from MS 293/2/2, Folder 19, ff. 1–7, where it shows the same title and text, but again, its title is not included in the manuscript scheme. The last chapter of *The Works of William Blake*, chapter 14, entitled "The Names" (*The Works of William Blake*, I, 327–329, until line 24, 'reveal their source in this way') still exists in MS 293/2/2, Folder 20, ff. 1–5 (Yeats's hand), but it turns out to be incomplete. The text of MS 293/2/2 does not contain the previous 11 chapters of "The Symbolic System". Furthermore, it does not show any reference to the titles of the MS scheme.

5.

In 2009, we approached the Yeats Estate via their literary agents A.P. Watt to enquire about the possibility of publishing an electronic edition, which would present facsimiles of UoR MS 293/2/2 and NLI MS 30,289 and 30,584, together with critical commentary, taking advantage of recent advances in digital humanities (see Robinson 1993). The Department of Comparative Languages, Literatures and Cultures of the University of Florence, which has a digital publication laboratory, The Open Access Publishing Workshop, supported the project. As expected, we were redirected to Cornell University Press, which has over a number of years been publishing manuscript editions of Yeats's complete works, and were informed that Yeats and Ellis' edition of Blake was not part of their editorial strategy, which only included "creative" work by Yeats. As a result, we were subsequently granted permission from A. P. Watt, on behalf of the Yeats Estate, to proceed with the publication, but unfortunately only in print, and not online.[4]

The decision not to include full transcriptions of the facsimiles was made for a variety of reasons. First, both UoR MS 293/2/2 and NLI MS 30,289 and 30,584 are not hard to read or difficult to understand, and the majority of the folios is not damaged or torn. Scholars and readers can approach the documents afresh, without the experience of the Yeatsian scholar or editor. Furthermore, the "Critical Apparatus" provides clear textual and explanatory annotations, while the textual notes deal with changes between the manuscript cluster and the Quaritch Edition, and also provide several transcriptions (especially of those few illegible sheets). Furthermore, the explanatory notes give literary and historical information that sheds light on the missing parts of the manuscript.

Second, the facsimile should immediately appeal to scholars and readers *tout court* for its fidelity to the original. Pages are reproduced in exact size, in high quality paper and printing. The colors of ink and paper closely match the original, and the variations in ink and pen on the manuscript enable a scholarly analyst to differentiate the phases of inscription within each section. Moreover, the decision to reproduce the text in polychrome was made to allow scholars to access a clear facsimile copy of the original and thus to contribute to the critical exegesis of the material, without being potentially misguided by a transcription.

Third, publishing the facsimiles of UoR MS 293 and NLI MS 30,289 and 30,584 as extant will allow research into the current status of the original manuscript, in particular regarding the autograph corrections by both Ellis and Yeats. Indeed, many chapters forming the final version of *The Works of William Blake* are still debated as far as their authorship is concerned, and by giving full access to facsimiles scholars will be able to ascertain whether our own interpretation of the handwriting is accurate and even propose alternative readings

---

[4]   A full-access electronic edition would have certainly helped readers to delve into the facsimile, enhancing their level of engagement.

of a text. In this context, and his own copy of the Quaritch edition, Yeats wrote (under the date "3 May 1900"):

> The writing of this book is mainly Ellis's. The thinking is as much mine as his. The biography is by him. He wrote and trebled in size a biography of mine. The greater part of the "symbolic system" is my writing; the rest of the book was written by Ellis working over short accounts of the books by me, except in the case of the "literary period," the account of the minor poems, and the account of Blake's art theories which are all his own except in so far as we discussed everything together.

Furthermore, as Ian Fletcher already noted in his 1972 essay on the manuscript, "on occasions [...] it is impossible to distinguish Yeats's deletions from those of Ellis" (Fletcher 1972, 81), even though the differences in color of ink, and slope and pressure of hand and pen which remain distinguishable in the facsimile allow the differentiation of Ellis's hand from Yeats's. The color of ink, in particular, comes out in red, faded greyish-black, pencil and shades of brown throughout the facsimile. Yeats largely used inks which now appear as greyish-black or brown, while Ellis mostly used pencil or red for corrections. Pencil marks and erasures can be easily recognized from inked ones. Interestingly, folders 3, 4, 6, 8 and 25 of MS 293/2/2, all in Yeats's hand, have marginal space for textual additions and deletions. The identification of the author is obviously an important issue that needs to be clarified, as it will further our understanding of the development of Yeats's and Ellis's reception of Blake's work, and the way in which it subsequently informed their writing.

An accessible, user-friendly edition of these manuscripts, in accordance with modern editorial practices, would greatly encourage further research on the Quaritch edition as well as scholarship in Blake's and Yeats's symbolism and poetics. We have tried to demonstrate that an exact reproduction of the original data, together with a critical apparatus which always constitutes a point of information and comparison, will result in a first full-scale, self-contained print edition of the manuscript cluster, which hopefully one day will be expanded within an electronic environment. It is our hope that this edition will yield new insights and discoveries about the genesis and the composition of *The Works of William Blake,* provoke new critical discussions, and give the reader a sense of how the manuscripts cluster fits into the larger *Works of William Blake.*

Bibliography

Adams, Hazard. 1968. *Blake and Yeats: The Contrary Vision.* New York: Russell & Russell.

Antonielli, Arianna. 2008. "William Butler Yeats's 'The Symbolic System' of William Blake". *Estudios Irlandeses*, 3, pp. 10–28.

———. 2009. *William Blake e William Butler Yeats: Sistemi simbolici e costruzioni poetiche.* Firenze: Firenze University Press.

Blake, William. 1966. *The Complete Writings of William Blake.* Ed. Geoffrey Keynes. London: Oxford University Press.

Fletcher, Ian. 1972. "The Ellis-Yeats-Blake Manuscript Cluster". *Book Collector*, 21, pp. 72–94.

Masterson, Donald, and Edward O'Shea. 1985. "Code Breaking and Myth Making: The Ellis-Yeats Edition of Blake's Works". *Yeats's Annual*, 3, 53–80.

Robinson, Peter. 1993. *The Digitization of Primary Textual Sources.* Oxford: Oxford University Office for Humanities Communication.

Yeats, W. B. 1955. *Autobiographies.* New York: Macmillan Company.

———. 1986. *The Collected Letters of W. B. Yeats: Volume 1: 1865–1895.* Ed. J. S. Kelly and Eric Domville. Oxford: Clarendon Press.

BOOK REVIEWS

Book Reviews

Stephanie A. Viereck Gibbs Kamath, *Authorship and First-Person Allegory in Late Medieval France and England.* Woodbridge, Suffolk and Rochester, NY: D. S. Brewer, 2012. 226 pp. ISBN 978-1-84384-313-9.

Many critics have studied the influence of the *Roman de La Rose*, which was highly popular in the middle ages, on Middle English literature. Stephanie A. Viereck Gibbs Kamath succeeds in providing a fresh perspective on the matter, by tracing the *Roman*'s influence on French and English writers' authorial representation and by considering how they re-employed the authorial strategies of the work to craft a "new I". To this end, her study examines authorial representation and self-knowledge in the works of Guillaume de Deguileville, Geoffrey Chaucer, Thomas Hoccleve and John Lydgate. She purposely limits her focal point to Chaucer and his fifteenth-century followers, which ties in with the recent attention that has been paid to these late medieval authors. She draws upon a wide range of examples which emerge from a European corpus of medieval literature and cross-references to the *Roman de la Rose*, and Deguileville's works form a thread which weaves its way through her study.

An analysis of the establishment of authorial self-representation in *Roman de La Rose* and Deguileville's allegories forms the basis for the rest of Viereck Gibbs Kamath's work. She discusses the authors chronologically, starting with Chaucer. The author points out that Chaucer's dream visions adapt three strategies of authorial self-representation which can be found in French allegories, namely the attribution of the author's name to the narrator, characters serving as scribes to allegorical personifications, and the embedding of documents, lyrics, and prayers in a fictional account to emphasize the "relationship of textual attribution and interpretation" (p. 73). Then she goes on to demonstrate how Hoccleve and Lydgate widen the allegorical tradition. Discussing Hoccleve's translations of Christine de Pizan and Deguileville, as well as his *Series*, she demonstrates how Hoccleve is influenced by some of these writers' strategies and alters them to fit his own means, which she considers to be the creation of a particular English response to French allegories.

Her discussion of Lydgate's works is particularly refreshing, as the influence of the French allegorical tradition on his strategies of self-representation has not yet received much scholarly attention. She points out how Lydgate "extends and transforms allegorical passages" (p. 141) in his English translations of *The Pilgrimage of the Life of Man* and *The Fall of Princes* to draw attention to self-authorization. Moreover, she demonstrates how the *Roman*, although references to the work are not explicit, serves as an underlying source, through which Lydgate establishes the authority of the author-as-translator protagonist.

One of the strengths of her work is its multifacetedness. Viereck Gibbs Kamath's study draws upon several emerging as well as established fields in the study of premodern literature, such as translation studies, authorship, allegory, the influence of French literature on English literature, and theories of reading. In this way, she successfully meets her aim of providing "a cohesive working model of the tradition for future study" (p. 15) which will appeal to those researching Chaucer and fifteenth-century poetry. Through its wide scope and its re-occurring focus on the influence of Deguileville's underexplored allegory on English authors, *Authorship and First-Person Allegory in Late Medieval France and England* succeeds in offering a fresh perspective while building on established work by leading scholars in the fields of medieval authorship and Anglo-French relationships, such as Alastair Minnis's *Medieval Theory of Authorship* and Ardis Butterfield's *The Familiar Enemy*. Viereck Gibbs Kamath successfully illustrates how the roots of many examples of vernacular authorship lie in the tradition of first-person allegory.

Sarah Laseke

Michael Calabrese, Hoyt N. Duggan, and Thorlac Turville-Petre, eds., *The Piers Plowman Electronic Archive, 6: San Marino, Huntington Library Hm 128 (Hm. Hm²): William Langland, SEENET, A.9.* (Woodbridge and Rochester, NY: Boydell and Brewer, for the Medieval Academy of America and SEENET, 2008). CD-ROM. ISBN 978-184384-092-3.

Readers of *Variants* will enjoy using this electronic edition of Piers Plowman *edited by* Michael Calabrese, Hoyt N. Duggan and Thorlac

Turville-Petre. This volume is a welcome addition to *The Piers Plowman Electronic Archive*, which, thus far, has published six volumes and promises more to come. This edition, like the others in the series, does not disappoint. It offers a variety of material and functionality which can have multiple uses in teaching and research. Not only does this electronic edition contain a plethora of information on the text of *Piers Plowman* as copied in San Marino, Huntington Library Hm 128 (Hm. Hm²), but it also includes important linguistic and codicological observations which are relevant to linguists, textual and manuscript scholars alike.

The CD-ROM will work on Windows 98 or later, and opens on a Macintosh with some difficulty. On launching the edition, users are greeted by the familiar logo of the Archive and the opportunity to choose the feature of the edition which is of interest. The JR Viewer launches the full edition including a Table of Contents, Preface, Copyright, License, Instructions for first-time users, Introduction, appendices on the encoding of the text and other technical material. The JR viewer also allows users to access the images and the fully transcribed text of *Piers Plowman* in San Marino, Huntington Library Hm 128 (Hm. Hm²). Abundant notes are available in this part of the edition to guide the user through linguistic and editorial decisions. The Elwood Viewer displays images and text at a higher resolution, and allows readers to search the text in different ways. In order to use the Elwood Viewer, users are advised to change the screen resolution to a higher spec (1280 x 1024 pixels); unfortunately not all computers have such a high-resolution screen and without the higher resolution the Elwood Viewer will not launch. Apart from this little technical glitch, the navigation bar provides easy and intuitive access to the material. A navigation tab facilitates the perusal of long documents, such as the introduction and the *passus* in the texts with complete reference to the folio numbers.

Most of the paratextual information is available in the introduction, which is divided into four main parts. Part one contains a detailed description of the manuscript, part two is devoted to a detailed explanation of the text, part three considers the editorial method, and part four focuses on the linguistic description. All parts offer an erudite account of the most recent codicological observations on Hm, and on some of the thorny issues of the textual transmission of *Piers Plowman*. The manuscript description offers a stimulating discussion on the composition of the manuscript, its sequence of construction and the number of scribes who copied it. Hm contains more than one text: a "southern" recension of the *Prick of Conscience*, ff. 1-16v, 25-32v, 17-24v, 33-94r; a B version of *Piers Plowman*, ff. 96r-v, 95r, and then ff. 113-205r; the Latin *Expositio sequentiarum*, ff. 97-112v; *The Siege of Jerusalem*, ff. 205r-216r; and *How the Good Wife Taught her Daughter*, ff. 216v-219r. The discussion mainly focuses on those parts of the manuscripts which include Langland's text, but the overall observations are contextualized with an eye to the codicological composition of the manuscript as a whole. The editors suggest that

> [i]t is possible that the two main scribes of *Piers Plowman*, Hand A and Hand D, worked as distinct craftsmen each with his own assignment, not necessarily knowing the other's work or consulting the other, for neither of the main scribes made any contribution to the quires for which the other is responsible [. . .] Perhaps, then, some sort of rather loose collaborative effort informed the production of this manuscript in the (probably religious) community in which it was created.

This could certainly be a likely scenario which, as the editors point out, is seen elsewhere. The editors ask: "Do these [hands] come from one centre of collaboration and, if so, clerical or lay? An answer may come through pursuit of the hands. The purposes of Hm 128 look partly pedagogic". So, if this is the case, are we here able to make broader conclusions about a particular mode of medieval book production and textual transmission? These are stimulating questions which scholars and students alike using this CD-ROM will be able to follow up and research further. It is precisely this type of close detailed studies of medieval manuscripts which will bring us a wealth of informed evidence on an issue still too broad to be properly dissected. I am here thinking about a more specific understanding of medieval book production and the many milieus in which bookmaking was undertaken and texts, such as *Piers Plowman*, circulated. Similar provocative questions come to mind when reading the excellent section on the textual transmission of the text and the linguistic description, which, coupled with the easily accessible transcriptions of the text of *Piers Plowman* and the beautiful colour images of Hm, will offer new ways of approaching and exploring Langland, its manuscript tradition within and beyond its textual transmission.

Orietta Da Rold

Thomas Middleton, *The Collected Works*. Ed. Gary Taylor and John Lavagnino. Oxford: Oxford University Press, 2007. 2016 pp. ISBN 978 0 19 81569 7

Thomas Middleton and Early Modern Textual Culture: A Companion to the Collected Works. Ed. Gary Taylor and John Lavagnino, Oxford: Oxford University Press, 2007. 1183 pp. ISBN 978 0 19 818570 3.

The *Collected Works* of Thomas Middleton is a massive volume, over 2,000 pages and weighing in at nearly three kilos. It contains contributions from more than 70 scholars, and, together with its not much smaller *Companion*, was many years in the making. This is evident from the fact that some of the bibliographies and discussions of the plays in performance (e.g., for *The Roaring Girl, The Changeling*) were obviously completed several years before publication. There is a sense of rivalry with the Oxford Shakespeare and its Textual Companion (first published in 1986 and 1987), on which Gary Taylor also served as a General Editor. In a phrase typical of the grand ambition but also of the confusion of purpose of the *Collected Works*, he refers to it as "the Middleton First Folio". But what Taylor calls the "federal" approach of the Middleton edition undermines this claim and also sets it apart from the Oxford Shakespeare, which is unified by a common editorial policy set out in the general introduction by Stanley Wells, who also wrote all the individual introductions to each play. There are more than 50 separate texts, including juvenilia, in the *Collected Works*, and each is separately edited, sometimes with two or three individuals involved. The editors range from scholars with the highest credentials in this field to those whose first work of this kind appears here. In his preliminary section entitled "How to use this book" Taylor avoids any suggestion of an overall editorial policy, stressing that the variety and lack of consistency resulting from different approaches are to be regarded as intrinsic to the nature of the project. Different editorial practices "make a virtue out of multivocality" by illustrating a range of possible approaches to annotation; and the editorial process itself is foregrounded by the particular choices of certain editors; Jeffery Masten in *The Old Law* and Taylor himself in his editing of two separate texts of *A Game at Chess* are special exemplars of this. Some editors, Taylor observes, "are more interested in detecting error, and more adventurous in correcting it, than others". Some may have their own critical perspective to put forward; for instance, certain of them (e.g., Coppelia Kahn, Valerie Wayne) have been chosen to demonstrate a feminist stance and thus enhance Middleton's credentials in manifesting "a masculinity defined by non-violence", as Taylor puts it (conveniently ignoring the misogynist elements that many have found in tragic plays like *The Revenger's Tragedy* and *Women Beware Women*). This edition aims not just to present all the surviving texts in which Middleton can be claimed to have had a hand (sometimes not such a large one), in a reader-friendly, modern-spelling fully annotated form — no mean aim — but also to act both as a demonstration of the range of editorial practices currently available for early modern texts, and as a manifesto for the basis of these practices in the recognition of the instability of the text.

It seems appropriate for this edition to draw attention to the materiality of Middleton's texts since he was, at least in the later part of his career, considerably involved in the publication of his works. Taylor makes a big point of this in his essays, "Thomas Middleton: Lives and Afterlives" in *The Collected Works* and "The Order of Persons", in the *Companion*; and John Astington, in his fine piece entitled "Visual Texts: Thomas Middleton and Prints", argues convincingly for Middleton's active input into the engraved illustration, the first ever for a quarto play-text, for the title-page of *A Game at Chess.* John Jowett in his informative essay on "Middleton's Early Readers" regards the playwright as "unusually aware of the reader". Yet the means by which the editorial process is made visible is often of dubious value. Running titles are recorded in various forms to remind the reader of the instability of early modern texts; this may serve some purpose, as in the variation between "The Ladies' Tragedy" and "The Lady's Tragedy" for the play most commonly known by the misleading and adventitious title of *The Second Maiden's Tragedy*, but the use of "No, Witt, no helpe like a Woman", "NO Wit Like a WOMANS", "The Almanacke", and "The Almanak" all for the same play is at best whimsical and at worst tiresomely distracting. And the use of various kinds of early modern handwriting, as in *The Old Law* and *The Witch,* makes, as Michael Neill noted in his review for the *London Review of Books,* a "fetish of instability".

The editorial presentation of *The Old Law,* to which Taylor draws attention in "How to use this book", is so obtrusive as to make the text distinctly secondary to the apparatus. Not only does Masten mix "textual apparatus with annotation and photography with type"; he sets out the annotation in a variety of different relations to the text, sometimes in three columns beneath it, sometimes above it, sometimes in a single column beside it. His stated aim, given postmodern theoretical underpinning from Roland Barthes, is to provide a version of the play "that can be read as reconstructing a performance", questioning the whole act of interpretation; his commentary "insists on the multiple interventions that editorial process makes in the text". For the reader of this not especially well-known play the look of the text, with its immense mass of footnotes, constantly rearranged in different formations on the page, may be daunting. Some may admire its playfulness, its Barthesian *jouissance,* but anyone with the humble aim of getting to know an unfamiliar play so as to augment what he or she knows of Middleton's works might find it easier to do so elsewhere.

The editorial style of *The Old Law* is not typical, and many texts are impeccably — and more conventionally — presented, for instance *The Changeling, The Roaring Girl, The Revenger's Tragedy, More Dissemblers Besides Women, Hengist, King of Kent* and the pageants edited by David Bergeron. It is excellent to have parallel texts of *The Lady's Tragedy,* one a reconstruction of the original version, the other the text as it was performed after incorporating the cuts and alterations made by the censor in the surviving manuscript. Taylor's edition of *A Game at Chess* in two versions, one of which, a reconstruction of the manuscript that constituted Middleton's first draft, has never been published before, represents a heroic feat of scholarship and deserves a review to itself. Taylor is right to call it "the most complex editorial problem in the entire corpus of early modern English drama". The extent of the problems he faced in extrapolating the relationships between the six extant manuscripts of the play and the three printed quartos so as to produce his reconstruction is fully described in his long essay in the *Companion.* This play, which adds in so many ways to our understanding of what theatre in this period could do, represents one of Middleton's most important achievements, even if it is hardly the masterpiece to match Shakespeare's history plays that Taylor claims.

A website is promised which will contain all the texts, and much additional material including a concordance. This has appeared in a rather vestigial form, and does contain a smallish list of errata, though not as yet either concordance or texts. It will be of particular value in instances of the greatest textual complexity (like *A Game at Chess*), or where manuscript versions exist (as in the case of *The Lady's Tragedy, The Witch* and *Hengist King of Kent*). It may also be a more appropriate medium than print for what are referred to here as the "genetic" texts of Shakespeare's *Measure for Measure* and *Macbeth.* To justify this description, the plays are printed in an ingenious way that is not at all easy to negotiate, with (in *Macbeth*) "passages apparently added or rewritten by Middleton [. . .] in bold type; passages apparently deleted or intended for deletion [. . .] in grey; transposed passages [. . .] in grey where Shakespeare probably placed them, and in bold where Middleton apparently moved them". The look of the *Macbeth* text is further defamiliarized by the removal of all punctuation, except for apostrophes, a decision spuriously justified by the claim that the Folio punctuation bears little or no relation to Shakespeare's intentions. The hypotheses from which these texts have been constructed can be challenged on many counts; but a reader wishing to assess the various states of the text as postulated by Taylor (*Macbeth*) and Jowett (*Measure for Measure*) would be much better served by the resources of a digital format.

"The Middleton canon had a weak authorial underpinning", as Jowett puts it, and everyone interested in early modern English literature can be grateful to the team behind the *Collected Works* which has endeavoured to remedy this deficiency. As a playwright Middleton did not succeed in all the genres that Shakespeare did, and some of his major successes were in a genre Shakespeare hardly attempted, city comedy. But he also wrote prose, religious, comic, satirical and political, city entertainments and masques, and had a larger literary presence in the public life of London than Shakespeare. What the *Collected Works* demonstrates for the first time is the multifariousness of his achievement, and together with the *Companion*, it greatly enlarges our understanding of his role in the world of early modern textual culture, manuscript as well as print. There is a mine of riches here for future research.

Sandra Clark

Charles Dickens, *The Manuscript of Great Expectations: From the Townshend Collection, Wisbech*. Cambridge: Cambridge University Press, 2011. 278 pp. ISBN 978-1-108-03440-1

Literary manuscripts belong to a nation's literary heritage. However, unlike other heritage objects, manuscripts usually remain inaccessible to a wider audience. Anyone can visit a museum or gallery to view some of the greatest works of art in a nation's public ownership, but manuscripts preserved in archives and libraries are shielded from the public by access policies and reading room restrictions. The manuscripts of the best-known literary works are usually the highest guarded, requiring not only a library pass but special dispensation from head curators before one can see the item in question.

Given the rarity and fragility of many manuscripts, these restrictions are understandable. This is why the publication of facsimile editions — whether in print or online — is of such great importance. The facsimile edition of Charles Dickens's *Great Expectations* published in the Cambridge Library Collection series of Cambridge University Press is doubly beneficial, for not only does it contain a full colour reproduction, in actual size, of the entire manuscript, but also, as a paperback (and coffee table book of sorts), it is affordable. This is a book for all readers who want to acquaint themselves with Dickens's writing methods.

I do recommend a magnifying glass, however. Dickens's hand is fairly small and regular, and the frequent cancellations and interlinear revisions create a bit of a puzzle at times. In fact, one may wonder what his printer made of it. Apart from some rudimentary notes — too rudimentary even to constitute a proper outline — Dickens appears to have poured out his novels in one go, the extant manuscripts being both first draft and fair copy from which the printer of the periodical *All the Year Round* would set up type. The job, to say the least, must have put the compositors really to the test. The proofs then would be subject to further revision, with Dickens frequently adjusting the length of his chapters to fit the number of pages in the weekly serial. (For *Great Expectations*, only partial proofs survive, which are held at the National Arts Library of the Victoria and Albert Museum, London.)

One may wonder if Dickens did not first compose a rough draft that was later copied and revised in the present manuscript. From a palaeographical perspective the hand is very even indeed and the lines, though sloping downward, are absolutely straight — all of which may suggest that the manuscript was copied from an earlier, now-lost version. The letters are sometimes imperfectly formed, which indicates that the writing progressed at a pace; in itself this is neither an argument for or against copying, but the apparent paucity of slips of the pen — such as instances of eye-skip or dittography — would militate against its being copied. What makes it likely, however, that the manuscript of *Great Expectations* is the only autograph document is Dickens's routine. Writing in installments, he was adept at producing copy for a tight weekly deadline; but to produce a rough draft as well as a fair copy (followed by the normal proofreading and further revision) would have been scarcely possible within such short time span.

The Cambridge facsimile makes studying the vigour and concentration with which Dickens created *Great Expectations* possible, but the edition itself is a somewhat strange item. It has no transcription, which will create a significant obstacle for most readers. Furthermore, it has no introduction or preface contextualizing the manuscript, nor is there any detailed catalogue description or codicological analysis of the form of the manuscript and its construction, nor even a date of composition. Only a short blurb mentions that Dickens presented the manuscript to his friend Chauncy Hare Townshend, that Townshend bequeathed the manuscript, with the rest of library and art collection, to the Wisbech and Fenland Museum (in Cambridgeshire) in 1868, where it is still kept, and that the facsimile is accompanied by two companion volumes: the serial (though alas not the revised proofs) and the triple-decker first edition. Such scant treatment of an absolutely fascinating manuscript of one of the best-known nineteenth-century English novels is rather negligent, particularly from a world-class publisher such as Cambridge University Press.

Wim Van Mierlo

David Butterfield and Christopher Stray, eds. *A. E. Housman: Classical Scholar*. London: Duckworth, 2009. ISBN 978-0715638088

Despite the numerous digital resources available to researchers, classical scholarship is not exactly thriving. The disappearance of Latin and Greek from the secondary school curriculum and the lack of institutional support have turned representatives of the discipline into an endangered species. This is even truer for the more arcane specialities such as codicology or textual scholarship, ironically precisely those sub-disciplines that have been revolutionized by the new media. Manuscripts are no longer expensive objects jealously guarded; they are available in a digital format that is easily transferred. New texts or variants can immediately be checked against vast databases of available texts: the Indiana Jones romance may have gone, but the efficiency with which this kind of work can be done today must have increased a hundredfold.

This is a book about the heroic age of textual scholarship in classical studies, a century ago, when gentlemen scholars at Oxbridge dominated the field, when boatloads of newly found papyri from Egypt were streaming in and a new professionalism had set in that flew in from Germany and that replaced the amateurism of parson scholars in the second third of the nineteenth century. Of that new generation A. E. Housman was probably considered the greatest, although not all contributors to this book wholeheartedly agree.

The book is a fitting tribute to a poet/scholar on the occasion of this birth 150 years ago: this is an academic book that has been edited and produced with a care that has become uncommon in publishing, and the contributors include some of the best classical scholars working in the United Kingdom. It is divided into three parts. The first focuses on Housman's own work as a scholar, with five contributions on Latin authors, in each case assessing how much of his work is still accepted a century later; the other two parts look at his work on metre and prosody on the one hand and on the role of manuscripts in his generation. Some of the contributors have edited works by authors that Housman worked on (S. J. Heyworth has just finished a new edition of Propertius) and they usually come to the conclusion that Housman's contribution to the study of this author was not only considerable, but that quite a few of his suggestions still stand, despite the fact that his unpublished edition was burned after his death at his explicit request. Heyworth goes through all the evidence in Housman's library, in the published miscellaneous articles and notes, and even in annotations in Housman's own copies of different editions by other scholars.

After the idea of turning the Propertius edition into his monument was given up, Housman turned to Manilius, an author for whom there was a lot less competition. This work would occupy him for more than three decades, and then there was also Juvenal, and Ovid, and Lucan. In the latter cases, Housman was often in active dialogue with other major scholars, reviewing their editions and arguing against their work.

The second part of the book discusses Housman's "scholarly environment" and especially his contacts with other scholars of his time, which had already been a constant theme in the first part as well. The third part collects three more general and more whimsical pieces, *laudationes*, by E. J. Kenney and G. Luck, and a short piece by James Diggle, who can call himself the proud owner of Housman's cap and pen.

Housman was a funny kind of textual scholar: he disdained manuscript work, did not like collating and never went out of his way to look at a manuscript. In addition, he hated what the Germans called *Überlieferungsgeschichte*, the history of the transmission of texts, telling the admittedly not always exciting story of how a work written twenty centuries ago survived into our own time: how the surviving witnesses were related to each other and to the author's version and what each of these manuscripts could teach us that could help us distinguish between the elements that the scribe was copying and what he himself ended up changing in the text. All of this expertise was beginning to establish itself in Germany and elsewhere, and professionalism and scholarly collaboration led to the great dictionaries. But all of these Housman hated: he belonged to an older age; the work he liked doing and the work he was extremely good at was the kind of free-floating yet brilliant scholarship for which Joseph Scaliger and Richard Bentley had been famous, two scholars whose work Housman deemed superior to his own.

Conjectural critics take a part of a text that has been transmitted in manuscript copies, identify a possible error and then conjecture what the original text was like. This is a game most of us play when we read badly edited newspapers or student essays, but the mistakes are often glaring and the text most of the time does not make sense on its own. But in the case of a longer transmission, the initial errors have been cleaned up by subsequent scribes who all at some point play the conjectural game themselves to remedy the situation: in most cases, alas, this does not return the text to its original form (if the scribe's conjecture is wrong) but it removes the marker of the mistake, so that you need an extremely trained eye (and in the case of metre, a good ear too) in order to identify that there is a problem in the first place.

This particular game is intellectually as seductive as crosswords or Sudoku, and at the turn of the century a lot of people were playing it, so many that the journals were filled with notes suggesting emendations to Latin and Greek works. But to play the game well, as Housman did, was extremely difficult: you had to have an incredibly deep knowledge of the possibilities of language, of grammar, morphology, spelling, of rare and recondite words (in the case of later Latin writers), but also of historical changes in the meaning of words and, lastly, of course, a very good sense of an author's style, tics and reach. You also had to know something about *Überlieferungsgeschichte*, because the mistakes scribes were likely to make fell into certain categories and some of these at least had to do with the fact that they no longer shared the same sense of the language that they were transcribing. Yet Housman did not like this new German science, of which he famously wrote that is was "a longer and nobler name than 'fudge'".

This leads us to something that even a book about Housman as a scholar written by well-wishers cannot leave out. Like Bentley before him (and like a lot of textual scholars, if you believe what textual scholars tell you), he seems to have been a particularly nasty reviewer who could be incredibly scathing of other critics' work, even when that critic was his junior and even when that critic was no longer on this side of the Styx. Of a defunct predecessor he wrote in his introduction to the edition of Lucan that hardly a page of his work "can be read without anger and disgust. Francken was a born blunderer cross from the womb and perverse", and that is not even the worst of it. Especially in the section on Housman's intellectual milieu there are lots of instances of the poet/scholar being vitriolic: at some point one of these critics points out that Housman and another scholar had "an almost polite disagreement" in the *Classical Review* over a passage of Persius.

It is only normal that some of Housman's contemporaries seem to have preferred him to pass over their work in contemptuous silence rather than being the victims of one of his extremely well-written rants. It is no coincidence that he edited Ovid's *Ibis*, a work consisting almost entirely of an incredibly detailed and varied set of curses and insults.

Housman seems to tower over his contemporaries in classics and that is not only the result of his considerable achievements: he knew he was the best and did not hesitate to tell his contemporaries, repeatedly if need be; but he also knew that he was inferior to Bentley, the giant of all conjecturers, who had conjectured an entire Greek letter out of nearly nothing. Housman seems to have been an extremely lonely individual. His earliest work was done in the evenings at the British Museum, while during the day, like Einstein, he worked at the Patent Office. Judging from his incredible output, he seems to have been always at work.

Geert Lernout

Mark Nixon, ed. *Publishing Samuel Beckett.* London: The British Library, 2011. 252 pp. ISBN 9780712358262

Publishing Samuel Beckett, edited by Mark Nixon, is one of those rare comprehensive essay collections that never stray from the topic and draw on a selection of the finest researchers in the field. The non-finite form of the verb "to publish" is aptly chosen in relation to Samuel Beckett. First of all, it conveys the sense of adventure involved in taking on a brilliant but daunting author who had the potential to yield spectacularly disappointing returns. In addition, the title underlines that the Beckett business is booming, with new editions of existing texts and posthumous publications appearing still. This polysemy of "publishing" is nicely reflected in the collection's multiple focus on the past, present and future of the Beckett canon.

Nixon's collection is divided into four sections, the first two dealing with the 1930s publications and Beckett's road to fame in the

1940s and 1950s. Although this chronological approach is methodologically justified, there is a downside. As the early chapters discuss a period in Beckett's career that was quite extensively covered
in *Damned to Fame* (1996), James Knowlson's authorized biography,
they offer the least refreshing insights. Nevertheless, a good selection
from new archival sources adds more texture and flavour to what
was already known. Also, the essays on Chatto & Windus (Andrew
Nash and John Pilling), the early prose and poetry publications with
Samuel Putnam and Nancy Cunard (Seán Lawlor) or Edward Titus
and *This Quarter* (Lois More Overbeck), and the relationship with
Beckett's first literary agent George Reavey (Mark Nixon), closely
interlock and provide a solid basis for what is to follow.

The first section concludes with an essay by Seán Kennedy on
Beckett's publishing history in Ireland. He rightly states that "[e]
ven now, after the extensive Irish celebrations of Beckett's centenary
in 2006, it remains difficult to assess Ireland's significance to his life
and work, with recurrent anxieties about any overstatement of the
case leading, at times, to an unnecessary reticence" (p. 57). By using
Pierre Bourdieu's theoretical framework on cultural production
Kennedy seeks to investigate "how Beckett's early publications demonstrate his 'ontological complicity' with his Irish habitus even as he
sought to assert his independence from it in iconoclastic gestures"
(p. 58). Although an ambitious enquiry of this kind would have to
include a thorough discussion of Beckett's postwar work in French,
Kennedy provides a good example of the tone in which such questions could be pursued.

Equally refreshing is Dirk Van Hulle's article on the publication
of "The End" (as "Suite") in *Les Temps modernes*. Whereas Knowlson
focused on the controversy surrounding the incomplete publication
of Beckett's story, Van Hulle establishes a very plausible link with
the next Beckettian fragment — this time from *Malone meurt* — to
appear in the magazine: "While Simone de Beauvoir interrupted
'Suite', 'Quel Malheur …' opens with the narrator's recapitulation
after he has interrupted himself. In the novel, the line 'Ah yes, I have
my little pastimes and they' is interrupted abruptly and is followed
by a blank line. After a break, the narrator notes that he must have
dropped his pencil" (p. 79). In this way, Beckett had possibly found
a creative outlet for his frustration.

The other two articles in the second section deal with Beckett's contributions to the avant-garde journal *transition* (Pilling and Lawlor), and his relationship with Olympia Press and the Merlin Juveniles (Justin Beplate). Although the latter essay offers little new information, focusing mainly on the already amply covered publication of *Watt* instead of the somewhat neglected translation of *Molloy*, Pilling and Lawlor corroborate Knowlson's earlier claim that "Beckett did far more translations than anyone has ever realised".[1] All in all, they believe that "Beckett had a hand in the translation of some thirty of the articles and poems published in successive issues of *Transition*" (p. 88), which opens up new avenues of research for those interested in Beckett's poetics of translation.

The third section features excellent accounts of Beckett's relationship with his major publishers. Shane Weller's portrait of Jérôme Lindon is the richest and most intimate to be found anywhere, owing to his excellent use of the Minuit archives preserved at IMEC. It even includes sales figures to sketch the financial implications of Beckett's growing critical success. This pecuniary aspect of Beckett's persona relates directly to the subject of S. E. Gontarski's essay on Grove Press, who claims that the "link between art and commerce has been under-examined by cultural critics in general and analysts of Beckett's work in particular" (p. 140). Although the partnership with Rosset is a canonical item in Beckett studies, Gontarski provides a new and refreshing angle by focusing on Beckett's mostly responsive and accepting attitude towards marketing trends and mechanisms. Peter D. McDonald does an admirable job of trying to make a fair assessment of John Calder's relevance for Beckett's career in Great Britain, beyond the cliché that he was "producing inaccurate editions" of the prose and "failing to market them adequately" (p. 161). Although these claims are partly true, McDonald situates them within the British cultural field.

Because the Faber and Faber archive is currently unavailable to scholarly enquiry, Chris Ackerley offers instead "a reflection of the impossible problems that arise from attempts — authorial, commercial and scholarly — to deal with the Beckett 'text'" (p. 172), notably the drama. In contrast to most of his prose, Beckett kept revising his

---

[1]   James Knowlson, *Damned to Fame: The Life of Samuel Beckett* (London: Bloomsbury, 1997), p. 369.

plays, often under his own direction, so that they are "difficult" to present in stable form. This has urged Faber and Faber to venture into the "minefields of textual editing" (p. 178) with their *Theatrical Notebooks* series, the editorial policy of which has been questioned by various scholars. Moreover, the "revised texts" they contain were not used for the most recent Faber editions, casting further doubt on their authorial status. As Gaby Hartel notes, not only did Beckett's German publishers, Suhrkamp, incorporate revised scripts into future editions; they also issued them in a multilingual format. Upon the publication of *Dramatische Dichtungen,* Siegfried Unseld rightly told Beckett that "the French original can [now] be seen in a new light through its reflection and mirroring in the English transposition" (p. 133), which Beckett greatly liked.

This multilingual aspect — and its hermeneutic consequences — is the topic of Sam Slote's splendid article, in the fourth and final section of the book, on the afterlife of Beckett's texts. Starting from the observation that they "exist *between* the French and the English versions" (p. 205), Slote emphasizes their sometimes playful interaction, which is somewhat obscured by monolingual publication. As bilingualism gradually became a more important factor in Beckett's oeuvre, the writing and translation processes began to interact, which is shown by the interesting changes to the drafts of *Company / Compagnie.* This relationship between what French *critique génétique* calls *avant-texte* and *texte* is further developed by Van Hulle in his article on Beckett and electronic publishing. He is the co-director of the *Beckett Digital Manuscript Project,* which "performs the functions of both a digital archive and an electronic critical edition" (p. 220), which "allows for an approach that shows the work literally as 'work' — a form of labour, instead of just its final product" (p. 224). How the *BDMP* is to influence the future of Beckett publications in print remains unclear.

As David Tucker's article on the posthumous publications of *Eleutheria* and *Dream of Fair to Middling Women* makes clear, the last word on the Beckett canon is far from having been said. Although Ackerley is right to stress that "readers (as well as publishers) need a reading text" (p. 180) and that it is impossible to say "precisely what the relationship will be between [electronic editing] and the more traditional modes of publication, let alone the commercial and

copyright implications" (p. 183), the future publishing of Beckett —
and the scholarly debate about it — promises to be exciting.

Pim Verhulst

Dirk Van Hulle. *The Making of Samuel Beckett's Stirrings Still/Soubresauts
and Comment dire/What is the Word.* Brussel: University Press Antwerp,
2011. 152 pp. ISBN: 978-90-5487-9121.

Samuel Beckett. *Stirrings Still/Soubresauts and Comment dire/What is
the Word.* Eds. Dirk Van Hulle and Vincent Neyt. The Beckett Digital Manuscript Project 1. Brussel: University Press Antwerp, 2011.
http://www.beckettarchive.org.

The twofold purpose of this book is to offer a genetic reading of
Beckett's two last works, and to serve as an expository introduction
to the *Beckett Digital Manuscript Project* (*BDMP*). The volume is conceived as the first of twenty-six codices to accompany the twenty-
six research modules into which the *BDMP*'s digital archive will be
divided. Apart from the neat logic of treating the end of the Beckett
œuvre at the beginning of the digital manuscript project, by opening with *Stirrings Still/Soubresauts* and *Comment dire/what is the word*,
Dirk Van Hulle is able to draw on two illuminating and contrasting
case studies of Beckett's late compositional practice, and especially
to highlight the chronological interspersion of writing and translation that characterizes many of the author's works. The Beckett
texts under consideration here are both discussed in their own
right and used to illustrate the series' editorial and critical procedures. The *BDMP* is a conspicuously ambitious programme to gather
and present Beckett's manuscripts in digital format, by way of an
online application and coding protocols that are deliberately geared
towards genetic research (p. 7). The transcription work and editorial research involved in this project has been divided into modules,
which will be released incrementally at a rate of one a year. This is a
long-term project which involves a number of textual scholars and
Beckett specialists working through the substantial body of extant
manuscripts. In contrast to the recent Faber and Faber reissues
of Beckett's published works, the *BDMP*'s editorial principles will

remain consistent for each module, though they will involve different editors and researchers. What this module represents, therefore, is a first taste of what will eventually be an extremely extensive digital archive, a major work of genetic editing, and an invaluable resource for Beckett scholarship.

As the first of the series, Van Hulle's codex has as one of its main purposes to highlight the aims and rationale of the editorial project. Following the MLA Committee on Scholarly Editions' guidelines, the volume includes a textual essay which details the project's editorial principles. There are three key features of the *BDMP* that shape the edition: it is bilingual, genetic and digital. Beckett studies already has a history of bilingual variorum editions in codex form, following the work of Charles Krance (on *Company, Ill Seen Ill Said* and *A Piece of Monologue*) and Edouard Magessa-O'Reilly (on *How It Is*). Full genetic editions (with variants and revision campaigns presented *in extenso*) were previously deemed unfeasible, due in large part to the constraints of the codex and to the editorial board's reservations about electronic editions. As Van Hulle describes it, recent developments in electronic editing have created the conditions for "an easily searchable environment, containing facsimiles and full transcriptions of all the versions": the digital enabling the genetic aspects of the project (p. 109). Van Hulle's essay shows the editorial work to be thoroughly grounded in theoretical and practical debates about both these fields. Its transcription practice, for example, takes into account the recommendations of the Text Encoding Initiative's Special Interest Group on genetic editions, supplementing its discussion of the relationship between "document" ("the physical object") and "text" ("the intellectual content of the document, the words written in their logical [...] sequence") with perspectives on the relative merits of topographic and linear transcription from Jean-Louis Lebrave and Claudine Quémar. The editorial decision in this case is characteristic: the technical capabilities of the *BDMP* allow both linear and topographic transcriptions to be offered alongside the digital facsimile, at the choice of the user (pp. 109-11). Nowhere does Van Hulle suggest that this capacity to offer different options absolves either the editor or the scholar of interpretative and evaluative decisions — quite the reverse — but throughout the essay it becomes clear that a prevailing inclination is to allow otherwise differing editorial approaches to complement one another.

In its form as well as its argument, the book reflects the explicit orientation of the project towards genetic scholarship. Besides the textual essay, by presenting a critical reading of the manuscripts presented in this first module of the digital archive, aimed at "reconstructing the genesis and exploring the hermeneutic potential" of these documents, the volume demonstrates an inclination for the project as a whole to integrate genetic editorial work and critical or hermeneutic analysis (pp. 19, 108). Van Hulle explicitly situates this inclination in relation to the historical divergence between textual scholarship and genetic criticism, with a diplomatic word on the complementarity of the two disciplines (pp. 107-8). The fact that each module of the *BDMP* will involve the publication of a critical essay alongside the release of the digitized manuscripts is a practical way of presenting them as interdependent. Likewise, the choice to publish codices in conjunction with each digital unit implies a valuation of complementarity at the level of the medium. The textual essay can be read on the digital manuscript site; the critical piece is exclusive to the codex. The book itself is a fine and distinctive object. In particular, the facsimile images are beautifully printed in full colour to accompany the critical reading. For using the digital archive itself, the book is clearly not essential; equally clearly, a mutual relationship between digital and codex, record and criticism is being presented. From the point of view of Beckett scholarship, the volume models the kind of contiguous and complementary use for which the archive hopes to provide. In short, the format of the publications reads as an invitation to bring genetic criticism into dialogue with other strands of critical work on Beckett, at the same time as it provides the resource for that kind of reading.

In the case of *Stirrings Still*, a catalogue of the extant manuscripts is accompanied by a narrative account of the publication history, including the financial situations of both John Calder and Rosset, the desire to produce a *de luxe*, illustrated edition, the approaches made to Joan Mitchell and Francis Bacon for accompanying lithographs, the text's dedications, limited print run, collectors' value and critical reception. In this respect Van Hulle keeps in play the circumstances of publication and a clear sense of Beckett's writing in the marketplace, alongside the volume's primary focus on the drafts and on writing as a practice. By doing so, the book implicitly offers a bridge between the manuscripts and a present interest within Beckett scholarship as to precisely such social and commercial concerns. Van Hulle characterizes the long process of this work's composition as one of myriad hesitations, but also as "linked to Beckett's concept of composition as a form of decomposition, according to the basic principle that each birth is the beginning of a process of dying" (p. 56). For his own part, Van Hulle moves between close genetic description, an erudite range of parallel or analogous cases (from within the Beckett *oeuvre* and without), compact references to contemporaneous letters, and critical readings that attempt to draw out prominent threads or recurring preoccupations. Observations about the emergence of a peculiar chiastic structure across the two languages (pp. 97-98), or the movement of subtraction mingling with a process of abstraction (pp. 82-83) are especially compelling. Illuminating though less closely argued are some of the essay's references back to questions of influence (Mani, Dante, Geulincx); these are tied back to specific earlier notes of Beckett, but the continuity is not always absolutely clear. That said, such moments, like the brief discussions of punctuation, or Adorno's reading of *The Unnamable*, work in a way as to point up existing discussions towards which a genetic reading might speak.

Comment dire/what is the word is a much more compact text with a less complex and lengthy record of its composition. In this case, the reading Van Hulle offers has uniquely to do with the unfolding of the writing process. Again, though, the questions widen to the "limits of the empirical" by way of the materiality of paralipomena and the topography of the page (pp. 102-103).

But the nature of the volume means that neither reading gives the effect of independence from the wider matter of the digital manuscript project. They supplement and serve it, and for all that offer distinctive new insights into these works. The digital component that the essays accompany gives a foretaste of the project's value for of Beckett scholars. The range of options for reading the manuscripts and transcriptions in different ways and in different combinations is very great. Accordingly, the interface takes a little getting used to, especially for the more microscopic and editorially involved functions such as comparing variants of a particular sentence. But the options are clear: views allow a user to work systematically through the catalogue, to browse by way of a chronology, to compare by document, variant or language at the level of sentence, paragraph or section. Choose to leaf through a notebook and the animations mimic something of the physics of turning the pages (less the habitual light touch of the archival researcher). In one sense, such features could be regarded as unnecessary, or worse a way of giving the new object its own fetish character, equivalent to the tactility of the facsimiled documents. Apart from being a nice touch, though, there is potentially a more serious value to the inclusion of this option among all the other kinds of view offered by the application. It is everywhere apparent that the object being viewed is no unmediated record. Van Hulle is at pains throughout his textual essay to assert that no digital representation is free from interpretation; all these options put the editorial work, the decision to segment the text at a given point in order to render a topographic transcription, the action of ordering documents in determinate ways, on display. In other words, the theoretical perspective Van Hulle proposes in his essay is borne out in the process of dealing with the digital archive. Besides that, the first module of the *Beckett Digital Manuscript Project* makes accessible to view, in high quality facsimiles, with an excellent zoom function, and with an array of scholarly aids, a set of manuscripts that document two exceptionally curious compositions. Van Hulle's book illuminates the potential value of these compositions for Beckett studies more widely, makes a convincing statement of the editorial principles, and elucidates the main features of a project that can offer a very useful touchstone for other editions of its kind.

Iain Bailey

Sukanta Chaudhuri, *The Metaphysics of Text*. Cambridge: Cambridge University Press, 2010. ISBN 978-0-521-19796-0.

In this lively and frequently compelling volume, Sukanta Chaudhuri combines theoretical reflection with an interest in bibliography, editing, and the history of the book, to explore the covert ways in which texts work. Chaudhuri wants to "look behind the text" to uncover the intricacies and processes through which meaning is produced. What he offers, with commendable if daunting ambition, is "a total enquiry into the nature of verbal constructs" (p. 6).

Two threads run throughout this richly varied book. First, Chaudhuri argues that material texts enact certain (often rather familiar) philosophical principles. Thus, if deconstruction has taught us that a sign points to a meaning and, by not attaining it, infinitely differs from, and defers, that meaning, so Chaudhuri argues that each new edition of a text "adds to the total material embodiment of the text" but defers any sense of a complete or finished text. The possibility of a definitive *Hamlet* "that embodies the conceptual scope of the whole" recedes with each text — "yet we cannot conceive of that whole except as inhering in the imperfect exemplars" (p. 57). Second, Chaudhuri thinks insightfully about the internet, arguing that it represents, in exaggerated form, tendencies that all texts possess: especially its receptivity to intervention and rewriting, and its running "together, with unprecedented clarity, the roles of not only author and reader but printer and publisher as well" (p. 36). "We read an e-text," Chaudhuri nicely notes, "as we read any other text, only more obviously so" (p. 37).

Chaudhuri has a happy knack for asking productive, fundamental questions. "Does a word have a substance?", he wonders in chapter 4. "What space does it occupy?" Such questions prompt a helpful discussion of the ways in which computers problematize textual space, in part because "the electronic text is not stored in the code in which we read it": as Shakespeare's works are translated into a series of zeros and ones which are meaningless to almost everyone except the computer scientist (and many of them, too), "the verbal text floats upon it as a kind of by-product" (p. 84). A survey of shape poems illustrates a broader interest in the material form of language and its often fraught relationship to meaning: this is illuminating, but too speedy, and we rush from Theocritus to George Herbert to William Blake ("I shall refer only briefly to William Blake's endeavours, as they are so well known" [p. 63]) to Apollinaire.

"When did anyone last *write* a book?", Chaudhuri asks in chapter 5, before discussing the always-overlapping, mutually-constituting media of manuscript and print. Chaudhuri is surely right to unravel any binary between individuating manuscript and socializing print, stressing, instead, participation by multiple agents across both media, and noting the ways in which printed texts encouraged manuscript culture (early modern commonplace books, for example, flourishing as a response to the great increase in printed books). Electronic texts, by enabling interactivity and participation, function here, and throughout, as heightened exemplifications of texts in general. (William Sherman's *Used Books* and H. J. Jackson's *Marginalia: Readers Writing in Books* are striking omissions in this chapter, and explain Chaudhuri's misleading statement that "[m]anuscript intervention in print is [. . .] little-studied" [p.112].)

Chapter 6 considers three "trajectories" or "paths" through texts: the material book which presents the text in a finite, physical form; the reader's navigation of the text; and the complexities of the written word, which "complicate, strain and finally challenge the fabric" (p. 113). There is an assumption, here, that the "narrow confines" (p. 115) of material form constitute a restriction against which literariness pushes. And while Chaudhuri stresses the need to recognize the "fluid, destabilizing features" of texts (p. 93), his weakness for Borgesian pronouncements ("[b]ehind every text is an infinity of other unrealized texts", "all texts link up with all other texts" [p. 114, 18]), which are of questionable meaningfulness, means that the concept of "destabilizing" becomes oddly uniform and inert.

Chapter 7 is strong on orality, a concept that "could arise only with the appearance of script as a binary" (p. 133), and especially on what happens to orality once it is recorded. (Chaudhuri's discussion would have been enriched by an engagement with Friedrich Kittler's *Gramophone, Film, Typewriter.*) In chapter 8, Chaudhuri provides a thoughtful account of the relation between book and performance in Shakespeare's drama, heavily indebted (as he notes) to Lukas Erne's *Shakespeare as Literary Dramatist* and Julie Stone Peters' *Theatre of the Book.* Chapter 9, on translation, is suggestive, not least in the observation that to translate "is to affirm one's conviction that something can be 'carried across' languages: that a verbal message does not inhere only in words" (p. 167) — but the by-now inevitable presence of Borges, in the form of "Pierre Menard, Author of the *Quixote*" (already discussed in chapter 1), lends moments of this chapter the quality of a joke already told.

The final chapter is in many ways the most stimulating, as Chaudhuri examines Rabindranath Tagore's habit of converting his manuscript deletions into doodles in the 1924 manuscript of the book of poems *Purabi*: "where the words are blotted out, a different visual form takes shape". Chaudhuri gives himself space to talk through a series of precise examples, and the shift from rapid synthesis to more patient analysis is richly rewarding. Chaudhuri is fascinating on the use of deletions — "rejected possibilities of form" (p. 183) — to produce something new: the writing on one page is scrawled out to create the shape of a crocodile, as the "cancelled is reinstated in another mode" (p. 180).

This is a rewarding, ambitious book, generously illustrated with 30 images. In brief but helpful footnotes, Chaudhuri nuances his arguments and cites further texts; and a full bibliography and index are included. But *The Metaphysics of Text* is not without faults. Chaudhuri rather underestimates the thoughtfulness of bibliographers and, indeed, of readers in general. "Not one user of MS Word in a thousand", he declares, implausibly, "may be aware" that computers store text not as letters but as the zeros and ones of bits and bytes (p. 22); and editors (he tells us) see variants as "species of aberration", he says, to be cleared away in pursuit of "a prior, as it were virgin, text" (p. 18–19). Throughout, Chaudhuri is admirably expansive in his interests and references: we move quickly between medieval scholasticism, contemporary European philosophy, Nigerian oral sagas, early modern English drama, Bengali poetry, European modernism, and much more. But the downside is, inevitably, a sometimes breathless haste: "I shall go as far back as Augustine and the Middle Ages" (p .42), Chaudhuri announces, but what we actually get in the following pages are a few hasty words. On Roger Bacon: one line; on William of Ockham: one line; on humanist grammar: one line. Perhaps unsurprisingly, Chaudhuri's conclusion is often that these various texts affirm the same central post-structuralist point that language is unstable and that meaning is produced through a series of deferred referents. Chaudhuri is eye-opening when making connections between periods and genres that few scholars can combine, but he is less convincing when everything ends up looking the same.

Adam Smyth

Joseph A. Dane. *Out of Sorts: On Typography and Print Culture.*
Philadelphia: University of Pennsylvania Press, 2011. 240 pp. ISBN
978-081224-294-2

Joseph A. Dane does not pull punches. In his 2003 study *The Myth of
Print Culture*, he deconstructed some of the most potent myths about
print culture and he does the same in his new book, *Out of Sorts*. This
time he accomplishes his mission in brief forays, a short introduction to the problem, and then a hard look at the available evidence:
punch, punch, punch, short hook: another myth down.

But unlike in the earlier book, the over-arching mission here is
less visible: the different short chapters do not seem to be battles in
a single war, just a set of disjointed guerilla-type raids. Dane's targets
here are diverse, though mostly related to print (and font) issues,
the result of the fact that at least some of these chapters seem to have
started life as articles or reviews.

The introduction opens with the invention of printing and with
the earliest and extremely imprecise descriptions of the novel process for which no suitable terminology had been invented yet and
that for quite some time was something of a trade secret. It was only
afterwards, when scholars began to inscribe these same descriptions
into their own, inevitably teleological narratives, that these descriptions began to make sense. The tension between "our speaking"
about such phenomena and what the material evidence provides is
the main theme of the book. Time and again we are confronted with
the insurmountable difference between what our historical narratives proclaim and what is available to us in terms of actual material
objects. And with the laziness of experts who simply copy the same
"facts" and interpretations of facts from earlier scholars.

Of course Dane applies this scrutiny in the first place to printing.
Out of Sorts is divided into two parts and the first addresses particularly the problem of the most basic classification of types and fonts.
Dane may have been tempted to use as a subtitle "shit happens",
because in most of the cases he studies here, this is really what seems
to have occurred. The world turns out to be a much messier place
than we would like to imagine and, inevitably, when things do go
wrong they do so in a big way.

The different chapters in this book are in essence exercises in
demythologizing aspects of print culture. As he did in his previous

book, Dane especially targets the grand narratives of the discipline, like Elizabeth L. Eisenstein's printing revolution or the Rise of Humanism (with capitals: in the index the word humanism has lost its capital but then it only appears as "humanism, myths of").

In the first half of the book, Dane targets both print culture and humanism and in the first two chapters he starts with Gutenberg, showing how most of our histories of early printing perpetuate the same set of old myths that silently assume that printing in the fifteenth century acquired a set of practices that remained essentially unchanged until the nineteenth century. Dane shows that this continuity is a myth: we should be looking at the material objects themselves and not create evidence through our stories about histories. In the third chapter Dane demolishes the myth that the return to gothic letter types had nothing to do with the supposed fact that gothic can accommodate more text. The argument is clear enough, despite the fact that on one occasion he writes "roman type" when he means "gothic". In the next chapter we look again at gothic which is not at all the letter type used on the title page of Percy's *Reliques of Ancient English Poetry*, as nearly everyone seems to have claimed, again because it fits so beautifully in an over-arching narrative that does seem to make sense.

After a brief interlude Dane then moves on to the section "Images and Texts" in which he first looks at the strange marginalia that were printed in the early Chaucer editions. He then moves to the Piers Plowman Archive to show that there is no real difference between editorial and typographical diplomacy, with a brief coda on the Blake Archive. This chapter ends with the characteristic deadpan conclusion: "Among the virtues of both the Blake Archive and the Piers Plowman Archive are those that contradict their apparent aims, those moments when the mediation of their editors comes most strongly to the forefront" (p. 140). In the next chapter the representation of visual perspective is deconstructed, as is, in the one after that, the representation of types in Thomas Frognall Dibdin's *Typographical Antiquities*. In his conclusion he once more rejects all "grands récits" and briefly discusses Walt Whitman's choice of the deathbed edition of his *Leaves of Grass*.

Dane problematizes all the issues that confront him and he tends to blame the (other) experts for misrepresenting the materials they work with, but then, as an expert himself, he also blames the experts for blaming the experts. As in the previous book, expert readers will relish the demythologizing moves that this book consists of, but even at only 240 pages this tends to get somewhat tiresome, because the author all too often seems to draw out a number of what are no more than short notes by resorting to minute descriptions of how exactly he arrived at his findings.

This is a self-indulgent book that at times seems to flirt with the inexcusable autobiographical tendency that I hoped had crested a decade or so ago. Simultaneously with this book, Dane did publish a memoir of his life in Maine (he now teaches at the University of Southern California), so perhaps some of this carried over from one book into the other. The two parts of this book are interrupted by a strange interlude in which Dane writes a short discussion of two "always interesting and amusing articles" by Randall McLeod on two poems by George Herbert. To some extent this piece fits into the general context of the book (shit happens), but at the same time the interlude reads like the letter of a jilted lover. In a coda to the interlude, included as a sort of footnote at the end, Dane adds a transcription of a jocular e-mail from McLeod (who addresses his colleague as "Dansk") which seems to be a part of an elaborate (but missing) correspondence between them. Unfortunately not all the shit that happens is relevant. Or even interesting.

Demythologizing a discipline is not too difficult (or maybe it is to Dane's credit that he makes it look so easy), but if we are no longer to have recourse to grand narratives or not even to the slightly less grand pockets of coherence we actually do find in our data, what are we left with? Let's hope that this amounts to more than just our own personal shit. But it seems that Dane has foreseen such reactions to his book, for he closes the introduction with the statement that if his "chapter succeed[s] only in producing the same quizzical stares I have seen in Huntington visitors, that is good enough for me" (p. 14). No shit.

Geert Lernout

Contributors

Tara L. Andrews is a post-doctoral researcher at the KU Leuven, Belgium. She holds a D.Phil. from the University of Oxford in Oriental Studies, for editorial and analytic work on the *Chronicle* of Matthew of Edessa. Her primary research focuses are Byzantine and medieval Armenian history and historiography, and text-stemmatological method. She is currently working with Caroline Macé on the *Tree of Texts* project, aimed at constructing an empirical model for medieval text transmission.

David Atkinson is the editor of *Folk Music Journal,* author of *The English Traditional Ballad: Theory, Method, and Practice* (2002), and co-editor of *Folk Song: Tradition, Revival, and Re-Creation* (2004). He has published widely on Anglo-Scottish ballads and is currently a Research Fellow at the Elphinstone Institute, University of Aberdeen, engaged in the preparation of a critical edition of the James Madison Carpenter folklore collection. He is also Executive Secretary of the Kommission für Volksdichtung (International Ballad Commission).

Arianna Antonielli is Assegnista di ricerca in English literature at the Università degli Studi di Firenze. She is the author of *William Blake e William Butler Yeats: Sistemi simbolici e costruzioni poetiche* (2009) as well as various article on W. B. Yeats and T. S. Eliot.

Iain Bailey is a part-time Lecturer in English Literature at the University of Manchester. He has published variously on the work of Samuel Beckett and is completing a monograph on the author for Bloomsbury Continuum.

Pietro G. Beltrami is professor of Romance philology at the University of Pisa; he is currently the director of the Opera del Vocabolario Italiano, a research unit of the Italian National Research Council in Florence. His publications deal with medieval French and Provençal literature (the troubadours, Chrétien de Troyes, Brunetto Latini), Dante, Italian and Romance metrics and textual criticism.

Sandra Clark is a Senior Research Fellow at the Institute of English Studies, School of Advanced Study, University of London. She has written widely on Shakespeare and early modern English literature. She is currently editing *Macbeth* for the Arden Shakespeare, third series.

Orietta Da Rold is Lecturer in Medieval Literature in the School of English at the University of Lecturer. She researches Medieval Literature *c.* 1100-1500, Geoffrey Chaucer and the digital humanities. Her most recent publication is *English Manuscripts before 1400*, co-edited with A.S.G Edwards (British Library, 2012).

Franz Fischer is research associate at the Cologne Center for eHumanities (CCeH), University of Cologne, and co-founder of the Institut für Dokumentologie und Editorik (IDE). His research interest is focused on digital scholarly editions of medieval Latin texts.

Giedrė Jankevičiūtė is an art historian and critic. She works as a leading researcher at the Lithuanian Institute for Culture Research and is professor at the Vilnius Art Academy. The main field of her interest is art and artistic life in the second half of the nineteenth and twentieth century.

Annemarie Kets is Senior Researcher in Textual Scholarship and Literary Studies at the Huygens Institute for the History of the Netherlands (Royal Netherlands Academy of Arts and Sciences). In addition, she is a Professor of Textual Scholarship at VU University Amsterdam. She has published editions of works of Dutch literature from the nineteenth and twentieth centuries, including both scholarly editions and popular editions. Her current research focuses on the digital edition of documentary sources (especially collections of letters).

Sarah Laseke is currently reading for an MSt in Medieval English Literature at the University of Oxford. She is particularly interested in romance, codicology and medieval readership.

Geert Lernout teaches English and Comparative Literature at the University of Antwerp. He is the author of *Help My Unbelief: James*

Joyce and Religion and he is co-editor of *The "Finnegans Wake" Notebooks at Buffalo.*

Teresa Marqués-Aguado is Lecturer in the Department of English at the University of Murcia (Spain), where she teaches English Language and English Historical Linguistics. She is currently involved with the preparation of an electronic edition of unedited late Middle English texts. Her work has been published in *English Studies* and *SELIM Journal,* and she has contributed to Benvenutus Grassus' *On the well-proven art of the eye: Practica Oculorum & De probatissima arte oculorum – Synoptic Edition and Philological Studies* (Peter Lang) and *The Handbook of Historical Sociolinguistics* (Wiley-Blackwell).

Kiyoko Myojo is Professor of German literature at Saitama University, Japan, In her research on the work of Franz Kafka she applies the methods of textual studies and genetic criticism. She is the author of *Atarashii Kafka* (Keio University Press 2002) and translator of several English and German mongraphs, including *Kafka* by Ritchie Robertson, *From Gutenberg to Google* by Peter Shillingsburg and *Electronic Textual Editing* by Lou Burnard et. al.

Mark Nixon is Reader in Modern Literature at the University of Reading, where he directs the Beckett International Foundation. He is the author of *Samuel Beckett's 'German Diaries'* (2011) and the co-director of the Beckett Digital Manuscript Project.

Veijo Pulkkinen (PhD, University of Oulo, 2010) is a literary critic at the Finnish Literature Society and holds a Postdoctoral Researcher Fellowship from the Academy of Finland. He is working on a study of Aaro Hellaakoski's typographically experimental work *Jääpeili* (1928). His research interests relate to Finnish poetry of the first half of the twentieth century, visual poetry, avant-garde, philosophy of literature, and the application of genetic and textual criticism to literary interpretation.

Peter Robinson is Bateman Professor of English at the University of Saskatchewan. He is currently leading development of the "Textual Communities" project, which aims to provide a platform for collaborative scholarly editing, building on his previous experience in the creation of digital tools for editors. He is active in the development of standards for digital resources, formerly as a member of the Text Encoding Initiative and as leader of the EU funded MASTER project, and he has published on Geoffrey Chaucer, scholarly editing, and digital humanities.

Mikas Vaicekauskas is a senior researcher of The Institute of Lithuanian Literature and Folklore in Vilnius, Lithuania. His recent book is *Motiejaus Valančiaus užrašų ir atsiminimų rankraščiai Lietuvių mokslo draugijoje: 1911–1914 metų istorija* (2009) [*Motiejus Valančius Manuscript Notes and Reminiscences in the Lithuanian Society of Science: The History of 1911–1914*]. Currently he is working on a documentary and critical edition of Kristijonas Donelaitis' *Metai* [*The Seasons*].

Wim Van Mierlo is Lecturer in Textual Scholarship and English Literature at the Institute of English Studies, School of Advanced Study, University of London. He has edited *Where there is Nothing and The Unicorn from the Stars: Manuscript Materials* by W. B. Yeats and Lady Gregory for the Cornell Yeats Series (2012).

Pim Verhulst works as a research assistant at the Centre for Manuscript Genetics at the University of Antwerp, Belgium. He is currently preparing a PhD on the draft versions of Samuel Beckett's radio plays and contributes to the Beckett *Digital Manuscript Project* (*BDMP*).

Jon Viklund is a Research Fellow at the Department of Literature at Uppsala University, Sweden.